Frozen in Time

Scotland Team, December 1910. Back Row; William Arnot (SIHA), David McGill (Match Referee), Archibald S Dunlop (Kings) and John B Wharrie (Corinthians). Front Row: J D Strathearn (Beavers), J Campbell

Frozen in Time
The Lost History of
Scottish Ice Hockey
1895-1940

William S. Marshall

The Grimsay Press

Published by:

The Grimsay Press
An imprint of Zeticula Ltd
The Roan
Kilkerran
KA19 8LS
Scotland
http://www.thegrimsaypress.co.uk

First published in 2014.

© William Marshall 2014

ISBN 978-1-84530-151-4

All rights reserved. No reproduction, copy or transmission of this publication may be made without prior written permission.

Acknowledgements

This book would have been very much harder to write without the work of others who have gone before in the field. I owe a great deal of gratitude to three historians of the sport in particular; Major Bethune Minet Patton, Martin C Harris and David Gordon.

Contemporary newspapers have been another major source of material for this book especially the *Glasgow Herald*, the *Evening Times* and the *Daily Record and Mail*. I am grateful to the ice hockey correspondents of these newspapers and others for their match reports, articles and comments regarding the sport's activities during the period under review. I can only hope that I have done justice to their efforts and commitment to ice hockey.

Websites were also a valuable source of useful information. Ice hockey is fortunate in having a number of first class sites dedicated to the sport. I found the websites of the Society for International Hockey Research, of which I am proud to be a member, the Ice Hockey Journalists UK and the French Hockey Archives to be of particular value and benefit.

I am extremely grateful to a number of individuals who have assisted me with my research for this book. This help has included reminiscences of their relatives who played ice hockey during the inter-war period and the provision of photographs of players and teams, some of which are precious family heirlooms and are reproduced in this book. I would especially like to thank Colonel Fraser Russell, Andrew R Dick, Jonathan Muirhead and Joy McLeod.

Obtaining photographs to illustrate this book proved a major challenge. I would like to acknowledge the assistance and goodwill I received from a variety of individuals and organisations and I appreciate their agreement to permit me to use their photographs. They include Martin C Harris, David Gordon, Stuart Wilson, Ian Dale, Alan McLellan, Sandy Clark of Bridge of Weir Community Council, Emma Yan and Lesley Richmond of Glasgow University Archive Services, Anne Swadel of D C Thomson and Company Limited, Grace Gough of Newsquest (Herald and Evening Times) Limited, Alison Lowson of the *Perthshire Advertiser* and Sara Ann Kelly of the A K Bell Library, Perth.

Most of the research for this book was undertaken in the Mitchell Library, Glasgow. I must acknowledge the patience and assistance I received from the staff in the Glasgow Room in particular. They were unfailingly helpful and always courteous despite my repeated requests for microfilm, newspapers and other material pertinent to this history.

I also thank Ann and Iain McClumpha for their patience and assistance in all matters relating to information technology.

Last, but by no means least, I thank my wife, Morag, for putting up with a part-time husband for a couple of years, while I was researching and writing this book, and it is to her that it is respectfully dedicated.

Contents

Acknowledgements	v
Illustrations	ix
Preface	xi
The Arrival of Ice Hockey in England	1
"Too Respectable For Glasgow"	7
The Father of Scottish Ice Hockey; William Pollock Wylie	17
The Establishment of the Scottish Ice Hockey Association	21
The First Home Internationals	27
The Wider Context: International Developments	33
In The Doldrums	37
The New Crossmyloof Ice Rink	41
The Revival of the Scottish Ice Hockey Association	45
The Amateur Game	51
Season 1929-30	57
Season 1930-31	73
Season 1931-32	93
Season 1932-33	113
Season 1933-34	133
Season 1934-35	153
Season 1935-36	175
Season 1936-37	197
Season 1937-38	221
Season 1938-39	251
Season 1939-40	285
Statistics	303
Glasgow Real Ice Skating Palace	305
Scottish Ice Hockey Association	306
Scottish Ice Hockey Association Player Squads	307
Scottish League Season 1929-30 Points Competition	308
Scottish League Season 1929-30 First Division	309
Scottish League Season 1929-30 Second Division	310
Scottish League Season 1929-30 Player Squads	311
Scottish League Season 1930-31 League Championship - Canada Cup	313
Scottish League Season 1930-31 Player Squads	315
Scottish League Season 1931-32 League Championship - Canada Cup	317
Scottish League Season 1931-32 Player Squads	319
Scottish League Season 1932-33 League Championship - Canada Cup	321

Scottish League Season 1932-33 Player Squads	323
Scottish League Season 1933-34 League Championship - Canada Cup	325
Scottish League Season 1933-34 Player Squads	327
Scottish League Season 1934-35 League Championship - Canada Cup	328
Scottish League Season 1934-35 Player Squads	330
Scottish League Season 1935-36 League Championship - Canada Cup	331
Scottish League Season 1935-36 Player Squads	333
Scottish League Season 1936-37 League Championship - Canada Cup	334
Scottish League Season 1936-37 Player Squads	336
Scottish League Season 1937-38 League Championship - Canada Cup	337
Scottish League Season 1937-38 Player Squads	339
Scottish League Season 1938-39 Points Competition	340
Scottish League Season 1938-39 League Championship - Canada Cup	342
Scottish League Season 1938-39 Player Squads	344
Scottish League Season 1939-40 Points Competition	345
Scottish League Season 1939-40 League Championship	347
Scottish League Season 1939-40 Player Squads	349
Scottish League	350
Scotland Competitive Record 1910 - 1938	355
Scotland Player Squads 1910 - 1938	356
Scotland Players 1910 - 1938	361
Players for Great Britain 1930-1939	365
Rules of Ice Hockey (1900)	367
Rules of Ice Hockey (1936)	373
Bibliography	391
Index	393

Illustrations

Scotland Team, December 1910	*Frontispiece*
Glasgow Real Ice Skating Palace, c1896	8
William Pollock Wylie, c1898	16
First Crossmyloof Ice Rink, c1908	23
Scotland and England Team Portraits, December 1910	29
Second Crossmyloof Ice Rink	44
Glasgow University Ice Hockey Club, 1930-31	78
Bridge of Weir Ice Hockey Club, 1930-31	83
Mohawks Players Practising at Rouken Glen Park, Glasgow, 1931	95
Scotland Team, December 1931	101
Scotland Team, March 1932	110
Scotland Team, November 1932	119
Bears Ice Hockey Club, 1932-33	128
Andy Dick, Kelvingrove	136
Kelvingrove Ice Hockey Club, 1933-34	141
Mohawks Ice Hockey Club, 1934-35	161
Scotland Team, December 1934	163
Jimmy Foster, Harringay Greyhounds, Scotland and Great Britain	188
Scotland and England Teams, March 1936	193
Billy Fullerton, Mohawks, Scotland and Great Britain	199
Les Tapp, Perth Panthers and Scotland	205
Joe Collins, Kelvingrove, Scotland and Great Britain	208
Jimmy Lightfoot, Perth Panthers and Scotland	223
Len McCartney, Perth Panthers and Scotland	229
Ronald Milne, Perth Black Hawks and Scotland	236
Don McLeod, Kelvingrove	243
Les Lovell, Perth Black Hawks and Scotland	248
Arnie Pratt, Perth Panthers and Scotland	260
Gerry Davey, Falkirk Lions and Great Britain	263
Gordon Cummine, Mohawks	267
Falkirk Lions Ice Hockey Club, 1938-39	268
Perth Panthers Ice Hockey Club, 1938-39	272
Tommy McInroy, Fife Flyers, Scotland and Great Britain	274
Dundee Tigers Ice Hockey Club, 1938-39	280
Ayr Raiders Ice Hockey Club, 1939-40	288

Preface

The main purpose of this book is to provide for the first time a comprehensive and informative history of Scottish ice hockey in its formative years.

Much of this early history has been neglected and forgotten. This has resulted in an important part of the sporting history of Scotland, and that of ice hockey in general, being metaphorically frozen in time, buried under the ice. This book seeks to address that situation by recovering this lost history as far as is possible with the aim of restoring Scottish ice hockey to its right and proper place in the early development and organisation of the sport.

Ice hockey, albeit in its most rudimentary form, was played in Scotland as early as 1896 at the Glasgow Real Ice Skating Palace. A year later, a team from Scotland, under the tutelage of William Pollock Wylie, played in Paris, France. These early pioneering efforts were amongst the very first undertaken in Europe for a sport which was still evolving and in its infancy outside of North America.

The original Crossmyloof Ice Rink was opened in 1907. Glasgow now boasted one of the finest artificial ice surfaces in the world. By this time a more recognisable form of ice hockey had developed; this led to the formation of ice hockey clubs at the rink. One of the first league competitions of its kind in Europe was established. In 1910, teams representing Scotland and England played each other in Glasgow and London, thereby initiating one of the oldest fixtures in international competition.

Ice hockey was not revived in Scotland until 1929 when the Scottish Ice Hockey Association (SIHA) was reconstituted in Glasgow. From then until 1939 a series of different teams were based at the second Crossmyloof Ice Rink. Various teams played in a thriving and popular league for ten seasons. Although strictly amateur for most of that period, competition between them was keen and entertaining for the many spectators who came to watch it.

In 1936, the character of Scottish ice hockey radically changed. It finally expanded beyond the confines of Crossmyloof Ice Rink. It arrived first in Perth and then spread over the next few years to Dundee, Falkirk, Kirkcaldy, Dunfermline and Ayr. This expansion led to the sport transcending its hitherto amateur status and adopting a fully semi-professional structure. Crowds of between 3,000 and 4,000 spectators regularly attended matches involving these new teams as Scottish ice hockey entered its first "boom" period.

This book covers all of these various developments although the core of it is devoted to the inter-war period. Here I have been able to provide a detailed commentary on every season of play, together with concomitant statistics comprising the fixtures and results of every match played in the league championship, final league tables and the player squads of every team in the competition. It represents a unique analysis of all eleven seasons of competition in the Scottish League between 1929 and 1940.

A bias in the book may be detected towards the amateur era. I make no apology for this. I want to put on record my admiration for the various players, coaches, officials and administrators who developed ice hockey in Scotland up to the mid 1930s, often at no little sacrifice to themselves and their families. For these sportsmen and gentlemen of a bygone era it was always "the game for the game's sake" and in the opinion of this observer at least that is as it should be.

The international scene is not neglected either. The SIHA was responsible for arranging all international matches. These matches involved teams variously described as "Scotland", "Scottish Select" or "Scottish League Select". More than mere semantics are involved here: these designations raise the question of what constituted a full international match as opposed to a representative match. Full international matches were played by "Scotland" whereas matches considered to be of lesser status were played by the "Scottish Select" or the "Scottish League Select".

There are a few occasions where this distinction is not entirely clear. Where this is the case I have taken the quite considerable liberty of determining myself whether it was Scotland who were playing or not. As guiding principles, I have considered the quality of the opposition faced by Scotland and the overall availability of players for squad selection. In view of this I am confident that the 22 full international matches cited in this book as involving Scotland were indeed those intended to be designated as such by the SIHA.

One cannot read this book but be struck by the remarkable contribution made by expatriate Canadians in the evolution of ice hockey in Scotland. That contribution cannot be overstated. It is a criticism of ice hockey from some quarters that it is an "imported" game not worthy of serious consideration in the sporting firmament of the nation. While such criticism is unworthy these critics may care to consider that many of these ice hockey missionaries from Canada were actually born in Scotland or were of Scottish ancestry.

Scotland has enjoyed a long and happy relationship with Canada on many levels. Over the centuries thousands of Scots, myself included, have crossed the Atlantic Ocean to seek a new life in that great country. Strong familial bonds have always existed between the two countries. The human traffic has not all been one way as many Canadians have come to Scotland to visit, work and study. It is not surprising that those who stayed sought to promote their national game in this country, a country where winter sports are not exactly unknown.

Readers who are more familiar with the rules of ice hockey today may find the Appendices of benefit. They are included because they correspond to the period covered by this book.

One of the most important sections of this book is the separate part on records. Here readers will find a definitive record of all of the major competition winners including the Canada Cup, Mitchell Trophy and President's Pucks. These records will end the confusion which exists in other publications and websites regarding Scottish League competition winners. Also included is a record of every competitive match played between those great Glasgow rivals, Kelvingrove and Mohawks.

I admit to ignoring the many local cup competitions initiated by the various ice rinks during the semi-professional era. These tournaments were primarily set up to maximise revenue and in my view had little intrinsic value. Apart from anything else they constituted a major impediment to the further development of representative and international competition at that time and they put a ridiculous amount of strain on the players. They were a menace and they continued to afflict Scottish ice hockey in the post-war period.

I have also provided a full records section for the Scottish international team, albeit with the caveats referred to above. There is a record of all of the international matches that Scotland played between 1910 and 1938 along with details on the squads selected for each game. Readers will also find a directory of all of the players who were selected for Scotland with details of their playing record.

Other historians of ice hockey will find the records section of real value. I hope it does offer clarity where there was once confusion. By way of example, it has been recorded in some sources that Dundee Tigers won the league championship in season 1939-40; I can now confirm that it was Fife Flyers who won that competition. Hopefully, these records will throw more light on previously dark corners of Scottish (National) League history.

It would seem that professional ice hockey is once again thriving in Great Britain and Northern Ireland. It enjoyed similar boom periods in Scotland and England in the late 1940s and the 1950s. It was good while it lasted but the new breed of people who were running the sport then badly overreached themselves and it all came crashing down in 1960. It is vitally important that the current crop of entrepreneurs and administrators running the professional game today learn the lessons of the past if history is not to sadly repeat itself.

William Marshall
Paisley, 2014

The Arrival of Ice Hockey in England

To place the origins and development of ice hockey in Scotland in its proper context, it is necessary to examine some key developments in England - where the sport first put down permanent roots in the British Isles. In its formative years in both England and Scotland, skating in general and ice hockey in particular were winter sports taken up by the wealthy. Ice hockey became a rather elitist pursuit.

It was no coincidence that the earliest participants in ice hockey were drawn from a strata of society which embraced professionals, military officers, Oxbridge students and a sprinkling of the aristocracy. It was often the custom of people in these particular social circles to indulge their passion for winter sports by taking holidays in the Alps. It was in these circumstances that affluent Britons first learned to skate, ski, slide on toboggans and play ice hockey or its "parent" sport, bandy.

Oxbridge students were amongst the earliest pioneers of the sport. Both universities claim to have ice hockey clubs dating back to 1885, making them amongst the oldest in the world. A record is said to exist of a match played between Oxford and Cambridge at the fashionable holiday resort of St Moritz in Switzerland, but most historians now accept that this contest was actually a bandy match. For the record, Oxford won 6-0. There are no further reports of any matches between the two universities until a decade later, in 1895. However, this too was in reality a bandy match played at Blenheim Lake, Oxford, the "Dark Blues" again prevailing by a score of 6-1.

By this time the distinction between bandy and what were emerging as the more rudimentary forms of ice hockey were becoming less blurred in Europe. Indeed, what is considered to be the earliest known surviving photograph of a bandy or "ice hockey" match in Great Britain was published in 1895, showing the players concerned in action on the frozen ice of Christ Church Meadow, Oxford, in February of that year.

According to Major Bethune Minet Patton, the first recognisable ice hockey match in Great Britain was said to have taken place on a frozen lake in the grounds of Buckingham Palace, London, in the winter of 1895. This historic match was arranged at the instigation of the sons of the ex-Governor General of Canada, Lord Stanley of Preston, who were keen exponents of what would soon become Canada's national game.

Lord Stanley's sons made up one team while their opponents were comprised of a number of British nobles and aristocrats with an interest in winter sports, including both the Prince of Wales (the future King Edward VII) and the Duke of York (the future King George V). The final score in this match is not given, but Patton noted that Lord Stanley's team scored numerous goals while the Palace team managed only one in reply. It appears that further matches were held, one of which had a Scottish connection.

Reminiscing about one such contest over forty years later, Colonel Thomas C Dunlop, a prominent Scottish soldier and ice hockey enthusiast, alluded to the participation of General Charles Fergusson, a fellow Scot, who in dashing up the ice became involved in what was described as a "rough and tumble" with the Duke of York who was keeping goal for the Palace team. At the after match *soirée* it was noted that while Fergusson was walking with a limp, the Duke of York was sporting a black eye!

Royal patronage no doubt assisted the fledgling sport's popularity, at least amongst those wealthy enough to participate, but the relative mildness of the British winter ensured that ice hockey would have no real future in the absence of artificial ice surfaces. A realistic start on that problem was made in early January 1895 with the opening of the Niagara Ice Rink in the Westminster district of London. Also known as Niagara Hall, the ice surface was 70 feet in diameter and circular in shape. While it was not particularly conducive to staging ice hockey, a team was nevertheless established at the rink. Their first match was played in the winter of 1896-97 with Lord Stanley's team of familial missionaries providing the opposition.

In January 1896, the National Skating Club leased premises previously used for promoting circuses and converted it into an ice rink. Known as both Henglers Ice Rink and the National Skating Palace, this venue was also located in the affluent west end of London, on a site where was situated a former residence of the Duke of Argyll. The larger ice surface there was more conducive for the promotion of ice hockey. Later in the year, on 7 November 1896, Princes Ice Rink became the third venue to be opened in the capital city within the past two years. It too was located in the west end, in the fashionable Knightsbridge district. The ice surface at Princes measured 210 feet by 52 feet.

Niagara, Henglers and Princes were not, however, the first ice rinks to have been built in London. At least two rinks had been previously constructed in the capital. One had also been erected in Manchester in the preceding decades, but none of these had survived, owing either to commercial failure or technical difficulties or a combination of both. The later ice rinks came along at the right time, both because the technology involved in artificially freezing ice was now more reliable and because skating had become an increasingly popular pastime, which could be commercially exploited.

The establishment of Princes Ice Rink was a very important development. Within a month of its opening Bethune "Peter" Patton had obtained permission from Admiral Friedrich ('Frederick') Augustus Maxse, a political writer, the proprietor of the Prince's Rink Skating Club, to form an ice hockey club at the rink. It would become the premier ice hockey club in England over the next decade.

Bethune Minet Patton was born in London in 1876 and was educated at Winchester and Wellington. He learned to skate while on holidays in Switzerland and became proficient in a number of winter sports as a result. The son of a Brigadier-General, Patton was himself a career soldier reaching the rank of Major. He was also to become a player, coach, administrator and historian of the sport and not for nothing was he considered to be the "father" of English ice hockey.

In 1936, Patton wrote "Ice Hockey", the first book published and specifically dedicated to ice hockey in Great Britain. While it provides an invaluable record of the sport's early development it is written in an almost diary and anecdotal style. Patton was clearly reminiscing, relying on his memory for much of the detail, some of which is rather vague and, on occasion, even inaccurate.

Princes Ice Hockey Club played their first match on 13 February 1897 when they defeated "Fenwick's Team" 6-3. During the next few years they would play matches against a small number of clubs including Niagara, Brighton and the Chatham-based Royal Engineers. There was of course no organised league structure at this time, but on the basis of results against each other Niagara were considered English champions in 1898 while Princes assumed that mantle in 1899, 1900 and 1901.

While the sport was taking off in London the two oldest ice hockey clubs in England, Oxford University and Cambridge University, decided in 1900 to compete against each other on an annual basis. The originator of this significant initiative seems to have been the Cambridge captain, J J "Jack" Cawthra, who was also a noted figure skater and lacrosse player.

The first of these Varsity contests took place on 16 March 1900 at the Princes Ice Rink in London. Oxford were captained by Bernard "Bosie" Bosanquet, a future Wisden cricketer of the year in 1905 and the inventor of the bowling action in cricket known as the "googly". Cawthra and Bosanquet were reported as being the best two players on the ice in an exciting match won by Oxford 7-6.

Canadian expatriates living, working and studying in England were of course a major potential source of recruitment for playing the game and for coaching the fledgling ice hockey clubs in the country. An undetermined number of exiles were scattered amongst the existing clubs often acting as missionaries for the sport. From amongst this source a new club, London Canadians, were formed in 1902.

The encouraging growth in the number of clubs and ice rinks in the London area led in 1903 to the establishment of an Ice Hockey League in England, the first of its kind outside North America. This important initiative arose out of a meeting held between the interested clubs at Henglers Ice Rink on 6 November 1903. The five founding clubs were Amateur Skating Club, Argyll, Cambridge University, London Canadians and Princes.

Patton, who played defence for Princes, became the first president of the new league, effectively an English Ice Hockey Association, in all but name. Amateur Skating Club and Argyll were both based at Henglers Ice Rink, the latter club having played a number of challenge matches in season 1902-03.

It is not immediately obvious why Oxford University were not involved in the new venture. Another famous name missing from the new set up was Niagara; they had unfortunately folded in the wake of Niagara Hall closing at the end of 1902. Cambridge University, who appear to have been a quite progressive club, won the unofficial championship in 1902, breaking the monopoly of Princes.

The new league championship in England was also significant for introducing a much more recognisable form of ice hockey based on the Canadian model of the game. Patton should be given credit for encouraging this development although the main instigators were really the London Canadians club. For really the first time in England, a puck was used in matches instead of a bandy ball and the players adopted long flat bladed sticks instead of the much shorter sticks previously utilised from bandy.

The first match in the new competition was played at Princes Ice Rink on 17 November 1903. London Canadians defeated Amateur Skating Club 8-5. Four days later, Princes defeated Cambridge University 9-6. The first match played at Henglers Ice Rink on 26 November resulted in a 4-2 defeat for Argyll at the hands of Princes. On 8 December, Argyll defeated their neighbours Amateur Skating Club 2-1. London Canadians were based at Princes Ice Rink; perhaps not surprisingly they were the strongest team. In the final match of the competition on 24 February 1904, the exiled Canadians defeated Princes 6-3 to win the championship with 14 points from 8 matches. Princes finished runners-up with 12 points. Argyll finished third, Amateur Skating Club were fourth and defending champions Cambridge University finished in last position.

Although deemed a success the Ice Hockey League was short lived. The closure of Henglers Ice Rink in the spring of 1904 resulted in the demise of both Argyll and Amateur Skating Club. London Canadians did not last much longer either the club playing its final match against Princes in November 1904. The next important development in the English game was the establishment of a new club, Oxford Canadians, in 1905. This club was composed of Canadian Rhodes scholars who were prevented from joining the existing Oxford University team because they were rightly considered too strong to compete in that club's usual round of competitive fixtures.

Oxford Canadians were to become a major force not just in England but in European ice hockey as well. Within a year of their formation they won the unofficial English championship, which had reverted back to its original format of the leading teams playing against each other in challenge matches for possession of the Admiral Maxse Challenge Cup.

The ultimate significance of Oxford Canadians laid in their role as missionaries for Canadian ice hockey in Europe; it was in that role that they made their greatest impact. They were the first ice hockey club to represent Canada abroad by wearing the maple leaf on their team jerseys, albeit in an unofficial capacity.

A similar ambassadorial role had previously been the sole prerogative of Princes, who had done so much to promote and popularise ice hockey in Europe with their annual round of winter tours. These two great clubs, both elitist in their own special ways, would become great rivals for ice hockey supremacy both at home and abroad. In time, Princes would regularly double as "England" in international competitions while Oxford Canadians would equally come to be regarded as "Canada" in the same and similar events.

"Too Respectable For Glasgow"

Scotland was not completely immune to the rash of ice rink construction which took place in London during the closing years of the 19th century. On 16 May 1896, a consortium of local businessmen fronted by Mr Arthur Hubner opened the Glasgow Real Ice Skating Palace by converting an existing theatre building in Sauchiehall Street into an ice rink.

According to contemporary newspaper reports no expense was spared in providing winter sports enthusiasts in Glasgow with a first class facility. It was indeed a veritable palace, certainly on a par with anything constructed in London. One side of the arena was entirely taken up with an ornate proscenium for the accommodation of an orchestra. The building was decorated with art work and included a tableaux of peacock blue velvet in gold trimmings.

The ice surface was enveloped by a handsome balcony for the use of spectators. Nine arc lamps were erected around the ice and when added to the reflecting lights under the balcony gave the arena a very brilliant appearance. The roof of the building was softened by a canopy, in the making of which 2,200 yards of cream and brown coloured calico material had been used. Indeed, almost all of the interior furnishings of the building were decorated with rich upholstery supplied by the local Glasgow firm of Wylie & Lochhead.

As to the manufacture of the ice itself, a local newspaper offers a fascinating glimpse of Victorian ingenuity and engineering at its best:

> "The ice formed is of absolutely homogeneous quality and of beautifully smooth surface. In order to cause the ice to form and to give it the necessary elasticity, the water tray is formed with a thin steel bottom beneath which is a strata of flowing brine. The brine is reduced to a low temperature before entering this space while a certain amount is being continually drawn out so that a continuous circulation is obtained. The brine, being also under a small pressure, acts as an elastic cushion and although forming an absolutely reliable support, it has sufficient elasticity to prevent a serious concussion. The effect produced is an exact reproduction of the natural ice when formed on the surface of a lake."
>
> (Evening Times: 13 May 1896).

Frozen in Time

Glasgow Real Ice Skating Palace, c1896

"Too Respectable for Glasgow"

The actual dimensions of the ice surface are not recorded but it seems to have been of a reasonable size and circular in shape, perhaps akin to that of the old Niagara Hall in London. Facilities, both for refreshments and for skate hire, were provided separately for ladies and gentlemen. Apart from skating other entertainments would be offered at the venue including the new art of "cinematography".

None of this came cheap. Admission charges reflected the costs involved in the construction and maintenance of the building. Prices for skating at the venue were fixed at rates which were prohibitive to all but the seriously wealthy. Skating was offered in three distinct sessions. The morning and evening sessions cost two shillings and the afternoon session three shillings; a weekly ticket cost patrons seven shillings and six pence — all substantial amounts of money for indulging a pastime.

The management of the new ice rink seem to have been aware from the outset that there might be financial risks associated with their enterprise. In essence, there seems to have been a nagging suspicion that there might not be a market in Glasgow for such a facility. In a private ceremony held two days before the official opening of the venue, Major Tye, one of the consortium's directors, acknowledged these doubts when he was reported as saying that ". . . if it did not succeed he would be forced to the conclusion that it was too respectable for Glasgow."

Major Tye was of the opinion that the venue would mainly cater for the respectable and wealthy denizens of the city's affluent west end. In this assessment he was almost certainly correct; it was only people in the well-to-do suburbs of Glasgow who had the money and leisure time available to avail themselves of the facilities on offer. It remained a moot point, though, whether there were enough of them with a sufficient interest in skating to make the venue a financially viable proposition for that purpose in the long run.

"Hockey On The Ice?"

It was not too long before the management of the Glasgow Real Ice Skating Palace were considering the promotion of other winter sports at the venue. On 4 June 1896, an advertisement appeared that stated "applications for the use of the ice floor for curling, hockey, etc, may be addressed to the managing director."

Time for curling was subsequently allocated in the early mornings. Partick Curling Club became the first in Scotland to play on locally produced artificial ice when they held a match at the rink shortly after the advertisement appeared. While the size of the ice required for curling was considered short of the optimum, the experiment proved a great success and soon more curling clubs applied to use the rink.

The reference in the advertisement to "hockey" is intriguing. Its inclusion may have been owing to the influence of George Alfred Meagher, the world champion figure skater and pioneering ice hockey enthusiast. One of the best known figures in winter sports, he was briefly engaged at considerable expense by the management of the Glasgow Real Ice Skating Palace to give skating exhibitions and offer tuition in figure skating.

Meagher was a native of Kingston, Ontario, and was 29 years of age when he arrived in Glasgow. An ice hockey missionary without peer, he had introduced the sport to Paris in 1894 before being employed at Niagara Hall in London a year later. His stay in Glasgow was short. He later travelled throughout Europe competing in figure skating competitions and promoting ice hockey at the same time. He would have encouraged the promotion of a series of what were termed "bandy" matches arranged at Glasgow Real Ice Skating Palace between 6 June and 8 June 1896. These contests were being held under the auspices of the Scottish branch of the National Skating Association of Great Britain, who proposed that a local team should be put together in order to accept a challenge laid down by the London Bandy Club. There was great interest in these matches since bandy was an almost unknown sport north of the border.

Where would the Scottish team come from? It was highly unlikely that there were any bandy clubs in existence in Scotland at this time, although it is possible that any number of individuals could have learned to play the game while abroad on winter sports holidays. In any event, a team was assembled under the direction of an acolyte of Meagher, William Pollock Wylie, who was not only a champion speed skater but the Honorary Secretary of the Scottish branch of the National Skating Association.

Newspaper correspondents covering these matches seemed to be uncertain as to just what exactly they were witnessing at the Glasgow rink. One has some sympathy with them because the terms "bandy", "hockey on the ice" and "ice hockey" were almost interchangeable at this time yet in their purest forms quite different games. The correspondent of the *Evening Times* obviously gave up, since he headed his match report of the first two games he saw as "shinty"! No doubt this was a more familiar stick and ball game to him. In contrast, the correspondent of the *Daily Record and Mail* was convinced he had been watching "hockey on the ice." Interestingly, neither seemingly thought it was "bandy".

Whatever these games actually were in reality they were nevertheless undoubtedly historic occasions and as such worthy of report:

> "The first match under National Skating Association rules ever played in Scotland took place at the Real Ice Skating Palace on Saturday. Two games were played, one at three o'clock in the afternoon and the other at eight o'clock at night. In the first game, the London men fairly walked around the Scotch *[sic]* players, the latter never really proving themselves dangerous. The result was ten goals to nothing in favour of London.

In the evening the Scotchmen, improving by their afternoon's experience and cheered by a crowded gallery, played a much better game and on several occasions energetically attacked the London goal. During the first half of this game the score stood London three, Glasgow nil, compared with London six, Glasgow nil, in the corresponding half of the afternoon game.

In the second half the Scotch, headed by Bayne, the Kinross skater, made vigorous attacks on the London goal and in spite of the brilliant forward play of Messrs Cooper, only once was the "puck" put past Pollock Wylie.

During the last three minutes of the game the London men surrounded the Glasgow goal and some beautiful dribbling and passing was shown by S B Cooper who had hard luck in not scoring putting in no less than five hard shots which were stopped by Wylie. This display of attack and defence was loudly cheered by the spectators who numbered over 1,000. The game ended London four, Glasgow nil.

The return games will be played on Monday at three o'clock in the afternoon and eight o'clock at night. The Scotchmen will visit London in three weeks.

Teams:

Glasgow: Goal - William Pollock Wylie; Back - A G McLaurin; Forwards - Jack Bayne, J Sloan and W Thomson.

London: Goal - R H Whyte; Back - Lieutenant-Colonel Barrow; Forwards - S B Cooper, W B Cooper and A H Tyler."

(Daily Record and Mail: 8 June 1896).

Duly chastened by these heavy defeats the Scots made a number of team changes for the next two matches played on 8 June 1896. They were also permitted to ice an extra player which says much for the confidence of their opponents. As it transpired that confidence was entirely justified:

"Considerable interest was manifested in the return games between teams representing London and Scotland which took place yesterday at the Real Ice Skating Palace. It was expected that the Scotchmen would make a big effort to retrieve their lost laurels and give a display in keeping with their reputation. The first game was played in the afternoon before a crowded attendance and resulted in a win for the London representatives by eight goals to one.

In the evening the second and last game was played. Play became fast and furious right away and both goals were hotly stormed. The Englishmen, notwithstanding that they had six opponents to face, exhibited much better combination than the Scotchmen and had the honour of opening the scoring. Wylie, the Scotch custodian, was very clever and chiefly to his exertions the London players were baulked of success.

Occasionally the Scotch forwards got well in on Whyte, the London goalkeeper, but do as they liked they could not score. Before half time the London team scored a second point and led at the interval by two goals to nothing.

On resuming the London players went into their work in grand style and by means of some really clever combinations beat Wylie on four occasions. The Scotchmen lacked the resource and skill of their opponents and were outplayed at all points save goal. Wylie kept a good goal notwithstanding the score against him. The fact that no goals were scored by the Scotchmen is the best tribute to the abilities of the London goalkeeper and the back.

There was again a large and fashionable turnout of spectators and the game appeared to be greatly appreciated.

Teams:

Glasgow: Goal - William Pollock Wylie; Back - W Thomson; Forwards - J Sloan, George Douglas, Martyn B Kay and Jack Bayne.

London: Goal - R H Whyte; Back - Lieutenant-Colonel Barrow; Forwards - S B Cooper, W B Cooper and A H Tyler.

Mr Walter H Hutchins, resident engineer at the Real Ice Skating Palace, acted as referee."

(Daily Record and Mail: 9 June 1896).

What is one to make of these matches? Perhaps the best explanation one can offer is that some kind of hybrid ice sport was played at the Glasgow Real Ice Skating Palace those two days in June. It was certainly not real bandy since that was primarily an outdoor game usually played on an ice surface the size of a football field. It may also be indicative that it was the National Skating Association which suggested these fixtures, and not the National Bandy Association which had been established in England in 1891.

Was it then "hockey on the ice" by what is meant a version of field hockey played on ice? Possibly, but certainly not in its purest form. For one thing a "puck" is specifically mentioned in one of the newspaper reports and in field hockey a ball is used and not a puck. This is one of the first references to the use of a puck in a game in Great Britain - notwithstanding one was noted in use at Henglers Ice Rink in London that same year.

The influence of Meagher in preparing the way has already been noted and in Pollock Wylie he had a loyal local lieutenant. It is quite likely that it was Meagher who supplied pucks to the National Skating Association for use in such matches, as he was known to carry both these and ice hockey sticks with him wherever he went on his travels. The revelation that pucks were used in these four matches may well strengthen the claim that Meagher made in his book, "Lessons in Skating", published in 1900, that he introduced "ice hockey" to Glasgow in 1896. That may be stretching it a bit. Ice hockey in Europe was still evolving and no where near its level of development in Canada but what one can say about these four historic games is that they were an important and until now neglected part of the process by which ice hockey finally became established as a distinct sport not only in Scotland but in Great Britain and in Europe.

The Scottish Bandy Club

It is open to doubt whether the proposed return fixtures in London ever took place since no record of these matches appears to exist. However, that was not the end of "bandy" or "hockey on the ice" fixtures at the Glasgow Real Ice Skating Palace. Shortly after the four matches between Glasgow and London, the Scottish Bandy Club was formed, with the stated if somewhat confusing objective to "promote the game of bandy or hockey on the ice." It was established under the control of the Scottish branch of the National Skating Association and its Honorary Secretary, Pollock Wylie, also became the Honorary Secretary of the Scottish Bandy Club as well. Both of these bodies shared the same address at Bath Street, Glasgow.

The Scottish Bandy Club's first fixture at the Real Ice Skating Palace was against a team styling themselves "Glasgow All Comers" on 3 July 1896. They were reported to be under the captaincy of a Mr Gratten, who in fact may actually have been Mr W H Gittens. The newspapers of the day were not always entirely accurate when reporting the names of players. Unfortunately, the result of this particular contest has been lost to posterity.

At the end of July 1896, the winter sports season finished somewhat abruptly at Glasgow Real Ice Skating Palace. The venue closed for extensive alterations before re-opening again on 24 August 1896 as a cinema and vaudeville theatre. The ice surface was covered with wooden flooring upon which additional seating was installed. From the outset the venue had made a point of promoting other attractions besides skating and ice sports. The early art of cinema was one such venture and had proved extremely popular with the public. It was almost as if the management were hedging their bets given the doubts some clearly had over the financial viability of promoting only ice sports at the venue. Motion pictures were the next "big thing" in the world of entertainment and the films on show at the Real Ice Skating Palace had proved very profitable.

The experiment of promoting vaudeville had also proved a success but the venue was reconverted into an ice rink again and re-opened as such on 12 December 1896. The morning skating session was dropped and the whole of this time was allocated to curling. Prices were also reduced, with the afternoon skating session now costing two shillings and the evening skating session one shilling. Spectators were still charged one shilling to watch from the balcony but at least that was now heated since the recent installation of radiators.

On 19 December 1896 an advertisement appeared in the local newspapers for a "hockey on the ice" match at the Real Ice Skating Palace. This fixture was to be played between the Scottish Bandy Club and Glasgow University Bandy Club at 9.15pm on the Monday evening of 21 December 1896. Once again the actual result of this contest was not subsequently reported.

It was not until 23 April 1897 that the Scottish Bandy Club again took to the ice at the Glasgow venue. They were due to play the "Rest of Scotland" but the arrangements for this match did not go entirely to plan:

> "A bandy match between teams representing the Scottish Bandy Club and the Rest of Scotland was played at the Ice Palace last night. A large audience turned out in anticipation of a good game. Unfortunately, the Rest of Scotland team were not forward and to satisfy the spectators a scratch game between two teams of the Scottish Bandy Club engaged in a friendly match.
>
> The "A" team was captained by Mr W H Gittens and the "B" team by Mr J A Harby. At half time the game stood at one goal each. The second half opened with some very fast play on both sides in which Mr Harby for the "B" team and Mr Bell Scott for the "A" team showed up best. The result was "A" team two goals, "B" team three goals.
>
> Teams:
>
> "A" Team: Goal - J L Jowett; Back - Martyn B Kay; Half-Back - W H Gittens; Forwards - Bell Scott and F Kay.
>
> "B" Team: Goal - Stanley Glanfield; Back - "A N Other"; Half-Back - George Douglas; Forwards - J A Harby and A G McLaurin.
>
> Referee: John Clark Junior.
>
> *(Evening Times: 24 April 1897).*

This was the final match the Scottish Bandy Club ever played at the Glasgow Real Ice Skating Palace. The venue itself was closed only six days later on 1 May 1897, ostensibly "for the season." When it eventually re-opened it was not as an ice rink but as Glasgow's first dedicated cinema. The management of the venue had done their sums and had finally concluded that the screening of motion pictures was a more profitable business than the promotion of winter sports. Thus ended Glasgow's first experiment with an artificial ice rink. The doubters within the management of the Glasgow Real Ice Skating Palace were ultimately proved correct. There was indeed no market for such a grand enterprise in the "Second City of the Empire."

However despite its short life the venue deserves to be remembered as a pioneer of the sports that would eventually evolve into ice hockey.

"Too Respectable for Glasgow"

Scottish Bandy Club

Established: 1896
Headquarters: 102 Bath Street, Glasgow
President: Sir Archibald Campbell, Lord Blythswood
Honorary Secretary: William Pollock Wylie
Membership: Sir Archibald Campbell,
Lord Blythswood,
William Pollock Wylie,
J L Jowett,
Martyn B Kay,
W H Gittens,
Bell Scott,
F Kay,
Stanley Glanfield,
George Douglas,
J A Harby,
A G McLaurin,
Jack Bayne,
J Sloan,
W Thomson.

William Pollock Wylie, c1898

The Father of Scottish Ice Hockey; William Pollock Wylie

If Bethune Minet Patton was the "father" of English ice hockey then William Pollock Wylie must surely be a contender for his Scottish equivalent.

The son of a Baptist minister, Wylie was born in the small seaside town of Gourock in Renfrewshire in 1869 and later lived in Glasgow. He became a journalist by profession and was the editor of a religious newspaper called the *Christian Leader* which had been established by his father.

The very epitome of Victorian "Muscular Christianity" he was a keen sportsman. He was not only involved in athletics but was also an active participant in a number of winter sports including bandy, "hockey on the ice", curling and speed skating. Speed skating was Wylie's real passion and he was very good at it. In 1895, he became the champion of Scotland when he won the mile event on the frozen ice of Loch Leven. It was his great interest in winter sports which led him to become the Honorary Secretary of the Scottish branch of the National Skating Association; he held the same position with the Scottish Bandy Club, whose membership included one of his great speed skating rivals, Jack Bayne of Kinross.

Wylie was instrumental in helping to organise the four historic bandy or "hockey on the ice" matches held at the Glasgow Real Ice Skating Palace in June, 1896, where his enthusiasm for these sports had no doubt been strongly encouraged by George Alfred Meagher during his short time at that venue. These were all significant achievements but Wylie may have yet another string to his bow.

The Scottish ice hockey historian, David Gordon, has uncovered exciting evidence of Wylie's major contribution to the development of ice hockey as a quite distinct sport from either bandy or "hockey on the ice" and much earlier in time than had otherwise been generally accepted.

In 1933, when Wylie was 64 years of age and obviously writing from memory in Switzerland, a letter from him was published in *The Scotsman* in which he referred to an "ice hockey" match in Paris, France, which he had played in and had actually helped to organise as early as 1897! The text of this important and historic letter is worth repeating in full.

"Who introduced ice hockey to Europe is a question now being discussed freely at the Swiss winter sports resorts.

Ice hockey as at present played on small enclosed rinks of either natural or artificial ice with a puck was first introduced to the Continent of Europe by the Scottish Ice Hockey Club in December 1897.

In November of that year, the secretary of the club received a request from the manager of the Palais de Glace in Le Champs Elysees, Paris, to forward a bundle of hockey sticks, such as the Scottish club used on their artificial rink at the Panorama [Glasgow Real Ice Skating Palace], Glasgow. These were sent and shortly afterwards a challenge was received to play the match in Paris during the last week of 1897. This challenge was accepted.

The French sportsmen had the opportunity of receiving a certain amount of tuition in the game from Mr George A Meagher of Montreal, the then champion figure skater of the world, who was residing in Paris.

The Scottish team left on Christmas Eve and after four days practice on the French rink, the match came off on the evening of 31 December. It resulted in a win for Scotland by twelve goals to one. Mr Meagher captained the French team and scored the only goal himself, individually; I captained the Scottish team.

Our teams in Scotland were mostly drawn from Edinburgh and Glasgow University students with a sprinkling of students from the engineering schools of Glasgow. This was the first match played on the Continent of the game as we now know it, and with a puck.

It might be as well for me to also mention that another form of hockey was introduced on the Continent prior to the game in Paris, namely, Fen country "bandy." Mr Charles Goodmand Tebbutt, the famous international amateur speed champion, took a team of bandy players over to Haarlem in Holland under the auspices of the athletic association there in the winter of 1891 when he captained the Bury Fen Bandy Club.

This game, of course, is entirely different to present day hockey and had been played for many years in the Fens on ice when available; it was played in the open air and the ground was a right angled parallelogram 200 yards long and 100 yards wide, the ball used was of solid India rubber not less than two and a quarter inches in diameter - a polo ball was preferable.

Mr Tebbutt's Bury Fen team won, I think, by fourteen goals to one.

Mr Tebbutt has also to his credit the introduction of bandy to Sweden, Norway and Denmark.

Hence, Great Britain can fairly claim to have introduced both forms of hockey on the ice to Europe."

(*The Scotsman: 17 January 1933*).

This is a truly fascinating letter but it actually raises as many questions as it answers. Wylie's reference to the use of pucks is affirmative. Pucks were used in the bandy or "hockey on the ice" matches played at the Real Ice Skating Palace in June 1896 and he has confirmed their use again in this match played in Paris a year and a half later.

The reference to "hockey sticks" is perhaps a bit more problematic. In using this term is Wylie actually referring to ice hockey sticks or field hockey sticks? He has implied that there was a "bundle" of these sticks in Glasgow which were subsequently sent to Paris for this match. One does have to wonder though whether there would have been such quantities of ice hockey sticks available in Glasgow at this time. How likely was that? Unfortunately, given the passage of time and the lack of corroborative evidence, one will never know for sure; however, if the members of the "Scottish Ice Hockey Club" were playing with ice hockey sticks rather than bandy sticks and with pucks rather than balls in 1897, then they deserve to be properly recognised as amongst the very earliest practitioners of "ice hockey" in Europe albeit in its most rudimentary form.

It is unfortunate that Wylie does not furnish any more details about the Scottish Ice Hockey Club, beyond the statement that the players were composed of students who attended Glasgow and Edinburgh Universities as well as some engineering schools in Glasgow. Given the result of the match it would seem that the Scottish team were much more familiar with the game than their French counterparts and this rather suggests that some, if not most, may well have been expatriate Canadians studying in Scotland.

It is unlikely that there was any organised or structured ice hockey competition in Scotland at this time. Rather, there were obviously a few enthusiastic individuals at both universities who had the ambition and the expertise required to play the game. It is not beyond the realms of possibility that, if some of these zealots were Canadian exiles, they could have brought the necessary pucks and sticks with them from Canada on settling in Scotland.

It has been noted that Glasgow University Bandy Club was certainly in existence by at least mid-December 1896. It is therefore quite probable that when the ice hockey club was formed it was from this group of players that it originated — particularly if, as suggested, they also had the necessary equipment by early 1897 for playing the newer game.

Wylie states in his letter that the Scottish Ice Hockey Club had the use of the artificial ice at the Panorama or Glasgow Real Ice Skating Palace in Glasgow. It is interesting to speculate as to when this might have occurred. The venue had only been available for ice sports between mid-May and end July 1896 and again between mid-August 1896 and early May 1897. It is therefore being suggested that the Scottish Ice Hockey Club would only have had access to the ice for the first five months of 1897 at best. Indeed, given the management of that venue's prevaricating attitude to promoting any ice sports outside figure skating and curling, any time set aside for "ice hockey" would presumably have been very limited.

The great outdoors offered the only other realistic alternative for playing ice team sports in Scotland; even that was similarly limited. As skaters and curlers knew only too well, depending on the unpredictability of Scottish winter weather was an exasperating and frustrating experience. The occasions when it was actually cold enough for solid and safe ice to form on frozen lochs and ponds were not that often, so those ice-hockey-playing students would have to take their opportunities for playing the game as and when they came along.

Despite the lack of opportunity for playing and for practice, the establishment of the Scottish Ice Hockey Club was a very significant development. It confirms that players in Scotland were amongst the very first to develop the sport in Great Britain and it is even more noteworthy that they undertook a pioneering missionary role in taking the game to Europe.

These achievements and the considerable part played in them by William Pollock Wylie in successfully bringing them to fruition deserve to be formally recognised by the sport's official historians and administrators in the same manner and reverence that Bethune Minet Patton and George Alfred Meagher are rightly regarded.

It now seems quite clear that William Pollock Wylie was also one of the founding fathers of British and European ice hockey.

The Establishment of the Scottish Ice Hockey Association

The conversion of the Glasgow Real Ice Skating Palace into a cinema in May 1897 effectively ended any further organised bandy or ice hockey activity in Scotland. For the foreseeable future bandy and ice hockey enthusiasts would have to hope that the winters would be cold enough to freeze lochs and ponds long enough for them to play some recreational sport. Such opportunities were therefore rather limited.

It was to be another decade before Glasgow experimented with an artificial ice rink again:

> "One of the most important developments in recreation and sport is that of the Scottish Ice Rink Company who have built and equipped at Crossmyloof, Glasgow, what is believed to be the largest artificial ice rink in the world.
>
> It is a reasonable lament almost every year that our fickle climate yields only disappointment to those devoted to the skating and curling pastimes. Indoor skating rinks are of course no novelty while enthusiastic urban curlers have adopted the artificial outdoor rink and by means of spraying a concreted surface obtained with a few degrees of frost, a tolerably good playing ice.
>
> The Glasgow enterprise is of course entirely independent of atmospheric conditions. The pavilion adjoins Crossmyloof railway station and is also within a penny tram ride from the centre of the city.
>
> The ice surface, oblong in shape, extends 1,525 square yards. The freezing plant has been supplied by a well known firm of engineers, the Haslam Foundry and Engineering Company, Derby. The public are thus put in possession of a skating and curling pavilion available at all times and free from disagreeable changes in the weather.
>
> There are dining, tea and smoking rooms attached to the rink, all comfortably furnished and heated. Each day will be divided into periods of three hours, say from 10.00am to 1.00pm, 2.00pm to 5.00pm, and 7.00pm to 10.00pm. In the summer months the pavilion will be closed and the refrigerating plant used for the manufacture of ice for sale.
>
> Skating clubs are already in the process of formation while curling competitions and bonspiels will be promoted. It is but fitting that the

inauguration of the pavilion should take the form of a competition in the national game of curling, the opening game taking place tomorrow."
(Glasgow Herald: 30 September 1907).

It is clear from contemporary newspaper reports that the main impetus behind the founding of the Scottish Ice Rink Company and its subsequent construction of Crossmyloof Ice Rink came from curling interests. Curling clubs were integrally involved in various fund raising activities for the project. The chairman of the company, George Hamilton, a native of Peebles but then resident in Glasgow, was noted as a keen curler as were most of the other company directors.

Crossmyloof Ice Rink was formally opened on 1 October 1907. In one of the many speeches given during the opening ceremony it was noted that "the kindred pastimes of skating and ice hockey will also be prosecuted." This public recognition of "ice hockey" was significant as a statement of intent for those few enthusiasts in Scotland who could play the game and for any of those who still remembered (or had even participated in) the sport's brief existence at the old Glasgow Real Ice Skating Palace a decade earlier.

By 1907, "ice hockey", as opposed to "bandy" or "hockey on the ice", had finally developed, although still somewhat rudimentary in form, into a distinct sport in England. There were probably no more than five or six clubs in existence, all socially exclusive and concentrated in London and the south east of England.

A curious feature of Crossmyloof Ice Rink, much referred to ever since, was that a bandstand resting on four pillars was erected in the centre of the ice surface. This must have been a very odd feature indeed for not only would it have restricted the movements of the skaters around the ice but presumably it would have also seriously impeded curling competition by restricting the number of lanes in use. The existence of a bandstand and four pillars in the centre of the ice surface would also have made it difficult to play competitive ice hockey at the venue. The pillars would have not only presented a major obstacle to the players but would also have seriously restricted any passing movements in that zone of the ice. Unless these pillars were somehow movable the ebb and flow normal to ice hockey matches would have been curtailed. It is remarkable that such an unusual feature should have escaped the notice of the *Glasgow Herald* in its report of the opening of the rink. There is absolutely no reference to the bandstand. One is left to conclude that it was a later addition.

It should be noted that the *Glasgow Herald* was indulging in some uncharacteristic hyperbole when it suggested that the ice surface at the rink was believed to be the largest in the world. That was certainly not the case but at 149 feet by 89 feet, the ice surface was a reasonable size, and bandstands apart, large enough to play ice hockey.

The Establishment of the Scottish Ice Hockey Association

First Crossmyloof Ice Rink, c.1908

It is almost certain that no organised form of ice hockey was played at Crossmyloof Ice Rink in what may be termed season 1907-08. This is not really surprising, given the dearth of competent players. It could be possible that some exhibition matches involving teams from south of the border were held at the venue but if this did occur no records have survived.

The rink re-opened for business on 1 October 1908 when it was noted that

> "Skating and curling are again in season at the Scottish Ice Rink, Crossmyloof, Glasgow. Although the rink has been in existence for only one year it has already secured a large measure of popularity among those who engage in these fascinating pastimes.
>
> Many new members have joined the skating section and several of the clubs have attained their maximum membership roll of 350. Last year curlers to the number of 800 were attached to the rink and during the present season it is expected that this total will be exceeded."
>
> *(Glasgow Herald: 2 October 1908).*

It may be instructive that unlike the previous year no mention is made in this report of the possibility of any ice hockey at the rink. Yet the formation of what were obviously a large number of skating clubs was an encouraging development. These clubs would in time provide a cadre of dedicated ice hockey enthusiasts who, when numerous enough, would go on to establish teams who would then compete against each other.

Membership of these skating clubs would have been boosted by the recruitment of expatriate Canadians resident in Scotland, some being students at local universities or professionals engaged in business or commerce. They would have been crucial to the formation of ice hockey clubs at the rink both as players and coaches, as well as instructing the locals in the rules of the sport. Unfortunately, a definitive date for the establishment of the first ice hockey clubs at Crossmyloof Ice Rink remains a matter conjecture, in the absence of hard evidence.

One man who might have known, J R (Jack) Gilmour, failed to throw any light on the subject in his written contribution to Patton's book, "Ice Hockey". Gilmour contributed a chapter on the history of ice hockey in Scotland but he did not address in any meaningful way the earliest period of the sport's development north of the border.

Writing some thirty years later the ice hockey correspondent of the *Glasgow Herald* recalled that the sport was introduced to Glasgow in 1910. This statement remains a valuable piece of local evidence but according to the Society of North American Hockey Historians and Researchers, Crossmyloof Ice Rink had staged its first ice hockey matches two years earlier in 1908, an assertion probably based on a less than conclusive statement made by Jack Gilmour in Patton's book.

The Establishment of the Scottish Ice Hockey Association

The problem with suggesting 1908 is that no real evidence has been offered - nor is any seemingly available - to support this claim. Neither is there any evidence to hand of matches being staged in the early months of 1909. In view of this, it would appear that season 1908-09 can also be rejected as the possible starting point for the promotion of any formally organised ice hockey being staged at Crossmyloof, beyond the possibility of a few enthusiasts indulging in purely recreational matches behind closed doors.

An important indicator in this matter may be that the management of Crossmyloof Ice Rink frequently placed advertisements in local newspapers. These advertisements always cited skating and curling as attractions at the venue but there was never any reference to ice hockey being staged at this time.

Since the standard of play would not have been very proficient, owing to the players lack of experience and opportunity, it is understandable that the rink management may not have considered ice hockey a spectator sport at this time. Given these circumstances, and on the balance of probabilities, one is led to conclude that the most likely date for the commencement of formal competition between organised clubs would have been season 1909-10.

Ice hockey clubs, or skating clubs which also played ice hockey, were certainly in existence at Crossmyloof Ice Rink by the winter of 1909. These clubs formed the nucleus of the Scottish Ice Hockey Association (SIHA) which was established either late in 1909 or early in 1910.

Amongst the founding clubs of the SIHA were Beavers, Corinthians, King's, Star and Wanderers. The names of these five clubs are on record but precious little else is known about any of them. There were probably more of whom no record has so far come to light. It is likely that the known clubs were all based in Glasgow and they would have played their matches at Crossmyloof. In reality, the competition between them was no more than a private "house league" played behind closed doors but nevertheless it was a beginning and that was what was important.

In spite of this dearth of information some conclusions can be drawn. As in England, these clubs would have attracted only the wealthier sections of society, middle class professionals and business people in the main, along with a sprinkling of expatriate Canadian students. It was only persons from these social groupings who had the money to indulge what was an expensive sport.

It is likely that most of the ice hockey clubs at Crossmyloof simply evolved out of pre-existing skating clubs. An exception though might be Wanderers, since there was already in existence a well known field hockey club of the same name in Glasgow, and the ice hockey club may well have been a winter sports offshoot of its parent.

One may also speculate as to whether Beavers suggested a specifically Canadian connotation? In the absence of any club records from the period, or any surviving eye witnesses to these events, the origin and development of these pioneering teams may never be fully known.

House league or not, it was still one of the earliest ice hockey league competitions in the world. Outside of North America, the sport was only really formally established in any corresponding organised manner in a few countries including Belgium, Bohemia, England, France, Germany and Switzerland.

Ice hockey as a sport was itself still evolving at this time. Teams consisted of seven players. The positions were goaltender; point; cover-point; rover; right wing, centre and left wing. The two defence players, point and cover-point, never left their zone of the ice and the position of rover was, as the name suggests, one where the player in question attempted to link the play between defence and attack, in an era when there were many more restrictions on forward passing.

Matches in the Edwardian era seem to have consisted of only two periods, each of twenty minutes duration, with an interval of three minutes between. Gilmour points out that players in Scotland were now using "short sticks, after the fashion of bandy sticks" despite the existence of the longer ice hockey sticks which had come into greater use elsewhere. No nets were provided behind the goal posts at Crossmyloof.

In terms of kit, customised uniforms were yet to come. Most Scottish players were obliged to wear thick woollen rugby jerseys and white tennis flannels instead of team shirts, shorts and knee length socks. Gloves were usually worn. Ice hockey skates were almost unobtainable outside of Canada and in Scotland most players had to make do with figure skates.

Protective equipment for players was also very primitive with various forms of thick padding used for shins, knees and elbows much of it being adapted and improvised from other sports. Goaltenders often resorted to wearing cricket pads. The concept of protective equipment specifically designed for ice hockey players was still a long way off, at least outside of North America.

The First Home Internationals

It was not too long before the mettle of the recently established Scottish Ice Hockey Association (SIHA) was tested because early in 1910 an invitation was received from Princes Ice Hockey Club to play them in London.

The fact that the invitation was so readily accepted suggests that the Scottish authority was confident that the standard of play at Crossmyloof Ice Rink had at least reached a level where it was thought they could give the aristocrats of the sport a decent match. Perhaps not unnaturally, the contest was considered to be a full international between Scotland and England. Thus commenced one of the oldest and most enduring rivalries in the ice hockey world.

The actual date of this fixture has always been the subject of some uncertainty due in the main to Major Patton who suggested in his book that it was played in 1909. One would have thought that he should have known, since he actually played for and captained England in this match, but even the normally reliable Patton could get it wrong on occasion. This truly historic fixture was actually played on Saturday 26 March 1910.

The SIHA obviously brought the impending contest to the attention of the local press in Glasgow, because the *Glasgow Herald*, the *Evening Times* and the *Daily Record and Mail* all carried more or less the same press release about the match. This one humble paragraph is of some significance because it was the first time any of these mass circulation newspapers had made any reference to the existence of domestic ice hockey.

The paragraph ran as follows:

"The following team, chosen from clubs affiliated to the Scottish Ice Hockey Association, will represent Scotland at Princes Rink, London, on Saturday; Goal - J B Wharrie (Corinthians); Back - A S Dunlop (King's); Half-Back - J Campbell (Corinthians); Rover - A J McGuffie (Wanderers); Forwards - T Taylor (Wanderers); G Pettigrew (Star) and Captain and J D Strathearn (Beavers); Reserve - J Melvin (Wanderers). Mr William Arnot will travel as honorary official of the Association."
(Evening Times: 24 March 1910).

By way of clarification, the positions cited "back" and "half-back" in this article actually equated to the positions of point and cover-point. Either the journalist concerned was not familiar with the correct terminology or that was indeed the names by which these positions were known in Scotland.

Unfortunately it is typical of the period that having reported on the Scottish team for this match, not one of the aforementioned newspapers subsequently gave the result of the contest, let alone any account of the play! For a contemporary report of this and the return match played in Glasgow later in the year historians have had to consult foreign winter sports magazines and in particular, the German *Deutscher Wintersport* and the French *Sports d' Hiver*.

The fact that Scotland could ice a team at all indicated the progress the sport had made north of the border. Since it was likely that the Scottish club sides had only been playing in regular competition from the autumn of 1909 the experience of the players selected for the national team must have been quite limited. That stated what is not known is whether any of these players were Canadians. The comparative inexperience of the Scottish team appears to have been borne out by the result of the match; England 11 Scotland 1.

In fairness, the English team was of course entirely composed of players from Princes who, only two months earlier, had won the first official European Championships at Les Avants in the Swiss Alps. Not only were they a very experienced group of players, but they were also playing on their home ice. Apart from Oxford Canadians, Princes were still arguably the strongest club side in European ice hockey.

The two teams which contested the first ever home international match were:

England: Thomas O M Sopwith; Thomas J Unite; Bethune M Patton; Nigel Haig; Charlie Napier, Hugo Stoner and C M G Howell.

Scotland: J B Wharrie (Corinthians); A S Dunlop (King's); J Campbell (Corinthians); A J McGuffie (Wanderers); T Taylor (Wanderers), G Pettigrew (Star) and J D Strathearn (Beavers).

Inexperience, lack of time playing together and the strength of the opposition were all significant factors in explaining the margin of the Scottish defeat. Yet, perhaps the most significant factor was the fact that the Scottish team played the match with their "short sticks, after the fashion of bandy sticks" while their opponents used ice hockey sticks. This gave an obvious advantage to the English team as it was more difficult for the Scottish players to control the puck with their shorter sticks.

Not much is known about the players. The goaltender, John Wharrie, was certainly still playing ice hockey some twenty years later, as he kept goal for Glasgow Skating Club during seasons 1929-30 and 1930-31. He was a native born Scot and was quite possibly connected to a family run textile business of the same name then operating in Glasgow.

Similarly, Archibald S Dunlop was another native Scot and was almost certainly connected to the family of the same name who owned the Doonside estate on the outskirts of Ayr. He was in all probability related to Colonel

The First Home Internationals

Scotland and England Team Portraits, December 1910
Top Row - Archibald S. Dunlop (Scotland), T. Taylor (Scotland) J. Campbell, junr. (Scotland), A. J. McGuffie (Scotland), John B. Wharrie (Scotland)
Second Row - Gordon Pettigrew (Scotland), J.D. Strathearn (captain) (Scotland), B. M. Patton (captain) England, Percy Lambert (England)
Bottom Row - H. Paul (England), B.R. Waite (England), Hugo Stoner (England), A.F. Austin-Smith (England), R. Greenway (England).

Thomas C Dunlop who played ice hockey himself and went on to establish the short lived Doonside Ice Hockey Club in 1929.

Crossmyloof Ice Rink re-opened for the new season on 1 October 1910. The management placed advertisements in the local press but again they referred only to skating and curling as attractions at the rink. There was no reference to ice hockey, which was being played behind closed doors. Matches most probably took place in the late evening, after the final skating sessions had ended, given that competition for ice time at the venue was so intense.

During the summer months of 1910 a number of structural improvements had been made to Crossmyloof including the extension of the tea rooms and offices and the creation of a new lounge for the use of ladies. It is quite clear from contemporary newspaper reports that the ice rink was popular and paying its way. A number of carnival evenings were held for various local charities in which the presence of ice hockey players was noted.

On 24 October 1910 the *Glasgow Herald* carried an advertisement for Crossmyloof Ice Rink which gave notice of a "First Division Ice Hockey Match" being staged at the venue. This is the first contemporary reference found to the actual existence of a league competition at the rink. However, it is a reference which raises more questions than it answers.

To begin with the advertisement failed to detail the time of the match, which teams were involved and any reference to admission charges. This seemed to imply that while the public were being invited to watch a match, almost certainly for the first time, they were not expected to pay for the privilege.

What is one to make of the fact that it was a "first division" match? It does probably confirm that there were indeed more than five ice hockey clubs in existence at the rink (unless there was perhaps a junior league in existence). If the latter was the case then it might have been a most encouraging development for the future of the sport at the Glasgow venue.

Irrespective of how many ice hockey clubs there may have been at Crossmyloof, the local newspapers continued to ignore their activities. Neither the fixtures nor the results of matches between these clubs were ever reported in the press. The notice referred to above was the only occasion between 1907 and 1914 where ice hockey was specifically mentioned in a newspaper advertisement for the ice rink. It is not entirely clear why this should have been the case.

Ice hockey was certainly a minority sport, probably viewed as somewhat elitist, but that never prevented the *Glasgow Herald* or other local newspapers from giving a decent amount of coverage to sports such as polo and lacrosse, equally socially exclusive. Perhaps ice hockey was seen as a foreign import not worthy of attention, or simply as a passing fad of a few wealthy individuals. Whatever the reasons, it did not register on the radar of local sports journalists.

The First Home Internationals

In fact the only occasion that ice hockey again merited any reference in the local press was when a return international match was arranged between Scotland and England at Crossmyloof Ice Rink. There has been some confusion as to when this fixture was actually played. The match took place on Friday 16 December 1910.

The SIHA gave a vote of confidence to the team which had played in London earlier in the year by selecting it again for this fixture. The only changes in personnel were on the substitutes bench where J W Melvin of Wanderers was missing with H Paul and S E Sage coming in as replacements.

A studio photograph of the Scottish team was taken to mark this historic occasion and it is reproduced in this book. The first team players are seen wearing what appears to be rugby kit consisting of a single colour jersey with a white open neck collar, shorts and socks although it is very unlikely that the team actually played in these shorts and socks. The goaltender, John Wharrie, is also wearing cricket pads and crucially the players have ice hockey sticks. The match referee, D McGill, is also in the photograph along with another gentleman who is most probably William Arnot of the Scottish Ice Hockey Association.

There is some evidence that the England team which arrived in Glasgow for this fixture was not that which was expected. They were also a player short. As a result, one of the Scottish substitutes, H Paul, was obliged to turn out for the visitors. A contemporary magazine picture shows portraits of the two teams where Paul is listed as an England player. In agreeing to play for the "Auld Enemy" he had clearly put the interests of the sport before national sentiment.

As in the first fixture between the two countries, England were wholly represented by players from Princes with the exception of H Paul. Only Bethune Patton and Hugo Stoner played in both matches. The Princes players came into this match off the back of a 7-5 defeat from their great rivals Oxford Canadians only three weeks earlier and may not have been in the best of form.

The two teams were:

Scotland: J B Wharrie (Corinthians); A J McGuffie (Wanderers); J Campbell (Corinthians); A S Dunlop (King's); T Taylor (Wanderers), G Pettigrew (Star) and J D Strathearn (Beavers).

England: R Greenway; Bethune Patton; Hugo Stoner; Percy Lambert; B R Waite, A F Austin-Smith and H Paul.

Referee: D McGill (SIHA).

Of course the Scots did not have the luxury of a large squad of competent players from which to select, but they had clearly learned one important lesson from their earlier match with England. The shorter bandy type sticks were abandoned. They took to the ice this time with ice hockey sticks with which they had, as Jack Gilmour commented, "put in much assiduous practice."

That practice certainly paid off because a rejuvenated Scottish team soundly defeated their more illustrious opponents 8-3 to record a truly historic victory. Unfortunately no match report has yet surfaced of this game but the pattern of scoring is known. Scotland led 4-1 at the end of the first period and won the second period 4- 2. The goal scoring was as follows; J D Strathearn 1-0; J D Strathearn 2-0; G Pettigrew 3-0; J D Strathearn 4-0; B R Waite 4-1; J D Strathearn 5-1; G Pettigrew 6-1; T Taylor 7-1; B R Waite 7-2; B R Waite 7-3 and J D Strathearn 8-3.

It was undoubtedly an impressive performance by the Scottish team who were clearly in control of the match from start to finish. A first half hat-trick from the slightly built left wing, J D Strathearn of Beavers, put the home side firmly in the driving seat. He capped a fine performance by scoring two further goals in the second half and was obviously the star of the show.

The occasion must have resulted in an enormous boost for ice hockey in Scotland although incredibly it passed the local press by. Not one of the mass circulation newspapers in Glasgow even managed to publish the result of the match, let alone report any details of it. What an extraordinary state of affairs! Sporting history being made on their doorstep but the players might as well have been playing on the moon for all the notice that was taken of them.

It is difficult to determine on the basis of the limited evidence available what the actual standard of ice hockey in Scotland was in the Edwardian era.

There is little doubt though that real progress had been made. The establishment of the Scottish Ice Hockey Association had been a very positive development. This led to an organised club competition at Crossmyloof Ice Rink and the creation of a national team. The recent defeat of England was highly significant. It demonstrated that Scotland possessed players of genuine ability and proficiency in the sport.

How many of those playing ice hockey in Scotland at this time were actually Scots-born, or had learned to play the game in their native land must remain a moot point. It was quite possibly the majority; one can only really speculate on this question. Some would undoubtedly have learned to play ice hockey while on Alpine holidays and others from the coaching of expatriate Canadians at Crossmyloof Ice Rink.

The number of expatriate Canadians playing ice hockey in the Glasgow area is unknown but they would no doubt have been well to the fore in encouraging and developing the sport locally - as was occurring in other parts of Europe where they were domiciled. These ice hockey 'missionaries' were the first of several waves of future generations who would similarly cross the Atlantic Ocean and play their national game in the towns and cities of Scotland.

By the end of the Edwardian era, a foundation of sorts had been laid. It had not been easy, for those involved had been obliged to look to their own resources but there was much for these early puck-chasing pioneers, whether Scottish or Canadian in origin, to be proud about. Competitive ice hockey was being played on a regular basis and on an artificial ice rink in Scotland. Not too many countries could boast that.

The Wider Context: International Developments

On 15 May 1908 a number of representatives from Belgium, France, Great Britain and Switzerland held a meeting in Paris, the purpose of which was to establish the Ligue Internationale de Hockey sur Glace (LIHG), the forerunner of what is now the International Ice Hockey Federation (IIHF). Representatives from Germany and Russia were also invited to the meeting but they did not attend. Bohemia joined the LIHG later in the year as its fifth member.

The initiative for this important development came from France so perhaps it was fitting that two Frenchmen should occupy the leading positions on the new body with Louis Magnus as President and Robert Planque as General Secretary. Both men were heavily involved with the pioneering Club de Patineurs de Paris, the premier ice hockey club in France.

Great Britain was represented at this meeting by E E Mavogodato, an official of the National Skating Association — not, as might have been expected, by Bethune Patton. This may have been because ice hockey was still under the jurisdiction of the National Skating Association at this time. It was still a year before the Scottish Ice Hockey Association would be formed and fully five years before the establishment of the British Ice Hockey Association.

The main aims of the LIHG were to standardise the rules and statutes of the sport across Europe, no mean feat in itself, and to promote international competition between member countries. An initial tournament was held in Berlin, Germany, in November 1908 which was won by England (Princes). At a second tournament held at Chamonix, France, teams from all of the founder countries competed. In both competitions the teams used Canadian ice hockey sticks and Canadian pucks and the playing time consisted of two twenty minute periods.

In January 1910 the LIHG organised the first official European Championships in the Swiss winter resort of Les Avants, not far from Montreux. The participating countries were Belgium, Great Britain, Switzerland and Germany, the latter nation joining the LIHG in 1909. France and Bohemia were also expected to take part in the competition but both countries withdrew only two weeks before the first matches were to be played.

The players stayed at the same hotel in Les Avants and all of the matches were played outdoors on a rink specially set up on some open ground in front of the building. According to Patton, who captained the Great Britain team, unseasonably mild weather meant that the ice was extremely bad for the three days that the championships were held. As was the norm, the British team was made up entirely of players from Princes.

In the first game Great Britain and Belgium drew 1-1 in front of about 400 spectators, many of whom were British tourists. Great Britain then defeated Germany 1-0 in a match marked by the brilliant goaltending of Thomas Sopwith in the British goal. Switzerland were then beaten 5-1. This unbeaten sequence of results was enough for Great Britain to be declared European Champions. The winning team was:

Thomas O M Sopwith; Bethune M Patton; Bevan C Cox; Harold H Duden; Hugo W Stoner, Robert Le Cron and P Sydney Cox.

It was the crowning achievement in the history of Princes who presented a somewhat cosmopolitan appearance. Only Sopwith and Patton were definitely known to be of English birth. Of the others, Robert Le Cron was an American and Harold H Duden was Belgian. The nationalities of the remaining players are not known but it is most likely they were Canadians.

The LIHG also invited Oxford Canadians to Les Avants in what seems to have been a semi-official capacity or as Patton rather more eloquently phrased it "hors concours". The idea was to give the European teams and the spectators the opportunity of seeing how a Canadian team played. Although this illustrious side took no part in the official tournament they did play all of the competing countries with the exception of Great Britain.

Against the competing nations Oxford Canadians defeated Switzerland 8-1, Germany 4-0 and Belgium 6-0 but they also played a large number of other matches against local club and representative teams. In total, they played 17 fixtures in 21 days and won every single match. The "Rhodies", as they were informally known, outscored their various opponents by a staggering 204 goals to 17! In such circumstances it is very difficult not to regard Oxford Canadians as the best ice hockey team in Europe, despite Princes winning the official title.

There had been some suggestion that Princes had deliberately avoided a confrontation with them at the European Championships. The two sides met a year later at a club tournament also held at Les Avants. Oxford Canadians registered an emphatic 12-0 victory. A day later they met again at the annual Coupe de Chamonix where the "Rhodies" confirmed their superiority with an 11-1 win.

These encounters were followed by what was described as the "British Championship Final" between the two teams. This match was played on 18 February 1911 in London, presumably at Princes Ice Rink. Home advantage counted for nothing. Oxford Canadians put in another devastating display to defeat Princes 11-2.

Amongst the players to turn out for this magnificent team were goaltender Gustave Lanctot, defenders W M Martin and Christopher A Adamson, rover Ernest A Munro and forwards Howard R L Henry, John G Higgins, Robert Tait and John Gillis. Both John Higgins and Robert Tait were from

The Wider Context - International Developments

Newfoundland (not part of Canada until 1949) and Gustave Lanctot was as his name suggests a French-Canadian.

Scotland's position in relation to the LIHG was something of an anomaly. There is no record of the Scottish Ice Hockey Association ever seeking recognition from or any formal affiliation to the LIHG. It would seem that Scotland was simply subsumed under the umbrella of Great Britain and one is left to ponder whether the international body was even aware of the separate existence of the sport north of the border.

This was unfortunate. Scotland deserved recognition in its own right as one of the pioneering nations in the international development of ice hockey going back to the late 19th century. Scotland was one of only a small number of countries in Europe to have an organised league structure in place and one of the first to produce a national team.

By 1911, Bohemia had eleven ice hockey clubs in operation, more than any other country in Europe. They took to the game very quickly and went on to win the second European Championships held that year in Berlin. Great Britain (Princes) declined to defend their title (for reasons never explained) and would not compete again in the European Championships until 1926.

The annual Oxbridge varsity matches had been resumed in Wengen, Switzerland, in 1909. Oxford won 5-3 and repeated that score the following year at Murren, Switzerland. Despite that initial setback, Murren proved to be a good change of venue for Cambridge who won the next three annual matches up to the outbreak of the First World War in 1914.

International politics reared its ugly head in ice hockey in 1912 following Bohemia's successful defence of their European Championship title. Their achievement was later annulled by the LIHG due to a dispute over Bohemia's actual status as a satellite nation within the Austro-Hungarian Empire. The following year Belgium won the title. In 1914, Bohemia won their third European Championship in four years by playing what was considered to be "Canadian style" ice hockey.

With all of this formal activity going on in Scotland and Europe one might ask what was going on in England? The British Ice Hockey Association (BIHA) was only established during the 1913-14 season. It seems astonishing that it took so long to organise a governing body for England. Up to this point both the National Skating Association and Princes Ice Hockey Club acted for ice hockey matters in England in a semi-official capacity - always a rather unsatisfactory state of affairs.

The founding of the BIHA led to a situation where it was responsible for governing ice hockey in England and Wales, while the SIHA remained the governing authority for the sport in Scotland. The later relationship between the two bodies was generally good although tensions could and did arise from time to time. The two bodies would eventually reach agreement on the mutual recognition of player registrations and player transfers in and between the two countries.

Only five clubs were involved in founding the BIHA and these were; Cambridge University; Manchester; Oxford Canadians; Princes and Royal Engineers (Chatham).

The composition of the BIHA reflected the widespread changes that had occurred in English ice hockey during the first two decades of its development. Many of the original clubs such as Niagara, Argyll and London Canadians had not survived whereas Manchester was a relative newcomer to the sport, having been formed as recently as 1910. Their home ice was the new state of the art Manchester Ice Palace which had 1,100 seats and a maximum spectator capacity of 2,500.

As with the formation of the old Ice Hockey League in England in 1903, Oxford University was again surprisingly absent from the founding of the new body ten years later. It is not obvious why this should have been the case. Perhaps the involvement of their sister club, Oxford Canadians, was enough.

The participation of Royal Engineers was an interesting development since it gave an early indication of the growing interest of Canadian military personnel in domestic ice hockey. In the future many Canadian officers and servicemen stationed in England would take an active interest in British ice hockey and some of them would later go on to play for Great Britain in international competition.

It was very apparent though from the distribution of senior posts within the BIHA that Princes Ice Hockey Club still held great sway in the English game. Given his great standing in the sport it was really no surprise that Major Patton was appointed its first President. In addition, T G Cannon, another Princes man of long standing, was appointed Honorary Secretary and Treasurer of the new organisation. In such circumstances it made sense for the headquarters of the BIHA to be located at Princes Ice Rink.

In The Doldrums

The steady if unspectacular progress made by ice hockey in Scotland and England all came to a shuddering halt with the outbreak of the First World War in August 1914. Like almost every other facet of public and private life in Great Britain, sport in general - and ice hockey in particular - was seriously disrupted by the advent of hostilities only in its case almost to the point of virtual extinction.

The small number of ice rinks in Great Britain were generally commandeered by the government for war purposes. Two of the most important, Princes in London and Crossmyloof in Glasgow, were destined not to re-open. Princes Ice Rink closed in 1917, resulting not only in the ice hockey club losing its home base after twenty years, but also in the unfortunate loss of all of the early records of the recently established BIHA.

The eventual closure of Crossmyloof Ice Rink in 1918 administered the *coup de grace* to Scottish ice hockey, already in a moribund state since the outbreak of the war. It is very doubtful if any of the pre-war clubs survived beyond 1914; even if they did manage to struggle on, they were effectively killed off since they now had no home ice on which to practice or play matches. It would be another eleven years before ice hockey in Scotland was formally revived.

South of the border, Princes Ice Hockey Club were able to continue playing, primarily because of the social status of their members. They simply played all of their matches abroad - Switzerland in the main - until such times as new ice rinks were built in London. Similarly, the annual Oxbridge varsity matches were resumed in 1920, with the venue alternating between Murren and St Moritz in Switzerland for the remainder of the decade.

Fate was not so kind to England's other great club, Oxford Canadians, whose brief but highly successful history came to an end in 1914. Following the war it was decided that Oxford University Ice Hockey Club could now play their Rhodes scholars. In 1920, Canada formally affiliated to the LIHG and could therefore compete in future World and Olympic Championships.

By the early 1920s, Haymarket Ice Rink in Edinburgh and the Manchester Ice Palace were the only ice rinks still operating in Great Britain. Ice hockey was rarely played at the Edinburgh venue. An exhibition game involving soldiers from Newfoundland was played at Haymarket in 1915 but the management of the rink was always much more interested in promoting curling.

Only a handful of ice hockey clubs remained in England and they endured a nomadic existence. It left the sport appearing even more socially exclusive and elitist - only those with real financial means at their disposal and appropriate leisure time were in a position to actively participate.

Oxford University were to assume the mantle of the country's leading club in the early years of the 1920s. Seriously strengthened by the addition of their Rhodes scholars they swept all before them in the crisp Alpine air. Oxford played six matches in 1921 and won them all, scoring 87 goals in the process for the loss of only 2. This sequence of results included a 27-0 thrashing of Cambridge University!

Oxford defeated Cambridge again in 1922 by 8-1 and in 1923 by 3-0. This talented side contained a number of outstanding players including goaltender Ken Taylor and forward Edward Pitblado. Others would go on to make their mark in Canadian life including Lester Pearson, a future Prime Minister of Canada, Roland Michener, a future Governor-General of Canada and Dick Bonnycastle, of the Harlequin book publishing dynasty.

Apart from Princes, Manchester and the Oxbridge students, the other main participants in domestic ice hockey were the armed forces. A team largely composed of Canadian army officers stationed in England visited St Moritz in 1923, where they played and won several matches against Swiss opposition. This team became the basis of the Great Britain side which entered the joint World and Olympic Championships held at Chamonix in 1924.

This was the first time that Great Britain had participated in an LIHG event since the successful European Championships of 1910. Of the ten players selected for the British team, at least six were known to be Canadians including Blaine Nathaniel Sexton, who would go on to play a major part in the future development of ice hockey in Britain.

The only survivor from the 1910 side was the ubiquitous Patton, who was the reserve goaltender. He was the sole representative from Princes, with at least six of the other players furnished by the army team. Great Britain surprised many observers by how well they played; they finished the tournament in third place with the bronze medal. Canada, as expected, won the gold medal and the United States of America finished second with the silver.

During this period of history Canada were represented by their leading amateur club sides. In 1924 this was the Toronto Granites and they thrashed Great Britain 19-2. It was a measure of their superiority that this thumping victory was the second lowest they achieved in the competition. No country they played managed to score more than two goals against them.

By this time the LIHG had introduced two important rule changes. In 1923, it had been decided that an ice hockey team should only consist of six players; a goaltender, two defenders and three forwards. The position of rover was therefore eliminated. In addition, it was also decided that ice hockey matches should consist of three periods of fifteen minutes duration each.

In the Doldrums

In 1924, Blaine Sexton formed a new ice hockey club, the London Lions. Patton noted in his book that the new club made a very favourable impression on its debut tour of Switzerland that year by winning all but one of their matches. This was a portent of what was to come. The London Lions, composed almost entirely of expatriate Canadians resident in the city area, took over from Oxford University as the leading club side in England.

Following another successful season in Switzerland in 1925, the London Lions supplied at least five of the ten players selected for the Great Britain team which competed in the European Championships held at Davos, Switzerland, in January 1926. Amongst that group was Patton, still playing at almost 50 years of age.

Manchester supplied three players to a British team which struggled to find any form compared to the heroics of 1924. Standards had been rising in European ice hockey, with Sweden and Czechoslovakia in particular coming to the fore. While Great Britain finished rather disappointingly in fourth position, a fact Patton put down to a lack of reserve players, Blaine Sexton enjoyed a good tournament, accounting for 8 of his team's 26 goals.

Sexton had genuine star quality. He had learned and played the game in his native Canada before coming to London, where he ran a successful canned food business and settled down with an English wife. Equally comfortable playing in defence or attack, he was a superb stick-handler, famous for his exhilarating one-man dashes up the ice. A bit of a showman, Sexton was the first real personality to emerge in British ice hockey at a time when the sport was at last just beginning to revive.

British ice hockey finally came out of the doldrums in late 1926 with the opening of the Westminster Ice Palace in London. This development allowed both Princes and London Lions to play their matches at the new venue although the rink management seem to have been somewhat less than enthusiastic in their promotion of the sport at the venue.

Within a year though three further ice rinks were constructed and opened in London. These new rinks were located at Golders Green, Hammersmith and Park Lane. The last named was perhaps the most unusual of the three. It was actually located in the basement of the plush and expensive Grosvenor House Hotel in the fashionable district of Mayfair. Despite its unique abode the rink had a capacity for 1,500 spectators and eventually became the home ice for a new club, the Grosvenor House Canadians.

Frozen in Time

The New Crossmyloof Ice Rink

The first real moves towards building a new ice rink in Glasgow seriously emerged in 1925 amongst the skating and curling communities when an appeal for funding the venture was officially launched. The main impetus seems to have come from the local provinces associated with the Royal Caledonian Curling Club but it would be a couple of years before these initial steps came to fruition.

While ice hockey in Scotland remained in a moribund condition the situation in England was rapidly improving. In January 1927 there was great excitement at the arrival of the Montreal Victorias, the first Canadian club side to visit the country. The tourists defeated England 14-1 at the Westminster Ice Palace in London with Major Patton the only native born player selected for the English team.

In 1928, the United Services Ice Hockey Club supplied almost half of the twelve players selected for the Great Britain team which participated in the World and Olympic Championships held at St Moritz. Cambridge University, who were now enjoying a period of ascendancy over their varsity rivals, supplied three players. One name missing from the British team was that of Patton. Time had at last caught up with the grand old man of English ice hockey.

Canada, represented on this occasion by the University of Toronto, won their third successive World and Olympic titles thereby confirming their complete dominance of international ice hockey. Great Britain finished in fourth position behind Sweden and Switzerland. The gulf between Canada and everyone else was as wide as ever, given that Great Britain were defeated 14-0, Sweden 11-0 and Switzerland 13-0, a total of 38 goals scored for the loss of none!

In April 1928 came the news that winter sports enthusiasts in the West of Scotland had waited ten long years for.

> "Curlers and skaters throughout Scotland have evinced considerable interest in the efforts now being made for the construction on modern lines of the new ice rink at Crossmyloof, Glasgow, and so generous has been the public response to the invitation to take up shares in the Scottish Ice Rink Company (1929) Limited that the directors are confident that within a short time the full capital will be submitted.
>
> When the rink was in use before the war it was a popular centre for ice sports. Since 1918, when it was taken over for national purposes,

the restricted facilities in Scotland for indoor play coupled with the unsuitability of the weather for outdoor sport have created a keen desire among curlers and skaters for the securing of another rink. Efforts towards this end were begun but only recently were they successful and the property at Crossmyloof was purchased.

A company was floated a short time ago with a capital of £35,000 and the interest which the public has shown in the venture is manifest by the fact that applications for upwards of 30,000 shares have been received to date.

The work of reconstruction will be begun forthwith. Under the scheme of alteration, renovation and extension, the centre pillars formally existing will be a thing of the past. A new and higher one arch roof will be laid and galleries constructed to afford comfortable accommodation for spectators while perhaps the most important feature will be the extension of the ice surface by about 45 feet.

This increased ice surface while affording skaters much greater scope will permit of ice hockey being played, a sport which from a spectator point of view has already become extremely popular in the new London Ice Rink (sic) and one which will undoubtedly greatly increase the revenue earning capacity of the Glasgow undertaking."
(Glasgow Herald: 19 April 1928).

Unlike the situation in 1907, when the original Crossmyloof Ice Rink was constructed, there was now a clear commitment to promote ice hockey at the new venue. The rink management obviously realised that the money making potential of the sport made it a profitable commercial enterprise. This was very welcome news indeed for those older spectators who had not witnessed any formally organised ice hockey in Glasgow since before 1914, and for those younger and newer enthusiasts now drawn to "the fastest game on earth."

By the end of the decade ice hockey was almost fashionable. Large and enthusiastic crowds were being drawn to matches in England and the sport was starting to attract an increased level of newspaper coverage. These developments would have a knock-on effect north of the border, now that a venue was at last in place able and willing to promote the sport.

The great day came on 14 January 1929 when the new Crossmyloof Ice Rink was formally opened:

"The necessity of meeting the demand by young people for healthy recreation was emphasised by the Duke of Montrose yesterday in opening the new Scottish Ice Rink at Crossmyloof, Glasgow.

The rink has been constructed on the site of one which was in operation prior to and during the early years of the war. The structure erected at a cost of £40,000 has accommodation for about 3,000 spectators and skaters. The total area available for ice sports measures 186 feet by 97 feet and with six rinks devoted to curling the space at the disposal of skaters is 100 feet by 50 feet.

Almost nine and a quarter miles of piping have been laid underneath the ice surface, the depth of the ice being about three and one half inches. There is a large entrance hall and along the south wing a tea room, dining room and refreshment room. A balcony runs along four sides of the building to accommodate spectators and an orchestra which will render selections of music for the benefit of skaters and sightseers.

The Duke of Montrose said there seemed to be an impression south of the border that in Scotland - and in Glasgow particularly - the people took their pleasures sadly. He did not think that could be said in the future. Referring to the lack of sports facilities in the city, he said there was no opportunity for having a ride on a horse or of doing some serious rowing; until the rink was opened it had been impossible to indulge in curling to any extent.

There was no doubt that in these days they had to meet the demand of young people for healthy recreation. It seemed almost a scandal that people had to go to Switzerland to indulge in the old Scottish sport of curling. The Duke threw the first stone over the ice and as a memento of the opening ceremony he was presented with a curling stone.

Thereafter, a number of skating displays were given by Mr Sidney Charlton, the professional at the rink, and others."

(Glasgow Herald: 15 January 1929).

Frozen in Time

Second Crossmyloof Ice Rink

The Revival of the Scottish Ice Hockey Association

In March 1929, less than two months after the opening of the new ice rink, the *Glasgow Herald* reported that

> "A novel form of sport was introduced in Glasgow at the Crossmyloof Ice Rink on Saturday night when an ice hockey match between Bearsden and Canadians took place. The event met with great success. Bearsden were represented by several well known rugby men. The teams were:
> Bearsden: R G Walker; G C Scott and A S Dykes; R O MacDonald, J G Carruthers and J E Forrest.
> Canadians: F McLernan; E McLeod and G R Nodwell; S K Lindsay, H W Reid and D A Porter.
> The announcement of this event attracted a large number of spectators and the game was followed throughout with keen interest by all present.
> Several other ice rinks are expected to be opened by the time next season commences and it is the intention to form a league among the Scottish ice rinks which will make it possible to select a strong representative team to meet other countries.
> Considering the want of training, Saturday's game was remarkably fast. The Canadians, who are resident in Glasgow, were leading by two goals to nothing at half time. In the second half this advantage was increased to four."
>
> *(Glasgow Herald, 4 March, 1929)*

Thus was summarised the return of organised ice hockey to Scotland after an absence of at least fifteen years.

A couple of points arising from this report merit some comment. This occasion was not a "novel form of sport" since ice hockey had been introduced to the Glasgow public before at Crossmyloof Ice Rink, during the Edwardian era. Indeed, as noted, a rudimentary form of the sport had even been played in the city as far back as the late 19th century at the old Glasgow Real Ice Skating Palace.

The new LIHG ruling on icing only six players in a team had obviously been adhered to. However, its other important ruling about ice hockey matches being of three periods of fifteen minutes duration each had been ignored. It seems that two periods were played of uncertain duration and this may have been due to either a throwback to the pre-war era or simply the rink management restricting the time the players were allowed on the ice.

What seems really surprising about this match was that it took place at all. It was only two months since the rink had opened, yet already at least two ice hockey clubs had been established and were proficient enough at the sport to compete against each other in front of a public audience. This was astonishing progress in such a short space of time. It appears that the Glasgow area was not short of players.

One might ask how was this possible? Of the historic match in question, one of the two teams which participated, Glasgow Canadians, was entirely composed of expatriate Canadians resident in the city for either business or education reasons. What might be more difficult to explain is the fact that the other team, Bearsden, was only one of several other ice hockey clubs already in existence in the West of Scotland.

Where did all of these players emerge from? Did they all learn to skate and play ice hockey during winter sports holidays in Switzerland? For some the answer was yes - but surely not for all of them?

For those who had not learned the game abroad, it would seem that they had been very quickly coached in the arts of the game by more experienced players locally. It is more than likely that the Glasgow Canadians Ice Hockey Club undertook that key coaching role. To their leading players, Eric McLeod, Don Porter, Felix McLernan, Hugh Reid and Stewart Lindsay, an enormous amount of gratitude is due for a job well done.

In his contribution to Patton's book "Ice Hockey", Jack Gilmour sheds some more light on this matter. The opening of Crossmyloof Ice Rink coincided with fine but freezing cold weather during the months of November and December 1928. Some knock-about ice hockey games - played on frozen lochs in the Bearsden area and at Ardinning outside Strathblane - led a number of Glaswegians and expatriate Canadians to become acquainted.

These informal games led four of the participants - two Scots, J R (Jack) Gilmour himself and G C Scott and two Canadians, S K (Stewie) Lindsay and Hugh W Reid - to make initial contact with James Gourley, the newly appointed ice rink manager at Crossmyloof, about the possibility of promoting ice hockey at the venue. At this stage, the new rink had not formally opened and "little headway" was made as a result.

Undaunted by this initial setback these four ice hockey missionaries continued in their quest. They started to badger the board of directors of the Scottish Ice Rink Company, the owners of Crossmyloof, and were fortunate in finding two staunch allies for their cause in Frank Stuart and Andrew Mitchell. Both of these gentlemen were very keen ice hockey enthusiasts. Both realised the commercial potential the sport offered as a source of revenue for the venue.

The Revival of the Scottish Ice Hockey Association

In fact the match played between Bearsden and Glasgow Canadians on 2 March 1929 was the beginning of a very long lasting and fruitful relationship between ice hockey and Crossmyloof Ice Rink. This was just as well. The comment in the *Glasgow Herald* report that other ice rinks would be opening in Scotland for the start of the new season proved to be wildly optimistic. Rather, it was left to Crossmyloof - and to Crossmyloof alone - to promote ice hockey in Scotland for the foreseeable future.

Events, though, were moving quickly, as the local press observed:

> "At a largely attended meeting held in the ice rink, Crossmyloof, Glasgow, Mr Frank Stuart, chairman of the company presiding, a recommendation to form an Ice Hockey Association with a view to properly regulating and governing matches and tournaments which will commence immediately on the re-opening of the ice rink next season, was approved of. Mr D B A Carty was elected secretary.
>
> Mr Mitchell, one of the directors, said that in order to encourage the movement he would give a trophy for competition.
>
> Eleven clubs have already intimated their intentions of joining the Association. These are Glasgow Canadians, Bearsden, Bridge of Weir (Renfrewshire), Doonside (Ayrshire), Achtungs, Queen's, Glasgow High School, Dennistoun, Kelvingrove, Old Glasgow Skating Club and Scottish Corinthians.
>
> It is proposed to run two sections of a league and play knock-out tournaments."
>
> *(Glasgow Herald: 25 March 1929).*

What took place on 23 March 1929 was in reality a re-constitution of the Scottish Ice Hockey Association (SIHA).

This was a key development. The rate of progress made had been phenomenal. In the space of about five months, about a dozen ice hockey clubs had been organised in the West of Scotland. It is also quite clear from the various office-bearers appointed to the SIHA that the Scottish Ice Rink Company, owners of Crossmyloof Ice Rink, were an absolutely integral part of the new governing body from the start.

Within three days of the revival of the SIHA a twelfth club, Mohawks, also joined the new organisation. They first came to notice on 30 March 1929 when they played what was possibly their first competitive match. Mohawks opponents were Bridge of Weir, also known as Ranfurly at this time. The team from Renfrewshire won a one-sided contest 5-0.

One of the referees in this initial period of activity was a Mr D McGill of the Scottish Corinthians Club. This was the same gentleman who had refereed the historic Scotland v England match at the old Crossmyloof Ice Rink in

Frozen in Time

December 1910. He was one of a very small number of players from that time to have survived into the new era just dawning for ice hockey in Scotland.

This raises an interesting question. Was his club, Scottish Corinthians, connected to the older Corinthians Club which had co-founded the first Scottish Ice Hockey Association in late 1909 or early 1910? If - as seems likely - it was then it was the only club of the original known five from that time to have survived. Although the Scottish Corinthians joined the revived SIHA in March 1929, there is no record of them actually playing any matches before Crossmyloof closed for the season in April.

After the match between Bearsden and Glasgow Canadians on 2 March 1929, a further ten fixtures involving most of the other founder clubs of the SIHA were played at Crossmyloof. These were simply challenge matches but they gave the teams a taste of competitive ice hockey for the first time. It was a pity that the season was drawing to a close at the ice rink.

All of these matches were squeezed in either before or after the regular public skating sessions. The teams were allocated only half an hour to play the fixtures and the spectators were not charged anything to watch them. The rink management, gauging the level of public interest in the sport, were not to be disappointed as the games, truncated as they were, nevertheless attracted large and enthusiastic crowds.

Further excitement was generated when the two best teams in England, London Lions and United Services, agreed to play a grand challenge match at Crossmyloof on 13 April 1929. The *Glasgow Herald* rather patronisingly observed that Scottish ice hockey followers would now have the opportunity of "seeing how the game should really be played." Certainly the match would be played under more normal conditions with three periods of thirteen minutes duration spaced by two intervals of seven minutes each.

The teams for this match were:

London Lions: V Gardner; W H Brown and W H MacKenzie; R Bruce, B N Sexton and J C P Magwood. - H W Bushell, R Brelter and W Strubbe.

United Services: Flight Lieutenant V H Tait; Flying Officer D A Harding and Lieutenant H A Davis; Captain C R Cuthbert, Lord Lincoln and Captain W J Holme. - Flying Officer P C Fair, Captain E D Carruthers and J J Dunne.

Referee: Clarence S Campbell (Oxford University).

In a close contest full of thrills and spills London Lions defeated United Services 4-3. With ten international players and five members of the Great Britain team (which had finished fourth in the World and Olympic Championships held at St Moritz in 1928), including the charismatic Blaine Sexton, on show the match attracted a full house at Crossmyloof. The whole occasion was a great success and further enthused everyone connected with the sport in Scotland.

The SIHA held a further meeting at the end of April 1929 to consolidate its position. Frank Stuart was confirmed as President and D B A (Dave) Carty as Secretary. Hugh W Reid, who played for Glasgow Canadians and who had done so much to promote the sport, was appointed Vice-President. Andrew Mitchell was appointed to the position of Honorary Vice-President. The organisation was in very good hands.

The building blocks were now all in place. All was set fair. Ice hockey followers in Scotland had much to be pleased about. After enduring years of dormancy the sport was back, albeit at only one ice rink. Within two months of Crossmyloof Ice Rink formally re-opening, the Scottish Ice Hockey Association was revived and had affiliated twelve clubs. The progress made had been nothing short of remarkable as the sport looked forward to its first full season of formal competition for a generation.

Frozen in Time

The Amateur Game

As the eagerly awaited season 1929-30 approached the *Glasgow Herald* observed

> "At the end of last season ice hockey in Glasgow seemed set for a splendid run of popularity as attendances at the Crossmyloof Ice Rink proved and this year the Scottish Ice Hockey Association in conjunction with the management of the Crossmyloof rink are determined to take up where they left off. An ambitious but practicable programme has been mapped out and the Crossmyloof Ice Rink management have provided dressing and bathing accommodation for the players."
> *(Glasgow Herald: 19 September 1929).*

Further improvements made to the venue during the summer months included the extension of the ice surface by a further forty feet, a new tea room was added to the gallery and the cloak room accommodation was considerably extended. The decision of the rink management to invest further in the fabric and infrastructure of the venue augured very well. It demonstrated their belief that ice sports in general and ice hockey in particular had a future in Glasgow.

The twelve clubs now affiliated to the SIHA were set to compete in the first formally organised league competition held in Scotland for at least fifteen years. These clubs were; Achtungs, Bearsden, Bridge of Weir, Dennistoun, Doonside, Glasgow High School, Glasgow Skating Club, Glasgow University, Kelvingrove, Mohawks, Queen's and Scottish Corinthians.

One very significant name missing from this line up was Glasgow Canadians. The club was composed of expatriate Canadians and some of them would not be available to play a full season in Glasgow. Only two or three of the team were destined to remain in the city for the foreseeable future. In these circumstances, there was no point in entering a team in the league if they were going to lose half their players during the season.

The loss of this club was a blow but the expertise of their remaining players was not lost to the local game. Thus, Hugh Reid moved to Achtungs, Felix McLernan joined Glasgow Skating Club and both Eric McLeod and Don Porter strengthened Queen's, although the latter's stay with that club was to be all too short. Glasgow Canadians were replaced in the SIHA by Glasgow University.

While Glasgow University restricted its membership to current students, staff and alumni, some of these individuals were in fact already experienced players from countries where ice hockey was played, including Canada, the United States of America and Switzerland. Indeed, the captain and coach of the new club, J A (Jack) Easton, would become one of the finest players to grace the Scottish game.

It is worth reflecting on the character and social structure of the various clubs which comprised the Scottish Ice Hockey Association. The origins and development of some of the clubs remains obscure but enough is known about the others to allow for a picture to be painted of what the sport in Scotland looked like as it entered its new era.

An important point to be underlined is that ice hockey in Scotland during this period was a strictly amateur sport. The *players* involved with their clubs were certainly serious about their commitment but ice hockey was played in their spare time. It was not their full time occupation. Most of the players, particularly those born and brought up in Scotland, approached the game in the Corinthian spirit. It was "the game for the game's sake." The social background of these players simply reinforced such attitudes.

It is quite clear from the social composition and nuances of the clubs that the sport remained a largely middle class enterprise. It could not really have been otherwise, since the cost of club subscriptions and the purchase of skates, sticks, kit and other essential equipment required to play ice hockey would have been beyond the financial means of anyone outside the more comfortably well-off sections of society.

With the possible exceptions of the Canadian exiles, who permeated most of the clubs, the Scottish players shared a similar socio-economic background and outlook. Most of them had been raised in owner-occupied homes, educated in private and independent fee-paying schools, and earned their living in business or the professions. No doubt as a result of a school system which encouraged the values of physical education and team-work on the playing field for building character, many of these future ice hockey players shared a passion for sport in general.

This social exclusivity was reinforced by the fact that at Crossmyloof Ice Rink, where all the players practiced and played, everyone would more or less know everyone else. Many of these players were also involved in other winter sports promoted by the rink, including curling and speed skating. Crossmyloof became something of a social club as well as the venue where winter sports enthusiasts could indulge their interests.

It is also noteworthy how many of these ice hockey players were actively involved in other amateur sports, particularly rugby union. Rugby was and still is a staple in the curriculum of private and independent fee-paying schools in Scotland. Many of these schools had senior clubs for former pupils which were amongst the very best in the country. Amongst these clubs were

Glasgow Academicals, who were one of the dominant forces in Scottish rugby during this period.

Not for nothing were Bearsden Ice Hockey Club referred to as the "rugby men" by the contemporary press. No less than four of their players also played rugby regularly for Glasgow Academicals. These players were A S (Andrew) Dykes, J C (Jimmy) Dykes, G C Scott and J E Forrest. In addition, both Dykes brothers and J E Forrest also played rugby for Scotland. Another later Scottish international player, F H Waters, would also play a handful of matches for Bearsden.

There was no formal connection between Glasgow Academicals Rugby Club and Bearsden Ice Hockey Club beyond the fact that a number of the former club's players obviously decided to participate in another equally demanding physical sport. The fact they played for Bearsden was probably because that was the area where most of these players lived. It remains one of the most prosperous suburbs of Glasgow lying to the north of the city.

A rugby connection was also found at other SIHA clubs. At Dennistoun, the brothers W Waddell and H Waddell also played for Glasgow Academicals while at Doonside, I K M (Ian) Fair and G D (Guy) Parsons regularly turned out for West of Scotland, a club based in Partick in the West End of Glasgow. It is likely that other ice hockey players were involved with rugby clubs at lower levels of the sport.

In similar circumstances at least seven players of the Bridge of Weir Ice Hockey Club also played field hockey for the Bridge of Weir Hockey Club. These players were A R M (Ramsay) Muirhead, H J Telfer, W M (Wilbur) Muirhead, I S (Ian) McLeod, A N (Norman) Macfie, J K (Jimmy) Woodrow and A E (Alistair) McLeod. In this case, the ice hockey club was clearly an official offshoot of the field hockey club which had been formed in 1903. Some of these players were also involved with the Bridge of Weir Curling Club.

Glasgow University Hockey Club also supplied at least two players to the Glasgow University Ice Hockey Club. These players were C W de Visser and J S Carslaw.

Both Glasgow Skating Club and Scottish Corinthians were skating clubs which had spawned ice hockey offshoots. These two rather venerable old clubs had a number of players who had actually participated in ice hockey during the Edwardian era at the original Crossmyloof Ice Rink, including J B (John) Wharrie, H R Orr and W Ritchie. Indeed, John Wharrie had kept goal for Scotland in the two historic matches against England in 1910.

Of the twelve clubs comprising the SIHA for season 1929-30 only Bridge of Weir, from Renfrewshire, and Doonside, from Ayrshire, were based outside of the city of Glasgow.

A major employer in Bridge of Weir, an affluent and quiet small country town about twelve miles west of Glasgow, was the Bridge of Weir Leather Company, which had been founded by members of the local Muirhead family in the late 19th century. Three contemporary directors of this company, Earl, Wilbur and Ramsay Muirhead, were members of the Bridge of Weir Ice Hockey Club and Wilbur would go on to play for Scotland.

The Doonside Ice Hockey Club, the most socially exclusive club in the country, took its name from the large country estate, located on the outskirts of Ayr, owned by Colonel Thomas Charles Dunlop. Educated at Eton, Dunlop had pursued a successful career in the army. He excelled in several sports, especially cricket, and had learned to skate while on winter sports holidays in Switzerland. A great ice hockey enthusiast, Dunlop was the founding father of the Doonside Club.

Apart from Dunlop, the team included Colonel W A (William) Collins, who had been educated at Harrow and was a member of the prominent Scottish publishing dynasty; Commander K B S (Kenneth) Greig, who had completed his education in Switzerland, where he had learned to skate before joining the Royal Navy; the Rev H (Harry) Horton who had been educated at Cambridge University and was the curate of the Episcopal Church in Ayr, and G T (George) Cunningham who was a hosiery manufacturer, member of the Ayrshire Polo Club and the Eglinton Hunt and a lieutenant in the Ayrshire Yeomanry.

If the Doonside team read like a list of entries from "Who's Who", only the bizarrely named Achtungs Ice Hockey Club was able to boast a future peer of the realm. The Honourable John Scott Maclay, second son of Baron Maclay, educated at Winchester and Cambridge University and a future MP and government minister, turned out on a couple of occasions for the Glasgow team in 1929. He later became the first Viscount Muirshiel of Kilmacolm.

Scottish ice hockey in this period of its development was also characterised by strong family and kinship ties. Many of the clubs attracted members drawn from the same families. At Doonside, Colonel Dunlop played alongside his sons, W H (William) Dunlop and F H (Frederick) Dunlop. At Achtungs, there were two sets of brothers; H C Higginbotham and W R Higginbotham as well as A Rintoul and R Rintoul. At Dennistoun, the Waddell brothers played together.

The club with the closest family ties was Bridge of Weir. There were two sets of three brothers in this team; Earl, Ramsay and Wilbur Muirhead as already noted and they played with Alistair, Ian and Walter McLeod, who were all employed in their family textile business, which had headquarters in Glasgow. Walter was the youngest of these brothers and he went on to play for Scotland After retiring from ice hockey, he became one of Scotland's finest amateur golfers.

The most famous brothers in the pre-war era of Scottish ice hockey were John, Alec and Billy Fullerton from Newlands, in the south-side of Glasgow. All three, initially with different clubs, would make their mark on the game. All three would play for Scotland. John was the eldest. Billy, the youngest, employed as a stockbroker's clerk in Glasgow, was destined to become the best Scottish-developed player in the country, the equal of any Canadian import.

Although some of the players and clubs affiliated to the SIHA had connections with other sports, it is important to bear in mind that at least two clubs, Kelvingrove and Mohawks - and possibly a third in Dennistoun - were founded wholly as ice hockey clubs from the outset. Kelvingrove and Mohawks players were not distracted by participation in sports outside of ice hockey, as some of those in other clubs. This partly explains why these two great clubs in particular came to dominate the Scottish game in the amateur era.

One gets the impression that what became the Scottish League, in reality the "Crossmyloof" league, was in its formative years at least something of a gentlemen's club for amateur sportsmen. As such it must have exuded a rather clannish air to anyone interested in taking up ice hockey from outside this social milieu.

In summary, ice hockey in Scotland, or more precisely Glasgow and West Central Scotland, was a minority pre-occupation of a few native-born wealthy individuals complemented by a cadre of Canadian and foreign enthusiasts resident in the country for business or education purposes. The exclusivity of the domestic game was demonstrated by the shared class, social, familial and kinship relationships of its main participants and reinforced its strict amateur ethos and code of conduct. Yet despite these apparent disadvantages ice hockey would come to appeal to a mass audience attracted by its skill, speed, aggression and excitement.

The management at Crossmyloof Ice Rink were well aware of the sport's commercial potential, having seen evidence of it earlier in the year. In turn, the Scottish Ice Hockey Association was aware that the standard of play and coaching required general improvement. The clubs had come a very long way in a short space of time. If the product was right on the ice, there was no doubt that the sport had a future - not just in Glasgow but in other parts of Scotland as well.

Frozen in Time

Season 1929-30

"Considerable interest was taken to the ice hockey match played at the Scottish Ice Rink, Crossmyloof, Glasgow, last evening between Bridge of Weir and the Mohawks. The game marked the baptism of the Scottish Ice Hockey Association which comprises twelve clubs and this match was the first of the league competition which has been formed.

The teams were:

Bridge of Weir: A R M Muirhead; J K Woodrow and W M Muirhead; I S McLeod, A E McLeod and R E Muirhead. - R J G McDonald, H J Telfer and B Downes.

Mohawks: C Gammie; A Anderson and J McDonald; T Shearer, J Fullerton and G Holmes. - S Stevenson and C B Baird.

Referee: H W Reid (Achtungs).

The game was played in three periods of twelve minutes each with two three minutes intervals. Bridge of Weir were first to make headway. A E McLeod came near to scoring and soon afterwards I S McLeod had the same experience. The Mohawks at last broke away and J Fullerton shot into the net. The goal was disallowed owing to an infringement.

The second period opened with Bridge of Weir attacking and after two minutes R E Muirhead scored after dribbling from the centre of the ice. Each player adopted shooting in this period instead of passing. J Fullerton got away for the Mohawks but W M Muirhead intercepted. A E McLeod had another nice run but was held up for offside. Near the end of the period, J Fullerton levelled the scores.

The third period was fast and well played by both teams but with most of the play within the Mohawks ground and ultimately A E McLeod got a clever goal."

(Glasgow Herald: 5 October 1929).

So was reported the first official competitive match played under the auspices of the revived Scottish Ice Hockey Association.

Since the clubs comprising the SIHA were relatively inexperienced it was agreed that a Points Competition should be initially established whereby each team would play four matches. The teams finishing in the first six positions of this Points Competition would then form a First Division and the remaining six teams a Second Division.

This seemed a sensible way to proceed. It gave the clubs some genuinely competitive matches and the opportunity to establish settled formations and styles of play. The new Scottish League would therefore commence in January 1930. Whether a split into two divisions was entirely practical or even desirable at this stage of the sport's development was a moot point.

The SIHA formally adopted the LIHG rule that matches should be played over three periods and not two. However, time constraints imposed by the rink management at Crossmyloof Ice Rink reduced these periods to only twelve minutes duration with two intervals of three minutes duration between each. This development was not entirely satisfactory since it placed home players at a disadvantage when they were required to play in representative or international matches of more normal duration.

Although the rink management at Crossmyloof were keen to promote ice hockey there was nevertheless a great deal of competition from skating and curling interests for available ice time at the venue. The SIHA were allocated Tuesday and Friday evenings for matches but these had to be completed between 7.15pm and 8.00pm. This meant that matches were played through without the clock being stopped for penalties - another departure from the normal rules governing the sport.

The players required a high level of fitness. The size of the ice surface at Crossmyloof and the no stoppages rule was tiring enough but, in addition, the substitute rule was also different. Once a player was substituted he could not come back into the game, so the better players in each team tended to play in all three periods for the whole thirty-six minutes of the match.

The game was however slower than it is now. This was because there was no centre red line and forward passing was only allowed within each zone of the ice but not across the blue line. This meant that the team defending had to carry the puck over their own blue line in order to initiate an attack. Hard skating was therefore required for a role previously undertaken by "rovers" in the past.

Within a week of its first matches the SIHA encountered teething problems. The Glasgow High School club reported difficulties in getting a team together and as a result it was decided they be omitted from senior competition. It was also agreed that the Scottish Corinthians club, who had experienced similar problems, be merged with Glasgow Skating Club to form one team.

The SIHA were now left with ten clubs. By this time two fixtures had been played but the results in both were allowed to stand. Kelvingrove had beaten Dennistoun 6-0 four days after the match between Bridge of Weir and Mohawks. This reduction in the number of teams competing in the Points Competition meant that twenty fixtures would now be played to be completed by the end of December.

Initial hopes regarding interest in the sport were well founded. An attendance of 800 spectators was reported at the match between Bearsden

Season 1929-1930

and Mohawks on 18 October, but all of the matches were drawing decent crowds. Equally encouraging was the interest in the sport being shown by some mass circulation newspapers, including the *Glasgow Herald*, the *Evening Times* and the *Daily Record and Mail* amongst others.

Unlike the situation during the Edwardian era these newspapers were now giving ice hockey extensive and, more importantly, regular coverage. Although not quite as thorough as the *Evening Times*, the *Glasgow Herald* was producing brief match reports of every fixture played. A regular ice hockey column written by a correspondent styling himself "The Blade" was as entertaining as it was informative.

The management of Crossmyloof Ice Rink was also placing advertisements for ice hockey matches in the newspapers. Admission prices were quoted at 6d but it is not clear whether this charge included the public skating session which always followed the ice hockey match or whether a separate charge was made for that. In any event, the admission charge compared reasonably favourably with other spectator sports. For example, it cost 1s to stand and watch a senior football match in Glasgow and double that if one wanted cover and a seat.

With nine of the ten teams having played at least one match by the middle of October "The Blade" was fulsome in his praise:

> "Already there has been ample illustration of how the new teams have with remarkable speed mastered the art of ice hockey. There is little suggestion of novice work about the players. In fact, the surprising feature is the comparatively expert positional play and deft manipulation considering that the game is in its infancy here."
> *(Evening Times: 19 October 1929).*

This somewhat rosy picture of the sport's progress in Glasgow was supported to a certain extent when a team representing the SIHA met a Canadian armed forces side at Crossmyloof on 1 November. The home team certainly rose to the challenge by winning a tight contest 3-2 against a team styling themselves the "Atlantic Fleet Canadians". The visitors comprised officers and other ranks from *HMCS Emperor of India* which had recently docked at Rosyth Naval Dock Yard for repairs. This match represented an important milestone in that a Scottish representative side took to the ice for the first time in nineteen years.

Scots-born Canadian Don Porter, of Queen's, put the home team 1-0 ahead in the first period, a lead which was extended in the second period by fellow Canadian John Campbell of Mohawks. The visitors then scored twice to level the scores before the interval. An exciting final period produced a winning goal from another Scot who learned the game in Canada, Eric McLeod of Queen's, to secure an unexpected victory.

While this result and performance was an important confidence booster for the SIHA, it gave a rather misleading impression of the comparative strength of Scottish ice hockey. A much more accurate barometer of where the domestic game actually stood was provided by the first of what would become regular inter-city matches with Manchester at Crossmyloof on 24 November.

The Manchester team was captained by the experienced Great Britain player, F N (Neville) Melland, and also contained another British international forward, Joe Cock. The match attracted a healthy attendance of 1,000 spectators to Crossmyloof, despite an increase in admission charges of between 2s and 3/6d for what was considered to be a glamour game. Unfortunately for the home crowd, it was a totally one sided affair as the visitors thrashed Glasgow 9-1, Neville Melland scoring five goals.

The Glasgow team was largely unchanged from that which had beaten the Canadian sailors only three weeks before, but they found Manchester an altogether different proposition. The English side was superior in all positions. Despite losing nine goals, the beleaguered home goaltender, D (Dave) Cross of Mohawks, a local police officer, was commended for a brave performance. Glasgow's only goal was scored by the always busy Jack Easton of Glasgow University.

Of the eleven players selected for the Glasgow team at least seven were known to be Canadians. Some, like Don Porter of Queen's, had actually been born in Scotland but had subsequently been brought up in Canada where he had learned to skate and play ice hockey. Porter was another of the early stars of the Scottish game and his imminent departure to London where he had found employment was a blow not only to his club but to the Scottish League generally.

Bearsden won the Points Competition when they defeated Glasgow Skating Club 3-2 in their final fixture. No one could really argue with their success as they had won all four of their matches, the only team to do so. They finished with 8 points, a point ahead of Achtungs and Queen's, who shared second place. The "rugby men" comprised a well-organised unit. They had a decent goaltender in R G Walker and, while their defence was not the best in the competition, their forward line of Jack Gilmour, G C Scott and J G Carruthers was very effective. The latter player finished second top marksman in the competition with 9 goals.

Queen's had shown up very well in the Points Competition where they were the early leaders. The loss of Don Porter occurred after they had played all four of their fixtures from which they had gathered 7 points. Queen's had the best defence in the competition but the team was about to be further weakened by the departure of two more players, Swedish defender F Helgregan, and Norwegian forward, K Eddy-Larsen, who were returning to their respective countries.

The point conceded by Achtungs and Queen's came in a match they played against each other, an exciting 2-2 draw, early in the competition. In

Season 1929-1930

fact, Achtungs finished as the leading goal scorers with 22 goals, 5 more than champions Bearsden. They had some very good players including Canadian Hugh Reid who marshalled a sound defence and the two Rintoul brothers in attack.

Mohawks finished in fourth spot; Bridge of Weir, with an inferior goal difference, were placed fifth.

The scoring records remain incomplete; in four of the twenty fixtures the names of the goal scorers are not given. John Campbell of Mohawks finished as the top goal scorer in the Points Competition with 14 goals. The remarkable contribution of Campbell to his team can be seen in the fact that he scored all but two of their goals in the competition.

Satisfied that the Points Competition had separated the wheat from the chaff, the SIHA announced that the top five finishers - Bearsden, Achtungs, Queen's, Mohawks and Bridge of Weir - would constitute the new First Division of the Scottish League to commence in January 1930.

The remaining five finishers - Kelvingrove, Glasgow Skating Club, Doonside, Glasgow University and Dennistoun - would constitute the Second Division. It was hard not to feel sorry for Kelvingrove who finished the Points Competition on four points but they lost out on goal difference to both Mohawks and Bridge of Weir.

The format for both divisions of the Scottish League would be that each team would play the other only once. While this was not a particularly onerous programme for the clubs it was likely that competition for ice time from other sports at Crossmyloof dictated what was a somewhat truncated tournament for the SIHA. The issue of promotion and relegation does not seem to have been discussed, rather implying that the two divisions format was something of an experiment to be later evaluated as to its worth upon completion.

Before the end of the year Glasgow travelled to the Manchester Ice Palace to play the hosts in a return inter-city fixture. The Scottish team made a few positional changes from the side crushed 9-1 at Crossmyloof a month earlier. Eric McLeod of Queen's was moved to defence while Jack Easton of Glasgow University was brought into the first line to partner John Campbell of Mohawks and new boy, A J (Arthur) Tingley of Queen's.

Arthur Tingley had recently joined Queen's. Like his fellow countrymen, John Campbell and Jack Easton, he was destined to have a big impact on Scottish ice hockey. A native of Ottawa, Tingley had played for the local university before coming to Glasgow as a senior official in the Canadian civil service.

Glasgow took to the ice in Manchester resplendent in a new uniform consisting of navy blue sweaters, white shorts and white stockings with a gold band round the ankles. The new kit seems to have inspired the visitors for they gave a much improved performance despite losing 3-1. Of the nine players who made the trip to Manchester, at least seven learned to play the game in Canada.

Interest in promoting ice hockey at the Haymarket Ice Rink in Edinburgh was being expressed by local enthusiasts - Canadian students at Edinburgh University in the main - but their appeals fell on deaf ears. The management at the Haymarket venue were wholly committed to promoting curling and nothing else. That was a great pity; a team representative of and playing in Edinburgh would have been a great boon to the game in Scotland.

A number of very good players were studying at Edinburgh University but they were not lost to the Scottish game. Arthur Bazin joined Queen's where he would become a stalwart in defence for both his club and Scotland. Similarly, Mohawks acquired two players, S A MacDonald and A R (Art) Brady. The latter was a medical student who would go on to make quite a name for himself as a dynamic and tricky left wing with both Mohawks and Scotland.

Enthusiasm for the sport was also being noted from youngsters. Ice hockey is very much a young man's sport where speed and stamina are required in large measure. It was evident from the crowds flocking to Crossmyloof for matches that many of those in attendance were young men or boys excited by what was a new sport to the vast majority of them.

The SIHA decided to harness this enthusiasm positively by forming a junior ice hockey league in January 1930. As always though, ice time was a problem. The seniors had found it difficult enough finding available ice time at Crossmyloof for matches let alone practice but eventually early slots on Saturday mornings were found for the youngsters to play and practice.

Junior clubs were formed in a number of independent fee paying schools. At least two of these had a senior club affiliation. Glasgow High School, which had been a founder member of the SIHA a year earlier, entered a team as Junior Mohawks. Shawlands, Queen's Park and Hutcheson's Grammar Schools combined together to enter a team as Junior Queen's. Boys from Glasgow Academy and Kelvinside Academy joined together to form Mohicans and a fourth club, Sioux, was established by the end of the month.

The ages of the boys making up these teams ranged from eleven to fourteen years. It was of course no coincidence that they were pupils of schools in the private sector of education; this followed the socio-economic profile of the sport generally. Many of their older relatives now playing for senior clubs were themselves "old boys" of these very same schools.

The SIHA was to be commended for developing junior ice hockey in spite of the difficulties over ice time and expense. There was an early realisation that local talent had to be nurtured and encouraged if the sport in Scotland was not to be wholly dependent on Canadian and foreign imports. Ice hockey had to be developed at grass roots level if it was to have any lasting future in the country.

The eagerly anticipated opening fixture of the Scottish League was a First Division encounter between Mohawks and Queen's, played on 3 January 1930 in front of 1,000 spectators. Mohawks' new Canadian stars made an immediate impact as S A MacDonald with two goals and Art Brady with another gave them an impressive 3-0 victory over a very good Queen's side.

Three days later Glasgow University thumped Doonside 8-0 in the opening fixture of the Second Division. Jack Easton scored five goals in this match with line mate D W Lindsay grabbing a hat-trick. The students looked to have a useful team with C W de Visser in defence providing good support for the attack.

The opening fixture in the Mitchell Trophy between Mohawks and Queen's was played in mid-January. Queen's took this early opportunity to avenge their recent league defeat with both hands. A close contest was settled by a single goal scored by new boy Arthur Bazin.

The Mitchell Trophy would become the premier cup competition in Scottish ice hockey. It was an attractive and impressive trophy being made of solid silver, mounted on an ebony stand, around which were half a dozen shields suitable for inscription. An ice hockey scene was depicted on the plinth, the two figures standing on each side were artistic and novel and the figure adorning the top of the trophy was considered "a work of art".

Off the ice, the SIHA had sought affiliation to the BIHA while retaining its right to formally regulate and organise ice hockey north of the border. Under its energetic secretary, D B A Carty, it was making great strides forward. Dave Carty was very well thought of by his peers at the SIHA; they presented him with a suitably engraved cigarette case for his services to the sport in Scotland. One important issue currently exercising the secretary was that of referees. It is not clear whether this was the result of any unhappiness expressed by the clubs or whether it was a matter the SIHA simply deemed worthy of further consideration.

> "A suggestion has been made that an association of referees be formed and that it should be composed of men who are not members of any of the Scottish Ice Hockey Association's clubs. Asked his opinion on the subject, Mr Dave Carty, stated that no decision would be made on this point without full consideration being given to every aspect.
>
> "Too many men in a small show blot out that show" he remarked. "What we want is ice hockey, ice hockey worth watching and plenty of it. We have every confidence in all the men who have refereed matches since the Scottish Ice Hockey Association's initiation, confidence in their unbiased attitude and in their intelligent reading of the rules."
>
> *(Glasgow Herald: 8 February 1930).*

These remarks from the Secretary of the SIHA represented a ringing endorsement of the *status quo*. Each club nominated a referee. How they were allocated to the various fixtures was a matter for the ruling body to determine. It was obviously a system open to abuse but given the amateur ethos pervading the sport it was unlikely that cheating or favouritism was really perceived as a major problem.

In any event if the referees were not to be provided by the clubs themselves then where on earth would they come from? It was not as if there was a pool of unaffiliated officials readily available for appointment. Presumably, the SIHA would have been charged to find referees from somewhere but that seemed an entirely unrealistic option at that time.

There was certainly no shortage of players. In early February it was reported that the SIHA had received interest for affiliation from three more clubs. This group included Kelvingrove who wanted to ice a second team in the Scottish League. After due consideration, it was decided that these clubs could not be accommodated, the SIHA wisely determining that the season was too far advanced and should not be disrupted by the late entry of further clubs.

This enthusiasm for the sport was echoed by greater levels of spectator interest. It was noticeable that spectators were becoming more knowledgeable about the game, and were starting to identify strongly with their favourite teams. Cries of encouragement to the players and teams - not to mention vocal criticism of refereeing decisions! - were by now becoming commonplace at matches. A number of clubs were encouraging interest from people wishing to formally affiliate to them in a non-playing capacity. Kelvingrove, who seemingly had an abundance of players, were particularly active on this front. By the early months of 1930, the 'Grove - as they were nicknamed - had enrolled about 100 non-playing members, enacting what was to all intents and purposes an official supporters' club.

Other clubs, including Queen's, Mohawks and Dennistoun, quickly followed suit. This was a very encouraging development as supporters' clubs were not only great morale boosters for the players but an important source of revenue for the clubs. They contributed membership fees and raised other funds by means of selling raffle tickets, badges and scarves as well as promoting social occasions such as dances or dinners.

Given the structure of Scottish ice hockey, not all of the clubs had the opportunity to open their doors to non-playing members. It was much more difficult for clubs like Bridge of Weir or Glasgow Skating Club than it was for Kelvingrove or Mohawks. As noted, the latter were first and foremost "ice hockey" clubs from the outset whereas the former were only ice hockey offshoots of longer established sports clubs in field hockey and figure skating respectively and as such their room for manoeuvre in such matters was more restricted.

One also rather gets the impression that in certain other cases some clubs, - including perhaps Achtungs, Bearsden and Doonside - would not have been overly keen in admitting non-playing members in any circumstances and therefore preferred to remain private clubs. In such clubs the amateur ethos was more strictly maintained and they remained immune from any funding streams outside their own pockets.

Season 1929-1930

Scottish ice hockey received a huge boost with the visit of Canada to Crossmyloof Ice Rink on 14 February to play against Great Britain. It was of course the biggest match ever played at the Glasgow venue up to that point and it attracted a capacity attendance. Canada, represented on this occasion by Toronto CCM (Canada Cycle and Motor Company), were the newly crowned world champions.

No doubt with local interest in mind the BIHA diplomatically selected four players from the Scottish League for the British team. They were all Canadians; Art Brady and S A MacDonald of Mohawks, Arthur Tingley of Queen's and Jack Easton of Glasgow University. The Great Britain side were kitted out in blue and white sweaters with numbers on their backs and red and blue stockings.

Unfortunately, it was men against boys as Canada annihilated Great Britain 16-3. It was simply no contest as the British players were chasing shadows for most of the match. They could not live with the power, skill and speed of their opponents whose rapid movements between defence and attack left them bewildered.

Neville Melland of Manchester and Blaine Sexton of London Lions tried manfully to rally the British team but to no avail. Still at least Art Brady of Mohawks had the consolation of scoring one of the British goals. In fact, according to "The Blade", Brady was the best of the Scottish based players and the most popular since "he never failed to get a roar from the crowd when he essayed a flash through."

Despite the heavy defeat inflicted on Great Britain the visitors were generous in their summation of the progress ice hockey was making in Scotland. Their team manager, Howard Armstrong, stated that Crossmyloof was the finest ice rink that Canada had played on during their extensive European tour and that the SIHA had done a very good job developing the sport in such a short time. He was particularly impressed by the encouragement being given to junior ice hockey and his advice was "catch them young".

Only six of the twenty First and Second Division fixtures had been played by the time Canada visited Crossmyloof in mid-February but more progress had been made in the Mitchell Trophy.

As befitting a major cup competition it had produced a number of surprising results. Achtungs had fallen at the first hurdle losing 2-1 in a close match to lower division side Glasgow Skating Club, Canadian J O McCabe scoring both goals for the victors. Queen's, conquerors of Mohawks in the first round, also fell to Second Division opposition when Glasgow University defeated them 1-0, courtesy of a goal from C W de Visser. Bearsden successfully negotiated a potentially tricky tie against Kelvingrove with a comfortable 2-0 victory in front of about 800 spectators. J G Carruthers and Andrew Dykes scored the goals that counted. In the other tie, Dennistoun had an easy 4-0 win against Doonside with two goals from H (Harry) Reid and one each from J S Hay and A J Biggar.

With three First Division teams already eliminated from the competition Bearsden were firmly installed as favourites to win the Mitchell Trophy. Their position was further strengthened when Glasgow Skating Club took their second First Division scalp following a 3-1 defeat of Bridge of Weir in a re-played tie. The first match had ended 2-2.

In the semi-finals, Bearsden would play Glasgow University and Glasgow Skating Club would play Dennistoun. The matches were played before the end of February and both went to form. Bearsden had little trouble in disposing of the students 5-1 with J G Carruthers and Jack Gilmour helping themselves to two goals apiece. In the other match, Glasgow Skating Club defeated Dennistoun 4-2 with the versatile Felix McLernan securing a brace.

It was still early days in the two championships but in the First Division, Bearsden suffered their first defeat of the season when Achtungs won a close encounter 3-2. Achtungs were making the early running by winning their second match against Bridge of Weir 2-1. They eventually came unstuck in their next match when they lost 6-2 against Queen's for whom Arthur Tingley scored all six goals in a quite extraordinary display of skating and shooting.

In the Second Division, Kelvingrove made an impressive start by defeating their closest rivals Glasgow Skating Club 3-2, and followed that up by beating Dennistoun 4-0. In early March, Doonside avenged their Mitchell Trophy exit at the hands of Dennistoun when they defeated the Glasgow team 1-0 to record what would be their only victory in the championship. Ian Fair scored the decisive goal.

Kelvingrove continued to make headway off the ice as well. Under the astute leadership of their president, Mark Cohen, the progressive West End club had enrolled 280 non-playing members by the end of March. They were already providing a valuable source of funding for the club who were one of the smartest teams in the league with their green, white and black kit complete with a large "K" on their sweaters. Their first team was quite considerably strengthened by the capture of two resident Canadians, D Croll, a goaltender, and L (Lorne) Berlinquet, a defender.

The influx of players from Edinburgh University had encouraged moves towards an inter-city match being played between Glasgow and Edinburgh. A date early in March had been arranged for such a fixture at Crossmyloof but then had to be abandoned when it was discovered the date clashed with university examinations being held at the same time.

In March the SIHA announced plans for the formation of a speed skating club, an initiative undertaken to facilitate faster play. The recent international match with Canada had highlighted just how slow the domestic players were in comparison with Canadian opposition. The various clubs reacted well to this initiative as the first practice sessions were very well attended.

The final of the Mitchell Trophy was contested between Bearsden and their Second Division opponents Glasgow Skating Club on 25 March. The

Season 1929-1930

SIHA made it a gala occasion as the match was preceded by a fancy dress carnival and figure skating display. About 2,000 spectators were attracted, with the gate money going to local hospital charities.

Glasgow Skating Club had already taken two First Division scalps on the way to the final so the warning signs were clearly there for Bearsden. The favourites started very brightly and Skating Club's veteran goaltender, John Wharrie, had a busy first period, conceding only one goal to G C Scott.

Play was more even in the second period and it was no surprise when Skating Club drew level, following a brilliant individual goal scored by the ever dangerous Felix McLernan. This goal proved to be the turning point of the match as Skating Club further grew in confidence.

In the third period Skating Club took the game to Bearsden, putting in a great display of checking and counter-attacking which had the "rugby men" on the ropes. J O McCabe and Felix McLernan were combining really well in attack and both scored. Although Bearsden rallied towards the end of the match the damage had already been done and Glasgow Skating Club held out for a memorable victory.

Lady Weir presented the Mitchell Trophy to the winning captain, H R Orr. It was a splendid achievement for this venerable old club whose team certainly was a blend of youth and experience. Goaltender John Wharrie, left defence W Ritchie and right wing H R Orr were all veterans of the Edwardian era at Crossmyloof Ice Rink. Youthful Canadians J O McCabe and Felix McLernan formed a formidable duo in attack.

The cup competition had confirmed what most keen observers of the game already knew: there was not that much difference between the teams in the First and Second Divisions. The only exceptions were Dennistoun and Doonside who were both a bit off the pace from the others. Kelvingrove and Glasgow Skating Club were just as good as those in the higher division and on their day Glasgow University were more than capable of holding their own against anyone.

In early April yet another inter-city match was arranged between Glasgow and Manchester but this fixture was used to determine the northern representatives to compete against London in the final of the newly established but short lived British Championship. Glasgow had lost the two previous matches 9-1 and 3-1 but hopes were high this time that the team would perform better. This optimism was based on the premise that it would be a very different Glasgow side which would take to the ice at the Manchester Ice Palace on 5 April. New players included D Croll, Arthur Bazin, Art Brady and S A MacDonald. Of the nine players selected for Glasgow, eight had learned to play the game in Canada. The only home developed player in the team was John Fullerton, the captain of Mohawks.

In what was a pulsating encounter Glasgow earned a hard fought 1-1 draw. Art Brady put the visitors ahead in the first period with a shoulder high shot which found the corner of the net but thereafter they had to sustain considerable pressure from a resolute Manchester team. D Croll played magnificently in the Glasgow goal but was cruelly beaten in the last few minutes of the match when D M H Davies scored on a rebound. Despite that disappointment Arthur Tingley came very close to snatching a winning goal for Glasgow in the dying seconds.

In the championships, Kelvingrove clinched the Second Division title on 4 April when they defeated Doonside 5-0 in their final match. The West End team were worthy winners having gone through the league campaign unbeaten with 13 goals scored for the loss of only 2. They had the largest playing squad, infused with a great deal of quality, of any club in the Scottish League. The arrival of D Croll, Lorne Berlinquet and latterly, R L Noble, had given the 'Grove team a solid spine which was the basis of their success. Other players who had made an impact were A S (Andy) Dick in defence and line mate W M Phinney. Kelvingrove were an enterprising club both on and off the ice and their future prospects looked bright.

Glasgow Skating Club finished runners-up to Kelvingrove, only two points behind in the league table. They were the division's top goal scorers with 17, their Canadian centre J O McCabe accounting for 9 of them. He finished joint leading goal scorer with fellow-countryman, Jack Easton of Glasgow University. While disappointed at finishing second, Glasgow Skating Club had the quite considerable consolation of becoming the first winners of the Mitchell Trophy.

Glasgow University finished in third position, which represented a decent effort from the students. They had a genuine star in Jack Easton and another was emerging in C W de Visser. Their two defeats by the two teams who finished above them in the league were both by a single goal. The team lacked strength in depth, in what would become a recurring problem at the club.

Doonside had scored exactly one goal in their four matches yet incredibly that single strike by Ian Fair in the match against Dennistoun was enough to give them fourth position in the division. The Ayrshire team had struggled all season with the availability of players, which partly explains their loss of 21 goals, the worst record of any team in either division.

Dennistoun thought themselves unlucky to finish in bottom position but three defeats - two by a single goal - and a draw probably suggests otherwise. In J H Borland, Harry Reid and the up and coming W W (Bill) Russell, the East End club had some good players. A well run and solid club with an active fan base gave it a platform to build on for the future.

The dominance of Kelvingrove in the Second Division was matched by Mohawks in the First Division. They had to wait until the final fixture of the season on 15 April to secure the championship when they defeated Bearsden 4-1, thanks to a sparkling display from Art Brady who scored all four goals. The capture of Brady and S A MacDonald at the commencement of the league

Season 1929-1930

campaign had turned Mohawks' fortunes completely around. They were unbeaten in their four matches scoring 12 goals in the process for the loss of only one. Although the club had a small squad of players it was packed with quality. Dave Cross was a steady and reliable goaltender, Art Brady and Tom Shearer were rocks in defence and their forward line of John Fullerton, John Campbell and S A MacDonald was the best in the Scottish League. Five of these players had won representative honours; all in all, Mohawks presented a formidable unit.

Queen's ran them close. A very entertaining side, they were led by the phenomenal Arthur Tingley, who scored 15 of his team's 17 goals in the championship, an incredible achievement. Along with Art Brady and Jack Easton, he was arguably the best player in the Scottish League. It was not a one-man-band though, because they had other outstanding players in Arthur Bazin in defence and the versatile Eric McLeod.

Achtungs finished third in the division but as in the Points Competition they rather flattered to deceive. One gets the impression with Achtungs that they perhaps lacked a bit of commitment at times. The team were not without talent in Hugh Reid and A Rintoul but generally there was no drive about them. They played in fits and starts.

Bearsden were very disappointed with fourth spot following their success in the Points Competition. It all rather petered out for them, although in Jack Gilmour and J G Carruthers they retained a potent force in attack. Perhaps they peaked too soon and their cup final defeat in the Mitchell Trophy merely confirmed their late season malaise.

Bridge of Weir, after a good showing in the Points Competition, never got going in the First Division. With a record of played four, lost four, the Renfrewshire men finished the league campaign with the worst record of any team in either division - yet they were by no means the poorest side. Lack of coaching was a problem, but the club had some good players including giant centre Wilbur Muirhead and line mate Ian McLeod.

The end of the season statistics for both divisions brought out some interesting points. In the ten matches played in each division, 47 goals were scored in the First Division and 46 goals were scored in the Second Division. However, the matches in the higher division tended to be closer affairs than those in the lower division where Doonside had been at the end of some heavy defeats.

The replay of the British Championship northern qualifying final was held between Glasgow and Manchester at Crossmyloof Ice Rink on 26 April. This was the fourth meeting of the season between these two sides and the steady improvement in both performances and results for Glasgow was consummated when they finally beat their opponents for the first time 3-2.

Glasgow iced the same team which had drawn 1-1 at the Manchester Ice Palace in the previous match. Manchester were at full strength and the game developed into a keenly contested encounter. The lead changed hands twice before S A MacDonald, who had played well throughout the match, broke away to score what was his second and Glasgow's winning goal.

In the southern qualifying ties London Lions reached the final by eliminating fierce rivals United Services and then Princes. Blaine Sexton's team were an impressive combination of speed, power and aggression. Both he and N D Mulholland had played for Great Britain in the World Championships, held three months earlier, when the British side had disappointingly finished in tenth position.

United Services had been champions of England in both 1928 and 1929, despite there not being any organised league competition south of the border. That defect was finally rectified in January 1930 when the inappropriately named "British League" was established. It operated with a south and a north section but met with only limited success as a number of its fixtures eventually had to be scratched.

The challenge presented by United Services had led Blaine Sexton to seriously strengthen his club with the capture of two German international players, goaltender Gerhard Ball and his brother, Heinz Ball. In addition, two future Great Britain international players also joined London Lions, J C P (John) Magwood and H W Bushell.

The final of the British Championship was held at the Golders Green Ice Rink in London on 17 May. The choice of venue was a major advantage for the English side as Golders Green was now the home ice of London Lions.

The two teams were:

London Lions: G L Ball; N D Mulholland and W H MacKenzie; J C P Magwood, B N Sexton and H W Bushell. - H Ball.

Glasgow: D Croll (Kelvingrove); A R Brady (Mohawks) and A R Bazin (Queen's); A J Tingley (Queen's), J A Easton (Glasgow University) and S A MacDonald (Mohawks). - E R McLeod (Queen's) and J Campbell (Mohawks).

Referee: Major B M Patton (BIHA).

In what was described as one of the best matches of the season London Lions just managed to squeeze past their plucky opponents 2-1. Blaine Sexton, who had a brilliant match, put the home team ahead just before the end of the first period but early in the second session, S A MacDonald finished off some excellent combination by Glasgow to score an equalising goal. Shortly after H W Bushell restored London's lead but while there were close things at both ends of the rink there was no further scoring.

There is little doubt from the match reports of both *The Times* in London and the *Glasgow Herald* that Glasgow had more than held their own and were perhaps just a shade unlucky to lose the match. Nevertheless it was an extremely encouraging performance. A feature of the match had been that the home team had started to visibly tire in the third period and one is left

Season 1929-1930

to speculate what the outcome may have been had the match been played on the larger ice surface at Crossmyloof.

With that match concluded the season officially ended. The SIHA had much to be encouraged about. It had successfully established a ten team league albeit on a limited basis which was attracting keen interest from both the paying public and the press. A junior league had also been formed and the SIHA had promoted a number of good representative matches against both English and Canadian opposition.

The popularity of ice hockey had convinced the Scottish Ice Rink Company that it was worth promoting at Crossmyloof in the future. With this platform the SIHA had the opportunity to further develop the sport. With this in view it had appointed an assistant secretary, Gregor Holmes of Mohawks, to assist Dave Carty in the various tasks and projects earmarked for the future.

It is worth making the point, by way of comparison, that the sport was now much better organised in Scotland than it was in England. The attempt at a "British League" had ended in failure. In the next season there would still be no formal league structure in place, leaving the leading English teams with only the option of playing challenge matches against each other on an *ad hoc* basis.

The situation in Scotland was certainly not perfect but the sport had made truly remarkable progress during the past two years. All connected with Scottish ice hockey, the clubs, the rink management, the spectators and the sporting press, were fully committed to building on the progress made in the new season ahead. Next season could not come quickly enough.

Frozen in Time

Season 1930-31

"The steady rise in the popularity of ice sports last year has resulted in the introduction of several new features at Crossmyloof Ice Rink, Glasgow. Speed skating will be a prominent feature during the coming season but whatever favour it finds it will scarcely displace the established game of ice hockey. A new floor and a generally renovated rink has given an advantage to hockey players who will start the year with an optimism that promises good sport.

Several of the teams of last season have altered their playing list to great extent, the ebb and flow of experienced visitors causing changes but most of the men who distinguished themselves will once more chase the puck at Crossmyloof.

Of the teams in the league most is expected from the Kelvingrove club who won the Second Division championship and whose club could boast of having close on 300 non-playing members. Kelvingrove has made use of the summer to strengthen its ranks and improve its membership. Several surprises may be expected from other quarters but all the clubs are prepared for the opening.

This year the league will be composed of nine clubs one less than last season, Doonside having intimated their withdrawal through experiencing difficulty in collecting a powerful enough team.

The most prominent absentees in the playing strength of the SIHA are S A MacDonald (Mohawks), D Croll (Kelvingrove) and E R McLeod (Queen's). All three players, who have returned to their own homes in Canada, took a big part in fostering the game in Glasgow and the local players benefited from their experience.

The knock-out competition for the Mitchell Trophy, which aroused so much interest last season and of which the Glasgow Skating Club became holders after a series of thrilling contests, will again be held.

Another interesting item of news is that this year a second trophy will be put up for competition. The Canada Cycle and Motor Company who took a big part in arranging the tour of Canada, who visited Glasgow last winter, have intimated that they will present a cup to the winners of the league.

It has been agreed to fix the hours of play on the same lines as last season, that is, from 7.15pm to 8.00pm on Tuesdays and Fridays, while

the allocation of the rink for practices which were held on Mondays and Thursdays will also be unchanged."
(Glasgow Herald: 2 October 1930).

This informative and rather upbeat preview of the new season accurately reflected the optimism pervading the sport. While the SIHA did indeed have much to be pleased about, there were still a number of difficulties to be overcome not the least of which was the requirement imposed on the clubs to have their matches concluded within three quarters of an hour, in order to fit in with the timetable of the rink management at Crossmyloof.

That was no doubt considered to be a small price to pay for the regular promotion of ice hockey at the venue but it rather rankled that the players and spectators were being denied the full benefits of the game as it should have been played. Not stopping the clock for the normal breaks in play meant that the Glasgow based players were partly playing a different type of game to their peers in England and Canada. It placed them at a disadvantage when meeting teams from these countries.

One should not dwell too much on the negative as there was a great deal to be positive about. The award of what became known as the "Canada Cup" to the winners of the league championship was a very welcome development and a most generous gesture from the Canada Cycle and Motor Company whose team Toronto CCM had of course won the World Championship in 1930 and had inflicted a 16-3 defeat on Great Britain at Crossmyloof in February.

Other positive developments from the SIHA included the decision to scrap the two division format of the previous season. This made a great deal of sense because most of the teams were of a similar standard and should therefore be allowed to compete against each other in a single league. It was also decided that a player who was substituted could come back into the game at any time as was the norm in other countries. Players could therefore come on and off the ice at the discretion of the coach.

The nine teams contesting the league championship this season were; Achtungs, Bearsden, Bridge of Weir, Dennistoun, Glasgow Skating Club, Glasgow University, Kelvingrove, Mohawks and Queen's.

The team missing from last season was of course Doonside from Ayr. It was disappointing that Doonside had been obliged to resign from the SIHA. Along with Bridge of Weir they had been the only team not based in Glasgow. Doonside had struggled to find consistency in team selection. Some of their players had found the travelling to Glasgow difficult for both matches and practice. The team had suffered some very heavy defeats in the Second Division and that would not have helped their morale. In total, they had played 9 official matches in season 1929-30 winning only 2 and losing 7. In these matches they had scored a total of 7 goals but had conceded 43. It was a tremendous blow to the club's patron and founder, Colonel Dunlop, who had

Season 1930-1931

done so much to foster the sport in Ayrshire. He was not lost to ice hockey, though and would in later years emerge again with a new club based in Ayr.

There would be no Points Competition this season, the teams immediately starting competition for the league championship. This would consist of each team playing the other only once for a total of 36 fixtures spread out over six months of the season. Even with the inclusion of at least one Mitchell Trophy tie it was unlikely that any team would play more than two or three matches per month.

There were too many teams playing out of one ice rink resulting in an infrequent and fragmented fixture list. This was exacerbated by a corresponding lack of available ice time at Crossmyloof, as ice hockey was obliged to compete with curling, figure skating and now it would seem speed skating.

At least there was no shortage of players. Each club affiliated to the SIHA was permitted to register up to twenty players, but few clubs met their full quota. Kelvingrove were an exception in having the capability to ice two teams but most clubs made do with icing a recognised first team, which was often on the ice for as long as physically possible, along with two or three substitutes.

A more worrying trend was the over reliance of some clubs on expatriate Canadians resident in Scotland. The SIHA had early recognised this as a potential problem for the future development of the domestic game, as the establishment of a junior league had clearly demonstrated. Canadian involvement had been and would continue to be an essential element in the continuing development of ice hockey in Scotland, but there had to be a balance struck within the various clubs between recruiting experienced Canadians and nurturing home based talent.

Kelvingrove were a case in point. They would take to the ice this season with an almost entirely Canadian team. Of their six recognised first team players namely Dave Cross, Andy Dick, William Phinney, W S (Sid) Montford, John Campbell and R L Noble, only Sid Montford had learned to play the game in Scotland, the land of his birth.

"Canadians" came in two varieties and Kelvingrove had both. There were those like John Campbell and R L Noble who were expatriate Canadians who just happened to be temporarily resident in Scotland through business or study. Then there were those like Dave Cross who were actually born in Scotland but who had subsequently moved to Canada as children and had learned to skate and play the game there before moving back to Scotland in later life. It was to be a major bone of contention in ice hockey that players who had been trained and developed in Canada often had dual nationality.

By comparison, Mohawks had a team which was almost wholly trained and developed in Scotland. This was partly due to the defections of Dave Cross and John Campbell to Kelvingrove during the summer which left Art Brady as the sole Canadian at the club. One aspect of going "native" as it were was that it gave local talent the chance to flourish and at Mohawks the Glasgow born and bred John Fullerton, amongst others, was to take full advantage of the opportunity offered to him.

To a certain extent Kelvingrove and Mohawks were at opposite ends of the spectrum regarding this issue. Most of the other clubs in the Scottish League had much more of a balance between Scottish and Canadian players. It was a fact though that every club regarded the procurement of Canadian talent as crucial to their credibility and to their prospects of success.

In looking at the prospects of the various teams for the season ahead it was doubtful if Mohawks would be able to repeat the success of the previous season. The departures of important players - like Dave Cross, John Campbell and S A MacDonald - left them quite considerably weakened. Mohawks had effectively lost half their team. While any team with Art Brady and the promising John Fullerton still posed a threat they could not do it all by themselves.

Kelvingrove, as ambitious as they were progressive, looked like favourites for the Canada Cup. The club had replaced departed goaltender D Croll with the reliable Dave Cross and in John Campbell had captured a proven goal scorer of real quality. Defensively the team looked particularly strong with Andy Dick and William Phinney forming a solid unit and they had abundant talent in reserve, Lorne Berlinquet, being a case in point.

The main challengers to Kelvingrove appeared to be Queen's. They had lost the services of Eric McLeod, but with Arthur Bazin in defence and Arthur Tingley at centre they had two of the best players in the Scottish League. The spine of the team was completed when the versatile F L (Fred) Reardon joined them, initially as a goaltender but he could really play anywhere. Queen's were an exciting mixture of youth and experience and in W (Billy) Fullerton, the younger brother of John, they had a great prospect for the future.

On the face of it none of the other teams in the league could be considered as title contenders. A lack of strength in depth was a general problem. Most sides had at least one outstanding performer whether it was Jack Easton at Glasgow University or Hugh Reid at Achtungs but one swallow does not make a summer. Success in the Mitchell Trophy offered a more realistic ambition for these teams.

The holders of the Mitchell Trophy, Glasgow Skating Club, had bade farewell to two of their veteran players, H R Orr and W Ritchie. Both had played ice hockey during the Edwardian era at the old Crossmyloof Ice Rink most probably for the Corinthians club. The only known survivor of that era still playing was John Wharrie who would again keep goal for Glasgow Skating Club in the coming season.

Some clubs made a serious effort to improve, Dennistoun amongst them. As the worst team in the league there was only one direction to go. Goaltender

Season 1930-1931

A Swan joined them from Kelvingrove where he had been understudy to D Croll and a promising youngster, Sam Stevenson, moved from Mohawks to team up with the useful but unsupported Harry Reid in attack. Dennistoun hoped for better things.

The league championship commenced on 7 October with a thrilling match between Glasgow Skating Club and Glasgow University won by the students 4-3. Jack Easton was the star of the show with a hat-trick. Glasgow University had been strengthened during the summer by the addition of two ex-Doonside players, William Dunlop and Guy Parsons, though neither would play regularly for the team.

Ten days later the first real heavyweight showdown of the season was held when Kelvingrove and Mohawks met. It was a terrific match decided by a single goal scored five minutes from time by Lorne Berlinquet of Kelvingrove. This was very sore on Mohawks, who deserved at least a draw. They dominated the first two periods thanks to a wonderful performance from Art Brady whose speed and stick handling continually troubled a busy 'Grove defence.

The match also featured some good goaltending from Dave Cross and W G (Greg) Lennox. While "The Blade" reflected in his newspaper column that the "Scottish" team had more than held its own with the "Canadian" team nevertheless it was the latter, Kelvingrove, who had ultimately prevailed. A very significant result, it was just a pity that such an important fixture was played so early in the season.

The various clubs continued to strengthen their teams during the opening weeks of the season. Kelvingrove procured the services of an Australian-Scots forward, J (Jimmy) Brown, who had been a speed skating champion in his homeland. Bridge of Weir made an important addition to their team when G D (Gordon) Rowley, a medical student from Montreal, joined them. Dennistoun secured another Canadian, T (Tom) Nisbet, who played on defence. All three were quality players.

With almost every team in the league having played at least one match, "The Blade" commented

> "One has only to look back on the closing stages of last year and compare the standard of play then with that of this season to appreciate the rapid progress which has been made. The players have demonstrated that they possess a better knowledge of the play, they have become acquainted with the art of controlling the puck and as a result the sport is becoming more spectacular and more exciting."
> *(Evening Times: 22 October 1930).*

This "rapid progress" was about to be severely tested because the SIHA arranged an international match against Berliner Schlittschuh Club of Germany at Crossmyloof. This famous old club from Berlin were regarded by

Frozen in Time

Glasgow University Ice Hockey Club, 1930-31
Back Row; J C Henderson, Dr R Parker, Robert H Gardiner and J W Barclay.
Front Row: C W de Vigen, Jock A Easton, James S Carolan, D W Lindsay and J R Erskine

many contemporary observers to be "Germany" in all but name and they were billed as such in the newspaper and ice rink advertisements for the match at Crossmyloof. The Germans had embarked on a short tour of England and their slight detour north of the border was testimony to the ambition of the SIHA.

It was Scotland's first full international match since defeating England in December 1910. Germany offered a formidable challenge. They had beaten Great Britain, Hungary, Poland and Switzerland on the way to winning the European Championship earlier in the year and although they had lost 6-1 to Canada (Toronto CCM) in the final of the World Championship that score did not reflect the closeness of the match. Germany had one world class player in Gustav Jaenecke and another in the making with Rudi Ball and both would be playing at Crossmyloof.

The match attracted a great deal of interest and excitement. There was much debate as to who should play for the Scottish team and the selectors certainly sprang one or two surprises. Thus, Fred Reardon of Queen's was preferred to Dave Cross in goal while fellow new boys Jimmy Brown of Kelvingrove, Gordon Rowley of Bridge of Weir and Tom Nisbet of Dennistoun came straight into the side after playing barely a month in the Scottish League. The late addition of the latter two players was at the expense of the Kelvingrove duo, John Campbell and Lorne Berlinquet who, having been originally selected, very generously agreed to stand down. With the exception of Brown, who was raised in Australia, all of the players selected for Scotland were Canadians.

The two teams for this historic match were:

Scotland: F L Reardon (Queen's); T Nisbet (Dennistoun) and A R Bazin (Queen's); G D Rowley (Bridge of Weir), J A Easton (Glasgow University) and A R Brady (Mohawks). - J Brown (Kelvingrove), A J Tingley (Queen's) and R L Noble (Kelvingrove).

Germany: G L Ball; Dr Holsbaur and G Jaenecke; E Roemer, A Heinrich and R Ball. - W Korff, H Ball, D Reichenheim and G Kummets.

Referee: D B A Carty (SIHA).

The match attracted about 2,500 spectators to Crossmyloof who paid 2s a head for the privilege. It turned out to be a very close and somewhat bad-tempered encounter. The German forwards were faster and their side generally showed much better teamwork and understanding than Scotland. Germany scored through Erich Roemer early in the first period and then Rudi Ball scored a second goal just before the interval. The second period was marred by a good deal of rough play. Tom Nisbet sustained a nasty fall and was obliged to temporarily retire from the game. At one point, Germany had two players in the sin bin. Scotland pushed hard and were rewarded when Arthur Bazin not only started a promising move but carried on to outmanoeuvre everyone and from an acute angle scored a magnificent goal to reduce Germany's lead. In the third period Scotland went all out for a deserved equaliser and almost got it but Bazin missed an open goal after great work from Jack Easton. Jimmy Brown was then injured and he too was forced to retire from the game. Tempers became increasingly frayed as full time approached and one gets the impression that the referee, Dave Carty, was only too glad to blow the final whistle.

Scotland had lost 2-1 but they had put in a very credible performance against the European champions. The match was clearly more physical than the home players were used to but they seem to have held their own in that department as well. Coupled with Glasgow's narrow defeat at London Lions in May these performances were nevertheless encouraging and augured well for the future.

On the domestic front the most improved team in the championship was Bridge of Weir, who by the end of November were sitting proudly at the top of the league with four wins out of four. The Renfrewshire men had scored eight goals with the loss of none in the process. This was a remarkable turnaround in fortune for a largely unchanged team that had not won a single match in the First Division the season before.

The catalyst of this new found success was the diminutive Gordon Rowley who was proving to be an outstanding player. Rowley had assumed the coaching duties at the club and the results had been immediate. Another important player in the team was the home developed centre Wilbur Muirhead whose all-round ability and eye for goal were now being brought fully to fruition. It was unfortunate for him that he had such strong competition for representative honours in that position from Jack Easton and Arthur Tingley.

Title favourites Kelvingrove were in second position, three points behind but with a match less played. They had dropped a point against Queen's in a disappointing match where the respective defences had been on top. It had ended 0-0, an unusual score in ice hockey, which rather summed up the fare on offer. The consolation for Kelvingrove was that they had now taken three points off Mohawks and Queen's, the two sides considered to be their main rivals for the title.

Queen's continued to be an enigma. They were a very attractive team but inconsistent. After only three matches their chances of winning the Canada Cup already looked doomed with a record of one win, one defeat and one draw. In Fred Reardon, Arthur Bazin and Arthur Tingley the building blocks were in place for success but they seemed to lack concentration at times and perhaps some organisation.

At the other end of the league table, Dennistoun continued to struggle despite the best efforts of their two Canadian stars, Hugh Reid and Tom Nisbet. The popular East End club had endured four defeats in four matches and had scored only two goals for the loss of eleven.

Bearsden seemed to be heading in the same direction with three straight defeats in which they had conceded thirteen goals and scored none before

Season 1930-1931

this free fall was reversed with a welcome 2-1 win over the ever unpredictable Glasgow Skating Club at the end of the month. The tricky Jack Gilmour scored both goals in this match but the team was missing J G Carruthers who was currently unavailable.

The first inter-city match of the season between Glasgow and Manchester was held at the Manchester Ice Palace only a week after Scotland's bruising encounter with Germany. This match gave the selectors the opportunity to blood a number of new players at representative level including Sid Montford and Lorne Berlinquet, who joined team-mate John Campbell for an all Kelvingrove attack, Wilbur Muirhead of Bridge of Weir and J O McCabe of Glasgow Skating Club. For his day job, Sid Montford spent his entire working life as a journalist for the *News* and *Record*. His criteria were simple - work hard, be objective, and get the facts right. His son, Arthur, followed in his journalistic footsteps.

The only survivors from the recent Scotland match were Arthur Bazin of Queen's, who captained Glasgow and defence partner Tom Nisbet of Dennistoun. Dave Cross of Kelvingrove returned as goaltender. The team was completed with the addition of A Rintoul of Achtungs. The match was a very close affair, only settled by a Neville Melland goal for Manchester scored in a period of extra time. The result only told part of the story. Glasgow were very aggrieved over a number of matters, not the least of which was the appearance in the Manchester team of Peter Fair of United Services, as well as Neville Melland and John Magwood of London Lions. Glasgow rightly considered their selection for Manchester to be improper conduct. They were further annoyed at the state of the ice which had remained cut up following a public skating session prior to the match.

In addition, Arthur Bazin had not been consulted regarding the playing of extra time - when Manchester secured the winning goal. These various grievances led the SIHA to send a formal letter of protest to the Manchester club. Quite what John Magwood made of it all would have been interesting to know. Apart from being one of the offending "guest" players for Manchester, he was also the current secretary of the BIHA!

That Manchester had felt obliged to strengthen their side with guest players was a backhanded compliment to Glasgow. There is no doubt that the Scottish game was being taken more seriously south of the border, the recent results and performances of Scottish representative sides being much improved. Scottish ice hockey was on the up and the SIHA was hopeful of arranging prestigious fixtures with London Lions and Oxford University before the end of the year.

One player starting to make a big impression was Tom Nisbet who led struggling Dennistoun to only their second win in the thirteen competitive matches the team had played since the resumption of ice hockey the previous season. Tall, well built and very fast, Nisbet scored all five goals in his side's 5-1 defeat of Bearsden in a league match played in early December. Dennistoun had been described as a clever team but lacking in leadership and organisation so perhaps Nisbet would be just the man to pull them together.

This was the last league fixture until mid-January as the remainder of the time in between was primarily devoted to playing the early rounds of the Mitchell Trophy. The holders, Glasgow Skating Club, were amongst the teams given a bye in the first round and would not play in the competition until they met Bearsden in the second round.

The best looking tie of the first round was that between the unbeaten league leaders Bridge of Weir and the mercurial Queen's. The match did not disappoint. A close encounter was decided 2-1 in favour of the Glasgow team, courtesy of an Arthur Tingley brace within a minute of each other in the second period. Wilbur Muirhead got his customary goal for Bridge of Weir in the final session but Queen's held out for a deserved if unexpected victory.

There was almost another surprise in the tie between the improving Dennistoun and a rather lethargic looking Mohawks which finished 2-2 after a period of extra time. John Fullerton put Mohawks ahead twice only for Tom Nisbet to twice level the scores with well taken solo goals. In the replay held ten days later, Mohawks put the shackles on Nisbet, who was marked out of the game, allowing them to progress to the next round with a 2-0 win thanks to goals from Art Brady and John Fullerton.

The tie between Achtungs and Kelvingrove also went to extra time. John Campbell and R L Noble gave 'Grove a 2-0 lead going into the third period and they appeared to be cruising but goals from Hugh Reid and A Rintoul brought the scores level before the end. A complacent Kelvingrove reasserted themselves in extra time, John Campbell scoring twice to secure his hat-trick and a 4-2 win but Achtungs had given a highly commendable performance. Not only were they missing R W Higginbotham in defence, but they had no substitutes available either so their starting six had to play the entire match.

In the first of the two second round ties, Bearsden exacted a measure of revenge for their final defeat of the previous season when they defeated holders Glasgow Skating Club 3-0. One could never be sure which Skating Club side would turn up for matches such was their unpredictability. They were a very disappointing and well beaten team in this game. It was an encouraging result for Bearsden, who were not enjoying the best of seasons.

In the other second round tie, Queen's had little difficulty in disposing of Glasgow University with an emphatic 8-1 victory. The students cause was not helped by their stand-in goaltender, R T Myers, who had a nightmare of a match, but Queen's were running into a rich vein of good form. Arthur Tingley scored four of his team's goals and their latest Canadian recruit, M J (Martin) Hall, marked his debut in impressive style with a hat-trick.

In the semi-finals, Queen's would play Kelvingrove, in what looked like the final before the final, and in the other, Bearsden would play Mohawks.

Season 1930-1931

Bridge of Weir Ice Hockey Club, 1930-31 Left to Right: Ramsay Muirhead, Walter McLeod, Earl Muirhead, Jimmy Woodrow, Alistair McLeod, David Carty (SIHA), Norman Macfie, Wilbur Muirhead, Gordon Rowley, Pat Brennan, Ian McLeod, ?, ?, John Anderson (Manager).

Frozen in Time

The year ended at Crossmyloof with a challenge match involving two teams made up of junior players. Amongst those taking part were several who would make a name for themselves in the game including J (Jack) Johnston, A (Andrew) Gray, F (Fred) Hems, K (Ken) Hurll, E L (Eric, brother of Sid) Montford and future international players, D D (Don) Edwards, Walter S McLeod and J H (Joe) Collins.

Kelvingrove, as dynamic as ever, arranged to play a challenge match in London against Hammersmith on New Year's Day. Such was the interest in this fixture that a number of carriages were booked on the London train by the club to take the players, officials and supporters down for the occasion. Hammersmith were a new club who were only formed that season but they had acquired some useful players including Dr T M Kellough and G A Strubbe. The match was played at the Hammersmith Ice Drome and was an even affair until the third period when Dave Cross, the Kelvingrove goaltender, sustained a bad injury which impeded his movement. Hammersmith fully capitalised on this misfortune by scoring three goals without reply but most observers agreed that the Glasgow team had given a good account of themselves and that the final score flattered the home side.

At Crossmyloof, a day later, Glasgow defeated West Renfrewshire 3-1 in a rather meaningless challenge match. The latter team was essentially Bridge of Weir but with the addition of Arthur Tingley of Queen's, Jack Gilmour of Bearsden and Tom Shearer of Mohawks. Glasgow were on familiar lines but took the opportunity of icing new boys Greg Lennox of Mohawks in goal, Harry Reid of Dennistoun and the young Billy Fullerton of Queen's.

The speed skating initiative promoted by the SIHA was proving popular as a number of clubs furnished players. Amongst the most enthusiastic were John Fullerton and T (Tom) Craig of Mohawks, E Fincham of Kelvingrove, Arthur Tingley and Billy Fullerton of Queen's, Jack Easton of Glasgow University and Tom Nisbet, Harry Reid and Sam Stevenson of Dennistoun. Harry Reid was appointed Secretary of the Scottish Speed Skating Association.

The SIHA was beginning to come under some pressure to recognise women's ice hockey. A number of female members from the various clubs were desirous of forming ladies' teams but - despite a modicum of resistance to the idea from the men - the stumbling block remained lack of available ice time at Crossmyloof. The SIHA pointed out with some justification just how difficult it was for the league clubs to procure adequate ice time at the rink not only for matches but for practice as well. In addition, the juniors had only recently been similarly accommodated after something of a struggle so the chances of further accommodating the ladies seemed remote in such circumstances. The ladies however were made of sterner stuff. Not taking the hint, they would continue to badger both the SIHA and the management of Crossmyloof Ice Rink for ice time. A ladies' ice hockey team had recently been formed at the Park Lane

Season 1930-1931

Arena in London and this development only encouraged the Glasgow ladies all the more in their determination to play the game.

The league championship resumed on 13 January when Queen's defeated Glasgow University, 4-1 only a week after their Mitchell Trophy tie. While Queen's did not find this match as easy as their previous encounter it left a rather sour taste in the mouth. A complaint was registered, either by Glasgow University or the match referee, over the behaviour of some of the Queen's players during the game. It seems that during the match Arthur Bazin, Fred Rearden and Martin Hall were treating it like a "practice session". One assumes from this description that they were, to use the modern parlance, "showboating". If correct, it was totally unacceptable. The SIHA were always likely to take a dim view of such antics for it not only brought the game into disrepute and showed a complete lack of respect for one's opponents but it also went against the spirit of the amateur code governing the sport in Scotland.

The league championship was developing into a dog-fight between leaders Bridge of Weir and title favourites, Kelvingrove. The Renfrewshire side dropped their first point of the campaign, when they could only draw 0-0 with Glasgow Skating Club, but Kelvingrove blew the opportunity to draw level with them at the top when they then drew 0-0 with Dennistoun in what "The Blade" described as "a game in which every art of the sport was displayed with polished skill". Not every art, though, since there were no goals!

Bridge of Weir appeared to be losing form at the wrong time, for their next match on 27 January was against Queen's, who had not yet given up hope of winning the title themselves. Both sides were missing important players for this fixture as both Arthur Bazin and Gordon Rowley were unavailable.

Queen's, who were already skating on what may be termed thin ice, indulged in yet another questionable action when they iced two guest players for this match, P Peltier and J Barnes. Both were Canadian sailors attached to *HMCS Calgarolite* which was berthed for repairs at the Govan dry dock in Glasgow. If Bridge of Weir were concerned about this incident it has not been recorded.

As to the match itself, Bridge of Weir clearly missed the influence of their coach. In what was a physical contest they were unable to cope with the dash and skill of Arthur Tingley, whose two goals gave Queen's a deserved 2-0 victory. It completed a wretched month for Bridge of Weir, who had now lost three points from their last two league matches. The chief beneficiaries of their recent discomfort were likely to be Kelvingrove, still a point behind but with three matches left to play, one more than Bridge of Weir.

A day later, Glasgow played a team representing *HMCS Calgarolite* although it had to be supplemented by the addition of four local players, Norman Macfie, Gordon Rowley, Tom Nisbet and Tom Shearer. There was one new player in the Glasgow team, the locally born and developed Sam Stevenson of Dennistoun.

In an interesting match, Tom Nisbet put the visitors ahead in the first period but Arthur Tingley brought the scores level after the interval. Nisbet then scored a brilliant solo goal in the final period before Hugh Reid took advantage of a mix-up in the *Calgarolite* defence to equalise. Shortly after, John Fullerton scored the winning goal for Glasgow to secure a fortunate 3-2 win.

Any victory against Canadian opposition, or in this case largely French-Canadian opposition, was welcome but not too much was read into this particular triumph. The visiting team were obviously not all that well prepared and their need to enlist the assistance of local players only added to their difficulties. Although it appears they could still have beaten Glasgow, it had not been a full strength home side which had taken the ice.

On the international front, Great Britain competed in the World Championships being held in early February in Poland. As would become the norm, no players from the Scottish League were deemed good enough for selection to the British team. Canada, this time represented by the Manitoba University Graduates, won the world title yet again. Great Britain finished in eighth position.

The eagerly anticipated Mitchell Trophy semi-final between Kelvingrove and Queen's was played on 6 February. It did not disappoint as an enthralling encounter was effectively settled in the second period with goals from John Campbell and Sid Montford within two minutes of each other, the latter score being disputed by the opposition. Queen's pulled a goal back in the final period through guest player, P Peltier, but 'Grove held on for an impressive 2-1 victory.

The talk was now of a possible "double" for Kelvingrove of both the Mitchell Trophy and the Canada Cup. They certainly had the playing squad to achieve this milestone and had further strengthened that squad by taking a leaf out of Queen's book by capturing another forward, C A Franette, from *HMCS Calgarolite*. He made his debut against Queen's and looked to be the best of the players available from this source.

Mohawks would provide the opposition to Kelvingrove in the final of the Mitchell Trophy. They had comfortably disposed of Bearsden 4-0 in the other semi-final, Art Brady helping himself to a hat-trick. Mohawks were 3-0 up in the first period and although Bearsden tried hard to recover the situation there was really no way back for the "rugby men". The final of the Mitchell Trophy would not be played until 28 March but before then the league championship would provide plenty of interest.

Kelvingrove at last took over the leadership by a point when they defeated Glasgow University 4-0 on 13 February, but only four days later Bridge of Weir got back to the top again, when they won a thrilling match 4-3 against Dennistoun, the Glasgow club fighting back from being 4-0 down at one stage. A week later, Kelvingrove returned to the top following an exciting

Season 1930-1931

8-4 victory over Glasgow Skating Club, C A Franette proving his worth to the team with a hat-trick.

Although the proposed challenge match against Oxford University had failed to materialise the SIHA announced that Scotland would be playing against the world champions, Canada (Manitoba University Graduates), at Crossmyloof in March. This would be the Canadians' last match before they returned home from their extensive European tour. The announcement of this fixture gave everyone associated with Scottish ice hockey an enormous buzz.

Arrangements were also made for Glasgow to play Manchester at Crossmyloof in their second fixture of the season on 14 February. Ticket prices for spectators were 2s and 1s for balcony seats and 6d for downstairs seats. In the previous match a largely experimental Glasgow side had lost 1-0 but this time the selectors, perhaps with an eye on the forthcoming match with Canada, decided to ice what looked like a full Scotland team.

Fred Reardon was again preferred to Dave Cross in goal with Gordon Rowley and Arthur Bazin completing the defence. John Fullerton was given his chance in the forward line along with Arthur Tingley and Art Brady. The substitutes were Hugh Reid, Jack Easton and Tom Nisbet. It was a strong line-up and it proved far too good for Manchester who were well beaten 4-0, Brady securing a hat-trick and Easton netting the other goal.

The league championship race was reaching an exciting climax. A depleted Queen's lost any real hope of at least finishing runners-up when they could only draw 2-2 with Bearsden on 3 March. The SIHA suspended Fred Reardon, Arthur Bazin and Martin Hall for this match, the consequence of their 'showboating' earlier in the year. This proved too much of a handicap for Queen's. Bearsden took to the ice with yet another rugby man in their team, the Scotland international player, F H Waters of Cambridge University and London Scottish.

All attention was now firmly fixed on the league championship decider between Bridge of Weir and Kelvingrove on 10 March. It was the final match of the season for both teams. Kelvingrove were top of the league with 12 points but Bridge of Weir were only a point behind. Nothing less than a win would do for the Renfrewshire team but 'Grove could afford a draw.

The match attracted 1,000 spectators to Crossmyloof and they watched a thrilling spectacle. Bridge of Weir started the match well, being more convincing in attack and in checking, so it was no surprise when danger man Wilbur Muirhead scored at the end of the first period, with a shot some observers thought Dave Cross might have saved. The loss of this goal seemed to galvanise Kelvingrove, who had struggled to get out of first gear. 'Grove adopted a more physical approach in the second period, but Bridge of Weir continued to look the better team as they strove to find a second goal. It did not come. In the third period 'Grove took the game to their opponents, and John Campbell took advantage of some sloppy defending to score an equalising goal with a hard drive amidst "tremendous cheering". Both teams could have scored again but the match finished 1-1 - a result which gave Kelvingrove the title and the Canada Cup.

While Bridge of Weir had been unlucky not to win this match, not too many observers grudged Kelvingrove the championship. They were the only unbeaten team in the league with five wins and three draws. Their success was based on a solid defence and a formidable array of attacking talent who between them had scored 25 goals, easily the highest total in the league. In fact, they had not lost a league match since 1929!

Their first team was entirely Canadian with the notable exception of Sid Montford. Within that squad were players like R L Noble, W M Phinney and Lorne Berlinquet, who were versatile enough to play comfortably in either defence or attack; this was a key to their success. Having such a large squad of players also afforded 'Grove the luxury of being able to cope better than other teams with absences, injuries or suspensions. They had a strong foundation. They had the largest supporters club in the league and derived a steady stream of funding for equipment and other necessities from this source. They also had a number of notable individuals in honorary positions in the club including Sir Matthew Montgomery, Lieutenant-Colonel Archibald Douglas McInnes-Shaw and Colonel G P Linton; it is not beyond the realms of possibility that some of these gentlemen may have assisted the odd fund-raising effort as well.

Barely had the excitement of the league championship decider died down when three days later world champions Canada visited Crossmyloof to play Scotland. The Manitoba University Graduates were a great side, having played a total of 39 matches in England and Europe, winning 38 and drawing the other. They represented a daunting challenge to a Scottish team not short of confidence or ability but fully aware of the gulf in class between them.

One of the real stars in the Canadian team was centre Dr Blake Watson. He had travelled to Vienna in 1925 to study medicine and became not only the player-coach of local side Wiener EV but the inspiration of Austrian ice hockey. Watson was one of the best known players in Europe, having also played for clubs in Prague and Zurich. Outside the sport, as a gynaecologist he would count amongst his future patients the Hollywood actresses, Greta Garbo and Rita Hayworth.

Needless to state Scotland selected their strongest team for this match. It was the same squad of players who had played against Manchester in February. Despite ticket prices ranging from 7s 6d to 2s, a total of 2,500 spectators packed into Crossmyloof for the match. Canada suffered a minor pre-match upset when their goaltender had to return home early and John Campbell of Kelvingrove took his place between the posts.

That was to be Canada's only set back as they thrashed Scotland 11-1. Arthur Tingley at least had the consolation of scoring the final goal of the match and denying John Campbell a shut-out.

Season 1930-1931

Try as they might Scotland could not live with the skill, speed and aggression of their opponents. The home side was constantly caught out of position. Canada gave an exhibition of controlled, disciplined and tactically aware ice hockey. The Scottish defence had been horribly exposed but they had not been helped by the inability of their forwards to back-check properly.

This tactical naivety and lack of positional play had not been quite as obvious in the earlier international match against Germany but the lessons of that defeat had clearly not been learned. Such matters were really down to coaching. If this match taught Scotland anything, it was that the SIHA's long-stated aim to engage the services of a full time coach with Canadian experience was now a matter requiring action.

A week after the match with Canada, a less-than-full-strength Glasgow side travelled to Manchester to play the home team for the third time that season. Each team had a win under their belt, although the earlier match at the Manchester Ice Palace had been marred by controversy. Glasgow were without a number of regular players including Arthur Bazin, Art Brady and Arthur Tingley but added the popular Achtungs forward, George Reid, who had been knocking on the door for representative honours for some time. In a fast and interesting match Glasgow came back from 2-0 down to draw level with goals from Tom Nisbet of Dennistoun and John Campbell of Kelvingrove. All of the goals in this match were scored in the second period. Despite a period of extra time being played it ended 2-2 which in the circumstances was a reasonable result for the visitors.

The show-piece game of the domestic calendar was the final of the Mitchell Trophy held on 28 March between champions Kelvingrove and their great rivals, Mohawks. The match gave Mohawks an opportunity to avenge their earlier league defeat and to finish the season with some silverware. For 'Grove it represented an opportunity to win a unique "double" of the league championship and the cup.

The contest attracted about 2,000 spectators to Crossmyloof. Kelvingrove were without their captain Andy Dick in defence, obliging them to move the versatile R L Noble into his position. Jimmy Brown, "the flying Australian", came back into the forward line after missing a few matches and for Mohawks, young Andrew Gray was given his chance at centre playing between John Fullerton and Art Brady.

In an exciting first period Sid Montford scored to put 'Grove ahead but Art Brady equalised following good work from John Fullerton. The second period was more scrappy, both sides having chances but finding the two goaltenders in good form. Jimmy Brown had been causing the Mohawks' defence problems with his lightning speed and deadly shooting but he had so far drawn a blank.

That situation changed within a minute of the third period, when Brown scored what turned out to be the winning goal. In a rapid flowing movement he gathered a pass and, beating an opponent by deft stick work, shot the puck past a helpless Greg Lennox in the Mohawks goal. Despite nursing a bad cut above an eye, the dashing Brown bravely remained on the ice to cap a wonderful individual performance.

Victory in the Mitchell Trophy was the icing on the cake for Kelvingrove. It had been a great season for the West End team - the first to win the "double" of league and cup. It was a fitting reward for their ambition, commitment and forward planning. The club had set the benchmark for other clubs to follow both on and off the ice.

The domestic season petered out following the conclusion of the Mitchell Trophy. Crossmyloof remained open for the month of April and it was a pity that competition had all but effectively ceased by the end of March. The clubs filled in the remaining few dates allocated to them with a series of challenge matches against each other and while these offered the opportunity to give more ice time to substitutes or juniors they were of little importance otherwise.

The only outstanding fixture was the northern semi-final of the British Championship between Glasgow and Manchester at Crossmyloof. The SIHA offered the English side a number of dates and after much prevarication from them the match was eventually scheduled for 25 April. Having agreed to the fixture Manchester announced - about a week before it was due to be played - that they had changed their mind and had agreed to play London Lions in a challenge match on that evening. Manchester suggested that the fixture with Glasgow be played a week later on 2 May but since Crossmyloof would be closed for the season by that time the match would then have to be played at the Manchester Ice Palace.

The SIHA were absolutely furious, not for the first time that season, at the actions of the Manchester club. They issued an ultimatum to the effect that if Manchester did not play Glasgow on the agreed date of 25 April then they would consider the English team as having scratched from the tie with the result that Glasgow should go straight to the final. In any event, Glasgow would not be travelling to Manchester. For their part, Manchester refused to come to Crossmyloof and in consequence their match with Glasgow never took place. A nonplussed SIHA laid the matter before the BIHA but the ruling body in England stalled on taking any effective action over the incident. The SIHA were rightly very upset over this turn of events and threatened to disaffiliate from the BIHA in protest.

A couple of weeks passed. Despite all the bluster and rancour Glasgow never got to play in the final of the British Championship. The SIHA remained in the BIHA, but the affair highlighted a growing tension between the two governing bodies which had been simmering all season. The BIHA was seen as toothless and unable to stand up to the more powerful clubs in England. There was probably an element of truth in this assertion. The sport was

Season 1930-1931

going through a major period of transition in England, causing the BIHA to reassess its own position in relation to a growing number of member clubs.

The season formally ended at Crossmyloof with a challenge match between Glasgow and Edinburgh on 28 April. All of the players selected for the Edinburgh team were of course based at the Glasgow rink and the match was little more than a glorified practice session. For the record it ended 2-2.

The English season ended in May with London Lions being considered the champions as they had gone through the season undefeated. This fine achievement marked the swansong for Blaine Sexton's talented team. Their mantle was about to be taken over by Oxford University, who had put together a very good side, augmented by the inclusion of a number of Rhodes scholars from Canada, so reminiscent of the old Oxford Canadians teams.

Indeed it was all change generally for ice hockey south of the border. The BIHA had decided to restore a league system for season 1931-32 which would be divided into two divisions according to merit. In addition, the establishment of the Grosvenor House Canadians and the Queen's clubs in London effectively ushered in the era of semi-professional ice hockey as both actively recruited Canadian players with the stated intention of paying them for their services.

Ice hockey in Scotland remained strictly amateur. Yet despite its apparent limitations the domestic game was in a buoyant state. There was no lack of interest from the public and the press and it was a measure of the continued progress being made that both Germany and Canada had agreed to play Scotland in representative matches. All in all it had not been a bad season, though the SIHA would have to address the issue of somehow elongating the fixture list, to ensure meaningful matches for all of the dates allocated for ice hockey at Crossmyloof Ice Rink in the future.

Frozen in Time

Season 1931-32

Crossmyloof Ice Rink re-opened for the new winter season on 1 October 1931. Ice sports generally were enjoying enormous popularity and the local press noted that competition between curling, figure skating, speed skating and ice hockey interests at the venue would be as fierce as ever. This situation obliged the SIHA to accept the status quo in terms of format and organisation for the season ahead.

In a rare period of stability, the composition of the Scottish League was unchanged from the previous season. The same nine teams - Achtungs, Bearsden, Bridge of Weir, Dennistoun Eagles, Glasgow Skating Club, Glasgow University, Kelvingrove, Mohawks and Queen's - would compete for the Canada Cup and the Mitchell Trophy.

While the basic format of the league championship would remain whereby each team would play the other only once, the SIHA had learned from the mistake of the season before; the competition would now be stretched by commencing in mid-October with a finish date scheduled for mid-April. The Mitchell Trophy competition would not begin until early February.

Unfortunately, matches would continue to be played within the allocated slot of three quarters of an hour. The face-off would commence at 7.15pm and the game would be expected to finish by 8.00pm.

Despite the public being obliged to watch a somewhat truncated version of ice hockey at Crossmyloof, the ice rink management decided to increase the admission charges to all matches. No doubt cashing in on the obvious popularity of the sport prices jumped from 6d to 9d, an increase of 50%. This still represented reasonable value since attendance at a senior football match in Glasgow would cost a spectator at least 1s but then it could be argued that football matches lasted twice as long.

In any event the increase in charges did not seem to deter too many spectators as attendances at the various practice matches held in early October indicated. In addition, most of the clubs which encouraged non-playing memberships - including Dennistoun, Kelvingrove and Mohawks - all reported increases in numbers, an encouraging development.

Any review of a team's prospects for the new season had to take account of player movements. As would become the norm, with so many transient Canadians in the domestic game, players would come and go. Some clubs were more affected than others by this process but those like Kelvingrove, who had been largely dependent on Canadian talent, tended to suffer more when the expatriates moved on.

Indeed the defending champions would start the new season without the services of two of their best players, Jimmy Brown and R L Noble. The loss of these players was a definite setback and this situation was exacerbated when Lorne Berlinquet and William Phinney both intimated that they would not be available for selection for every match the team would play in the season ahead.

Kelvingrove still presented a formidable challenge with Dave Cross in goal, Andy Dick in defence and John Campbell and Sid Montford up front but there was little doubt that their player squad was significantly weaker from that of the previous season with the key ingredient of versatility greatly diminished. On the plus side was the emergence of young Joe Collins in defence who looked a good prospect.

The other main contenders for the Canada Cup were likely to be last season's runners-up, Bridge of Weir, along with Mohawks and Queen's.

The Renfrewshire side was largely unchanged although the goaltender, Norman Macfie, was no longer available. He would be replaced by A (Angus) Ross. While any team with Gordon Rowley and Wilbur Muirhead deserved respect Bridge of Weir seemed to depend rather too much on these players although in young Walter McLeod they also appeared to have a star of the future.

Mohawks were also largely unchanged with a settled and well organised team. The club continued to operate with a small squad of mainly home produced players who had noticeably improved in the latter half of the previous season. Mohawks had a sound defence and an impressive and very fast forward line consisting of John Fullerton, Tom Craig and Art Brady. Provided they steered clear of injuries they looked set fair for a good season.

The other main contenders for the title, perhaps as an outside bet, were the highly entertaining Queen's. The club received a heavy blow with the departure of Martin Hall to his native Canada and it became clear that Fred Reardon would only be available at certain times during the season. Queen's were another club which did not have a large squad of players but they did have quality in Arthur Bazin and Arthur Tingley and much was expected of young Billy Fullerton who was making great progress. None of the other teams in the league could realistically expect to win the title.

There were a number of changes at Dennistoun not the least of which was the name of the club. From this season onwards the East End team would be known as Dennistoun Eagles perhaps in the hope that a change of name might bring a change of fortune. Such expectations were almost immediately dashed with the departure back to Canada of talisman Tom Nisbet. The loss of Nisbet was not just a blow to Dennistoun but to Scottish ice hockey in general since players of his ability and character were very hard to replace.

Season 1931-1932

Mohawks Players Practising at Rouken Glen Park, Glasgow, 1931

Another very notable absentee from the local game this season was John Wharrie, the veteran goaltender of Glasgow Skating Club, who had at last decided to hang up his skates. John Wharrie was the last of those who had played during the Edwardian era at the original Crossmyloof Ice Rink. He had been a player with the old Corinthians club and had kept goal for Scotland in the two historic matches against England in 1910.

The league championship formally commenced on 13 October when Achtungs defeated Glasgow University 3-2 in front of a large number of spectators which included the football teams, Rangers and Queen's Park. The match did not spring into life until the third period by which time Achtungs were leading 3-0 but Jack Easton pulled two goals back for the students to ensure an exciting finale.

Only three days later an SIHA representative side were in action having been invited to play a North of England select team in a match organised to formally open the new Liverpool Ice Rink. This fixture came rather too early in the season for the SIHA who decided to play safe by selecting a squad of the tried and tested. The match attracted about 3,000 spectators to the new venue.

It was an evening when just about everything clicked into place for the Scottish team, who thumped the North of England 9-0. The value of playing a settled side was clearly demonstrated as the forward line ran amok with John Fullerton helping himself to four goals. When the English team did attack they found Dave Cross in the visiting goal in great form - something which could not be said of the experienced Stan Bookbinder, in the opposing goal, who did not have one of his better matches.

Both the performance and the margin of victory had exceeded Scottish expectations, but there were those south of the border who remained unimpressed. They pointed out that the North of England team had been cobbled together with hardly any practice from clubs which were not in the top drawer of English ice hockey. While there was certainly some truth in these assertions the home side had included Bernard H Fawcett of Cambridge University and Joe Cock of Manchester, both of whom had played for Great Britain.

Despite the negativity from some quarters the performance of the Scottish team did not go wholly unappreciated. The SIHA received an invitation to play two matches against the English champions, London Lions. The matches were scheduled for early November at Liverpool and Birmingham. Given the calibre of the opposition these fixtures were considered full international matches and would be a good barometer of how far ice hockey had really come in Scotland.

In the league championship the leading teams had all got off to a good start by winning their opening matches. While Bridge of Weir, Mohawks and Queen's all recorded relatively easy victories, defending champions Kelvingrove had laboured somewhat to finally overcome Achtungs 1-0 in what was described as a defensive and physical encounter.

Season 1931-1932

In fact some dissatisfaction was being expressed regarding the overall standard of play in the domestic game.

> "For nearly a month now ice hockey has been in progress but so far play has not reached the high standard of last season and a number of games have been somewhat dull and uninteresting. Only in sides that include full internationals has real interest been evoked and it must be said that but for the efforts of these talented players the goodly number of spectators must have been disappointed."
>
> *(Glasgow Herald: 29 October 1931).*

This was a rather harsh judgement. In point of fact almost every team in the Scottish League had at least one established international player in their ranks and while every team had now played one match it was far too early in the season to be making such a negative statement. The fare on offer may not have been of a comparable standard in relation to England but it was competitive and it did undoubtedly contain a number of players of genuine quality.

In a further effort to improve standards the SIHA announced that a select side would be making an extensive tour of England in early January. A total of eight fixtures would be played in as many days at a variety of rinks from Liverpool in the north to Southampton in the south. This represented an ambitious project for the SIHA but it became the focus of yet another dispute with the BIHA. The Secretary of the BIHA, John Magwood, pointed out that Great Britain would be undertaking a tour of Poland at exactly the same time as the Scottish tour of England was taking place and in view of this he suggested that the SIHA might wish to reschedule its visit accordingly. Given the unlikelihood of any Scottish based players being selected for the British team it was not immediately apparent to the SIHA what the problem was.

In any event the SIHA stuck to its guns and confirmed that its tour of England would proceed as planned. It was unfortunate that the relationship between the two ruling bodies in Great Britain appeared to be deteriorating at a time when the sport was gaining in popularity and prestige in both countries. One gets the impression that something akin to "turf wars" was a prime motivator in their recent conflicts and perhaps in the fullness of time these sorts of disputes would become less pronounced. On a more positive note the two Associations announced that Scotland would play England at Crossmyloof Ice Rink on 12 December. The resumption of this fixture after an absence of twenty one years was welcome news indeed. The hope was expressed that this would become an annual event.

The amateur code governing Scottish ice hockey was perfectly encapsulated by an interesting and highly indicative incident which took place in November. A league fixture between Bridge of Weir and Dennistoun was postponed because Wilbur and Earl Muirhead of the former team were attending their late uncle's funeral on the same day. It says much for the spirit, ethos and sportsmanship pervading the local game that Dennistoun and the SIHA so readily agreed to the postponement in what was fairly short notice.

For Scotland's "double-header" against London Lions regular players Fred Reardon, Arthur Bazin and Art Brady were unavailable. They were replaced by Dave Cross, Jack Gilmour and A Rintoul, the latter two joining John Fullerton as the only home developed players in the squad. John Campbell was also selected for Scotland for the first time.

The Scottish return to Liverpool Ice Rink on 6 November turned out to be a most chastening experience. London Lions simply blew Scotland away. From the moment Blaine Sexton scored in the first minute of the match the writing was on the wall. London Lions cruised to an easy 7-0 victory with the Scottish team confined to shooting from long distance but they never at any point seriously threatened their opponents goal. It was a shell-shocked Scottish team which skated on to the ice of Birmingham Ice Rink the following evening to face London Lions again. John Campbell started this match in place of John Fullerton as the only change in the Scottish side but it made little difference as the powerful English champions ran out winners again by 4-1. Scotland did play a little better in this match and A Rintoul managed to grab a consolation goal in the final minute but the gulf in class was there for all to see.

Both matches were a sobering experience for a relatively full strength Scotland side who were comprehensively out-skated and out-played by a rampant London Lions. It was noticeable that the Scottish players were constantly caught out of position every time their opponents broke away up the ice. Once again the lessons of last season's defeats against Germany and Canada had still not been learned.

Although on the wane London Lions remained a class act. They exuded quality with a number of Great Britain players including John Magwood, Neville Melland, H W Bushell and the imperious Blaine Sexton still going strong. They also had a couple of other notable personalities in their team including the future character actor, James Robertson Justice, and a member of the Austrian nobility, Baron H von Trauttenberg.

Away from the excitement of these representative contests the league championship was starting to hot up. The first big confrontation of the season arose on 13 November when defending champions Kelvingrove took on challengers Queen's. In a thrilling match, young Joe Collins gave 'Grove a 1-0 first period lead but two goals from the ever dangerous Arthur Tingley swung the momentum Queen's way by the end of the middle session. Despite a huge effort by the champions to salvage the game in the final period, Queen's held out for "a most popular victory" to win 2-1.

Queen's then faced another stern examination of their title credentials in their next match when they met Mohawks. Mohawks came into this encounter in very good form having scored nine goals in their previous two matches and it was most unfortunate for Queen's that neither Arthur Bazin nor Fred Reardon, essentially the team's defence now that V (Val) Carty was playing in goal, were available for this important fixture.

In a dour and disappointing game Tom Shearer secured the goal that mattered in the first period to give Mohawks a crucial 1-0 win. Arthur Tingley came close for Queen's in a hectic third period, but the handicap of missing two of their best players and meeting a very organised and confident Mohawks side proved too much for them. The result gave Mohawks sole leadership of the league as they remained the only team with a 100% record.

Bridge of Weir had also made a good start to the season but lost a critical point when they could only draw 1-1 with Dennistoun Eagles at the end of November. Their star player remained Gordon Rowley and apart from offering tuition to the juniors he was also actively involved in trying to raise standards in the senior game by hosting what were termed "master classes". It was noted that

> "Gordon Rowley, the Bridge of Weir and Scottish ice hockey internationalist, gave a comprehensive talk on the improvement of ice hockey to all members of Scottish clubs on Saturday evening in the board room at Crossmyloof. The talk lasted nearly two hours and was mainly directed towards the advantages of combination, team work, passing and the correct method of delivering the puck at goal. Further talks will take place in due course."
>
> *(Glasgow Herald: 26 November 1931).*

Rowley was clearly a figure who commanded respect, particularly if he was lecturing his fellow players on some of the finer points of the game. He combined his medical studies with being the European representative of the Montreal Amateur Athletic Association, one of the best amateur ice hockey clubs in Canada. This famous old club was about to embark on a tour of Europe and it was hoped that they might be able to fit in a match in Glasgow.

Expectations - not to mention great excitement - were mounting for the visit of England to Crossmyloof on 12 December. Ticket prices were fixed at 5s for the most expensive seats to 2s and a big crowd was expected. Scotland's two recent defeats by London Lions had led to much soul searching within the SIHA and it resulted in the selectors adopting radical measures.

For the first time the SIHA selected players based in England. The players in question were D A Porter and K Thomson, who were both forwards with the Grosvenor House Canadians in London. Don Porter, born in Milngavie but brought up in Canada, was no stranger to local ice hockey having played for both the old Glasgow Canadians and then Queen's before moving to England. Keith Thomson had been born in Edinburgh but like Porter learned to play ice hockey while growing up in Canada.

The inclusion of these "Anglo-Scots" attracted both favourable and adverse comment in equal measure. Porter and Thomson had been selected at the expense of regular international players Jack Gilmour and Arthur Tingley. The exclusion from the team of Tingley in particular raised a few eyebrows, especially since he was currently in very good form, and had never let Scotland down in the past.

The BIHA intimated that the home international would be regarded as a trial match, in that any players who did well would merit serious consideration for the Great Britain team being put together for the forthcoming European Championships to be held in Berlin in March 1932. This statement was probably taken with a pinch of salt by the SIHA, since no players from the Scottish League had ever really been seriously considered for the British team in any of the major LIHG competitions held thus far.

No matter. The match was the first time Scotland had played England since 1910. The teams were:

Scotland: D Cross (Kelvingrove); G D Rowley (Bridge of Weir) and A R Bazin (Queen's); D A Porter (Grosvenor House Canadians), K Thomson (Grosvenor House Canadians) and A R Brady (Mohawks). - J Fullerton (Mohawks), J A Easton (Glasgow University) and J Campbell (Kelvingrove).

England: V G C Gardner (London Lions); H E Mayes (Grosvenor House Canadians) and B N Sexton (London Lions); F N Melland (London Lions), J C P Magwood (London Lions) and B H Fawcett (London Lions). - E J Ramus (Princes), L Bonnycastle (Oxford University) and F A de Marwicz (London Lions).

Referee: H W Reid (SIHA).

Despite an improved performance Scotland came up just short against a very strong and experienced English team, losing 2-0. The local press were divided on how well the home side had coped with their more illustrious opponents. The ice hockey correspondent of the *Glasgow Herald* suggested that England were superior in almost every position except goaltender where Dave Cross had given an inspired display.

"Inside-Edge", the ice hockey correspondent of the *Daily Record and Mail*, noted that while England had about three-quarters of the play, Scotland's defence had performed magnificently in keeping the score down. They had been considerably assisted in this by John Fullerton and Don Porter, who back-checked properly, a facet of the game many Scottish forwards were yet to learn.

"The Blade" took a more sanguine view of Scotland's efforts.

> "England won by 2-0. Granted, but the progress of the Scottish team is the thing to marvel at. Their technique has advanced beyond all expectations. England won because they had more experience, better combination and greater skating speed and also because they

Season 1931-1932

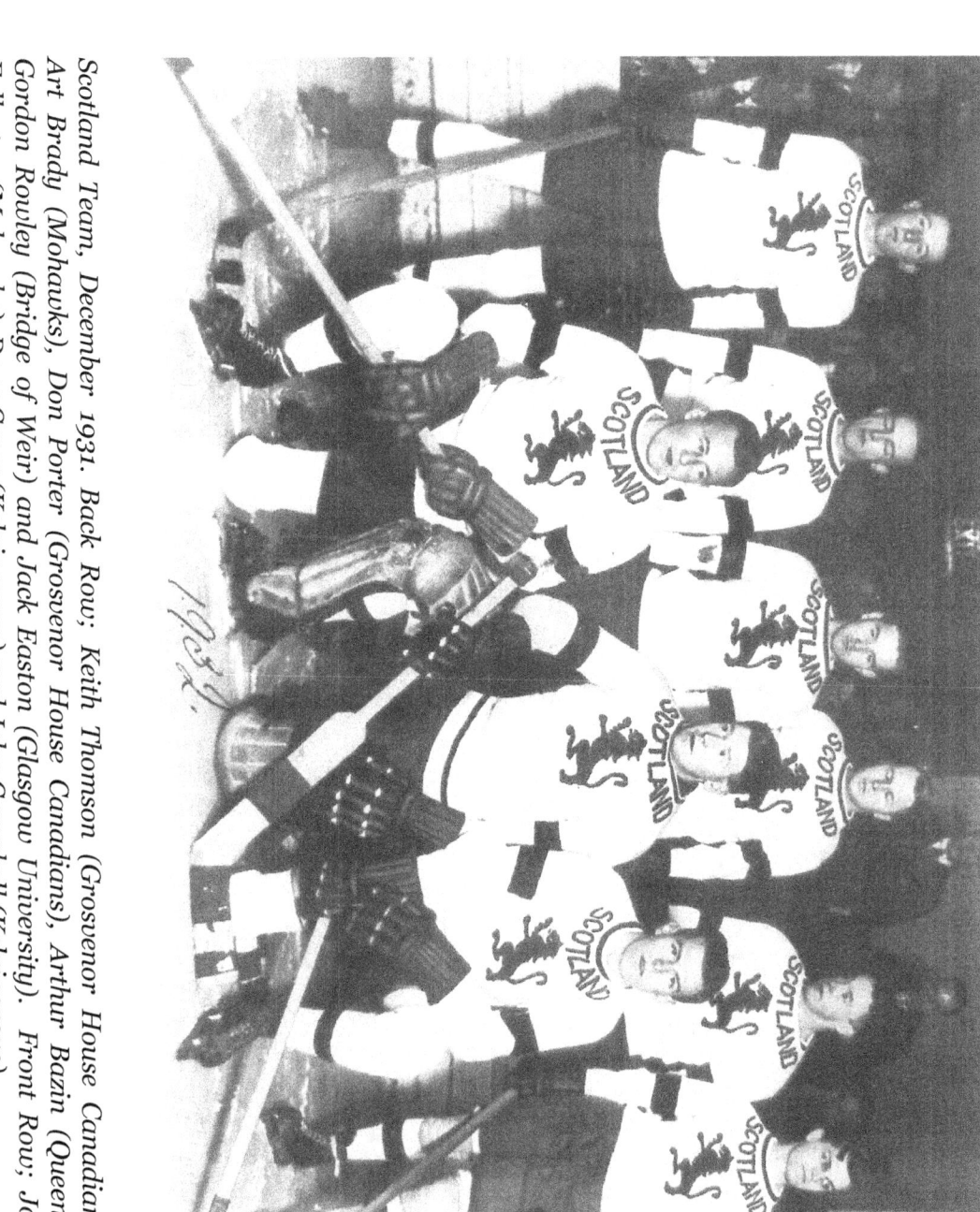

Scotland Team, December 1931. Back Row; Keith Thomson (Grosvenor House Canadians), Art Brady (Mohawks), Don Porter (Grosvenor House Canadians), Arthur Bazin (Queen's), Gordon Rowley (Bridge of Weir) and Jack Easton (Glasgow University). Front Row; John Fullerton (Mohawks), Dave Cross (Kelvingrove) and John Campbell (Kelvingrove).

had Bonnycastle. He is undoubtedly the greatest exponent of the game in this country today."

(Evening Times: 14 December 1931).

There was no doubt that the standard of ice hockey being played in what was now the English League Division One remained much better than that of the Scottish League but Scotland was still able to put together a representative side capable of at least competing at this level. The Scottish team was of course totally reliant on itinerant Canadians but it was hoped that would not always be the case. John Fullerton was really the only born-and-bred Scot who had thus far made the breakthrough, but the SIHA was confident that more would follow in the fullness of time.

The league championship reached the halfway stage on 22 December when an increasingly impressive Mohawks side defeated Achtungs 5-0, thanks to star players John Fullerton grabbing a hat-trick and Art Brady a brace. Indeed, Fullerton had scored 8 of his team's 15 goals up to that point. The Mohawks captain was deadly in front of goal and was known for his very deceptive body swerve, coupled with a fine turn of speed.

Mohawks sat proudly at the top of the league with eight points, the only team retaining a 100% record of played four, won four. They were looking a very good bet for their first Canada Cup. Bridge of Weir and Queen's shared second place on five points although the Renfrewshire men had played one match less. They were really Mohawks strongest challengers especially since Queen's lost further ground when they could only draw 2-2 with Bearsden in their next fixture. Once again Queen's had to play without Arthur Bazin and Fred Reardon and the continued unavailability of these players was wrecking their title challenge.

At the other end of the league table Glasgow Skating Club were struggling in bottom place. They had lost all three of their matches having scored only two goals for the loss of twelve. The team was clearly missing the steadying influence of a number of experienced players who had retired the previous season. The main problem was in defence for in Felix McLernan and J O McCabe, Skating Club had decent forwards but they received little support from the back line.

The New Year commenced with the scheduled tour - a rather punishing schedule of eight matches in almost as many days - of England by a Scottish representative side. The SIHA billed their touring team as a "Scottish League Select" rather than "Scotland" even though the squad of players selected for these matches was on the usual lines. One might have thought that the opportunity would have been taken to ice a few fringe players but the SIHA erred on the side of caution by selecting the best they had available in the hope of obtaining some good results.

The itinerary and results of this 1932 tour were as follows:

Season 1931-1932

1 January	Golders Green	London Lions	2-2
2 January	Hove	Sussex	1-1
4 January	Streatham	Princes	3-0
5 January	Southampton	London Select	2-5
6 January	Park Lane	Grosvenor House Canadians	1-1
7 January	Oxford	English League Select	1-1
8 January	Birmingham	English League Select	1-2
9 January	Liverpool	Lancashire	4-1

A total of twelve players comprised the Scottish League Select for this tour although only four of them - Dave Cross, Jack Gilmour, A Rintoul and John Campbell - played in every match. Arthur Bazin was not available for most of the fixtures and as a result he only played in the final two matches. Taken as a whole, the results obtained by the tourists were quite encouraging, particularly those against London Lions, Princes and Grosvenor House Canadians. A feature of the tour had been the consistently impressive performances put in by Dave Cross and Jack Easton. In fact, Easton had really caught the eye of observers south of the border so much so that he was actually selected to play for England in their forthcoming matches against Canada on 18 and 20 January. This was a singular achievement for the diminutive and wiry Canadian whose deft stick-handling and deadly finishing had now been recognised beyond the confines of the Scottish game.

On 22 January, an important league match was played between a thus far unbeaten Bridge of Weir and the defending champions, Kelvingrove. In a bruising encounter Sid Montford, developing into a fine player, put the Glasgow team ahead in the first period, a lead extended by John Campbell in the final session. Gordon Rowley then reduced the deficit but it was not enough as Kelvingrove ran out winners by 2-1.

There had not been much between the two teams, although Bridge of Weir had been guilty of bunching up too much in the middle of the ice while Kelvingrove had used their wing men to greater effect. This welcome result brought the champions back into contention for the title; while they remained four points behind leaders Mohawks and one point behind Bridge of Weir and Queen's they had played one match less than all of them.

Four days later Queen's moved solely into second place when they crushed Glasgow University 6-1, Arthur Tingley scoring four of these goals. Tingley had played in only three of the Scottish League Select's matches on their recent tour and was taking the opportunity to remind the selectors what they were missing. Kelvingrove then lost the chance to draw level with Queen's when they were surprisingly held 0-0 by a stuffy Bearsden in early February. That was to prove a very costly dropped point for the champions.

The Scottish League Select saw action again on 23 January when they entertained Manchester at Crossmyloof. The visitors were almost identical to the team iced as Lancashire in the recent Scottish tour match and the result was the same. This time the Scottish side posted an easy 6-0 victory against what was a rather lacklustre and disappointing visiting team.

Off the ice the SIHA was continuing to look seriously at how the game in Scotland might be further improved. There was a widespread recognition that something had to be done as the existing structure of the sport was not quite right. Unfortunately, Crossmyloof would remain the only ice rink in the country willing to regularly promote ice hockey for the foreseeable future and given that reality any reforms would be limited to what was or what was not possible at the Glasgow venue. Most informed observers of the Scottish game agreed that there were too many clubs in existence for the pool of available playing talent at Crossmyloof. This led the SIHA to conclude that there should be a reduction in the number of teams competing in the circuit. This could have proved very difficult to implement but fortunately common sense and good will prevailed. With next season in mind it was agreed that Achtungs and Bearsden would merge as would Glasgow Skating Club and Glasgow University.

A second strand of what was a radical re-construction of Scottish ice hockey was the creation of a distinct junior team. The intention was that this team, composed of young men up to the age of 18 years, should compete against the senior teams in all competitions. The experienced and respected Gordon Rowley agreed to leave Bridge of Weir at the end of the season to become the player-coach of this new team. On the face of it, the SIHA had come out with a sensible package of reforms but of course only time would tell. The reduction in the number of clubs, albeit by only one in the final analysis, was a regrettable but necessary step to take if the sport in Scotland was to move forward. It would mean that existing talent would not be so thinly spread as it was at the moment but nurtured and hopefully developed to its full potential by clubs fully committed to playing and promoting ice hockey.

The re-construction of the league was an acknowledgement of existing realities. The past two seasons and the current season demonstrated that there were really two leagues in operation. A top tier consisting of four clubs, Kelvingrove, Mohawks, Bridge of Weir and Queen's, who were capable of competing for the honours and the rest, the remaining five clubs who were almost just making up the numbers. The structured development of junior ice hockey was an encouraging and bold initiative. The future of the sport depended on getting this right. While the continuing injection of Canadian talent was both welcome as it was necessary it could not by itself sustain and develop the sport in Scotland. Most of this Canadian involvement was of a transitory nature but the sport required a firmer and more local input if it was to survive and prosper.

Although no one probably realised it at the time this package of reforms was the first perceptible break with the sport's strictly amateur ethos in Scotland. While the SIHA was no doubt undertaking these reforms in order to improve

Season 1931-1932

overall standards as they insisted, the main driving forces behind them were undoubtedly the rink management at Crossmyloof, the paying public and the local press. The sport was becoming a victim of its own success and as a result factors above and beyond "the game for the game's sake" were making their influence felt for the first time. Of course, ice hockey in Scotland would remain amateur for the foreseeable future but the fortress had suffered its first breach with the removal of teams for the sake of making the game more of a competitive spectacle for the paying customers who attended it. The die had been cast; one might have asked where might it end?

The league championship went into abeyance in early to mid-February as attention turned to the opening rounds of the Mitchell Trophy. The outstanding tie of the first round was that between trophy holders Kelvingrove and the current league leaders Mohawks. The match gave Mohawks the opportunity to avenge their trophy final defeat by Kelvingrove the previous season. That opportunity was not taken as Kelvingrove continued to dominate their fiercest rivals. A very close contest was not settled until the final minute of the match when John Campbell netted the winning goal on an assist from Sid Montford to clinch a 1-0 victory.

Four days later Glasgow Skating Club defeated Glasgow University 4-3 in another exciting match. Two goals from Felix McLernan contributed to a 3-1 first period lead for Skating Club but the students fought back to tie the game 3-3 by the end of the second session. Both teams had chances to score in the final period but it was J O McCabe who found the net to give Skating Club the win.

Achtungs and Queen's were both without key players for their second round tie on 12 February. Missing for Achtungs were goaltender Billy Dunlop and captain Hugh Reid while Arthur Bazin and Fred Reardon were once again absent for Queen's. This rather detracted from the occasion resulting in a dull and uninspiring game effectively settled 3-2 in favour of Queen's thanks to an Arthur Tingley hat-trick.

Bridge of Weir had a real struggle in overcoming a plucky Dennistoun Eagles who were unfortunate not to earn at least a replay. Gordon Rowley scored with a deflected shot mid way through the second period before Earl Muirhead sealed a 2-0 victory with a goal in the final session. Don Edwards, the left wing of Dennistoun, confirmed his status as one of the most promising juniors in the country in this match.

The final tie of the second round saw Kelvingrove take on Bearsden. The holders had little trouble in seeing off their opponents with a 4-1 win although the score did flatter the West End team. Bearsden were disjointed in their approach; their defence was unable to cope with an inspired display from John Campbell, who bagged a hat-trick.

The semi-final draw pitted Queen's against Glasgow Skating Club and Kelvingrove against Bridge of Weir. Both ties would be played in mid-March.

The league championship resumed in early March with Mohawks still top of the pile on a maximum ten points from five matches played. Bridge of Weir and Queen's shared second place on nine points but with one more match played than the leaders. In third place were Kelvingrove with seven points but they too had only played five matches and their next fixture just happened to be against Mohawks.

For Kelvingrove the aim was crystal clear. They had to defeat Mohawks to stay in the championship race. The two sides met on 1 March, almost a month after their Mitchell Trophy match. The outcome was the same. For Mohawks the jinx continued, as the defending champions posted an emphatic-looking 4-0 defeat upon them. The game had been a very close affair until the third period. Mohawks were severely disadvantaged by the absence of Art Brady and their cause was not helped either by having only one substitute available. Their defence coped well until Sid Montford scored an early goal in the third session; this seemed to break any further resistance. It was Mohawks' first league defeat of the season and their fourth consecutive loss to Kelvingrove in all competitions.

Bridge of Weir took over the leadership of the league three days later when they thumped a weakened Queen's 6-0. The Glasgow side were yet again minus important players - Arthur Bazin, Fred Reardon and the in-form Arthur Tingley - and paid the price. The game was notable for young Walter McLeod's first goal in senior ice hockey.

On 8 March, Mohawks returned to the top of the league by one point when they annihilated Glasgow University 9-3 in the highest scoring match of the season. John Fullerton turned in a sensational performance in scoring six of his team's nine goals. Mohawks were again without Art Brady who had now graduated from university and qualified as a doctor. Art Brady had actually moved to St Helens in Lancashire to take up a post in general practice. His departure from Mohawks was a serious blow to the club and to the Scottish League in general. The flying wing man was a perfect foil for John Fullerton and the team would not only miss his accurate passing, superb finishing and calming influence on the ice but his overall experience which was invaluable.

The first semi-final of the Mitchell Trophy was played on 11 March when rank outsiders Glasgow Skating Club took on Queen's. Although the latter were once again below full strength they were still too strong for their opponents. Queen's received an early alarm though when Felix McLernan gave Skating Club a first period lead but a hat-trick from Billy Fullerton and a brace from Arthur Tingley in the next two periods secured a 5-2 victory and their passage to the final.

Away from domestic competition the SIHA arranged another full international match for Scotland with the visit of English League Division One side Grosvenor House Canadians to Crossmyloof on 12 March. Ticket prices for this contest were fixed at 3s and 2s for balcony seats and 1s for all

Season 1931-1932

other spectator accommodation. In the absence of Arthur Bazin, Hugh Reid and Arthur Tingley, the SIHA took the opportunity to bring in some new faces. Wilbur Muirhead of Bridge of Weir, who had been knocking on the door of international honours for some time, was at last given his chance. Perhaps more surprisingly, young Don Edwards of Dennistoun Eagles was selected. The Scottish League Select side had drawn 1-1 with Grosvenor House Canadians during their recent tour of England and it was essentially the same team which took the ice against them in this latest encounter. The visitors were to all intents and purposes semi-professional and in Flight-Lieutenant Harry Mayes, Bob Rogers, Peter Fair and Keith Thomson had four players who had been selected for the Great Britain team about to compete in the forthcoming European Championships in Berlin.

The match did not quite live up to everyone's expectations as the two defences dominated. Ironically enough it was a Scot, Keith Thomson, who put Grosvenor House Canadians ahead in the first period. Of course both he and line-mate Don Porter had played for Scotland against England in December. Dave Cross was having his usual sterling performance in the Scottish goal and the second period finished blank. Scotland put in a determined effort in the final period. They were rewarded when John Fullerton broke through the visiting defence, to send a hard drive past goaltender J Elkins who, though he got a hand on the puck, could not stop it entering the net. As the excitement mounted Fullerton struck again two minutes from time, when he received a perfect pass from Jack Gilmour, who had skated the length of the ice, and scored a magnificent goal with a first time shot. The match finished 2-1. It was Scotland's first international victory since 1910. It was to be their last international win until after the Second World War.

The second Mitchell Trophy semi-final between Bridge of Weir and holders Kelvingrove was played a week later. The Renfrewshire side were missing Gordon Rowley and Earl Muirhead from their team but they still managed to give Kelvingrove a very hard fight. The match was effectively settled in the second period with a goal from John Campbell, a player who had the knack of scoring important goals.

The final of the Mitchell Trophy between Kelvingrove and Queen's was played at Crossmyloof on 1 April. It was an eagerly awaited contest and it did not disappoint. As "The Blade" pointed out "it undoubtedly must go down in history as one of the keenest and thrilling games yet witnessed at the rink." That was quite a compliment for a match which ended 0-0 but it seemed to have everything except goals. Queen's were almost at full strength and when that happened they were a match for anyone. The welcome return of the hard hitting Arthur Bazin gave their defence much more solidity and the propensity of Arthur Tingley to back-check, still something of a rare occurrence in Scotland, meant that the dangerous Kelvingrove forwards, John Campbell and Sid Montford, struggled to get into the match. Indeed,

Queen's looked the likelier team to win but found Dave Cross in sparkling form. The re-play was set for 15 April.

The excitement had barely died down before what was effectively the deciding match of the league championship was played a week later between Mohawks and Bridge of Weir. Mohawks were top of the league with 12 points but both Bridge of Weir and Kelvingrove shared second position on 11 points, the West End team still having one match to play. It was a thrilling finale to the league competition. For Mohawks, the objective was quite clear. If they defeated Bridge of Weir they would win the championship and the Canada Cup. That was quite an incentive and the Glasgow team left nothing to chance as Art Brady returned from England to play in this match. With Bridge of Weir also at full strength, a rousing contest was almost guaranteed.

It was an absorbing encounter. In a match full of incident and intensity checking was a major feature to the extent that broken sticks had to be replaced on three separate occasions. Mohawks made their intentions clear from the start by taking the game to Bridge of Weir in the first period and Art Brady almost scored but was denied by an outstanding full length or "sprawl" save by Angus Ross. Ross could do nothing at the start of the second period when John Fullerton opened the scoring on a rebound off a shot from Tom Craig which had been only partially saved by the goaltender. Ian McLeod then restored parity for Bridge of Weir. J G Fyfe restored Mohawks lead with a fine solo goal when he skated the full length of the ice before despatching a crisp drive past the helpless Ross. In a nervous final period Art Brady thought he had scored Mohawks third goal but it was disallowed by the referee, Dave Carty. No matter, despite the best efforts of the Renfrewshire team, Mohawks held out for a narrow but fully deserved 2-1 win against very worthy opponents. With that result they secured the league championship and the Canada Cup for the first time.

Mohawks fully deserved to be champions. They had won more league matches and scored more goals than any other side although, in the end - as had happened the previous season - the title was won by only one point from the team which finished second. It perhaps rankled Mohawks that their only defeats of the season had both been against Kelvingrove but at least they had the ultimate satisfaction of taking the Canada Cup from the West End club. Mohawks had an economy of style about them. Greg Lennox was a steady goaltender and J G Fyfe and Tom Shearer had developed into a sound and much underestimated defensive duo with cover now being provided by the tough Alec Fullerton, brother of John and Billy. Mohawks attack consisting of John Fullerton, Tom Craig and Art Brady was the most potent in the league. The champions had scored 29 goals of which 15 had come from the stick of the talented John Fullerton who finished the season as the leading goal scorer in the competition. Mohawks operated with one of the smallest playing squads in the league. There was little room for manoeuvre if any of their regular

Season 1931-1932

players were injured, suspended or otherwise unavailable through work or study commitments. The departure of Art Brady represented a serious loss for the future as players of his calibre were very difficult to replace.

The Mitchell Trophy final re-play between Kelvingrove and Queen's took place on 15 April and attracted about 3,000 spectators to Crossmyloof, the largest attendance of the season. Queen's took a leaf out of Mohawks' book by ensuring they had their full team available for this match with Fred Reardon answering the call to partner Arthur Bazin in defence. Queen's started where they had left off in the first match by taking the initiative from the opening face-off. In truth, the two teams were very well matched but the superior teamwork and discipline of Queen's eventually prevailed. The first period ended goalless but in the second session, Arthur Tingley, who else, broke the deadlock when he scored with a brilliant long range shot which beat Dave Cross all ends up. In a hectic final period, John Campbell almost secured an equalising goal for 'Grove but was denied by Val Carty in the Queen's goal who brought off an exceptional save. Sid Montford then almost scored but it was the deadly Tingley who gift wrapped the Mitchell Trophy for Queen's with a second goal to give them a deserved 2-0 victory.

Although Kelvingrove were bitterly disappointed to relinquish both of their titles, not many observers grudged Queen's their cup success. Some thought Queen's, when at full strength, the best team in the Scottish League. While not wishing to diminish Mohawks achievement in winning the Canada Cup, one is left to speculate what might have happened had Queen's been able to ice their three international players in all of their league matches.

For Kelvingrove, it was a season of what might have been. Runners-up in both the league and cup was not what their large support expected. The team had the meanest defence in the league having conceded only 5 goals all season but they had not scored enough goals. The loss of R L Noble and Jimmy Brown affected them more deeply than they thought and with hindsight they should have attempted to reinforce their attack at the start of the season.

In England, Oxford University reigned supreme. The experiment with the new league competition was deemed a success. Almost all of the Oxford University team were Canadians but they had exceptional players in goaltender Herbie Little and forward Larry Bonnycastle, the man who had so tormented the Scottish defence in the home international played in December.

Just before Crossmyloof Ice Rink closed for the season it hosted a speed skating competition which attracted a number of younger ice hockey players. Those who participated included Billy Fullerton and Jack Johnston of Queen's, W J Towers of Glasgow Skating Club and Don Edwards of Dennistoun Eagles.

All in all it had been an interesting and significant season. There had been new winners of both the Canada Cup and the Mitchell Trophy and the interest

Frozen in Time

Scotland Team, March 1932. Back Row; Arthur Tingley (Referee), John Fullerton (Mohawks), Wilbur Muirhead (Bridge of Weir), Dave Cross (Kelvingrove), John Campbell (Mohawks) and Gordon Rowley (Bridge of Weir). Front Row; Art Brady (Mohawks), Jack Easton (Glasgow University), Don Edwards (Dennistoun Eagles) and Jack Gilmour (Bearsden).

Season 1931-1932

of both the paying public at matches and the press had been sustained. On the international front Scotland had won its first match since 1910 and the Scottish League Select side had more than held their own during an intensive and tough tour of England.

One of the finest players in European ice hockey, Blake Watson, had recently accepted a medical post at a Glasgow hospital. He was of course no stranger to Crossmyloof Ice Rink having played and starred for Canada when they thrashed Scotland 11-1 at the Glasgow venue the previous season. Watson had attended a number of local matches and gave an interview to "Inside Edge" on the current state of the Scottish game.

> "He (Watson) was delighted to see how the game has progressed at Crossmyloof, although he admitted that we have a long way to go before the Canadian amateur standard is reached. He pointed out that the forwards must learn to combine better, leaving the centre man to make the play and to be more incisive in attack. The wing men are too easily forced to the boards."
>
> *(Daily Record and Mail: 19 April 1932).*

Watson, who was himself a forward, had made a number of valid points. It is clear from reading contemporary match reports that there was still too much emphasis on individual play and not enough on teamwork. Better coaching was required and this was an issue the SIHA was determined to address.

Frozen in Time

Season 1932-33

The Scottish Ice Hockey Association approached the new season with high hopes that the changes it had introduced would result in better competition for the teams and more entertaining matches for the spectators. The number of teams had been reduced from nine to eight. Although that bare statistic masked the fact that five clubs had been affected by the new structure in place, only time would reveal whether this reorganisation would bring the hoped for benefits.

There was some scepticism amongst keen observers of the Scottish game that not much had really changed. The reduction in the number of clubs was in the final analysis only one, and it was felt that eight clubs were still too many for the pool of talent available at Crossmyloof Ice Rink.

It is perhaps difficult to argue with this view. On looking at the player movements from the previous season one is led to conclude that the overall standard appeared to be in decline. Four players of international class, Arthur Bazin, Fred Reardon, Hugh Reid and Art Brady, had departed the local scene for different reasons and Scottish ice hockey was the poorer for it.

Of these four only Hugh Reid was not entirely lost to the Scottish game. Capped once for Scotland against his native Canada in 1931, he had played a major part in the revival of ice hockey in Scotland and in the re-formation of the SIHA in 1929. Reid had played for the pioneering Glasgow Canadians and then Achtungs and though he was still registered as a player he now intended to concentrate on refereeing and on his latest role as president of the new Bears Ice Hockey Club, formed from the old Achtungs and Bearsden clubs.

On the positive side the creation of Juniors Ice Hockey Club, under the astute tutelage of Gordon Rowley, for players up to the age of 18 years was encouraging and rightly regarded as an important development in the evolution of the local game. Although it would deprive several teams of their most promising youngsters it gave those young men the opportunity of playing regularly in senior competition and hopefully learning from the experience.

It was widely recognised by everyone associated with the sport that the future of ice hockey in Scotland in the long run depended on nurturing and developing local talent. No less an authority than Howard Armstrong, the team manager of world champions Canada in 1930, had urged the SIHA to "catch them young", advice the ruling body was now putting into practice. They trusted that the creation of the Juniors club represented as good a method of achieving this objective as anything else.

Gordon Rowley left Bridge of Weir to take up the position of player-coach at Juniors and his partner in defence would be the extremely promising and solid checking Joe Collins previously with Kelvingrove. The key position of goaltender was entrusted to Billy Turnbull from Bearsden and in attack the club would rely on Don Edwards from Dennistoun Eagles and Andrew Gray and Fred Hems from Bearsden.

The other new clubs on the circuit also provided some interest. One always got the impression that neither Bearsden nor Achtungs were wholly dedicated to ice hockey per se. Achtungs tended to exude an apparently dilettante air while Bearsden were distracted by so many of their players being involved in rugby. That stated, Bearsden had been the more successful of the two having won the initial if somewhat limited Points Competition in 1929 as well as reaching the final of the Mitchell Trophy in 1930.

The new Bears team would not be without talent. They would have two international players in their ranks with Jack Gilmour and A Rintoul. Hugh Reid might also be available for the odd match or in an emergency and they had acquired a good young player in Jack Johnston, who arrived from Queen's. It certainly looked like Bears would be more capable of providing a challenge than when the previous two sides were separate entities.

This was also true of Glasgow University, whose amalgamation with Glasgow Skating Club appeared to be more of a complete takeover. For the students surely things could only get better. Although the statistics indicated that Varsity had been the worst team in the league championship the previous season, they had in Jack Easton, club president, coach and captain, one of the finest players in the country.

Easton would now be joined by fellow Canadians, Felix McLernan and J O McCabe, as well as the useful home produced R H (Robert) Gardiner from Skating Club. Although McLernan and McCabe were proven goal scorers the intention was to move the former player back to bolster a fragile defence with the latter partnering Easton and C W de Visser in attack. The new team thus appeared to have a better balance than before.

One player missing from the Glasgow University team was the regular goaltender of three years, James S Carslaw. He had played his first two seasons as a medical student at the university and his final season as a qualified junior doctor at the Western Infirmary in Glasgow. Carslaw accepted a medical post in England in the summer of 1932 and therefore left the club for good. He later joined the Royal Air Force and reached the rank of Group Captain before returning to medical practice.

Of the other teams outside the leading four, Dennistoun Eagles seemed to have the most problems. Indeed it was reported that the East End club had experienced some difficulty in retaining a viable squad of players for the new season. An already weak side was further diminished by the departure of international player Don Edwards to Juniors. Much would therefore depend

Season 1932-33

on the form of J H Borland, Sam Stevenson and Bill Russell but there was not much else in reserve to support them.

It would be fair to state that all of the main contenders for honours this season were significantly weaker. Defending champions Mohawks had lost the services of Art Brady, considerably reducing their potency in attack. The team had also lost the hard hitting Alec Fullerton in defence and although he had rarely figured in the first team his departure to Kelvingrove represented a further depletion in the size and quality of Mohawks' squad.

Kelvingrove had lost their two best youngsters following the departure of Joe Collins to Juniors and Ken Hurll to a teaching appointment in Spain. In addition, there were serious doubts as to the regular availability of Lorne Berlinquet, William Phinney and E Fincham leaving the team with fewer options all round. These changes meant that the newly acquired Alec Fullerton would partner Andy Dick in defence while last season's regular substitute, R D (Bert) Gemmell, would be given his chance in attack.

Queen's were the most badly affected of all the clubs. They had lost their outstanding international defence, Fred Reardon and Arthur Bazin, the latter having graduated in medicine and returned to Canada. Young Jack Johnston had opted to go to Bears for the new season. Billy Fullerton and Arthur Tingley remained at the club but at least they would be briefly joined by the nomadic Blake Watson who agreed to play for the team until his departure from Glasgow at the end of October.

Despite the unfortunate departure of the brilliant Gordon Rowley, Bridge of Weir were largely unchanged from previous seasons and were hopeful that continuity in team selection would at last bring some reward. Their chances however were certainly not helped by the temporary absence of Wilbur Muirhead, still recuperating from a bout of rheumatic fever, but on the plus side the club had managed to obtain the services of W G McDonald, yet another Canadian student from the conveyor belt of ice hockey talent that was the Faculty of Medicine at the University of Edinburgh!

The new season would commence with the following eight teams; Bears, Bridge of Weir, Dennistoun Eagles, Glasgow University, Juniors, Kelvingrove, Mohawks and Queen's. It was of course sad to have witnessed the demise of Achtungs, Bearsden and Glasgow Skating Club, the latter club being the last real link with the Edwardian era of ice hockey at Crossmyloof, but it was hoped that these sacrifices would benefit the game in the long run.

Although most of the teams were weaker, at least there was the hope that that might provide closer contests between them all. The gulf in class between the top four and the rest did not seem as wide this season. Once again in the league championship each team would play the other only once giving a total of 28 fixtures to be played between mid October and the end of February. The month of March would be largely taken up by the Mitchell Trophy competition.

Frozen in Time

The opening match in the league championship was played on 11 October between those great rivals Kelvingrove and Mohawks. Early notice of the kind of season the defending champions were likely to have was indicated when they lost for the fifth consecutive time against 'Grove, this time by 3-1, an indignity compounded by the fact that Alec Fullerton scored the clinching goal against his old team.

Four days later Queen's recorded an encouraging 3-0 victory against Bridge of Weir in another heavyweight contest. Although the score flattered the Glasgow team the match was notable for what turned out to be the one and only appearance for Queen's of Blake Watson, who made his usual impact by scoring a brace. The wandering medic was about to be off on his travels again, this time finding employment at a hospital in Zurich, Switzerland.

The third fixture of the season on 18 October was the encounter between two of the new teams, Bears and Juniors. "The Blade" writing in his column in the *Evening Times* was fulsome in his praise of the youngsters, who displayed "excellent control of the puck while they swerved in and out in a manner perplexing to their opponents." The perplexed Bears were put to the sword 2-1 with goals from Gordon Rowley and a late winner from Andrew Gray.

The fourth match in the first round of fixtures resulted in a disappointing 1-1 draw between Glasgow University and Dennistoun Eagles. Both of these teams would have been hoping for a winning start but the game was scrappy and featureless. C W de Visser scored for the students while the improving Bill Russell replied for Dennistoun.

The opening round of fixtures had been awash with big matches and yet another came along on 25 October. In a portent of things to come Queen's only had five players available for a match with 'Grove, but no matter. Trailing 2-1 at the beginning of the third period, Billy Fullerton scored an equalising goal before Arthur Tingley scored the winning goal in the final minute. Queen's had defeated Kelvingrove 3-2 in quite remarkable circumstances!

"The Blade" noted that "unprecedented scenes of enthusiasm" greeted this victory at the final whistle. The heroes for Queen's were Val Carty in goal, R G (Roy) Webster and G R Forsyth in defence with Billy Fullerton and Arthur Tingley in attack. Apart from the stamina and levels of fitness required it was an even more impressive feat in view of the strength of the opposition. The result confirmed Queen's very impressive start to the season.

Glasgow police officer Dave Cross, the Kelvingrove and Scotland goaltender, followed in the footsteps of Jack Easton, the previous season, when he was selected to play for England against France in two international matches arranged in London. While he was noted as nervous in the first match he nevertheless gave a good account of himself in both. France won both contests, the first 9-4 at the Queens Ice Rink in Bayswater and the second 3-2.

Cross would be facing the French again on 29 October but this time in the colours of Scotland as the SIHA accepted a welcome invitation to play France

Season 1932-33

at the Palais des Sports in Paris. This was Scotland's first international match of the season and only their second against European opposition, following their rugged home encounter with Germany in 1930.

The match was unique for another reason: it was the only occasion on which Scotland would travel abroad for an international match until after the Second World War. It is notable that the Scottish team flew to Paris from Croydon Airport in London and that this was possibly the first time that any ice hockey side from Great Britain had ever travelled by air to fulfil a fixture in Europe. France were a good team, having finished ahead of Great Britain in sixth place in the European Championships of 1932. The French had decided against competing in the World Championships to be held in Prague in 1933 and were therefore keen to play as many challenge matches as possible against foreign opposition.

The squad selected by the SIHA for the match in Paris was on familiar lines. The one curiosity was the place allocated to the Zurich based Blake Watson. This seemed to be a case of wishful thinking on the part of the SIHA for - as some sceptics had rather suspected - the good doctor failed to turn up for the match leaving Scotland short-handed.

The two teams were:

France: J Morrison; C Michaelis and M Claret; G Geran, J P Hagnauer and P Bessone. - M Delesalle, R D Oblonsky and J Cholette.

Scotland: D Cross (Kelvingrove); G D Rowley (Juniors) and J R Gilmour (Bears); J Fullerton (Mohawks), J A Easton (Glasgow University) and A R Brady (Liverpool). - J Campbell (Kelvingrove) and A J Tingley (Queen's).

Referee: ?

Scotland opened the match in confident fashion and took a first period 1-0 lead courtesy of a Jack Easton goal. It proved to be a false dawn however as the French side eventually asserted themselves following an equalising goal at the start of the second session. France led 4-1 going into the third period and with the Scots seemingly unable to get out of their own defensive zone, the home team skated to a comfortable 7-1 victory.

The performance and the result were a disappointment. Scotland simply lost the place in the second period. Only desperate defending by Gordon Rowley, Jack Gilmour and the back-checking Arthur Tingley seems to have prevented an even worse defeat. The events at the Palais des Sports confirmed what many observers already thought - that the overall standard in Scottish ice hockey had declined from that of previous seasons.

In the league championship, Bridge of Weir secured an important victory when they defeated Mohawks 4-2 in early November. Their new Canadian replacement for the departed Gordon Rowley, W G McDonald, scored his first goal for the team to make it 3-1 at the beginning of the second period. It was a much improved performance by the Renfrewshire side and just to prove that it was no flash in the pan they followed it up with a 1-0 win over Kelvingrove two weeks later.

This match was a much tighter affair settled by a solo Ian McLeod goal in the opening minutes of the game. Bridge of Weir had much the better of the first period but Kelvingrove came back strongly in the middle session and should have equalised when Sid Montford shot past an open net. The pace, if not the effort, slackened in the final period but the score remained unchanged.

The more perceptive of observers would have noticed the improvement in form being shown by Bridge of Weir. They had now played three matches against their main rivals in the championship and had gained four points. This augured well for their title prospects and was particularly impressive given that their best player and captain, Wilbur Muirhead, was still absent because of illness. He was expected to return to the team in the near future.

Another team making a good impression were Juniors. They gave Mohawks their third consecutive defeat of the season in mid-November when they prevailed 3-2. Gordon Rowley was making an impact, leading "The Blade" to observe that "not only is there shown a fine understanding between the players but their speed and checking abilities quite apart from being pretty to watch are most effective and disconcerting to their opponents."

With three matches played by 18 November both Juniors and Bridge of Weir shared second place in the league table with four points. Queen's were top on five points. Having defeated Bridge of Weir and Kelvingrove, they would have been disappointed at dropping a vital point, drawing their third match 3-3 with Glasgow University. At one point in this game Queen's were 3-0 down but fought back well.

Disappointing was not the word to describe the start to the season made by defending champions Mohawks. Catastrophic was more like it as they had succumbed to three straight defeats. Goaltending problems due to the temporary unavailability of Greg Lennox had certainly not helped the cause but John Fullerton also seemed out of sorts ploughing a lonely furrow in attack following the departure of Art Brady.

Scottish ice hockey received a major boost when the SIHA announced that Edmonton Superiors would play at Crossmyloof on 26 November. Glasgow would be the first stop on an extensive two months long European tour being undertaken by the team from Alberta in Western Canada. Edmonton were a young side which included a couple of players not yet adults. In addition, two of their players had been born in the United Kingdom, namely Johnny Lammie from Carluke and Jimmy Graham from Londonderry.

All teams from Canada deserved the utmost respect and the SIHA selected their strongest possible team to face Edmonton. Scotland were therefore on the usual lines. The only addition to the squad which had faced France a month earlier was young Billy Fullerton of Queen's who was enjoying a fine season.

Season 1932-33

Scotland Team, November 1932 Back Row; John Fullerton (Mohawks), John Campbell (Kelvingrove), Arthur Tingley (Queen's), Hugh Reid (Referee), Billy Fullerton (Queen's), Dave Cross (Kelvingrove) and Gordon Rowley (Juniors). Front Row; Jack Gilmour (Bears), Jack Easton (Glasgow University) and Dr Art Brady (Liverpool).

Frozen in Time

The occasion, billed incorrectly as a match against Canada, had prices ranging from 7s/6d for the best seats to 1s for standing room. About 3,000 spectators packed into Crossmyloof for the match and within a minute of the face-off John Fullerton put Scotland ahead amidst great excitement. Alas, that was as good as it got for the home side. Dave Cross was then subjected to a siege on his goal as the visitors poured forward finally equalising just before the first interval. In the second period Edmonton started to live up to their name when they scored four goals without reply and then added another three in the final session for an emphatic 8-1 victory. As was by now the norm against such opposition Scotland were simply unable to cope with the speed, stick-handling and general teamwork of their opponents.

The match had actually followed a similar course to that of the recent contest against France where after an encouraging start Scotland just evaporated in the face of superior opposition. Defensively, the Scots again did relatively well where it was noted that Gordon Rowley and Jack Gilmour were "worked to death" but the forwards had failed to shine in both attack and in their back-checking responsibilities.

Another key factor continuing to work against Scottish prospects of success in representative matches was their duration. Scottish based players were not used to playing the normal three periods of fifteen minutes each. The truncated version of the game played at Crossmyloof mitigated against the home based players who were mentally and physically unprepared for the extra nine minutes required on the ice. It was no mere co-incidence that most Scottish representative teams always noticeably tired in the third period.

Bridge of Weir moved to the top of the league championship table on 2 December when they defeated Glasgow University 3-0, with a brace from Ian McLeod. A week later their closest challengers, Queen's, lost ground. Dennistoun Eagles won 1-0, Bill Russell scoring the match winning goal. In mitigation though, for the second time in four fixtures, Queen's were unable to ice a full team, but on this occasion they could not repeat the heroics of their match with Kelvingrove.

The fixture list for the remainder of December was disrupted by an influenza outbreak in the West of Scotland. Kelvingrove could only ice five players for their match against Glasgow University and, like Queen's, paid the price with a 3-1 defeat as Varsity recorded their first victory of the season, Jack Easton scoring all three goals.

It was rather unfair that clubs were expected to fulfil their fixtures when they were shorthanded through no fault of their own. The influenza outbreak was starting to take a real toll and the SIHA at last took cognisance of that situation when it postponed a couple of upcoming fixtures. Despite that the results of the previous two fixtures were allowed to stand. The main beneficiaries were Bridge of Weir who profited from the joint misfortune of their main rivals.

Season 1932-33

Bridge of Weir managed to sneak in another match against Juniors just before the round of postponements was introduced in mid-December. To a certain extent it backfired as the Renfrewshire side dropped a point in a 2-2 draw but then again they had the points in the bag and remained in first position in the league. With three matches left and most of their potentially difficult fixtures already played, Bridge of Weir looked set fair for the Canada Cup.

On 17 December, a Scottish League Select team travelled to Liverpool to play the home side in a representative match. Perhaps with recent results in mind the SIHA took no chances and selected what was in reality not far off a full international team. Billy Fullerton retained his position as one of the substitutes and he was joined by Sid Montford of Kelvingrove and A Rintoul of Bears.

It was disappointing that the SIHA were not more adventurous in their squad selection but their conservatism was justified as the Scottish League Select won the match 4-2. In truth they made rather heavy weather of it but a win on English ice was always welcome. Art Brady, now playing for the home side, was their star man but it was Dave Cross in the visitor's goal who was the man of the match.

In the league championship, Bridge of Weir consolidated first position with a 2-0 win against Dennistoun Eagles at the end of December in what was described as a poor match. No matter, the Renfrewshire men were grinding out the results and they now had the added bonus of welcoming back Wilbur Muirhead who played his first match of the season against the East End club.

At the end of the year the SIHA announced plans for another tour of England in early January but in actual fact these plans eventually came to nothing as did a proposed fixture against the English champions, Oxford University. All was not lost however as Oxford Ice Rink would provide the venue for the next home international against England to be played in March or April.

The league championship was heading towards a conclusion by mid January. Queen's kept in the hunt with a good 3-0 victory over Bears, Billy Fullerton scoring a brace but in their next match against Juniors they lost 1-0 to a Joe Collins goal scored in the final minute of play. That late winner was a killer blow to Queen's title hopes for if Bridge of Weir won their final match against Bears on 24 January no one else in the league could catch them.

The day of destiny arrived for Bridge of Weir but it was a tricky match because the unpredictable Bears were no pushover. It proved to be an exciting game characterised by sound defence and some heavy checking. Bridge of Weir were nervous throughout and the game was not settled until minutes from the end when Ian McLeod scored by forcing the puck past Billy Dunlop from close in.

It was enough to give Bridge of Weir a 1-0 victory and with that result the league championship and the Canada Cup were secured for the first time.

Although some observers suggested that it had not been a vintage season, Bridge of Weir deserved the title. After losing their first match they had consolidated to become the most consistent team in the league. The Renfrewshire men finished on 11 points, three more than eventual runners-up, Mohawks. The new champions had won more and lost fewer matches than anyone else and they had the best defence in the league.

Bridge of Weir had benefited from continuity in team selection in comparison to most of their main rivals. Their team was not only bonded by familial relationships but its core had remained largely unchanged since the initial season of 1929-30. While the loss of Gordon Rowley had certainly been a blow it remained the case that the Renfrewshire side had avoided the player disruption evident at other clubs.

Bridge of Weir were essentially a stuffy and physically robust team. Their success was due in no small measure to a no-nonsense style of play allied to a great sense of esprit de corps. That success was all the more meritorious when one takes account of the fact that their captain and leading goal scorer, Wilbur Muirhead, had been sidelined by illness for most of the season. Fortunately, some other players had stepped up to the plate, particularly Ian McLeod who had scored match winning goals against Kelvingrove and Bears and the Canadian student W G McDonald who was a real star in the making.

There were still four league fixtures to be played when Bridge of Weir secured the title. These matches would be played over the next two months. It was however a somewhat incongruous situation to have the major domestic competition of the season done and dusted before the end of January. In view of this it was back to the drawing board once again for the SIHA who really did need to find some way of stretching the league championship over most of the season.

Attention became focussed on a return visit from Edmonton Superiors to Crossmyloof on 27 January. This wonderful side had commenced their European tour in Glasgow with an 8-1 victory against Scotland two months earlier and they were now going to conclude their travels with another match in the same city. During their gruelling tour Edmonton had played 34 matches and had lost only once!

No doubt mindful of these rather daunting statistics the SIHA suggested that a Great Britain side should take on Edmonton. This was agreed by the BIHA but one gets the distinct impression that their commitment to the contest was less than enthusiastic. In spite of this, interest in the match from the public remained high with ticket prices fixed between 5s and 1s.

The British team selected was essentially the normal Scotland side with the addition of three players from England, Harold Sursock, Peter Churchill and Ivor Nesbitt. The injection of this talent from south of the border made little difference to Edmonton who ran out easy winners by 7-0. Great Britain were simply outclassed with the only pass marks going to Dave Cross, Jack Gilmour and Harold Sursock.

Season 1932-33

Back on the domestic front, the Scotland international right wing, John Campbell, sprung a major surprise when he moved from Kelvingrove, where he had been for the past two seasons, back to Mohawks, his first club. It is not known why Campbell moved back across the city one can only assume it was for personal reasons. In any event, it was a huge blow for Kelvingrove but a massive boost for Mohawks, who had been labouring for most of the season.

The opening rounds of the Mitchell Trophy commenced with a tie between Bears and Juniors on 31 January. Gordon Rowley's youngsters had won the corresponding league match 2-1 in October but on this occasion it was Bears who prevailed 3-2, albeit in controversial circumstances. It was 2-2 going into the final period before Jack Gilmour scored a splendid solo goal just on full time. Juniors claimed this goal was scored over time but the match referee, Arthur Tingley of Queen's, disagreed and allowed it to stand.

Glasgow University put up very spirited resistance in their tie against Mohawks, for whom John Campbell made his debut. The students missed several chances to take the lead. It remained 0-0 going into the third period. They paid the price for their profligacy in front of goal when John Fullerton scored for Mohawks. This setback seemed to unsettle Varsity and it was no surprise when J G Fyfe clinched a 2-0 win for Mohawks with a second goal.

The tie of the first round was that between Kelvingrove and Queen's, the holders of the Mitchell Trophy, in a repeat of the previous season's final. The West End team came up with a definite game plan to contain Queen's two danger men, Billy Fullerton and Arthur Tingley, and it succeeded as both were restricted to shooting from long distance. Bert Gemmell put Kelvingrove ahead in the first period and Sid Montford sealed a good all round performance by scoring a second goal in the final period for an impressive 2-0 victory.

The champions, Bridge of Weir, were involved in a particularly bruising encounter with Dennistoun Eagles. In a match marred by various infringements and illegalities, the young and promising Walter McLeod put the Renfrewshire side ahead after a clever assist by Wilbur Muirhead in the opening period but Dennistoun equalised in the next session with a goal from J H Borland. The final period deteriorated into a succession of penalties and a poor match ended 1-1.

The first semi-final of the Mitchell Trophy was played between Bears and Mohawks on 17 February. The two sides had met only three days earlier in a league match won easily by Mohawks 4-1. Bears gave a much more resilient performance in the cup-tie and were in fact unlucky not to win. At one point in the match they were leading 3-1 but goals from Tom Shearer and John Campbell secured a 3-3 draw for Mohawks, and a replay they barely deserved.

Scotland returned to international duty when a match was arranged against Grosvenor House Canadians at Crossmyloof on 24 February. Despite two heavy defeats already this season at the hands of France and Edmonton Superiors hopes were high that last season's success against the London team could be repeated. This optimism was really misplaced because Grosvenor House Canadians were a better side this season and were going well in the English League Division One.

The SIHA threw caution to the wind and selected two new players for the Scottish squad. In the absence of the injured Gordon Rowley, J G Fyfe of Mohawks was brought in to partner Jack Gilmour in defence and the versatile W G McDonald of Bridge of Weir was brought in as a substitute. Wilbur Muirhead also returned to the international squad after a year's absence.

It is worth pointing out that out of a squad of 11 players, 5 were home developed. The native Scots were J G Fyfe, Jack Gilmour, Billy Fullerton, John Fullerton and Wilbur Muirhead. It was the first time that so many had been selected and while the core of the squad remained Canadian, the SIHA were always keen to promote as many home bred players as possible as long as they were good enough.

But it was to be a disappointing evening for the Scottish team and the spectators. "The Blade" noted that "the game lacked that spice which we generally associate with such a distinguished visit and though hard-fought was somewhat below standard." In truth, Scotland seemed more intent on not losing than they were on actually going all out to win the match. Grosvenor House Canadians avenged last season's defeat by winning 2-0 and Scotland could have little complaint.

The re-played first round Mitchell Trophy tie between Bridge of Weir and Dennistoun Eagles took place on 3 March. It was another thoroughly bad-tempered affair only settled in favour of the Renfrewshire side in the final minute of two periods of extra time. The winner came from Walter McLeod, exhibiting a confidence which belied his tender years, who beat the opposing defence, skated round the goaltender and slotted the puck home for a brilliant solo goal.

Four days later the final league match of the season was played between Juniors and Glasgow University. Bridge of Weir had of course already won the championship but second place was yet to be decided. If Juniors won they would cap a very good first season by securing the runners-up position. It was then doubly unfortunate that they had to face Varsity without the still injured Gordon Rowley or any substitutes. The fates had conspired against them and they lost 2-0.

This result meant that Mohawks remained clear in second position with 8 points, 3 behind Bridge of Weir. Mohawks' form had improved dramatically in the latter part of the season with four straight victories following on from three consecutive defeats. Three teams ended the season with 7 points, Queen's, Kelvingrove and Juniors, but they finished in that particular order owing to goal difference.

Mohawks were hopeful of carrying their good late season form into the Mitchell Trophy but it was not to be. The semi-final replay against Bears took

Season 1932-33

place on 14 March and it was an enthralling match. The first two periods remained goal-less but then six goals were traded in the final session with Jack Gilmour scoring his second and clinching goal for Bears close to the finish to ensure a completely deserved 4-2 victory.

Bears' opponents in the final were still not known, as Kelvingrove and Bridge of Weir had fought out a surprisingly exciting 0-0 draw in their semi-final four days before. It was a match the Renfrewshire side should have won given the number of clear cut scoring chances they had created. The hero for Kelvingrove, though, was the stand-in goaltender, E Fincham, who gave an inspired performance in the absence of Dave Cross.

For the replay on 17 March, Dave Cross resumed his normal position in goal, but even he could do nothing to stop Bridge of Weir this time, as they totally dominated the match. There was no scoring in the first period. Walter McLeod, who was in the midst of a rich vein of form, scored for Bridge of Weir at the beginning of the second period. W G McDonald added a second goal later to secure a deserved 2-0 win.

Bridge of Weir now had the opportunity to achieve the "double" of Canada Cup and Mitchell Trophy and thereby emulate Kelvingrove who had accomplished that very feat in season 1930-31.

Apart from the final of the Mitchell Trophy to be played on 31 March, the fixture list had now been completed, with six weeks of the winter season still left at Crossmyloof Ice Rink. The SIHA took the opportunity to introduce a new knock-out cup competition to be known as the President's Pucks. As the name suggested this was an initiative of Frank Stuart, the president of the ruling body. He bought and paid for the small silver-plated ceremonial pucks to be awarded to the players of the winning team.

It was a most generous gesture from Frank Stuart but it rather reinforced the view that the current fixture list remained disjointed and required reform. It was not made clear at this stage whether the new competition was to be a regular feature of the ice hockey calendar; in point of fact it did. Unfortunately, only seven clubs would be competing for the President's Pucks; in a deeply sad development, Queen's had been obliged to withdraw from the SIHA because of a lack of players.

The demise of Queen's represented a serious loss to Scottish ice hockey. Unfortunately Queen's had often been struggling for the past two seasons to ice a full team let alone fill the substitutes bench. The unavailability of key players like Arthur Bazin and Fred Reardon had wrecked the team's title challenge in the previous season and their ultimate departure from the club left a huge void which was never filled. This season had seen the team seriously short-handed in a number of fixtures.

In their final match against Mohawks on 21 February, Queen's only had five players available and these were Val Carty, Roy Webster, Billy Fullerton, Arthur Tingley and H S Finnie. It could not go on and the remaining players and officials took the awful decision about early March to disband the club after four good seasons in the Scottish League.

It was a terrible end for one of the better and more entertaining teams in the Scottish game. Rarely out of the top three in the league championship and winners of the Mitchell Trophy in 1932, Queen's had always striven to play attractive ice hockey and had been one of the most popular teams at the Crossmyloof rink. The club had iced a number of outstanding players in its short history including Eric McLeod, Don Porter, Arthur Bazin, Fred Reardon, Arthur Tingley and one in the making, Billy Fullerton.

In their four seasons, Queen's had played a total of 41 competitive matches for an overall record of 24 wins, 11 losses and 6 draws. In the Points Competition, First Division and Canada Cup their record was 18 wins, 8 losses and 5 draws and in the Mitchell Trophy their record was 6 wins, 3 losses and 1 draw.

Queen's misfortune became Kelvingrove's gain as they moved quickly to secure the services of star forward, Arthur Tingley. The capture of the talented Canadian was a major coup for the West End club who now had a more than adequate replacement for the departed John Campbell. Tingley was of course both a maker and a taker of goals and was more willing than most forwards in the domestic game to back-check and work hard for the whole team.

Arthur Tingley's influence on his new team was felt immediately when in his first match for Kelvingrove against Bears in the first round of the President's Pucks on 21 March, he scored the winning goal in a 1-0 victory. In what was described as a drab game dominated by two strong defences, Tingley fired the puck into the net with a hard low drive in the first period.

Three days later Dennistoun Eagles played Glasgow University in another first round tie. As expected, it was a close match settled in favour of the East End club with a Bill Russell goal early in the opening period. The students with Jack Easton in great form dominated the third period but, try as they might, they could not find a way past an inspired J F (Jack) Logan in the Dennistoun goal.

The first round ties were completed when Mohawks defeated a plucky Juniors side by 2-0 thanks to a brace from John Campbell. Juniors were without Gordon Rowley but they drafted in Jack Gilmour as a temporary replacement and gave a very disciplined performance, characterised by good checking and passing. The match was notable for the first appearance in Mohawks colours of Billy Fullerton who had joined his brother John at the club.

Bridge of Weir had been given a bye in the first round of the President's Pucks. They were drawn against Mohawks in the semi-final leaving Dennistoun Eagles to play Kelvingrove in the other tie. Both semi-finals would be played in early April.

Before those particular contests the not inconsiderable matter of the final of the Mitchell Trophy between Bridge of Weir and Bears was yet to be decided on 31 March. As anticipated, it turned out to be a thrilling if controversial match keenly fought and full of interest. Bridge of Weir were of course chasing the "double" but in Bears they faced mercurial opponents.

Bridge of Weir attacked from the start and Billy Dunlop, the ex-Doonside and Achtungs goaltender, made two brilliant saves from Ian McLeod and Earl Muirhead. Despite this pressure it was Bears who made the breakthrough when R F Winfield gathered the puck cleanly from A Rintoul and crashed it past Angus Ross from a narrow angle.

Walter McLeod missed a great opportunity to equalise at the start of the second period, then Dunlop saved magnificently from Ian McLeod. By the third period the game had developed into a virtual siege of the Bears goal but their defence held firm. The match ended amidst great controversy as Bridge of Weir had two late goals disallowed by the referee, Dave Carty. The first decision was correct, as there had been an obvious infringement, but the second decision was much more open to debate.

Despite the furore, it was a deserved victory for Bears, even though Bridge of Weir had the bulk of the play. Although they had plenty of possession the Renfrewshire team were not as co-ordinated as they usually were; the loss of that first period goal clearly unsettled them. Bears gave a great defensive display and the cup win was an appropriate reward for their captain, Jack Gilmour, who was enjoying an outstanding season for both club and country. Bears were now the fourth different winner of the Mitchell Trophy in as many seasons.

The cup final does not seem to have been one of Dave Carty's better performances as a referee. Apart from the controversy over the two disallowed goals he had also ended the game a minute early! On recognising his mistake Carty had to re-call the players back on to the ice to play out the time remaining. In fairness, everyone has an off-night and Carty was recognised as one of the most efficient and experienced referees in the Scottish League.

The first semi-final of the President's Pucks between Kelvingrove and Dennistoun Eagles was played on 7 April. As was generally expected the West End club prevailed but not without a real fight from Dennistoun. Arthur Tingley was again the match winner for Kelvingrove as he was in the first round with two well-taken goals in their 2-0 win.

The other semi-final between Bridge of Weir and Mohawks was a fast, thrilling and physical encounter. D (Duncan) MacLachlan of Mohawks was the busier of the two goaltenders, with several excellent saves, although both sides came close to scoring. It was the Glasgow side who eventually broke the deadlock when John Fullerton scored on an assist from his brother Billy in the third period to give them a narrow 1-0 win.

Mohawks had only three days to recover before their appearance in the final of the President's Pucks against Kelvingrove. They must have looked forward to this match with some trepidation. Since the re-establishment of ice hockey in season 1929-30, Mohawks had yet to defeat their great

Frozen in Time

Bears Ice Hockey Club, 1932-33. Back Row; A Rintoul, Charlie Russell and R F Winfield. Third Row; R G Walker (Vice-President) and J Riddell (Trainer). Second Row; N C MacKenzie, A Frame (Honorary President), Jack Gilmour, Hugh Reid (President) and Ronald MacDonald. Front Row; L W Sproule and Jack Johnston. Inset; Billy Dunlop.

Season 1932-33

rivals in a competitive game. The two teams had played each other on five occasions, three times in the Canada Cup and twice in the Mitchell Trophy, and Kelvingrove had won all five.

Nevertheless, the final was an exciting match. It ended 0-0; not even a period of extra time could separate what were two evenly matched sides. The two goaltenders, Dave Cross and Duncan MacLachlan, were in great form. Kelvingrove had sprung a pre-match surprise when they iced Gordon Rowley in defence and pushed Alec Fullerton into the forward line. The re-play was set for 28 April.

It is notable that the referee in this match was one John Hanley who had just been appointed as a coach by the SIHA. This represented a major initiative by the ruling body. The need for a dedicated coach had been recognised for some time and was probably accelerated by the fact that the Association's unofficial coach, Gordon Rowley, would be leaving Scotland later in the year. John Hanley had been born in Kilsyth but had emigrated to Canada as a youngster. He played semi-professional ice hockey in his adopted country before going into coaching. Prior to joining the SIHA, Hanley was the coach of Milan Ice Hockey Club in Italy for a few years. Although his experience of British ice hockey was limited he came to Scotland with a respectable *curriculum vitae* in the sport. One of Hanley's first tasks was to take charge of the Scottish international side for their forthcoming match with England at Oxford Ice Rink on 20 April. This was something of a baptism of fire for the new coach but being entirely new to the Scottish game he inherited a squad of players selected by the SIHA. It was Scotland's fourth international match of the season and, historically, their fourth against England.

The Scottish squad was missing a few regulars including Jack Easton, Arthur Tingley and Art Brady. As replacements, three home developed players were brought in for the first time, Sid Montford, Bill Russell and Walter McLeod. Indeed, seven of the ten players selected in the squad were native Scots, a record. In another interesting development, the Scottish forward line would consist of the Mohawks trio, Billy and John Fullerton along with John Campbell. Jack Gilmour would captain the team.

The two teams were:

England: A Holmes (Grosvenor House Canadians); H E Mayes (Grosvenor House Canadians) and C A Erhardt (Princes); J G Carr (Grosvenor House Canadians); G Davey (Princes) and P C Fair (Grosvenor House Canadians). - F A de Marwicz (London Lions), G H Johnson (Oxford University) and W McGuire (Grosvenor House Canadians).

Scotland: D Cross (Kelvingrove); W M Muirhead (Bridge of Weir) and J R Gilmour (Bears); W Fullerton (Mohawks), J Fullerton (Mohawks) and J Campbell (Mohawks).- W S Montford (Kelvingrove), W G McDonald (Bridge of Weir), W W Russell (Dennistoun Eagles) and W S McLeod (Bridge of Weir).

Referee: Baron H H von Trauttenberg (Vienna).

Frozen in Time

The English team was of course very strong and coupled with the unfamiliarity of the Oxford arena, Scotland struggled in the first period losing a goal to Gordon Johnson. The visitors improved in the middle session and Bill Russell came close to equalising. It was a fast game and as usual the Scottish team started to visibly tire in the third period. England then capitalised and scored three goals without reply for a rather flattering 4-0 victory.

Although apparently well beaten if one just looked at the score, Scotland had actually given an encouraging performance. Dave Cross injured himself in the pre-match warm-up, but that had not hampered his performance unduly. Given that the team was mainly composed of home-developed players the match was good experience and would hopefully have benefited those concerned.

The final match of the domestic season was the replayed President's Pucks final between Kelvingrove and Mohawks on 28 April. As in the first match the teams could not be separated, even after another period of extra time. Incredibly, this game also finished 0-0 and it was agreed that the two captains should toss a coin to decide the winner. Sid Montford guessed correctly so Kelvingrove were awarded the spoils.

This was of course a most unsatisfactory way of determining the outcome of a major competition, a point recognised by everyone concerned. After some due consideration, Mohawks were also later awarded the silver plated pucks thanks to the generosity of a "wealthy enthusiast". The identity of this benefactor was not revealed but it was noted that a Mrs Ralston was involved in this arrangement.

Thus ended another season. At the commencement of the season the SIHA had hoped that it would provide greater competition and more exciting ice hockey for the paying public. The ruling body could be satisfied on both counts. Four different teams had shared the domestic honours and attendances at the various matches continued to be encouraging.

On the international front there was more to be concerned about as Scotland's results continued to disappoint. But that disappointment had to be tempered with a dose of realism, since the opposition Scotland faced in these matches - in the main from Canada and England - was of the highest calibre. In a sense it was not a level playing field but it was important that Scotland should continue to play against these sides for the experience it brought and for keeping the country actively involved in international competition.

On a more optimistic note the appointment of a dedicated coach by the SIHA was a positive and very necessary development, if the Scottish game was to progress and improve. Similarly, the establishment of the Juniors club to foster young talent in a competitive environment, and the gradual introduction of more home developed players in international and representative matches was to be commended. Such developments augured well for the future.

In England, Oxford University won the English League Division One for the second successive season despite strong opposition from a number of teams on the cusp of semi-professionalism. Oxford were largely composed of postgraduate students of Canadian origin and included some wonderful players, Herbie Little, Gordon Johnson and Larry Bonnycastle. They were undefeated during their league campaign. It was a team well known to Scotland, Grosvenor House Canadians, who finished runners-up.

One significant footnote from the season in England was the effective demise of Princes Ice Hockey Club.

It says much for the way the sport in England was developing that there was no longer any room or future for this famous old club. Princes were of course the leading club in the early days of ice hockey in England and served as ambassadors for the sport in Europe. Times were changing though and they had struggled to find a new role in the dawning era of semi-professionalism. Princes were merged with a new club, Queen's, but in reality it signalled the end for one of the greatest institutions in the ice hockey world.

Frozen in Time

Season 1933-34

As Crossmyloof Ice Rink reopened for business, in October 1933, it was noted by a national newspaper that approximately 1,000 people from Glasgow and the West of Scotland regularly participated in curling at the venue. The obvious popularity of the "roaring game", not to mention recreational skating, served to remind the Scottish Ice Hockey Association that competition for available ice time at the rink between the various winter sports was always a given. Fortunately, ice hockey was also popular attracting generally healthy attendances from the paying public. The ice rink management were satisfied with the revenue accrued from promoting the sport and while that situation pertained its future at the venue was secure. It remained regrettable, however, that Crossmyloof was still the only ice rink in Scotland where spectators could watch competitive ice hockey.

Prices for watching normal league championship and cup matches remained at 9d for the new season. This still represented good value in comparison to other sports. Domestic matches were once again expected to finish within the three-quarters of an hour time limit imposed by the rink management despite the recent LIHG ruling that matches could now be extended to three periods of twenty minutes duration each.

Press interest in the sport also remained high. The *Glasgow Herald* continued to offer regular and detailed match reports as well as other news while the ice hockey correspondent of the *Daily Record and Mail*, "Inside Edge", now had a weekly column of news and views in addition to providing match reports. In the *Evening Times*, coverage had become more erratic but "The Blade" still produced an occasional column and the odd match report.

The important point was that most of the main circulation newspapers in West Central Scotland, both at the quality and the popular ends of the market, were now covering the sport on a regular and informed basis. This gave ice hockey a much higher profile and helped to enthuse everyone connected with the Scottish game.

With the new season on the horizon the ice hockey correspondent of the *Glasgow Herald* offered his readers a very upbeat preview.

"The Scottish ice hockey season, which commences at the Scottish Ice Rink, Crossmyloof, Glasgow, next week promises to maintain the steady progress which the game has made since its inception in

Glasgow four years ago.

In that time the standard of play both in representative and club matches has been raised immeasurably and Scotland can now challenge, with fair hopes of success, all but the most outstanding exponents of the game.

A crowded season is in prospect in club hockey. The reduction in the number of clubs in the league to seven, owing to the disbandment of Queen's, has made it possible for each club to fulfil two fixtures with all the others, an arrangement which makes for a test in the championship.

A change is announced in the Mitchell Trophy tournament, which will be concluded in the first half of the season and not in the closing months as previously. The generosity of Mr Frank Stuart, President of the Scottish Ice Hockey Association, again ensures the knock-out tournament for the President's Pucks which will be held after the completion of the league programme."

(Glasgow Herald: 7 October 1933).

While it was certainly true that club ice hockey in Scotland had come a long way in just four years, the suggestion that the national team was almost ready to take on the world was well wide of the mark. In the ten international matches played since 1930, Scotland had lost nine and won only one. The national team had lost 48 goals in the process and scored only 7 in reply. Given these statistics it was important to retain a sense of realism when discussing Scotland's position in the ice hockey world.

In point of fact, it could be argued that the overall standard in Scotland appeared to be declining if anything. Crucially, the number of Canadians playing for Scottish teams was at an all time low. While more home developed players were coming into the sport - which was an encouraging development - they were obviously neither as proficient or experienced as their transatlantic counterparts in the arts of the game.

The new season would commence with seven clubs, the smallest number yet. The competing teams were; Bears, Bridge of Weir, Dennistoun Eagles, Glasgow University, Juniors, Kelvingrove and Mohawks. It was an ill wind, but the reduction in the number of teams meant that there was now room in the calendar for each side to play the other twice. This would ensure a much more competitive championship than hitherto with a total of 42 fixtures to be played between mid October and the end of April. It was a more punishing schedule than the clubs were used to but it did provide them with much more of a challenge, as well as giving the Canada Cup the importance it deserved.

The length of the fixture list also avoided the embarrassment of the championship petering out with months of the season still left. While that was a positive step, the move of the Mitchell Trophy competition to the beginning of the season was ill-judged. This tournament had really established itself as

Season 1933-1934

the "cup" competition in Scottish ice hockey and it would have been much more appropriate for the President's Pucks competition to have been brought forward instead.

The LIHG had introduced another important rule change in an attempt to speed up play and make the game more exciting for spectators. In future, players could pass the puck forward on the centre or neutral zone of the ice making it far easier to initiate attacks and move forward at a quicker pace. A fast game had just got faster and the SIHA readily adopted the rule change. There was not nearly as much player movement at the start of this season as had been customary in the past.

The current champions, Bridge of Weir, had good reason to look forward to another successful season. They would certainly miss Earl Muirhead who, had indicated his unavailability, for business reasons, for most of the season, but in Walter McLeod the club had unearthed a real star in the making. Bridge of Weir were hoping to add another Canadian player to what was a tried and trusted squad which was once again largely unchanged from that of previous seasons. Their main challengers were likely to be Kelvingrove and Mohawks both of whom were also generally unchanged from the previous season.

Kelvingrove had arguably the best and toughest defence in the league, with Dave Cross in goal behind Andy Dick and Alec Fullerton on the blue line. Indeed, "Inside Edge" considered that rearguard to be "the best ever produced at Crossmyloof". This statement may be going a bit too far but they undoubtedly constituted a formidable obstacle for opposing forwards to overcome. In attack, Kelvingrove were no slouches either, with Sid Montford, Arthur Tingley and Bert Gemmell forming an impressive forward line along with the more than useful Charlie McMillan and the promising J (Joe) Beveridge and W J Towers as back-up. The West End club did not have as many Canadians or substitute players as in previous seasons, but that was now a common trait throughout the Scottish League.

Quality rather than quantity had always been the theme at Mohawks, who never ever seemed to have enough players in reserve. The troublesome goaltending position was at last resolved following the decision to stick with Duncan MacLachlan He would have the reliable J G Fyfe and Tom Shearer in front of him. Mohawks looked to have the best, and without doubt the fastest, forward line in the country, with Billy and John Fullerton playing alongside the dangerous John Campbell.

Glasgow University were the team most affected by the movement of players. The club had lost the services of their two Dutchmen, C W de Visser and T A Proost, both of whom had returned to Holland and the long serving D W Lindsay. Goaltender, C N (Cowan) Young, would also be unavailable for a time, owing to an injury he sustained while playing rugby. On the plus side, A J McCabe, brother of J O McCabe, was joining the club and was considered a good prospect.

Andy Dick, Kelvingrove, one of the club's stalwart defenders and longest serving players.

Season 1933-1934

where, for example, the Mitchell Trophy had already provided some major surprises in the past.

One nagging worry though was that league matches between those teams outside the "big three" might start to prove less attractive to the paying public. It was noted that the recent match between Dennistoun Eagles and Glasgow University, which was won 1-0 by the East End club, had been very poor and "woefully slow". Too many matches like this in what was now an extended fixture list would not be conducive to maintaining spectator interest or winning over new fans to the sport.

The first round ties of the Mitchell Trophy commenced in early November, the main interest focussing on the first of an eagerly awaited cup and league double-header between Bridge of Weir and Kelvingrove. Both teams were so far unbeaten and playing well. As a result keen contests were expected. The largest crowd of the season turned up for the tie played on 10 November and they were not disappointed.

In a really thrilling encounter Kelvingrove prevailed 3-0 but that score did not accurately reflect the course of the match. In fact it had been very even throughout, but Bridge of Weir found Dave Cross in magnificent form, and as they furiously attacked gaps were left at the back which the deadly Kelvingrove forwards fully exploited. The first period saw early pressure by Bridge of Weir but it was Kelvingrove who scored when, following a clever run and shot by Arthur Tingley, Sid Montford pounced on the rebound. Tingley added a second goal in the middle period and, despite a barrage of pressure exerted by the Renfrewshire men in the third period, it was the Glasgow team who scored again when the majestic Tingley capitalised on a defensive error.

Four days later the two sides met again in the championship. Still nursing their wounds, Bridge of Weir made significant positional changes by moving Max Brennan and W G McDonald to their defence allowing the versatile Wilbur Muirhead to return to the forward line to partner the McLeod brothers. This gave the team a better balance allowing more mobility and creativity in turning defence into attack though it meant that team captain, Jimmy Woodrow, was consigned to the substitutes' bench. Within twenty five seconds of the match commencing W G McDonald put Bridge of Weir 1-0 ahead. That goal was the first conceded by Kelvingrove all season. The champions continued to dominate but were held at bay by a resolute 'Grove defence. The Glasgow men rallied in the final session and it was no real surprise when Sid Montford scored an equalising goal. The match ended 1-1, a result which, given the run of play, pleased Kelvingrove more than Bridge of Weir.

On either side of these two highly charged contests another two Mitchell Trophy first round ties were played. In the first the holders Bears had little trouble in disposing of a disappointing Dennistoun Eagles by 5-0, thanks to a brace each from Jack Gilmour and R F Winfield. It was noted of Bears

Of the other teams, Bears would have to start the season without their international forward, A Rintoul, who would not be available until the New Year. This was a serious blow to the Mitchell Trophy holders but at least in R O (Ronald) MacDonald and Jack Gilmour, the team had retained a stuffy and experienced defence. There were no major changes at Dennistoun Eagles but Juniors would be considerably weaker because of the continued unavailability of Gordon Rowley, who was expected to complete his studies at university and leave the Glasgow area later in the year.

The SIHA decided to establish a Board of Referees. The aim was to put refereeing on a more organised and formal footing with perhaps a pool of about half a dozen or so who would be appointed to officiate at all of the matches throughout the season. This development was enacted partly as a response to the controversial Mitchell Trophy final of the previous season when refereeing decisions had rather marred the occasion. Complaints about referees had been few and far between in the Scottish League, but their appointment to matches had always been a somewhat arbitrary affair. It was hoped that the new system would improve the situation by giving this pool of referees greater experience since they would be handling more matches. Ian McLeod of Bridge of Weir was appointed as the chairman of the new body.

The champions, Bridge of Weir, opened the new season on 10 October with an encouraging 3-0 win against Bears. The first period was goalless but within five minutes of the middle session W G McDonald scored. In the final period, the brothers Walter and Ian McLeod added further goals to seal the victory and give the Renfrewshire side a solid start to the campaign. Bridge of Weir followed up this initial success with a hard fought 1-0 victory against Dennistoun Eagles two weeks later. Walter McLeod scored the winning goal in the final minute of the match following an assist from Canadian new boy, M D (Max) Brennan, who was making his debut for the champions. Brennan, yet another student from the University of Edinburgh, would turn out to be an excellent signing for the club.

As anticipated both Kelvingrove and Mohawks kept pace with Bridge of Weir by also winning their respective first two matches. Kelvingrove made a very smart start by defeating Dennistoun Eagles 4-0 and followed this up with a 3-0 win against Juniors. Mohawks also beat Juniors but by 2-0 before thrashing Bears 5-0, a match where John Fullerton grabbed a hat-trick.

The opening rounds of the fixture list had confirmed the views held by most observers and pundits that the "big three" were going to be too strong for the rest of the league. Indeed, of the 20 goals scored in the first eight fixtures of the championship, 18 were shared between Bridge of Weir, Kelvingrove and Mohawks, none of whom had lost a single goal. The pattern was thus set for the season. Those three teams were expected to battle it out for the league championship while the other four teams were simply making up the numbers. Their best hopes for success lay in the two cup competitions that they had "cleverly combined in attack allied to grim defensive strength" despite missing A Rintoul.

With Mohawks receiving a bye, the other tie was contested on 18 November between Glasgow University and Juniors. In a scrappy and disjointed match, A J McCabe put the students ahead before Joe Collins responded with an excellent solo equaliser. The second period was goalless and the match was decided in the final session when J O McCabe scored the winning goal to give Varsity a 2-1 win.

Although neither of these teams had started the championship particularly well, the result was something of a surprise, given that Gordon Rowley had made his first appearance of the season for Juniors in this match. In any event, Glasgow University would play Mohawks in the semi-final and in the other, Bears were drawn against Kelvingrove.

Glasgow University sprung an even bigger surprise at the end of November when they defeated Bridge of Weir 3-1 in the league championship. The match turned into a nightmare for reserve goaltender W MacLachlan, who conceded three goals in the first period before being replaced between the posts by Jimmy Woodrow in the second period. Despite enormous pressure the students held out for a notable victory - their first ever against Bridge of Weir in four attempts.

By the end of November, Mohawks led the league with 6 points as the result of three wins from three matches. Kelvingrove and Bridge of Weir shared second place on 5 points, although the champions had played one more match. At the other end of the league table Juniors, the only team not to have recorded a win, were bottom following three defeats in as many matches.

The first semi-final of the Mitchell Trophy was held on 1 December between holders Bears and Kelvingrove. It was very unfortunate for Bears that A Rintoul was still not available, as their task was far from easy. From the moment that Sid Montford put the West End team 1-0 ahead in the first period there was never any real doubt about the outcome. It eventually finished 4-1 for Kelvingrove, the result accurately reflecting the course of the game.

If that semi-final went to script then that was most certainly not the case in the other semi-final played a week later between Glasgow University and Mohawks. In an exciting match the students registered their second major upset of the season when they defeated their more fancied opponents 1-0, albeit with a slice of luck. The match was settled in the second period when A J McCabe, who was improving in every match, drew the Mohawks defence and passed to Jack Easton, who made no mistake with a low hard drive. Try as they might, Mohawks were unable to break down a stubborn Varsity defence, in which Canadian goaltender, A G Garnock, was outstanding. For Mohawks it was yet another disappointment, in a competition in which they seemed destined never to do well.

Frozen in Time

Mohawks were probably not in the best fettle for their next league match a week later against Bridge of Weir. It was an important encounter for both teams, particularly the champions who had dropped three points in their previous two matches. Bridge of Weir persevered with their new formation and produced a narrow 1-0 win courtesy of a goal scored by Wilbur Muirhead. While Mohawks had played well, they had found their opponents' mostly Canadian defence a tough nut to crack.

The domestic programme was interrupted by the first representative match of the season when Glasgow entertained Manchester at Crossmyloof on 16 December. It was the first visit by the English side for almost two years and the occasion afforded the SIHA the opportunity to blood a number of new players at representative level. The newcomers selected were Alec Fullerton of Kelvingrove, Joe Collins of Juniors and Max Brennan of Bridge of Weir.

The match ended 0-0 but it was far from a boring game. Glasgow largely dominated the proceedings but a mixture of poor finishing and splendid goaltending by H N Bridge combined to make it a frustrating evening for the home side and the large crowd in attendance.

A notable feature of the match was the first appearance of all three Fullerton brothers, Alec, Billy and John, at representative level. "Inside Edge" noted that the Glasgow forwards were guilty of over-skating the puck allowing Bridge to come out of his crease to smother their goal attempts, but he was fulsome in his praise of Joe Collins who, at 18 years of age, "displayed a coolness which some of his older colleagues might have emulated with profit."

Kelvingrove and Glasgow University were due to meet in the final of the Mitchell Trophy on 22 December but in a rehearsal they met in a league match only three days before. With the cup final in mind Varsity rested three of their regular first team players and were subsequently beaten 5-0. While their caution was understandable, the margin of that defeat would have done nothing for the confidence of the players as they prepared for the final.

And so it appeared. In the most one sided final in the history of the competition Glasgow University were crushed 8-0 by a rampant Kelvingrove side. Although the score did flatter the West End team, there was never any doubt that the Mitchell Trophy would be bedecked with green, white and black ribbons for the second time. It was a shocking anti-climax for Varsity who completely failed to do themselves any justice in this match.

After an even start, Sid Montford put Kelvingrove 1-0 ahead in the first period. The contest was effectively decided in the second period as Glasgow University strove hard for an equalising goal, A J McCabe being thwarted at point blank range by Dave Cross on one occasion. But it was not to be, and further goals from Arthur Tingley and Montford again knocked the stuffing out of the students. Their resistance simply collapsed in the final session as Sid Montford completed his hat-trick and four other goals were shared by Bert Gemmell, W J Towers, Joe Beveridge and Andy Dick.

Season 1933-1934

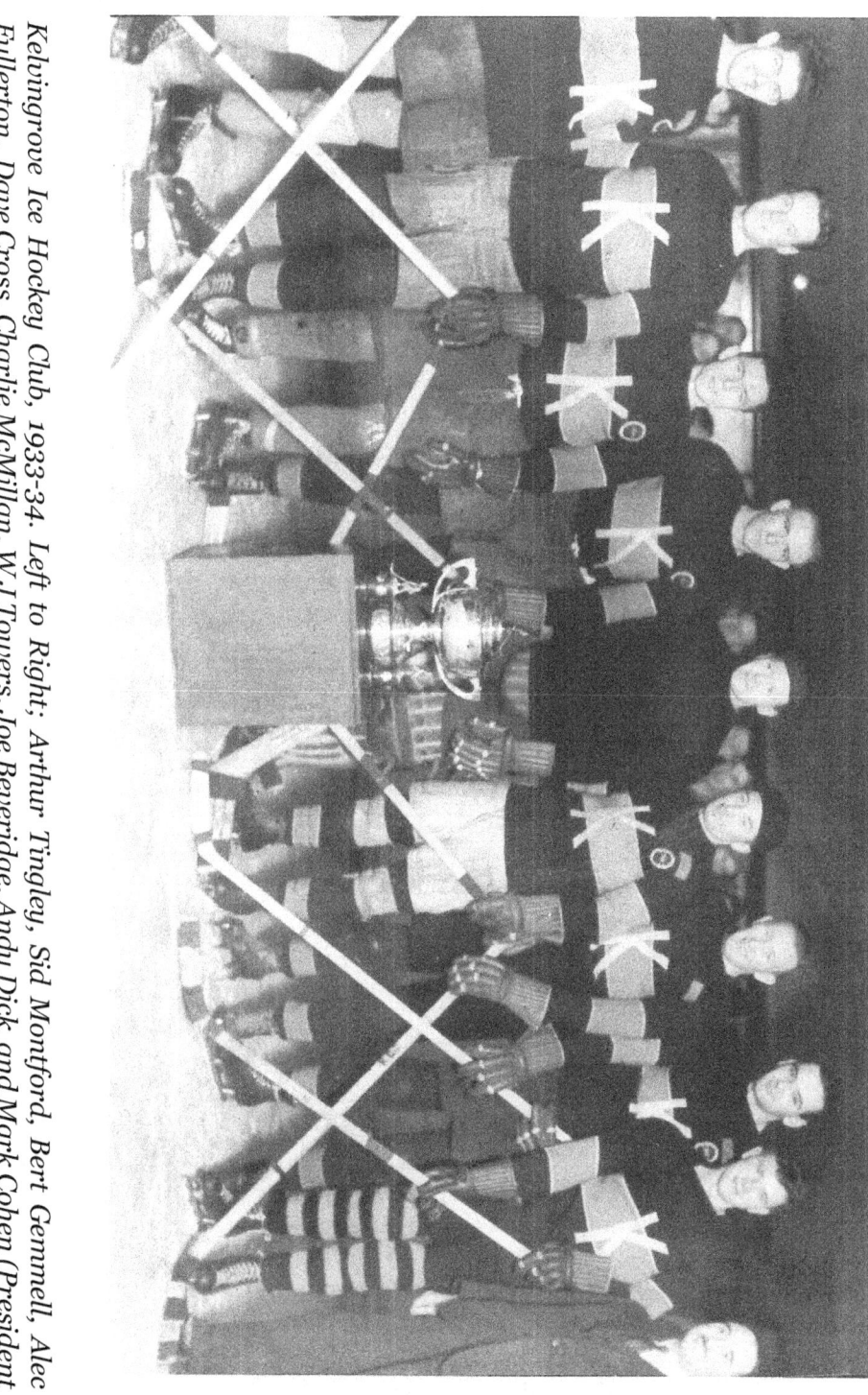

Kelvingrove Ice Hockey Club, 1933-34. Left to Right; Arthur Tingley, Sid Montford, Bert Gemmell, Alec Fullerton, Dave Cross, Charlie McMillan, W J Towers, Joe Beveridge, Andy Dick and Mark Cohen (President

The match was a particularly disappointing finale for Jack Easton, who had played his last game for Glasgow University prior to his imminent departure for Canada early in the New Year.

Easton was without question one of the finest players of this era in Scottish ice hockey. Small, sturdy, feisty, industrious, enthusiastic and skilful, he was the inspiration of the Glasgow University team for five years. It was unfortunate for him that he never played with a better side, because the honours he deserved eluded him - not that he ever complained. His overall contribution to the Scottish game had been immense.

On an individual level, Jack Easton had made his mark. He had been the leading goal scorer in the Scottish League three times, 1929-30 (Second Division), 1930-31 and 1932-33. He had played for Scotland on nine occasions between 1930 and 1933 and scored one goal against France in Paris. Not simply a big fish in a small pond, his talents had been recognised south of the border, where he played for England against Canada on two occasions in 1932 and also for Great Britain against Canadian opposition in 1930 and 1933.

Another huge loss to the Scottish game at this time was Gordon Rowley, who had decided to retire on gaining his medical qualifications. He had made a considerable impact at both Bridge of Weir and Juniors as a player-coach and had also readily assumed the mantle of unofficial coach to the SIHA for a time. Rowley had played on eight occasions for Scotland between 1930 and 1932, and once for Great Britain in the match against Edmonton Superiors in 1933.

Scottish ice hockey could ill afford to lose players of this calibre but for Glasgow University at least as one door was closing another was opening.

In January, O A (Orvald) Gratias joined the club from Oxford University where he was studying mathematics as a Rhodes scholar. A native of Saskatchewan, Gratias had been playing on defence with the brilliant Oxford University side for the past three years and the temporary capture of this highly accomplished athlete was a major coup for the Varsity team. He made his debut in a league match against Mohawks on 6 January but it was not to be a winning start as the students lost 1-0.

A week later, Mohawks faced their bogey team Kelvingrove in a top of the table clash. As expected, it was a keenly contested affair. Mohawks were more methodical in attack but found the 'Grove defence as formidable as ever. After a goalless first period, Arthur Tingley broke the deadlock in the middle session with a spectacular strike. Tom Shearer, playing in the forward line for the unavailable John Campbell, assumed his mantle by equalising for Mohawks in the final period. It looked like staying 1-1 but Bert Gemmell scored a winning goal for Kelvingrove just minutes from time.

So the long agony continued for Mohawks who had still never beaten Kelvingrove. This latest victory for the West End club consolidated their position at the top of the league. With the championship now at the half way stage, Kelvingrove had 11 points from six matches. They remained unbeaten

Season 1933-1934

with five wins and a draw. Defending champions Bridge of Weir were in second position with 9 points but Mohawks had slipped to third position on 8 points.

At the wrong end of the table were Juniors in bottom position with a record of played six, lost six. Gordon Rowley had only managed to play a couple of matches for the team prior to his retirement and obviously they were missing his influence as both a player and a coach. It was all a far cry from the previous season when Juniors almost finished second. The one bright spot on the horizon was the form of Joe Collins who seemed to be getting better with every game.

The domestic season was interrupted on 23 January for a glamour challenge match at Crossmyloof between "Canada" and the United States of America. The Canadian team was actually represented by the Ottawa Shamrocks and the match attracted a huge crowd who were treated to an exceptional contest. Ottawa won less easily than the 5-1 score line suggested their captain, Lou Bates, being the outstanding player on the ice.

Matches of this pedigree were few and far between in Scotland. Ottawa had already beaten the Americans twice before in similar challenge matches in England. Although Ottawa had been billed by the management at Crossmyloof as Canada this was poetic licence since the team which would shortly represent that country in the forthcoming World Championships in February were the Saskatoon Quakers and not the Ottawa Shamrocks.

Interestingly, and perhaps indicatively, the referee for this match was not provided by the SIHA as might have been expected. "Inside Edge" suggested that Andy Dick of Kelvingrove would have been an ideal candidate for the task but it was Albert Duncanson of the Grosvenor House Canadians club in London who was appointed, presumably at the insistence of the BIHA, who had organised this series of challenge matches.

In the league championship Mohawks lost further ground when they could only draw 2-2 with Bears in early February. They were without flying wing man Billy Fullerton who was competing in a national speed skating competition at Oxford the following day and regular goaltender, Duncan MacLachlan. Mohawks then received a more permanent blow when long standing defence man J G Fyfe announced he was moving to another part of Scotland to live.

On 16 February, leaders Kelvingrove faced Bridge of Weir in a crucial encounter. Both teams were sitting on top of the league with 13 points but the Renfrewshire side had played one match more. When the two teams had met earlier in the season, Kelvingrove had been fortunate to obtain a share of the spoils, and they were to ride their luck again in this latest match.

In a game dominated by heavy and effective checking Bridge of Weir outplayed their opponents in the first two periods but found Dave Cross an insurmountable barrier in the Kelvingrove goal, saving a series of likely shots. When he was beaten by Wilbur Muirhead that effort came back off a post. Kelvingrove improved in the final session. Following a clever dash, Andy Dick passed to Charlie McMillan who coolly steadied himself before firing the winning goal into the corner of the net.

The result was rough justice on Bridge of Weir who deserved to win. It represented a further dent to retaining their title with only three matches left. Kelvingrove were now firmly in pole position, with a two points lead and a vital match in hand over the reigning champions. It seemed that only a dramatic collapse in their remaining four games could deprive 'Grove of their second Canada Cup.

Four days later Juniors picked up their first league point of the season when they drew 1-1 with the unpredictable Bears. Jack Gilmour had given Bears the lead with a trademark solo goal in the second period and only the fine goaltending of the rapidly improving Billy Turnbull prevented further damage. In the third period, Eric Montford, capitalised on an assist from Joe Collins to give Juniors some joy at last.

The first round ties of the President's Pucks competition commenced on 23 February. Mohawks had little trouble in disposing of a lacklustre Dennistoun Eagles by 4-0 in a match dominated by Billy Fullerton who scored a hat-trick. They were hopeful of doing well in this competition following their shock exit in the semi-final of the Mitchell Trophy and their disappointing league campaign.

The two teams met again four days later in the championship and the outcome was the same. Mohawks won 5-1; this time it was John Fullerton who grabbed a hat-trick. In spite of these reverses, Dennistoun Eagles were an improved side from the season before. As "Inside Edge" observed they were "without much guile or experience but were game fighters" and with the diminutive and agile Jack Logan in goal and international Bill Russell in attack they were not without talent.

Attention became focussed on the first international match of the season as Scotland were due to play England at Crossmyloof on 3 March. It would be the fifth meeting between the two countries but thus far the Scots had only managed one victory against the "auld enemy" and that had been in 1910. The build-up to the latest confrontation was dominated by a great deal of debate around the thorny issue of nationality. Essentially, this was a question about what constituted a "Canadian". It was a problem which had tormented international ice hockey competition for years; despite numerous rulings and guidelines from the LIHG it had never been satisfactorily resolved. It was the case that individual national ice hockey associations simply interpreted the rules and guidelines as they saw fit and uniformity on this issue was almost impossible to establish.

For the forthcoming home international match, the SIHA insisted that only home-born players should be selected for both countries. In turn, the BIHA was not happy with this narrow stipulation and suggested that the

Season 1933-1934

most recent LIHG ruling on nationality be invoked whereby Canadian-born players could be selected provided they had lived in their country of adoption for five years.

Discussions continued. In the end the SIHA more or less got its way. While its intentions in this matter were honourable, in that encouragement should always be given to home-produced players where possible, one cannot help thinking that some self-interest was at work here. The Scottish League did not have either the quantity or the quality of Canadians that were playing in the English leagues so choices were much more limited north of the border.

The entire issue was complicated. Within a specifically Scottish context three players at Kelvingrove provided a good example of how the current rules and guidelines on nationality could be applied.

One could start with Dave Cross as an example of the "native born" rule. Although born in Scotland he had been brought up in Canada where he learned to skate and to play ice hockey. Cross then returned to Scotland as a permanent resident. As a result, he had dual nationality and could therefore quite legitimately represent either Canada or Scotland.

Andy Dick was an example of the new "residence" rule. He had been born in Canada where he learned to skate and play ice hockey but he now qualified to play for Scotland because he had lived in the country for at least five years. If the SIHA chose to ignore this ruling they would be turning their back on talented players like him.

On the other hand, Canadian born players like Arthur Tingley, who had already played often for Scotland in the past, would no longer be eligible for Scottish selection until they had resided in the country for the stipulated five years. Other Canadian born but potential Scottish international players such as W G McDonald and Max Brennan of Bridge of Weir would be similarly disqualified on a strict appliance of the residence rule.

This was the theory. The reality was often different. All national ice hockey associations managed to find ways around these rules and guidelines. In time, the SIHA would as well. Nationality was a minefield of obfuscation and slight of hand and the LIHG seemed powerless to do anything really practical about it.

Political machinations aside the SIHA, as it had done in the home international match the previous season, selected a squad of players who were mostly home developed.

Three new players came into the squad, Alec Fullerton and Charlie McMillan of Kelvingrove and A J McCabe of Glasgow University. Of the ten players selected only Dave Cross, John Campbell and A J McCabe had played and learned the game in Canada.

The English squad was very strong containing as it did five Great Britain international players. Apart from the goaltender, George Mason, who played for Purley in the English League Division Two, the squad was drawn entirely from only two clubs, Grosvenor House Canadians and Streatham, which meant that almost all of these players were semi-professionals. The match attracted much interest with ticket prices for spectators fixed at between 3s and 1s.

The two teams were:

Scotland: D Cross (Kelvingrove); A Fullerton (Kelvingrove) and J R Gilmour (Bears); W Fullerton (Mohawks), J Fullerton (Mohawks) and J Campbell (Mohawks). - W S McLeod (Bridge of Weir), W S Montford (Kelvingrove), C McMillan (Kelvingrove) and A J McCabe (Glasgow University).

England: G Mason (Purley); H E Mayes (Grosvenor House Canadians) and C A Erhardt (Streatham); F A de Marwicz (Streatham), J Borland (Grosvenor House Canadians) and E Jackson (Grosvenor House Canadians). - E J Ramus (Streatham), P Halford (Streatham) and R W Couldray (Streatham).

Referee: I S McLeod (SIHA).

As anticipated, England were the better side but the Scots put up a decent display. Indeed, Scotland took the lead early in the first period when Walter McLeod scored with a high shot from an assist by Charlie McMillan. Harry Mayes equalised for the visitors with a sensational individual goal leaving the opening session at 1-1. Dave Cross was playing his usual sound game in goal and he managed to keep the eager English forwards out in the second period.

England's superior tactics and forward combination came to the fore in the final period as the Scots began to tire. Goals from Ted Jackson and Carl Erhardt gave the visitors a 3-1 victory their overall play fully deserved. Scotland's defence had coped well but the all-Mohawks forward line had failed to make any impact and after the first period John Fullerton was replaced in the first line by Walter McLeod.

As the inquests into yet another Scottish defeat commenced "Inside Edge" noted

> "England's success on this occasion was chiefly due to their expert application of the forward pass, permitted in the centre zone this season for the first time, and it was obvious until the Scots properly develop this mode of attack they cannot hope for any real degree of proficiency."
>
> *(Daily Record and Mail: 5 March 1934).*

This was a telling comment. It was not the first time that lack of adequate coaching had cost Scotland dear. It was depressingly still the case that Scottish ice hockey lagged badly behind in basic technique and tactical awareness compared to other countries, a matter the SIHA had long recognised but had still failed to really successfully address. The match also demonstrated yet again that the fitness levels of players in Scotland were not at the level of their opponents but that was hardly surprising given the semi-professional nature of the game in England.

Season 1933-1934

The home international match was sandwiched between the two remaining first round ties in the President's Pucks. The struggling Juniors gave Kelvingrove something of a fright before the superior skills of the latter team eventually prevailed for a 2-0 win. The other tie also went to form as Bridge of Weir convincingly defeated Glasgow University 3-0.

Bears had received a bye in the first round of the competition but would now face Bridge of Weir in the semi-final. The other semi-final would be contested by Kelvingrove and Mohawks.

Bridge of Weir's success over Glasgow University on 9 March was revenge for a shock 5-1 defeat at the hands of the students in the league championship only three days earlier. In that particular match, the Renfrewshire side were missing their two Canadian stars, Max Brennan and W G McDonald, and an Orvald Gratias inspired Varsity took full advantage. It was the second time that Bridge of Weir had lost to Glasgow University in the league but this latest defeat ended any lingering hopes the reigning champions had of retaining the Canada Cup. The championship was now a clear two horse race between league leaders Kelvingrove and their fierce rivals Mohawks who were sitting in second place.

Kelvingrove had a healthy lead but it was eroded slightly in their next match when they had to come from behind twice to draw 2-2 with Bears. That result left them still top of the league with 16 points from nine matches. Mohawks had 13 points from the same number of games played.

Mohawks handed Bridge of Weir their third consecutive league defeat on 20 March when they won an ill-tempered and physical match 4-1. It was a notable victory for a rather makeshift Mohawks side who were obliged to play with John Campbell and E K Reid in defence and the now semi-retired Tom Craig partnering the Fullerton brothers in attack. Their lack of reserve strength continued to be a problem.

It was undoubtedly a factor in their next match three days later when they played Kelvingrove in the first semi-final of the President's Pucks. Mohawks were again short of substitutes, having none available for this tie. Despite that they put up a great fight but the stuffy 'Grove defence was giving nothing away. Goals from Sid Montford, Arthur Tingley and Alec Fullerton sealed a 3-0 victory for Kelvingrove to ensure their second consecutive appearance in the final of this competition.

Kelvingrove were no doubt cock-a-hoop at their latest win against Mohawks and this may have contributed to some complacency creeping in, for in their next match in the league they were beaten 2-1 by Glasgow University. It was the first defeat suffered by Kelvingrove in any competition all season but Varsity had been making a habit of producing shock results lately. Goals from the McCabe brothers gave the students some measure of revenge for their humiliation at the hands of Kelvingrove in the final of the Mitchell Trophy in December.

Kelvingrove had now lost three points in their last two matches but still remained at the top of the league on 16 points. Mohawks had now narrowed their lead to one point, with both teams having two matches still to play. As fate would have it, the two sides were due to play each other in their next fixture when the destination of the Canada Cup would almost certainly be decided.

On 31 March, Kelvingrove travelled south to Birmingham Ice Rink to play local team Warwickshire in a challenge match. Fixtures between Scottish and English club sides were a rarity. Warwickshire played in the English League Division One having won promotion from Division Two as champions the season before. They were more than holding their own in the top division and were a semi-professional club. On paper it looked like a mismatch but Kelvingrove took the precaution of including two guest players, Walter McLeod and Billy Fullerton, to strengthen their team. The Glasgow side rose magnificently to the challenge and shocked their more fancied opponents by recording a wonderful 4-2 victory. Warwickshire opened the scoring in the first period but Billy Fullerton equalised for Kelvingrove. Sid Montford then put the Glasgow men ahead pouncing on a rebound shot from Arthur Tingley. Walter McLeod scored a spectacular third goal before Charlie McMillan made it 4-1 at the end of the second period. Warwickshire pulled a goal back in the final session but Kelvingrove held out for a notable success.

The second semi-final of the President's Pucks between Bridge of Weir and Bears was played early April. Bears were seriously weakened by the absence of talisman Jack Gilmour from their team and were further handicapped when the other half of their defence, Ronald MacDonald, sustained a nasty head injury early in the game which rendered him "hors de combat". Bridge of Weir fully cashed in by winning the match 6-3 with both Max Brennan and W G McDonald in outstanding form.

Bridge of Weir would now play Kelvingrove in what was an attractive looking final on 13 April. The match presented the Renfrewshire side with the opportunity of salvaging some silverware from an otherwise disappointing season although in their three previous matches against 'Grove, two in the league championship and one in the Mitchell Trophy, they had yet to register a win against them.

On the other hand, Kelvingrove were now chasing a unique "treble" of all three major honours. They had already won the Mitchell Trophy and were in pole position for the league championship so winning the President's Pucks would give the West End club the clean sweep. The only fly in the ointment was that their form had dipped in recent weeks causing some concern amongst their large support. And so it came to pass. In the final, Kelvingrove never seemed to get out of first gear as Bridge of Weir set about them with their usual gusto. Their defensive pair of Max Brennan and W G McDonald were in an abrasive mood snuffing out the considerable threat posed by the Kelvingrove

Season 1933-1934

forwards and setting up numerous attacks for their own team. Bridge of Weir also made better use of substitutions in what was a fast paced game.

The first period was goal-less despite heavy pressure by Bridge of Weir. Sid Montford actually put Kelvingrove ahead early in the second period but the goal was disallowed by the referee, Ronald MacDonald. Max Brennan then set up a goal for W G McDonald and the same combination struck again at the beginning of the third session. A F Reid put the issue beyond doubt by scoring a third goal to give Bridge of Weir a 3-0 win and the President's Pucks.

Kelvingrove did not have much time to dwell on what had been a strangely inept and uncharacteristic performance. Within four days of that final disappointment they were facing what was to all intents and purposes the league championship decider against Mohawks. For Kelvingrove the aim, if not the task, was quite simple. A victory would give them the championship and the Canada Cup. If the match ended in a draw or a Mohawks win then the destination of the league title would depend on each team's final match of the season. The omens for Mohawks were not good, given their poor record against Kelvingrove, but they would have been heartened by the fact that the league leaders had lost a bit of form recently and that their captain, Sid Montford, would be unable to play in the match because of an injury.

The match did not disappoint the huge crowd who turned out to watch it. It was a fast, pulsating and thrilling contest worthy of the occasion. Mohawks started brightly, forcing Dave Cross to make a couple of great saves from Billy and John Fullerton. Then, following a hectic scramble in front of Duncan MacLachlan, Charlie McMillan bundled the puck over the line to give Kelvingrove that crucial first goal. The second period saw sustained attacking by Mohawks but the solid 'Grove defence held firm. At the start of the third period John Campbell missed a golden opportunity to draw Mohawks level. This was to prove costly as McMillan "stick-handling with baffling dexterity" skated through the entire Mohawks defence before planting the puck firmly behind MacLachlan for his (and Kelvingrove's) second goal to secure a hard fought 2-0 victory.

It was typical of Kelvingrove to come up with a big performance against their great rivals when it was most needed. Their defence of Dave Cross, Andy Dick and Alec Fullerton had put in yet another solid effort but it was also the willingness of their forwards to back-check and skate hard that made them such a difficult team to beat. Mohawks must have wondered what they had to do to defeat Kelvingrove. In ten competitive matches stretching back four years they had yet to record a single win!

Kelvingrove had now repeated their "double" success of season 1930-31 by winning both the Canada Cup and the Mitchell Trophy. No other team in the Scottish League had achieved this once let alone twice. While Mohawks had pushed them hard, there could be little debate that Kelvingrove deserved the league title. While both teams had won eight matches, Mohawks had lost three and drawn one whereas Kelvingrove had lost only once and drawn three. In addition, in the two head to head clashes, Kelvingrove had won both. The champions also had far and away the best defensive record in the league, having lost only seven goals all season, and that was the basis of their success.

Mohawks had to settle for second place eventually finishing two points behind Kelvingrove. It had been a disappointing season for the club but at least they had the consolation of having the two leading goal scorers in the league championship with John Fullerton scoring 14 goals and his brother, Billy, scoring 10. Indeed, of the 29 goals scored by Mohawks in the championship, the Fullerton brothers had scored 24 of them!

Defence was a continuing problem for Mohawks. Losing J G Fyfe was a blow; he was never adequately replaced. More generally, the club really needed to increase the size of their squad. For the league decider against Kelvingrove they were once again obliged to take to the ice with no substitutes on the bench. This placed an enormous burden on their team. It was an issue which would have to be addressed seriously if Mohawks were to progress.

Of the remaining fixtures in the championship the most notable result was Juniors 2-1 victory over Glasgow University on 24 March. Juniors first and only win of the season did not prevent them from finishing in bottom position in the league. The loss of Gordon Rowley had been too much to bear and it was clear that a coach of similar ability would be required if the team was to improve.

The season ended with another representative match when Warwickshire agreed to come to Crossmyloof on 21 April. The original intention had been that they should play Kelvingrove in a return fixture but the SIHA decided that their opponents should be a "Scottish League Select" side instead.

The SIHA took the opportunity to experiment. Orvald Gratias of Glasgow University and Joe Collins of Juniors formed a new defence with Walter McLeod, Max Brennan and W G McDonald forming an all Bridge of Weir second line of attack. The first line consisted of the Mohawks pair, Billy and John Fullerton, along with Arthur Tingley of Kelvingrove. Of the nine players selected for the Scottish League Select, only four were home developed.

Following Kelvingrove's unexpected win in Birmingham, hopes were high that the Scottish League Select would be able to secure another victory but it was not to be. Warwickshire won a close contest 2-1 mainly due to a combination of their speed and directness as well as the home team's profligacy near goal. Several excellent scoring opportunities were squandered, the main culprits being Walter McLeod and Max Brennan. The result was a major disappointment and for the SIHA it was back to the drawing board.

So another season drew to a close. Domestically, it had been rather dominated by Kelvingrove. The deposed champions, Bridge of Weir, at least

Season 1933-1934

found some consolation in winning the President's Pucks thereby denying Kelvingrove the opportunity of achieving a truly unique "treble".

On the international front nothing much had changed. The SIHA had decided to curtail the international programme to just one match against England but the result had been the same, a defeat. The ruling body had done this partly as a response to the extended domestic calendar but also in response to past heavy defeats by teams which were just too good for Scotland. There was a view that there was little benefit to be gained playing crack Canadian or foreign opposition only to be humiliated.

Overall, the impression held by most observers was that, while the standard of play in the Scottish League had generally declined, most of the matches remained competitive and entertaining for the paying public. There was a recognition that all of the teams required better coaching and greater tactical awareness but an encouraging sign was the number of good young home-developed players coming to the fore.

In England, Grosvenor House Canadians, who were to disband at the end of the season, became champions for the first and only time in their short but colourful history. They had lost only one of their twelve league fixtures scoring 75 goals in the process and conceding only 22. Their team was full of quality and included Harry Mayes, Jimmy Borland, Ted Jackson, Bob Wyman, and the Scottish-born Keith Thomson, all of whom were Great Britain international players.

Ice hockey was about to enter a golden age in England with the impending opening of the huge Wembley Arena in London. The stated intention was to promote two semi-professional teams from the venue. In addition, there were plans to build another two North American style arenas in London at Earls Court and Harringay. The English game at senior level was throwing off the last vestiges of amateurism: the days of the old Oxford Canadians and Princes clubs seeming like a bygone age.

Frozen in Time

Season 1934-35

The new ice hockey season commenced with only six clubs in competition, the lowest number since the re-introduction of the sport in season 1929-30.

This situation was indicative of a steady contraction from those heady days of 1929 when a total of 12 clubs re-constituted the Scottish Ice Hockey Association. Since then 9 clubs had come and gone in little under six years. These clubs were Glasgow Canadians, Scottish Corinthians, Glasgow High School, Doonside, Achtungs, Bearsden, Glasgow Skating Club, Queen's and the latest to disband, Bears. However, the ice hockey correspondent of the *Glasgow Herald* remained sanguine as he reviewed the season ahead:

"Scottish ice hockey, now entering its sixth season, has passed through a number of evolutionary stages associated with any new game. In the early years great strides were made but last season there was a decided check in its advance and ice hockey appeared to have reached a state of stalemate.

This was directly reflected in the disappointing displays of representative sides and by the quality of ice hockey played by a number of the clubs in the various tournaments. Too many games were drab and one sided with very little teamwork or skill in evidence.

Two remedies suggest themselves, the provision of more suitable and liberal facilities for practice and the appointment of an expert coach. No doubt the SIHA are faced with great difficulty in regard to the question of practice but they have shown considerable enterprise by engaging Pat Aitken who comes from Canada with splendid credentials as an exponent of the game.

No definite arrangements have yet been made for international matches but plans are afoot for bringing several attractive sides to Glasgow. The club programme will as usual comprise the league tournament, the Mitchell Trophy and the President's Pucks competitions.

The disbandment of Bears on account of difficulties in raising a suitable side while regrettable will probably benefit the remaining six clubs who are thus ensured of more frequent and regular appearances on the ice. There are those indeed who advocate the reduction of clubs to five."

(Glasgow Herald: 4 October 1934).

Frozen in Time

The demise of Bears was indeed regrettable and not without some irony as they were themselves an amalgam of two formerly disbanded clubs, Achtungs and Bearsden. The decision to call it a day was almost certainly the result of the club's two best players, Jack Gilmour and A Rintoul, intimating their intention to play much less in the season ahead. The remaining players in the team obviously thought it was not worthwhile continuing in these circumstances.

Bears had lasted only two seasons. Their league performance had been poor, finishing in penultimate position on both occasions. The club's one major success was winning the Mitchell Trophy in season 1932-33, when in a controversial game they defeated the more fancied Bridge of Weir 1-0 in the final.

On a more positive note, the appointment of another new dedicated coach by the SIHA was a welcome and long overdue development. Archibald S Aitken, known as "Pat", had been brought up in Canada to where his family had emigrated while he was still a baby. He arrived in Glasgow from Calgary, Alberta, having played the game at senior level in his adopted country. With almost no formal development infrastructure in place at Crossmyloof, Aitken had taken on quite a responsibility and one that would require the full co-operation of all of the clubs and officials connected with the sport in Scotland.

The six clubs which would be competing in the new season were Bridge of Weir, Dennistoun Eagles, Glasgow University, Juniors, Kelvingrove and Mohawks. In the league championship each team would play the other on three occasions for a total of 45 fixtures to be played between early October and the end of April. This represented the longest schedule of matches yet and would give each team a thorough examination of their abilities not to mention their stamina.

The SIHA retained the format whereby the Mitchell Trophy would be competed for earlier in the season than the President's Pucks. This remained unfortunate because the former competition was the more senior of the two; its conclusion previously provided one of the showpieces of the season. Placing the latter tournament at the end of the season was probably done to acknowledge the generosity of Frank Stuart, who continued to donate these silver-mounted pucks to the winning team.

There was a significant amount of player movement in the run-up to the new season. The most unaffected team was probably the defending champions, Kelvingrove, who were largely unchanged from the previous season. They had arguably the best defence in the league with the ever-reliable Dave Cross, a model of consistency, in goal and in front of him, the hard hitting and energetic Andy Dick and Alec Fullerton, the latter taking over as captain of the side.

Kelvingrove would start with Sid Montford, Charlie McMillan and Arthur Tingley as their first line in attack with Bert Gemmell, Joe Beveridge and new boy, A (Arthur) Gray, who had moved west from Dennistoun Eagles, as

Season 1934-1935

a second line. It was though something of a surprise that 'Grove did not do more to strengthen their squad but they clearly thought that what they had would be enough to give them another successful season.

Mohawks started the season without the considerable talent of John Campbell who had moved to England. He would be seriously missed since he had formed a very effective attack with Billy and John Fullerton. As replacements, Mohawks acquired the services of three ex-Bears players, Ronald MacDonald, R F Winfield and C J (Charlie) Russell.

For the first time in their history Mohawks seemed to have a genuine squad of players rather than having a first team with barely one or two reserves. It looked a reasonably strong line-up and the club was hopeful of securing another player with Canadian experience before the season was too old. Mohawks would also start the season in new colours. Since 1929 the club had played in a predominantly green outfit but the decision was taken to switch to a combination of red, white and blue for the future.

There were some major changes at Bridge of Weir. After five seasons as regular players, Ian McLeod, Earl Muirhead and Jimmy Woodrow, all intimated their desire to play much less often in the future. They would still be available for selection, but only if the team found itself short-handed. On the bright side, Jack Johnston joined the club from the disbanded Bears.

With Canadians W G McDonald and Max Brennan, Bridge of Weir retained two of the most versatile players in the league and in Walter McLeod and Wilbur Muirhead, they had two very different but equally talented forwards. The main question mark hung over the strength of their substitutes' bench. Was there enough strength in depth to sustain the team over the season?

There would of course be no Jack Easton at Glasgow University this season, and the club had also lost the services of fellow Canadians A G Garnock and A J McCabe, who had also returned to the land of their birth. These were heavy losses to sustain, but the club obtained two players from Juniors, Andrew Gray and the international forward, Don Edwards. In addition, the experienced Orvald Gratias would also be available at least for the early part of the season.

Of all of the teams in the Scottish League, Glasgow University were probably the least "coached". Individually, the team had produced some outstanding players but their overall play had tended to lack cohesion, combination and positional sense. They had never been a particularly physical side, either. Despite a general lack of tactical awareness Varsity were nevertheless always capable of springing a surprise or two.

What of Dennistoun Eagles? This was a team who had consistently disappointed their loyal band of followers. In four seasons of Canada Cup competition, Dennistoun had finished bottom of the league twice and third from the bottom on the other two occasions. The East End team had also failed to do anything of note in either of the two cup competitions. Yet, they remained a popular and hard working club who always attempted to play the game in the right spirit.

Hope springs eternal and Dennistoun would commence the season with a new defence in front of the capable Jack Logan in goal. The new partnership would comprise Eric Montford, brother of Sid at Kelvingrove, and Joe Collins. The signing of Collins in particular was a major coup for Dennistoun as he was one of the hottest properties in Scottish ice hockey. In attack, the club had also acquired a useful Canadian in R (Bobby) Mills and the promising G (Glen) Braid to complement Bill Russell and Sam Stevenson. All in all better things were expected in the East End of Glasgow.

Juniors were in dire straights. Most of their better players had moved to rival teams and it had left the remaining squad seemingly uncompetitive. There had been some debate the previous season about the future of Juniors but the SIHA had decided to continue with the club for another season. That decision looked flawed for unless serious reinforcements could be found, Juniors were likely to be on the end of some heavy defeats, a situation not conducive to encouraging younger players.

Although more of a challenge might be expected from Glasgow University and Dennistoun Eagles, it was likely to be the "big three" who would once again be contesting for the honours. With each team having to play fifteen fixtures in the league championship the eventual winners will certainly have deserved it.

The SIHA introduced two important rule changes to bring the local game into line with the latest LIHG directives. The first was the legalising of forward passing in all three zones of the ice as a further aid to speed up play. The second change was the introduction of the penalty shot as a deterrent to foul play in front of the goaltender's crease.

Mohawks opened the season on 9 October with a comfortable 3-1 win against Glasgow University, R F Winfield scoring one of these goals on his debut for his new club. Dennistoun Eagles opened their account with a 2-0 victory over Juniors, Glen Braid scoring both of their goals.

The next fixture pitched Bridge of Weir against reigning champions, Kelvingrove, in the first big match of the season. The Renfrewshire side continued where they had left off the season before in the final of the President's Pucks when they again defeated their opponents 2-0 thanks to a brace from Walter McLeod. Although Kelvingrove were disappointing, Bridge of Weir, with W G McDonald and Max Brennan in great form, dominated for most of the game and thoroughly deserved the two points.

The result was bad enough for Kelvingrove, but they would also have to cope with the temporary unavailability of star forward, Arthur Tingley. A senior civil servant, his term of office as an Assistant Trade Commissioner for Canada in Glasgow had now come to an end. He was returning home for an extended holiday, and was not expected to return to Glasgow until about March.

Season 1934-1935

Bridge of Weir continued their impressive start to the season with a 2-1 win against Mohawks. Having defeated their two main rivals the Renfrewshire side had clearly thrown down the gauntlet. Max Brennan was again the star of the show with both goals. The only consolation for Mohawks was a good debut performance from their new Canadian player, J (Jim) Kenny, who scored a brilliant solo goal in the final minutes of the match.

Kelvingrove's stuttering start to the season continued in their next match when they were held 1-1 by Juniors. It could have been worse: the youngsters had a goal disallowed minutes from full time. While Kelvingrove were again out of sorts, Juniors were boosted by the appearance of SIHA coach, Pat Aitken, who put in an exceptional performance.

The presence of Aitken in the Juniors team led Kelvingrove to make an official complaint to the SIHA, on the grounds that he was unregistered to play for the club and that he was of course a "professional". The West End club had a good case even if it did look a bit like sour grapes. After due consideration, the SIHA agreed with Kelvingrove and declared the result of the match null and void. It would be re-played at a future date.

Glasgow University found a more than adequate replacement for departed goaltender, A G Garnock, when R S (Ronald) Milne joined the club. Milne would become one of the best goaltenders ever to play in Scotland but one would not have known it at the time of his debut for Varsity as Bridge of Weir knocked five goals past him in a 5-1 victory at the end of October.

Ronald "Scotty" Milne was well-built and something of a character. Born in Glasgow, he had emigrated to Canada when a youngster; it was there that he developed his ice hockey skills. His last season in Canada was spent with the Prince Albert Mintos where he had impressed Pat Aitken. Milne was also a keen footballer, and had been training at Ibrox Stadium with Glasgow Rangers for whom he had hoped to get a trial as a goalkeeper.

The opening rounds of the Mitchell Trophy commenced on 2 November. "Fleet-footed" Mohawks flew past Juniors 5-0. The youngsters held out well in the first period but a brace each from Billy and John Fullerton sealed a comfortable win for Mohawks, in a poor match characterised by much scrappy play.

The two teams met again in the league championship only four days later. On this occasion, Mohawks annihilated their opponents 12-1, a record score in the Scottish League. Jim Kenny, R F Winfield and Billy Fullerton all helped themselves to hat-tricks as the hapless Juniors were simply swept aside. The result initiated yet another bout of navel gazing at the SIHA regarding the future of the Juniors club.

In the other first round tie of the Mitchell Trophy, Glasgow University defeated Dennistoun Eagles 3-0 in a closely-fought encounter. The score line flattered the victors as Dennistoun were the more polished team and attacked with vigour but found Orvald Gratias and Ronald Milne in fine form. J O

McCabe put Varsity ahead in the second period and further goals were added in the final period by I H Borland and Gratias.

In the league championship, Kelvingrove recorded their first win of the season when they defeated a spirited Dennistoun Eagles 1-0 with a goal from Charlie McMillan only four minutes from full time. Making his debut for Kelvingrove in this match was a young Canadian of Scots birth, R (Bobby) Brown, who had played at junior level in Montreal. The club hoped that in time he would become an adequate replacement for the departed Arthur Tingley.

Reinforcements were the order of the day at Juniors as well. The SIHA decided to waive their rules on age when they allowed an over-age player to join the club in an attempt to make them more competitive. The player in question was the Scots born Canadian, P (Pete) Stevenson. Another Canadian trained and Scots born youngster who joined at the same time was J (Johnny) Kelly. They made their debut against Glasgow University on 20 November but it was not to be a winning start as Varsity won 2-0.

Mohawks and Kelvingrove met in a league and Mitchell Trophy double header at the end of November. As "Inside Edge" noted "it is generally admitted that for sheer excitement nothing better than a clash between Kelvingrove and Mohawks can be provided in ice hockey." In their ten competitive matches to date, Kelvingrove had won seven and the other three had ended in draws.

Mohawks desperately wanted to break this sequence of domination but they were once again thwarted in the league match when they were held 1-1. It was a result which suited neither team. The real beneficiaries were Bridge of Weir who were maintaining their excellent start to the season at the top of the league table.

In the semi-final of the Mitchell Trophy, played only three days later, Mohawks were at full strength, with Ronald MacDonald and Tom Shearer forming the blue line and Jim Kenny was moved from defence to the forward line to partner Billy and John Fullerton. Kelvingrove were without the crafty Charlie McMillan, a big blow, but new boy Bobby Brown returned after missing the league match.

It was a typically thrilling and robust encounter between these two great rivals, settled five minutes from time, when Jim Kenny scored with a fine shot which struck a post before entering the net. After eleven attempts and four years Mohawks had their long awaited victory! The win was deserved, but the champions were simply not firing on all cylinders and seemed to be lacking the vim and vigour of the previous season.

At a meeting of the SIHA held on 4 December, a special presentation was made to Dave Carty, who had filled the position of Honorary Secretary since the ruling body was revived in 1929. Carty had also acted as a referee but he was now leaving the country to take up new employment in India.

Season 1934-1935

Carty's replacement as Honorary Secretary of the SIHA was J R Gilmour who was unanimously elected to the post. Jack Gilmour had enjoyed a long and distinguished career as a player with Bearsden and then latterly Bears and had also played on eight occasions for Scotland between 1931 and 1934. He was a well-kent and respected figure within the Scottish game who brought a great deal of valuable experience to his new job. The SIHA had chosen well.

The second semi-final of the Mitchell Trophy was played on 7 December between the high flying Bridge of Weir and the unpredictable Glasgow University. A keen match was expected and it did not disappoint. While Ian McLeod returned to play in his first match of the season, the lively and ever dangerous J O McCabe was an absentee for the students. In a very close and entertaining contest, Walter McLeod put Bridge of Weir ahead in the first period but Andrew Gray got a second period equaliser. Both teams went all out for the winning goal, but even after a period of extra time the two sides could not be separated. This stalemate was largely due to superb displays of goaltending from both Angus Ross and Ronald Milne.

The following day, a Bridge of Weir "select" team travelled to Birmingham to play Warwickshire from the English League Division One. Only four players from Bridge of Weir made the trip south, the remainder of the squad being made up of guest players from other Scottish teams. Although outplayed at times, the visitors gave a good account of themselves in a 3-2 defeat. The star of the evening was Ronald Milne who made no less than fifteen sprawl saves in the course of the match.

Glasgow University were dealt a double blow on the eve of their Mitchell Trophy semi-final re-play against Bridge of Weir on 14 December when it was announced that both Ronald Milne and Orvald Gratias were leaving the club. The popular Milne had accepted a business appointment in Manchester while Gratias was returning to his native Canada. Only Milne was available for the semi-final but he gave an inspirational performance as Varsity stunned Bridge of Weir with a 4-1 victory in front of the largest crowd of the season. Max Brennan put Bridge of Weir ahead in the first period but the students who were checking and close marking really well hit back in the middle session with two goals in quick succession from Andrew Gray. Bridge of Weir were clearly rattled and lost their discipline by taking a number of cheap penalties. They threw everything into attack in the final period but left gaps at the back which the young legs of Don Edwards and Andrew Gray fully exploited by adding two more goals for the students, the latter player completing a notable hat-trick.

Bridge of Weir were left bitterly disappointed; not only was this their first defeat of the season but they had harboured high expectations of winning the Mitchell Trophy - the only honour which had eluded the club. Glasgow University would now meet Mohawks in the final. For them it was an opportunity to make amends for their final humiliation of the previous season when they lost 8-1 to Kelvingrove.

Frozen in Time

The final of the Mitchell Trophy was played on 21 December and it promised to be an interesting contrast in styles. Mohawks had the fastest and most skilful forward line in the league but they would be up against a highly individualistic team always capable of springing a surprise. Varsity were boosted by the appearance of Ronald Milne who travelled back to Glasgow especially for this match.

It was an absorbing encounter. The teams were tied 0-0 at the end of the first period. In the middle session the deadlock was broken by the in-form Andrew Gray with a back flip shot which beat Duncan MacLachlan all ends up. Gray almost scored again immediately afterwards but the goaltender saved well before Ronald MacDonald scored an equalising goal on an assist from Billy Fullerton. Mohawks then took the lead when Jim Kenny lashed home a goal on another assist from the same player. In the final period Varsity went all out and both Andrew Gray and J O McCabe came very close to snatching an equaliser. In the final minutes, MacLachlan made a goal line clearance following a frantic scramble in his crease but Mohawks held on for a hard fought 2-1 victory. Although the students had played exceptionally well the superior combination of Mohawks told in the end and in Billy Fullerton they had the best player on the ice. Mohawks had finally won the Mitchell Trophy after five attempts!

A day later, Mohawks travelled to Birmingham to play Warwickshire. Like Bridge of Weir two weeks earlier they probably wished they had not bothered. Most of their first team made the trip but they were also bolstered by some guest players. It made little difference as Warwickshire triumphed by 10-4.

It is difficult to disagree with "Inside Edge" when he questioned the wisdom of playing matches like these. It was often the case that the Scottish teams were less than full strength and usually had to rely on guest players from other teams. There was no time for practice or for these players to familiarise themselves with each other prior to the match. The results of these contests were rarely good for the Scottish teams and merely served to undermine their prestige south of the border.

The first third of the league championship was almost completed by the end of the year. Bridge of Weir sat proudly if perhaps unexpectedly at the top of the league table with five wins from five matches for a total of 10 points. The reigning champions, Kelvingrove, were in second position with 7 points and Mohawks were some way back in third place with only 5 points.

At the other end of the table were Juniors who had played five and lost five. They had scored only 4 goals but had conceded a frightening 26! At least some attempt had been made to strengthen the team but it would take time for Pete Stevenson and Johnny Kelly, talented as they were, to turn things around.

The old year went out with something of a bang as the SIHA arranged for Scotland to play two international matches in as many days home and away. The opposition was provided by English League Division One teams,

Season 1934-1935

Mohawks Ice Hockey Club, 1934-35. Back Row; Tom Shearer, E K Reid, G A Porter, Gilmour Ayres, V A McCowan and Robert Carson (Manager). Front Row; Jack Gilmour, Ronald MacDonald, John Fullerton, Frank Thompson (President), Jim Kenny, Billy Fullerton and Charlie Russell

Frozen in Time

Wembley Canadians and Richmond Hawks. They were of course semi-professional outfits and they presented a major challenge for Pat Aitken who was in charge of Scotland for the first time.

The first match was against Wembley Canadians at the Empire Arena, London, on 27 December. The Scottish squad selected bore little resemblance to that picked to play against England earlier in the year. The only survivors from that squad were John and Billy Fullerton and Walter McLeod.

It would be a new look Scottish team which would take to the ice for these matches. In came Ronald Milne, now playing for Manchester, as goaltender, and the blue line would be protected by the Bridge of Weir pair, W G McDonald and Max Brennan. It was an all Mohawks first line of attack with Billy and John Fullerton and Jim Kenny. The second line of attack comprised Walter McLeod, Pete Stevenson of Juniors and Bill Russell of Dennistoun Eagles.

Wembley Canadians were an excellent team; the Scots put up a very encouraging performance, although they eventually lost a well-contested match 3-1. The home side scored two goals late in the first period, the second of which came from the stick of a player well known to Scottish ice hockey, Don Porter. Pete Stevenson pulled one back for Scotland in the second period but Jake Milford got his second goal in the final session to secure the win for Wembley Canadians. The match had not been as fast as expected, owing to the poor condition of the ice. The star of the Scottish team was Ronald Milne, though some observers thought that it had been rather unfair to drop Dave Cross who had never let the country down. Pat Aitken took the view that Scotland had played to their strengths which he interpreted as tight defence, effective checking and sound positional play. While no doubt true, the slower pace of the game undoubtedly suited Scotland more than it suited the swifter Wembley Canadians.

Hopes were raised that Scotland might spring a surprise in the next match against Richmond Hawks at Crossmyloof two days later. While Richmond were a good side they were not considered as strong as Wembley Canadians and it was thought that with home advantage the Scots might prevail. Unfortunately, the first choice defence of W G McDonald and Max Brennan, who had played so well at Wembley, were not available for this match.

Even worse was to follow as goaltender, Ronald Milne, failed to turn up for the match and young Billy Turnbull of Juniors was drafted in at literally the last minute as his replacement. This was of course far from an ideal situation and while Turnbull was a very promising goaltender, at only 17 years of age, it was obvious that he lacked the necessary experience required to face opponents of the calibre of Richmond Hawks.

Alec Fullerton of Kelvingrove and Joe Collins of Dennistoun Eagles completed the new defence, but Scotland's off-ice problems were only to be exacerbated as the chickens came home to roost. Scotland were 2-0 down at the end of the first period and 5-0 down by the end of the second. The visitors

Season 1934-1935

Scotland Team, December 1934. Back Row; Walter McLeod (Bridge of Weir), Billy Turnbull (Juniors), Jim Kenny (Mohauks), Pete Stevenson (Juniors), Billy Fullerton (Mohauks) and Pat Aitken (Coach). Front Row; Bill Russell (Dennistoun Eagles), Joe Collins (Dennistoun Eagles), Alec Fullerton (Kelvingrove) and John Fullerton (Mohauks).

Frozen in Time

added three more goals in the final period before Pete Stevenson scored a consolation goal just before the finish. It finished an embarrassing 8-1 for Richmond Hawks.

It would be easy but wholly unfair to solely blame Billy Turnbull for the margin of the defeat. It was noted that both Alec Fullerton and Joe Collins were often too easily outwitted besides being faulty in clearances but they had been overworked due to the lack of back-checking from the Scottish forwards. It seems that the tactical awareness so evident at Wembley went awry at Crossmyloof.

These latest reverses for the national team along with the defeats suffered by Bridge of Weir and Mohawks by Warwickshire in Birmingham brought the customary bout of soul searching by the local press and other observers over the state of the Scottish game compared to that south of the border.

This was not comparing like with like. The game in England at the highest level was now semi-professional. Their leading teams were full of imported Canadians specifically brought over from Canada to play ice hockey in England and to be paid for it. The game in Scotland remained amateur and the Canadians who played in the Scottish League still tended to be itinerant, players who just happened to be in Scotland working or studying. Crucially, they were of variable quality. In view of this situation was it really all that surprising that Scottish teams regularly failed against such opposition?

If there was disappointment at the continuing failure of the national team, at least one keen observer of the sport was more optimistic about the domestic game. In looking forward to the New Year, "Inside Edge" noted

> "One most satisfactory aspect of the present ice hockey season in Scotland is that dull games are few and far between quite different from previous years. There has been a definite levelling up of form among the clubs and for this no doubt, Pat Aitken, the coach, is largely responsible.
>
> There are now very few weaknesses apparent among the teams but there is still scope for stronger substitute lines. If that were achieved play could be maintained at a faster speed and the first forward line could be given longer rests."
>
> *(Daily Record and Mail: 8 January 1935).*

There was no doubt that the current set-up was competitive and generally entertaining but of the six teams comprising the league championship it remained the case that only three had any realistic prospect of winning it. Of the others, Dennistoun Eagles had certainly improved and Glasgow University remained unpredictable but problems continued at Juniors although positive steps had been taken to address these by recruiting better players.

The observation about substitute lines was well made. Lack of second forward lines in particular and adequate reserves more generally was a

Season 1934-1935

continuing problem at most clubs. There were simply not enough ice hockey players in the country of sufficient quality to fill the rosters of the various clubs though some teams were more affected than others.

Bridge of Weir were a case in point. The league leaders had played almost all season with only one substitute on the bench. Teams could just about get away with this provided they stayed clear of injuries, but ice hockey is a physically demanding sport and injuries are common. With only six players on the ice, a couple of injuries at the same time could decimate the playing strength of a team without adequate substitutes.

Bridge of Weir faced Kelvingrove in an important league match on 4 January with only seven players available. Their substitute was Earl Muirhead who had more or less retired from the sport due to business commitments in London. Nevertheless, the Renfrewshire side maintained their three point lead over Kelvingrove with a hard fought 0-0 draw in a match noted for poor play and an outstanding goaltending performance by the reliable Angus Ross.

A week later, a tired looking Bridge of Weir lost their first league match of the season when Mohawks defeated them 2-1 in a bruising contest. Mohawks were 1-0 down in the first period but John Fullerton restored parity in the middle session. It was left to his brother Billy to seal the win with a spectacular solo goal two minutes from time in the final period. It was a result Mohawks badly needed to stay in the championship race.

Mohawks had been gradually strengthening their team. Jim Kenny was turning out to be a first class addition to the squad. Small, bespectacled but sturdy, he was very fast and a brilliant stick-handler. Mohawks had originally played Kenny on defence but moved him to left wing in place of R F Winfield to partner the equally quick and skilful Fullerton brothers. In time, they would become the most deadly attack in the Scottish League.

Regular right defence, Ronald MacDonald, had been told to take it easier for a time as he had been experiencing a heart strain. The club acquired some very effective cover in the shape of G (Gilmour) Ayres and they also managed to coax Jack Gilmour out of semi-retirement for a few matches. Cover was also provided for goaltender, Duncan MacLachlan, when the reliable Greg Lennox re-joined Mohawks after an absence of two years.

Bridge of Weir's dip in form continued into their next match when they were held 1-1 by Glasgow University. Varsity had acquired a new goaltender, P (Peter) McKay, who replaced the departed Ronald Milne, but he was actually off the ice injured when Don Edwards scored their equalising goal late in the third period. McKay was a native of Hamilton, Ontario, and he looked a good prospect, having defied the Bridge of Weir forwards all evening with a string of great saves.

Bridge of Weir had now lost four points out of a possible six in their last three matches. That allowed Kelvingrove, following their successive wins over Juniors and Dennistoun Eagles, to catch up with them at the top of the league table. The latter match had been a thriller; it was testimony to how well the West End team were playing that they defeated a lively Dennistoun 4-1 without the injured Charlie McMillan and Bert Gemmell.

At the end of January, Kelvingrove and Bridge of Weir shared top position in the league championship with 12 points from 8 matches. Mohawks were in second position with 9 points from 7 matches. The second half of the season was shaping up to be quite a battle between these three traditional rivals although the momentum now seemed to be with the two Glasgow clubs.

At the other end of the table, Juniors finally got off the mark when they gained their first point of the season with a 2-2 draw against Glasgow University at the end of January. The result was also notable for the fact that they achieved it without star man Pete Stevenson. Varsity were also short-handed and this may have accounted for the appearance in their team of the experienced but semi-retired, A Rintoul, who scored one of their goals.

The absence of Pete Stevenson in Juniors recent matches had been the result of his remarkable call-up to the Great Britain team, which was participating in the European and World Championships in Davos, Switzerland.

An excellent player, Stevenson had not been in Scotland all that long, but his recent performances and goal scoring exploits against both Wembley Canadians and Richmond Hawks had clearly impressed the selectors at the BIHA. While no one in Scotland grudged Stevenson his elevation to the British team there was a view that there were other more likely prospects who also deserved such consideration. Thus Billy Fullerton and Walter McLeod, home-developed young men who played with a style and maturity way beyond their tender years, would have benefited enormously with involvement in the British set-up at this stage in their careers.

Nevertheless, it was a truly historic event: Pete Stevenson was the first player from the Scottish League to be selected for a Great Britain team participating in the European and World Championships.

Great Britain put in their best performance in the European Championships since the inaugural competition in 1910. The team finished second to Switzerland and that runners-up spot meant a third place finish in the World Championships, their best performance in that competition since 1924. Canada, represented on this occasion by the Winnipeg Monarchs, were the new world champions. Great Britain played a total of seven matches and Pete Stevenson played in all of them. He scored two goals in a 5-1 defeat of Latvia in the opening round of the competition. Another man with Scottish connections in the British team was the goaltender, Ronald Milne, who also played in all seven matches and gave a very good account of himself.

In the league championship, Bridge of Weir won their first match for nearly two months when they defeated Dennistoun Eagles 3-1 on 1 February thanks primarily to a brace from Walter McLeod who was in a very rich vein of form. Their closest rivals, Kelvingrove and Mohawks, met three days later.

Season 1934-1935

It was the West End team which prevailed yet again in this fixture. Charlie McMillan scored the winning goal in the third period for an important 1-0 victory. This result was a severe setback for Mohawks, who fell further behind in the title race.

Bridge of Weir maintained their winning ways with a laboured 2-1 victory over an improving Juniors side, but Kelvingrove slipped up when they were held to a 2-2 draw by Glasgow University in their next match. Indeed, the students were actually 2-0 ahead early in the first period but 'Grove, without Bert Gemmell and Bobby Brown, clawed their way back into the game and with a bit of luck might have snatched the victory near the end.

Attention became focussed on the third international match of the season as Scotland were scheduled to play Wembley Canadians in a return match at Crossmyloof on 16 February. Dave Cross, Max Brennan and W G McDonald came back into the side to form the defence and in attack Pete Stevenson replaced John Fullerton in the first line with Billy Fullerton and Jim Kenny. Walter McLeod and Bill Russell retained their positions. A place was allocated to Bobby Mills of Dennistoun Eagles but he unexpectedly returned to Canada a week before the match. Wisely the SIHA decided to allocate his place to an additional defender and Alec Fullerton was selected.

The match attracted a full house at Crossmyloof, but any hopes were dashed as they witnessed a very poor performance from a team completely outclassed by their opponents. Wembley Canadians won 7-0 and only the overworked Max Brennan, W G McDonald and Pete Stevenson gained any pass marks. Even the normally reliable Dave Cross had an off-night; it later emerged that he had not been fully fit, owing to a recent injury he sustained in the line of duty as a police officer.

There were few positives that the Scottish coach, Pat Aitken, could take out of this match. The team failed to function as a unit and seemed to lack any sense of tactical awareness. Of particular concern was the total failure of the forwards to make any impression. This was something that Aitken would have to take a long hard look at, though his options were limited.

The opening round of the President's Pucks commenced on 22 February with a match between Mohawks and Juniors. It was a disappointing affair settled in Mohawks favour with goals from the Fullerton brothers giving them a 2-0 win. Pete Stevenson played on defence for Juniors and missed two gilt-edged chances to score in the third period. Mohawks had been unconvincing but with their league title hopes diminishing this tournament gave them the opportunity to complete a unique "cup double".

Pete Stevenson more than made up for that disappointment by scoring five goals in Juniors' next league match, an amazing 8-1 demolition of Dennistoun Eagles. Juniors had gone ten matches in the championship without a win but they certainly broke their duck in some style. In truth, they had been improving of late, but the margin of victory raised a few eyebrows, not least at Dennistoun, who obviously missed the steadying influence and checking abilities of Joe Collins in this match.

With two-thirds of the league championship now completed Bridge of Weir remained in first position, with 16 points from 10 matches. Kelvingrove were pushing them hard in second place, only a point behind with the same number of matches played. In third place were Mohawks on 13 points from 10 matches. Bridge of Weir had managed to steady the ship following a recent dip in form; it may have crossed the minds of the two Glasgow clubs that the Renfrewshire side had come through this bad spell while retaining top position in the league.

The SIHA announced that the world champions, Canada, represented by Winnipeg Monarchs, would be visiting Crossmyloof in March. It was decided though that their opponents would not be Scotland but Great Britain. Given the track record of the Scottish team this decision smacked of discretion being the greater part of valour! The intention though was to select players from the Scottish League to ensure some local interest. "Inside Edge" also reported on some vague proposals to allow Scotland to compete in a re-organised English National League for next season. While a superficially attractive proposition, it was difficult to see how the Scots would be able to compete against semi-professional teams with any degree of parity. In any case the Scottish game remained strictly amateur, so such notions seemed merely fanciful.

Bridge of Weir took a major step towards winning the league championship when they defeated Kelvingrove 3-1 on 5 March. The match marked the return of Arthur Tingley to the reigning champions, but even he could not make any headway against a resolute Bridge of Weir defence. It was a typically punishing and keenly contested match and while 'Grove had the better of the exchanges in the final period the better team won. W G McDonald gave Bridge of Weir an early lead but Sid Montford equalised in the second period. Max Brennan deservedly restored the Renfrewshire side's lead. Despite incessant pressure from Kelvingrove in the final session, the effervescent Walter McLeod scored an opportunist third and clinching breakaway goal in trademark fashion to give the league leaders both points.

The result was a body blow to Kelvingrove, who had only three days to recover before playing Juniors in their next match. They were missing four first team regulars for this game including goaltender Dave Cross, but no one really expected them to slip up again. Juniors had not read the script, however, and with Pete Stevenson in brilliant form they raced into a 3-0 lead by the end of the second period. Arthur Tingley got two goals back for Kelvingrove in the final period but it was a case of too little too late. Juniors held out for an unexpected 3-2 victory. Those two reverses effectively ended the defending champions' title aspirations for the season.

Bridge of Weir were of course the real beneficiaries of this latest defeat. Already three points ahead of Kelvingrove they now had the opportunity to

Season 1934-1935

go five points clear of them if they won their game in hand. The Renfrewshire side also progressed to the semi-finals of the President's Pucks when in a rather laboured performance they defeated Glasgow University 2-1. Walter McLeod scored both of their goals after Andrew Gray had put Varsity ahead.

An interesting feature of this match was the appearance in the Bridge of Weir team of young Johnny Kelly of Juniors. The SIHA allowed him to turn out as a "guest" player because the Renfrewshire team was seriously short of personnel for this match and because Juniors had no further interest in this competition, having been eliminated by Mohawks.

Enormous interest was stimulated by the news that an international "double-header" had been arranged for 15 and 16 March. On the former date, Great Britain would play Canada, represented by the world champions, Winnipeg Monarchs, at Crossmyloof and the following evening Scotland would play England at the Empire Arena in Wembley, London.

Canada's visit to Glasgow was the final match of an extensive European tour where they had lost only three and drawn four out of 57 matches played. Their star players included goaltender Art Rice-Jones, brothers Albert and Tony Lemay, Norm Yellowlees and Vic Lindquist. The appearance of the current world champions at Crossmyloof attracted a full house, with each spectator paying 2s for the privilege.

Four players from the Scottish League were selected for the Great Britain squad. These players were the Bridge of Weir trio of Max Brennan, W G McDonald and Walter McLeod with Billy Fullerton of Mohawks. Additional Scottish interest was provided by the appearance of the Manchester based Ronald Milne in goal. Although Great Britain tried hard they were no match for Canada who won 7-2, the two British goals coming in the final minutes when the visitors were 7-0 ahead and cruising.

For the sixth home international, the SIHA and the BIHA agreed that only players born in Great Britain were eligible for selection. For Scotland this meant that the usual first team defence of Max Brennan and W G McDonald were ruled out, a serious handicap. Since Alec Fullerton and Joe Collins were not available either, the selectors decided that Pete Stevenson and Wilbur Muirhead should form a new and rather experimental defence in front of Ronald Milne. In attack, the all-Mohawks forward line of Billy and John Fullerton and Jim Kenny was again tried. The second line would comprise Walter McLeod, Johnny Kelly and Bill Russell. If Kelly's elevation to the Scottish team was a surprise it was nothing compared to the selection of Gilmour Ayres of Mohawks who completed the line-up.

The two teams were:

England: G Mason (Wembley Canadians); J Carr (Cambridge University) and C A Erhardt (Streatham); G Davey (Streatham), G Johnson (Manchester) and E J Ramus (Streatham). - R Wyman (Wembley Canadians), R W Couldray (Streatham), I Nesbitt (Richmond Hawks) and P Halford (Streatham).

Scotland: R S Milne (Manchester); P Stevenson (Juniors) and W M Muirhead (Bridge of Weir); W Fullerton (Mohawks), J Fullerton (Mohawks) and J Kenny (Mohawks). - W S McLeod (Bridge of Weir), J Kelly (Juniors), W W Russell (Dennistoun Eagles) and G Ayres (Mohawks).

Referee: ?

Every player selected by England had learned to play the game in Canada whereas about half of the Scottish team was home developed. The match attracted about 6,000 spectators to Wembley and they were treated to an extremely entertaining contest, in the main owing to a much better than expected performance from the visitors. Wilbur Muirhead put Scotland ahead after only two minutes but England recovered to lead 3-1 by the end of the first period. Gerry Davey completed his hat-trick at the start of the middle session to make the score 4-1 but then Walter McLeod scored after a bout of passing with Jim Kenny. J Carr scored again for England to give them a 5-2 lead at the interval. In an exciting third period, Pete Stevenson scored a magnificent solo goal to reduce the deficit but P Halford added another goal to give England a 6-3 victory.

While there was disappointment that Scotland had lost for the fourth successive time against England, most observers were heartened by their performance. Ronald Milne, Wilbur Muirhead, Walter McLeod and Pete Stevenson were all marked out for special praise. However "Inside Edge" noted that "the Mohawks trio, the Fullerton brothers and Kenny, opposed as they were to England's first line of attack, went through a gruelling ordeal and found it impossible to develop their usual combined game."

On the domestic front, Bridge of Weir consolidated their lead at the top of the league championship with a narrow 2-1 win against Glasgow University on 26 March. They were without Angus Ross and Max Brennan for this match but R G Walker, the ex-Bears goaltender, was an able deputy for Ross. Bridge of Weir were now five points clear of Kelvingrove. With only three matches left, Mohawks now looked to be their main challengers.

Three days later, Bridge of Weir faced Mohawks in the semi-final of the President's Pucks. The Renfrewshire side were once again seriously short handed for this important match with Max Brennan and W G McDonald absent from duty. Johnny Kelly was again drafted in to bolster the attack. It was too much of a handicap against an ever improving Mohawks team who ran out easy winners by 7-1. Billy and John Fullerton both secured hat-tricks.

Mohawks opponents in the final would be Kelvingrove, who also had an easier than expected passage in their semi-final when they defeated Dennistoun Eagles 4-1. The West End team were without Andy Dick and Charlie McMillan, but they were still too strong for a disappointing Dennistoun side. Arthur Tingley scored a hat-trick and new boy, C Nevitt, notched the other goal on his debut.

Season 1934-1935

Bridge of Weir entered the final phase of the league championship three points ahead of Mohawks and five points ahead of Kelvingrove with three matches left. All three teams won their next games, but then Mohawks met Kelvingrove in their penultimate fixture which ended in a thrilling 4-4 draw. This result suited neither team. It meant that if Bridge of Weir avoided defeat in their next match against Juniors, the Canada Cup would be heading to Renfrewshire for the second time.

Mohawks and Kelvingrove met again only three days later on 19 April to contest the final of the President's Pucks. Both teams were desperate to win, Mohawks to achieve a unique "cup double" having already won the Mitchell Trophy, and Kelvingrove to finish a disappointing season with at least some silverware. As expected the match was extremely close and required two periods of extra time to settle it. Both teams played cautiously with much checking and safety first tactics in evidence. John Fullerton put Mohawks ahead in the first period with a shot which deflected off the stick of Dave Cross. It looked like staying that way until ten seconds from time when his brother Alec equalised for Kelvingrove amidst great excitement. The first period of extra time was goalless. In the second session, John Fullerton made his way up the ice and drew the 'Grove defence enough for Billy Fullerton to exploit the gap and score the winning goal for Mohawks.

It had been a unique occasion in that all three Fullerton brothers had scored all of the goals in the match. Mohawks had now got a monkey off their backs with this latest success against Kelvingrove, albeit in the two cup competitions. The cut-and-thrust of cup tie ice hockey seemed to suit Mohawks, who played a fast and offensive game but who were often vulnerable at the back.

Defence was certainly not an issue for Kelvingrove, but they had spent most of the season searching for the right formula in attack. The club had tried various forward combinations without finding the right answer. Injuries to key players had played a part; the unavailability of Arthur Tingley for a large part of the season had been a huge blow, but given the overall talent at their disposal more had been expected from the West End club.

Arthur Tingley had departed Glasgow for the last time, and didn't play in the final of the President's Pucks. He would be sorely missed. Tall and well built, and a really outstanding player for both Queen's and 'Grove during his four and a half years at Crossmyloof, he was famous for his exciting one-man rushes up the ice, his industrious back-checking, his sportsmanship and his prodigious goal making and goal taking abilities. He finished leading goal scorer in season 1929-30 (First Division) and joint leading goal scorer in season 1932-33, on both occasions with Queen's. He scored both goals in Queen's 2-0 victory over 'Grove in the re-played Mitchell Trophy final in 1932. He played on seven occasions for Scotland between 1930 and 1933 and twice for Great Britain in 1930 and 1933, and scored two goals during his international career.

Frozen in Time

Bridge of Weir clinched their second league championship and Canada Cup on 23 April when they drew 2-2 with Juniors. The youngsters made a real fight of it taking the lead in the first period but goals from Walter McLeod and W G McDonald in the middle session steadied the nerves of the Renfrewshire side. They finished the season on 23 points; although there were still some matches to play they could not now be caught.

No one could seriously argue that Bridge of Weir did not deserve the title. They had the best defence in the league, thanks to the efforts of a much under-rated goaltender in Angus Ross and an exceptional blue line in Max Brennan and W G McDonald. Apart from their solid checking and sound positional play, which was of the highest order, the two Canadians were also brilliant at setting up attacks and finishing them. They had scored 17 of their team's 39 goals during the league campaign.

The versatility of Brennan and McDonald was matched by that stalwart of the Bridge of Weir team, Wilbur Muirhead. He could also play in either defence or attack; as a big man, his sheer physical presence was very intimidating to any opponents. The real star of the team though was the talented Walter McLeod who had enjoyed a wonderful campaign. He finished joint top scorer in the league championship with Billy Fullerton and Pete Stevenson on 14 goals and was, in most observers' opinion, the player of the season. Bridge of Weir had won the league championship despite the unavailability of key players at different stages of the season. On a number of occasions the champions had struggled to ice a full team and most times they had only one substitute player on the bench. Old campaigners like Jimmy Woodrow, Ian McLeod and Earl Muirhead had been obliged to come out of their semi-retirement and plug the gaps when necessary. It says everything about the ethos underpinning this great family club that these players did that so willingly.

Fixture congestion had caused a situation where the four remaining fixtures of the season had to be squeezed into the last week of April. Bridge of Weir having secured the league title against Juniors the evening before were obliged to face Mohawks the following evening! This was too much even for Bridge of Weir and they were forced to recruit a number of guest players to fulfil the fixture. This patch-work side defeated Mohawks 7-2. Not surprisingly Mohawks objected. The SIHA agreed that they had a case and the two points won by Bridge of Weir were forfeited and awarded to Mohawks. This action seemed reasonable in the circumstances but the ultimate responsibility for this shambles laid with the SIHA themselves who had not managed the extended fixture list in an efficient enough manner. Worse was to come. The two final fixtures of the season were played on the same evening! The second of these two fixtures was a match between Mohawks and Dennistoun Eagles. However, since neither club was able to ice a full team the SIHA agreed to scratch the fixture altogether. The two teams played an exhibition match instead with a number of guest players turning out for each.

Season 1934-1935

It was a farcical end to what nevertheless had been an interesting season. Although the "big three" had again dominated for the honours the other three teams had their moments. Juniors produced a late surge in form, but that did not prevent them from finishing in bottom position on goal difference from Dennistoun Eagles. That improvement in form was almost entirely due to the efforts of Pete Stevenson, with some assistance from Johnny Kelly.

Glasgow University were as usual unpredictable. Lack of coaching remained a problem at a club always capable of icing good individual players but short on teamwork and organisation. Their cause had not been helped by the departures of Ronald Milne and Orvald Gratias but a word of praise was certainly due to Felix McLernan, an institution at the club, a man who had played in almost every position for the team including goaltender!

What was one to make of Dennistoun Eagles? At the midway point of the season it actually looked as though they might seriously challenge the "big three" in the championship but then they simply fell away again. Dennistoun had arguably their strongest ever team, with international players in Joe Collins and Bill Russell along with the more than useful Bobby Mills and Glen Braid. Yet they failed to make the breakthrough. Again, lack of coaching was in evidence but one cannot help concluding that the team had seriously underachieved.

At the start of the season the hope had been expressed that Glasgow University and Dennistoun Eagles might close the gap a bit further on the "big three". Hope was one thing - reality was quite another. Unfortunately that gap had just increased. Glasgow University had finished fourth but 11 points behind Kelvingrove in third position. In season 1933-34, Varsity had also finished fourth but only 4 points behind Bridge of Weir in third place.

This season had more than ever emphasised the gulf in class between Bridge of Weir, Mohawks and Kelvingrove at the top and Glasgow University, Dennistoun Eagles and Juniors at the bottom. The Scottish League really consisted of two mini leagues, one for the "big three" and one for the "rest".

As for Scotland, it continued to be an uphill struggle with a record of played four, lost four. However, these bare statistics mask a couple of decent performances which gave some grounds for optimism in the future. Pat Aitken had made a difference but the transient character of the Scottish game which saw players coming and going so much did little to build stability and inspire confidence.

In England, a star-studded Streatham which included Carl Erhardt, Gerry Davey and Ernie Ramus won the English League Division One. Wembley Canadians, no strangers to Scotland, finished second and their stable companions, Wembley Lions, finished third. The sport in England was booming with the various teams in the top tier being staffed with well paid semi-professional Canadians. Attendances at matches were at an all time high. There were exciting plans to expand again in the season ahead when new clubs would join an elite English National League.

Frozen in Time

Expansion though was not confined to England. The game in Scotland received a huge boost with the news that plans were being put forward to construct a new ice rink in Perth capable of staging ice hockey matches. This was a long-awaited but nevertheless welcome development, as for the first time it seemed the sport might be able to expand beyond the rather restrictive confines of Crossmyloof Ice Rink and lay the foundations for becoming truly national in scope. It at last opened the possibility of a genuine "Scottish" League being formed.

Season 1935-36

At its Annual General Meeting held on 30 April 1935, the Scottish Ice Hockey Association re-elected its office-bearers for the coming year. The ruling body stayed with the tried and trusted as Frank Stuart remained as president and Andrew Mitchell retained his position as vice-president. Both of these gentlemen were also directors of the Scottish Ice Rink Company, the proprietors of Crossmyloof Ice Rink. Jack Gilmour was re-appointed as honorary secretary of the SIHA and confirmed his intention to try and retire from playing the game having enjoyed a brief cameo role with Mohawks the previous season. Ian H Borland, the ex-Glasgow University player, was appointed as treasurer and the executive council of the SIHA was completed with the appointments of Mark Cohen of Kelvingrove and a Mr J Porteus.

The administration of Scottish ice hockey was therefore in experienced and able hands. That was just as well as the sport commenced the new season in something of a crisis. During the summer months two clubs - Dennistoun Eagles and Juniors - had taken the decision to cease playing. A later proposal to establish a new club, to be known as Mustangs, only added to the turmoil encompassing Crossmyloof as the new season approached. The writing had been on the wall for Juniors for some time. The club had almost been disbanded the season before but the SIHA had agreed to persevere with it for a third season. The establishment of a junior team to compete at senior level had been a novel but ultimately flawed experiment. The club was always up against it, since its best players simply moved on to senior teams when the time was deemed right to do so.

The responsibility for bringing on any promising youngsters would now fall primarily on Graham Fraser, the newly appointed coach of the SIHA. He replaced the departed Pat Aitken whose tenure in the post had lasted only one year. Fraser was a native of Halifax, Nova Scotia, and had wide experience of the game.

The demise of Dennistoun Eagles was as unexpected as it was sad. Founder members of the revived SIHA in 1929, it was something of a curiosity that in six seasons of formal competition Dennistoun had never been serious contenders for any of the sport's major honours. The East End club had consistently failed to shine in the league championship, and they never reached the final of either cup competition.

It was perhaps that singular lack of success which ultimately led to the club's demise. Dennistoun never seemed to have been seriously short of players, but quantity is no substitute for quality and their constant underachievement sapped morale. That stated, some very good players had worn the club's colours over the years, none better than Tom Nisbet, but other players of note included Don Edwards, Bill Russell and Joe Collins.

The SIHA was set to start the season with only four clubs before the Glasgow-based Mustangs came along. The main instigator in founding the new club was Robert H Gardiner, who had also been instrumental in the establishment of Kelvingrove in 1929. He initially played for Kelvingrove before moving to Glasgow University in 1930 where he had been a regular for five seasons. Gardiner had been energetic in recruiting for his new club. From the ashes of Juniors and Dennistoun Eagles came goaltender Billy Turnbull and forwards Glen Braid, Bill Russell and Johnny Kelly. He also brought Don Edwards with him from Glasgow University but his biggest captures were the Bridge of Weir and Scotland defensive duo, Max Brennan and W G McDonald.

The defection of Brennan and McDonald in particular gave Mustangs a competitive look, but where it left defending champions Bridge of Weir was quite another matter. Why the two Canadian students left the Renfrewshire side has not been recorded; one might assume that personal reasons were involved. Their departure left a gaping hole in the Bridge of Weir team.

That was not the least of Bridge of Weir's problems. Long serving regulars Ian McLeod and Jimmy Woodrow had intimated their definite retirement as players from the sport but the real bombshell came with the news that Walter McLeod was also giving up the game to concentrate on his other great sporting passion, golf. Young Walter had received a nasty injury just above one of his eyes the previous season; this had made up his mind to devote his talents to the more sedate pastures of the golf course where he was already making serious headway as a first class amateur.

All of this was hardly ideal preparation for the defending champions, who were due to play Mohawks in the first league match of the season on 5 October. Would they be able to ice a team? The club held a meeting the day before the opening match to assess the situation but no one was really prepared for the outcome; disbandment!

"Inside Edge" reported the proceedings as follows

> "The decision to disband was made at a full meeting of the club on Thursday night, the chief reason being that any team they could put on the ice would not represent the Bridge of Weir community and they were not prepared to import players from other districts."
>
> *(Daily Record and Mail: 5 October 1935).*

Season 1935-1936

The statement issued by the club encapsulated everything they were about. Not only were Bridge of Weir a community club but they were also a family club. The core of the club had always been provided by two families in particular; the McLeods and the Muirheads. They were however being slightly disingenuous in suggesting that they did not like "importing" players. Max Brennan and W G McDonald had been exactly that, although they had been the exceptions to this rule.

Shortage of local players was undoubtedly the main reason for the drastic course of action taken by Bride of Weir but pride may also have played a part. They had been a very successful club, so the prospect of having to struggle in the lower echelons of the game perhaps did not appeal to the remaining players. Bridge of Weir would not have been able to compete on an equal footing with Kelvingrove and Mohawks as they had done in the past, and that fact would also have contributed to their decision to disband. A great pity and a disappointing end for the last non-Glasgow club in the Scottish League.

Founder members of the SIHA in 1929, when they were also referred to as Ranfurly, Bridge of Weir had completed six seasons at Crossmyloof. They had won the Canada Cup twice as league champions in seasons 1932-33 and 1934-35 and the President's Pucks in season 1933-34. The only honour to elude the club was the Mitchell Trophy. Although they did get to the final of that competition in season 1932-33, they lost to Bears in controversial circumstances.

In their six seasons, Bridge of Weir had played a total of 77 competitive matches for an overall record of 41 wins, 24 losses and 12 draws. In the Points Competition, First Division and Canada Cup their record was 34 wins, 16 losses and 8 draws out of 58 matches played. In the Mitchell Trophy they played 13 matches with a record of 3 wins, 6 losses and 4 draws and in the President's Pucks they played 6 matches with a record of 4 wins and 2 losses.

Some outstanding players had worn the colours of Bridge of Weir over the years including Wilbur Muirhead, Gordon Rowley, Walter McLeod, Max Brennan and W G McDonald. Known for a somewhat abrasive and robust style of play, Bridge of Weir would be sadly missed and their unfortunate demise was another black day for the SIHA.

The loss of Bridge of Weir, along with that of Dennistoun Eagles and Juniors left the SIHA with only four senior clubs in membership, its lowest number yet. The ruling body acted quickly and decisively by announcing that another new club would be formed by utilising the available spare talent left around the circuit. If this manoeuvre appeared to be something of a "patch-up" job that's exactly what it was.

In such circumstances were formed the Crossmyloof Lions Ice Hockey Club. In truth, Lions as they came to be known, were on a hiding to nothing from the start. Cobbled together at the last minute, what chance did this team have? They had never trained or practiced together let alone actually played with each other.

Lions' best known player was Earl Muirhead, who was now available to play on a regular basis again but most of the club's other recruits were or had been squad players with other teams. They included J M Newton and H S Finnie from Dennistoun Eagles, D Jackson from Juniors, Joe Beveridge from Kelvingrove, Charlie Russell from Mohawks and out of semi-retirement, L W Sproule, ex-Bears. The key position of goaltender was entrusted to G Henderson who had been the understudy to Billy Turnbull at Juniors. It was difficult not to conclude that the sole purpose of Lions was simply to make up the numbers.

Following all of this off-ice drama the new season would finally get underway with just five clubs; Glasgow University, Kelvingrove, Lions, Mohawks and Mustangs. In view of this, the SIHA decided that the league championship should consist of four rounds; each team would play the other on four occasions for a total of 40 fixtures commencing in early October and concluding at the end of April. Each team would play 16 fixtures, the most ever in the history of the league championship. The SIHA also decided to change the running order of the two cup competitions. The Mitchell Trophy was restored to its rightful position at the end of the season with the President's Pucks brought forward to the autumn. This gave a proper precedence to the former competition as befitting its status as the more senior of the two.

Of the established clubs, Mohawks appeared to be the least affected by changes. They had retained all of their regular first team players, giving the side a very settled look. The double cup winners had a good balance about them and their prospects for the season ahead were considerably enhanced by the signings of ex-Juniors, A G (Archie) Bogie and Pete Stevenson.

The arrival of Stevenson in particular was a major coup for Mohawks. The Great Britain international could play equally well in defence or attack, such was his ability. His presence gave Mohawks a number of tactical options, leading "Inside Edge" in the *Daily Record and Mail* to suggest that the club was entering the new season with its strongest ever squad.

Kelvingrove also managed to retain most of their key players although that had to be balanced against the loss of Arthur Tingley. Having won nothing the previous season, the West End club were very keen to improve on that situation leading them to sign a number of new players for the campaign ahead. Two ex-Dennistoun men were acquired in Eric Montford, now joining his brother Sid at Kelvingrove, and Sam Stevenson and from Juniors, Ken Hurll.

As for their prospects much would depend on whether they found the right blend in attack, a problem area the previous season. The signings of the useful Hurll and Stevenson gave Kelvingrove further options up front but the club were looking to strengthen further by acquiring a player with Canadian experience if possible. The defence remained on the usual solid lines.

Glasgow University had lost the services of a number of important players. Their Canadian goaltender, Peter McKay, had left and long standing right

Season 1935-1936

defence, Robert Gardiner, had defected to establish Mustangs. He had taken with him the impressive Don Edwards but perhaps the biggest blow of all was the decision of J O McCabe to retire from playing to concentrate on refereeing.

On the plus side, Glasgow University signed two ex-Mohawks, goaltender Duncan MacLachlan and left wing R F Winfield. Their biggest capture though was that man of many clubs, Joe Collins, who gave their blue line a much more solid look. The decision of A Rintoul and Felix McLernan to play another season also gave Varsity some much needed continuity.

The signing of Joe Collins, and possibly some of their other more recent players, was significant for another reason. He had never studied at Glasgow University nor had he any other connection with it. The original constitution of the club had apparently stipulated that only students, teaching staff or alumni could play for them but this was now evidently no longer the case. The club was obviously bowing to the pressure to become more competitive but in doing so perhaps something else equally important was being lost; the game for the game's sake.

It was with a sense of relief that the league championship finally got underway on 8 October with a match between Glasgow University and Mustangs. The new boys on the block got off to a winning start by defeating Varsity 2-1, the decisive goal coming from the stick of Max Brennan a minute from full time.

Kelvingrove opened their account with a rather laboured 3-0 victory against the other new team, Lions. Opinion was divided as to how well Lions had played in their first match. "The Blade" in the *Evening Times* suggested they were unfortunate not to get a draw whereas the ice hockey correspondent of the *Glasgow Herald* thought they were "far from impressive."

Mohawks started their campaign with an impressive 5-1 defeat of Glasgow University though perhaps surprisingly Pete Stevenson failed to find the net.

The ice hockey correspondent of the *Glasgow Herald* noted with disappointment that the colours worn by the new teams, Lions and Mustangs, seemed to be an unsightly "hotchpotch" of all the recently disbanded clubs, namely Bridge of Weir, Dennistoun Eagles, Juniors and Bears. He perhaps correctly went on to point out that "clothes may not make either man or team but unfortunately can play its part."

While the sartorial elegance of Mustangs was being called into question there were more pressing concerns in some quarters about their early season form following two successive defeats by Kelvingrove and Mohawks. Both matches were only lost by the odd goal; both could have been won. In fairness to Mustangs it takes time for a new team to settle.

In early November, Mohawks accepted an invitation to play Birmingham Maple Leafs away in a challenge match. This club was formerly known as Warwickshire but had changed their name in line with league re-construction in England where they now played in the English League Northern Section, effectively the Second Division. In the corresponding fixture the previous season the Midlands side had won 10-4; they repeated the dose again with a comprehensive 13-2 mauling of the Glasgow team.

Two days later Mohawks met Kelvingrove in their first confrontation of the season. Although Mohawks had finally broken their duck against their old rivals in the two cup competitions the season before, they had yet to defeat Kelvingrove in a league championship fixture. In their eight league matches to date, the West End club had won six and the other two had been drawn.

Kelvingrove managed to maintain this remarkable sequence of results over Mohawks with a tight but deserved 2-1 victory. Two early goals from Charlie McMillan, who was now centre to wing men Sid Montford and Bert Gemmell, unsettled Mohawks for the rest of the match. It was not until the third period that Billy Fullerton pulled a goal back but the formidable 'Grove defence conceded no more.

The first quarter of the league championship was completed on 8 November with each team having played four matches. Kelvingrove, the only unbeaten team, sat at the top of the league with 7 points. Mohawks were second on 6 points followed by Mustangs on 4 points. Glasgow University had accumulated 3 points but Lions had yet to get off the mark.

Indeed, Lions were already causing real concern. Lions had only managed to score 2 goals so far; they had conceded a staggering 28, an average of 7 per match! In one recent match Mustangs had thrashed them 11-1 with Bill Russell and Johnny Kelly helping themselves to four goals apiece. To rub salt into the wounds, Mohawks inflicted a 9-1 defeat in their next match, Jim Kenny scoring five of these goals. Lions' luckless goaltender, G Henderson, had been dropped after the debacle against Mustangs but his replacement, Joe Beveridge, had then fared little better against Mohawks. Such reverses sapped morale. More recruits were drafted in. Wilbur Muirhead, the ex-Bridge of Weir and Scotland international, joined his brother Earl at the club but even he would have his work cut out to try and improve the situation. Goaltending had of course been seen as a major problem at the club but Lions took steps to address that with the capture of an American student, T (Tom) Nicol, now studying in Glasgow. Nicol was a native of Philadelphia and came to the Lions goal having gained some college league experience in his native land.

Mohawks and Scottish ice hockey in general received a blow with the unexpected departure of Pete Stevenson who was moving to Manchester to live. An outstanding exponent of the game, he was equally adept in defence or attack, a dazzling stick-handler and a deadly finisher. Stevenson had played on four occasions for Scotland between 1934 and 1935 and remained the only player from the Scottish League to have been selected for Great Britain in the European and World Championships.

The SIHA introduced a couple of new initiatives to improve the game. The recent match between Kelvingrove and Mohawks had seen the introduction of two referees for the first time in a Scottish League match. In future a red light would be flashed to signal when a goal had been scored. In the past a goal judge stood behind the goal net but would now sit in the balcony immediately above the goal area for a better view. It was hoped these innovations, common elsewhere in the ice hockey world, would assist the match officials in avoiding controversial decisions as far as possible.

A new public address system was also introduced at Crossmyloof as an aid to better communication with the paying public. The idea was to assist and enhance the actual experience of spectators in watching matches and to explain refereeing decisions such as penalties. Attendances at matches continued to be encouraging. It was noticeable that more women and children were being attracted to the games as ice hockey was keen to brand itself as a family sport. With admission prices fixed at 9d for domestic matches spectators were receiving value for money.

Another important initiative undertaken by the SIHA was the establishment of a Junior League for boys aged between 14 and 17 years. Teams were attached to four of the senior clubs, Kelvingrove, Lions, Mohawks and Mustangs, but the players would actually be under the tutelage of the SIHA coach, Graham Fraser. The necessary ice time at Crossmyloof was found for both practice and matches, no mean feat in itself, with the four teams competing against each other in a formal league competition.

This was of course only the latest attempt by the SIHA to encourage and develop junior talent, previous experiments having fallen by the wayside. This initiative looked to have a better prospect of success. It linked junior development directly into the senior clubs, and had the added bonus of dedicated coaching from a fully qualified individual who had the time and patience required to undertake the task. The SIHA was to be commended for its perseverance in this matter.

Many of the younger players involved in ice hockey were members of the Glasgow Speed Skating Club including its honorary secretary, Joe Beveridge of Lions, along with his team-mates, H S Finnie and D Harvie. Membership of the club was restricted to 40 by the rink management at Crossmyloof. Its primary aim was to produce speed skaters capable of competing in official championships but for those who played ice hockey, it assisted in enhancing their speed and skill in playing the game.

John and Billy Fullerton of Mohawks were of course long-standing members of the speed skating fraternity at Crossmyloof. Both were very proficient at the sport. John had won the Scottish half-mile outdoor title in 1933 at Loch Leven and Billy won the mile event at the same venue early in 1935. He would repeat that feat on 15 February 1936.

Billy Fullerton also challenged for the British one mile indoor championship in May 1935 but finished in second place. However, success in this event was only delayed as he would win this prestigious title at Streatham Ice Rink on 29 February 1936 with a time of three minutes and thirteen seconds. Glasgow Speed Skating Club awarded him with an honorary life membership in recognition of this latest achievement in the sport.

Billy Fullerton was the only Scot possessing the National Skating Association Gold Medal, an award only given to those who had skated a mile in three minutes, fifteen seconds, or better. Not for nothing was Billy known as "The Flying Mohawk"!

The first round of the President's Pucks competition commenced on 19 November with a tie between Glasgow University and Mustangs. Varsity had lost two league matches 1-0 against this opposition; amazingly that score was repeated in this tournament. A goal from Bill Russell in the third period was all that separated the two teams. That was partly due to a brilliant display of goaltending from Duncan MacLachlan but the university men had played well generally.

Mustangs had been getting better with each match played and they underlined that improvement with an impressive 4-0 win over the thus far undefeated Kelvingrove in the league championship at the end of November. A match where everything clicked into place for Mustangs, it demonstrated just what a good side they could be. Max Brennan was the best player on the ice, capping a great performance with a sensational individual goal in the final period.

Mohawks kept pace with Kelvingrove and Mustangs as the championship developed into the expected three-horse race. They had moved quickly to strengthen their ranks following the sudden departure of Pete Stevenson by signing a fellow native of Port Arthur, Ontario, the 20-year-old W S (Walter) "Wally" Welch. He was a rugged left defence who packed a hefty shot, demonstrated by scoring a goal on his debut for Mohawks against Glasgow University in a 4-0 win.

Glasgow University had rather struggled thus far, their only victories in the league championship coming against the hapless Lions. Given the squad they had assembled, some observers thought they were underachieving but this view seemed unrealistic. The unavailability of Joe Collins in recent matches had not helped their cause, but the team was showing a greater degree of combination and passing than was usual for Varsity. Despite that, nothing other than a fourth place finish looked likely.

The first semi-final of the President's Pucks was played on 3 December when Mohawks defeated Lions 5-0. The result was not entirely unexpected ,given the current form of the two sides, but it masked a plucky performance by Lions who were unfortunate to lose by such a big margin. An interesting addition to their team was Walter McLeod, who would make the odd appearance for Lions as the season progressed.

The other semi-final, played three days later, was a very much closer contest between Kelvingrove and Mustangs. The latter were in a very good spell of

Season 1935-1936

form but the West End team were determined that there would be no repeat of their recent heavy league defeat. As a result, Kelvingrove adopted a safety first approach to the match based on close marking and solid checking. Ken Hurll opened the scoring for 'Grove mid way through the first period on an assist from Alec Fullerton. The middle session was an even affair. In the third period Mustangs exerted a great deal of pressure, but the Kelvingrove defence just managed to hold out to secure the 1-0 victory. Dave Cross had played splendidly in goal. Such was the intensity of the exchanges that at one point in the final period both teams had two players in the penalty box at the same time.

For the third time in the four years' history of this competition Kelvingrove and Mohawks would go head to head in the final. It was Kelvingrove's fourth successive final; they were desperately keen to win it, having lost the previous two encounters. On the other hand, Mohawks had defeated their old rivals in the final of the previous season and were keen to repeat the experience.

The final of the President's Pucks was contested on 20 December and as expected it was a thriller. Sid Montford put Kelvingrove ahead after only six minutes with a long range shot which some thought Greg Lennox might have saved. Mohawks improved in the second period and Billy Fullerton scored the equaliser following a melée in front of the unsighted Dave Cross. Kelvingrove protested that the puck had been kicked into the goal but the referees, Graham Fraser and Andrew Gray, disagreed and allowed the goal to stand. Mohawks dominated the final period but met with the usual stout resistance from a resolute 'Grove defence. Two periods of extra time were played in an attempt to separate the two teams but to no avail. Billy Fullerton almost snatched it in the final minute but was thwarted by a brilliant save from Dave Cross. The match ended 1-1. In many respects the final had been a classic Kelvingrove and Mohawks encounter, the solid and determined defence of the former largely containing the fast and skilful forwards of the latter. "The Blade" was of the opinion that Mohawks had been unfortunate not to win but not many observers grudged the West End team the draw. The replay would be held on 17 January.

Before then, the two teams met again on 3 January in a crucial league match. The first period was goalless but in the middle session John Fullerton scored for Mohawks on a rebound off the pads of Dave Cross. With Kelvingrove chasing the game in the final period, John and then Billy Fullerton added to Mohawks total. This was hard on their opponents, who did not deserve to lose by such a large margin. It was notable that Jack Gilmour played in goal for Mohawks, in the absence of the injured Greg Lennox. It was a historic victory for Mohawks. At long last they had beaten Kelvingrove in a league championship match. It had been a wait of six years. In the previous nine meetings between the two teams Kelvingrove had won seven and drawn two. The West End club had produced a quite remarkable sequence of positive results against their greatest rivals but it had now finally come to an end.

Frozen in Time

Mohawks followed up that excellent result with a 6-1 mauling of Lions. This fixture completed the first half of the league championship. Mohawks moved to the top of the league with 13 points from eight matches, having won six, lost one and drawn one. They had scored 30 goals in the process for the loss of only 7, underlining a much improved defensive performance thanks to the partnership on the blue line which had been established between Ronald MacDonald and Wally Welch.

Mustangs were in second position on goal difference from Kelvingrove as both teams had 11 points. Mustangs had lost only 5 goals so far, a tribute to goaltender Billy Turnbull, as well as the solid and versatile Max Brennan and W G McDonald. It was evident that Mustangs were becoming a suitable replacement for Bridge of Weir as one of the "big three" in the Scottish League, the results between them, Kelvingrove and Mohawks now being of paramount importance.

At the other end of the league table Glasgow University had attained a miserable 5 points having won only two matches - both against Lions. The latter team had scored 3 goals and conceded 44 but had not as yet won a single point in their eight matches. It was difficult to see how, in the absence of quality reinforcements, the club could possibly improve its desperate situation.

The first representative match of the season was played at Crossmyloof on 10 January when Glasgow entertained Manchester. This was the first fixture between these two sides since December 1933 when they had drawn 0-0 in Glasgow. Manchester had since been "relegated" to the English League Northern Section but they still presented serious opposition as almost all of their players were Canadian developed including Pete Stevenson, the ex-Juniors and Mohawks star. Glasgow were on familiar lines with a squad that was mostly home developed. Dave Cross was in goal behind a blue line consisting of Ronald MacDonald and Alec Fullerton. The all-Mohawks attack of Billy and John Fullerton and Jim Kenny comprised the first line with Wally Welch, Sid Montford and Ken Hurll making up a second line. Joe Collins was also included in the squad as cover for the defence.

The contest attracted 2,500 spectators to Crossmyloof and they were treated to an exciting encounter with heavy body checking and fast raiding much in evidence. It was not without controversy either, as Glasgow had two goals disallowed by the referees, Andy Dick and Gilmour Ayres. The first period was an even affair and goalless but in the middle session, L (Les) Tapp, the best player on the ice and someone who would soon become very familiar to Scottish ice hockey followers, put Manchester ahead. Sid Montford then thought he had equalised but the score was disallowed. Wally Welch did score a legitimate goal for Glasgow early in the final period but minutes from time Tapp scored the winner. In the final minute, Jim Kenny slammed the puck into the net but it rebounded out of the goal so quickly that the score was missed

Season 1935-1936

by both the goal judge and the referees! Manchester were the slicker team and deserved their 2-1 victory, despite an encouraging home performance.

A week later Mohawks collected the first domestic honours of the season when they defeated Kelvingrove 3-0 in the replayed final of the President's Pucks. The match attracted great interest as seats could be booked in advance for 1s and 6d, twice the normal price. It was a closer game than the score suggested though Mohawks were the better team. In the first period, Greg Lennox saved a certain goal by diving at the feet of Ken Hurll as he was about to pull the trigger. Wally Welch scored for Mohawks early in the second period but then Sid Montford almost snatched an equaliser thirty seconds later. Kelvingrove pressed hard in the final session but found the solid checking of Ronald MacDonald and Welch unyielding. The latter then scored a brilliant solo goal before Billy Fullerton wrapped it up for Mohawks with a typical breakaway effort. The result was a major blow to Kelvingrove since it represented their third successive defeat in the final of the President's Pucks and their second to Mohawks. They were still a very good team defensively but they had yet to determine what constituted their best forward line. The club had six good forwards and had tried various permutations to find the right blend between them but without lasting success. In a real sense the ghost of Arthur Tingley continued to haunt Kelvingrove.

In the league championship, Lions obtained their first - and as it would turn out their only - point of the season on 24 January when they drew 2-2 with Glasgow University. It should have been better for they led 2-0 at the end of the second period but allowed Varsity back into the game in the final session. Lions new goaltender, Tom Nicol, was earning some good notices for his performances.

Mohawks consolidated their position at the top of the league table with an impressive 2-0 victory over Mustangs at the end of the month. Mustangs may have been a bit rusty as they had not played a competitive match for about six weeks but they still managed to put in a decent performance. Goals from Jim Kenny and John Fullerton in the second period sealed the Mohawks win. Very much the team of the moment, they carried their great run of form into the first round of the Mitchell Trophy when they thrashed Lions 8-0 at the end of January. It was over as a contest from the moment Jim Kenny scored in the first minute of the match, despite the best efforts of Tom Nicol in the Lions goal. Mohawks would play Glasgow University in the semi-final.

Glasgow travelled to Manchester on 15 February for a return fixture with the English side. Billy Fullerton was unavailable as he was competing in the Scottish Speed Skating Championships at Loch Leven on the same day, where he would go on to win the mile event for the second time. Wally Welch took his place in the forward line with Max Brennan and W G McDonald returning to the defence. Earl Muirhead of Lions and Johnny Kelly of Mustangs were also called up to the squad.

Frozen in Time

In a close match Glasgow struggled to come to terms with the smaller ice surface of the Manchester Ice Palace as it restricted their normal forward passing game. The home team raced into a 2-0 lead at the end of the first period and then outscored Glasgow 3-1 in the middle session. The visitors staged something of a comeback in the final period but the match ended 7-4 in favour of a good Manchester team. The two best players on the ice were Wally Welch of Mohawks who scored a hat-trick and Gordon Johnson of Manchester, who scored four goals. The heavy body checking of the Glasgow defence had been a feature of the match but they were unable to wholly contain the skilful and speedy Manchester players for whom Les Tapp and Pete Stevenson were also prominent.

Domestic ice hockey both in Scotland and in England, not to mention British sport in general, received an enormous boost with the sensational and completely unexpected success of Great Britain in the European, World and Olympic Championships held at the twin Bavarian Alpine villages of Garmisch-Partenkirchen in Germany under the watchful eyes of the ruling Nazi regime. The Great Britain team was entirely composed of players competing in the new and highly successful English National League and while almost all of them had been born in England the vast majority had learned to play ice hockey while growing up in Canada. The only exceptions were the captain of the team, Carl Erhardt, and Bob Wyman, both of whom were home developed. The British side also contained one Scottish-born player, Jimmy Foster, who now played for Richmond Hawks in London.

In their qualifying group, Great Britain defeated Sweden 1-0 and Japan 3-0. The semifinals were also played on a sectional basis and the British team drew 1-1 with hosts Germany and then thrashed Hungary 5-1. The best British performance though was reserved for the reigning world champions, Canada, represented on this occasion by the Port Arthur Bearcats, who were defeated 2-1 in a tense match with goals from Gerry Davey in the first minute and Edgar Brenchley in the closing minutes. It was Canada's first defeat in 20 consecutive matches in Olympic competition.

Great Britain qualified for the final group stage along with Canada, Czechoslovakia and the United States of America. In what was a somewhat complicated format, because previous results against these opponents were taken into consideration, Great Britain found itself in a strong position having already beaten Canada. The British team then defeated Czechoslovakia 5-0 and in their final match, an incredibly nervy encounter which went to two periods of extra time, drew 0-0 with the United States of America. Unbeaten, this sequence of results meant that Great Britain were the European, World and Olympic champions for the first and only time in their history!

Under the astute coaching of Canadian, Percy Nicklin, the British team had played to their strengths which included tight checking allied to safety first tactics. Magnificent goaltending, solid defence and fast and tricky forwards were key elements in the British success. The squad which made history was:

J Foster (Richmond Hawks) and A Child (Wembley Lions); J Borland (Brighton Tigers), G Dailley (Brighton Tigers), C A Erhardt (Streatham) and R Wyman (Wembley Canadians); J Kilpatrick (Wembley Lions), A Archer (Wembley Lions), E Brenchley (Richmond Hawks), J Chappell (Earls Court Rangers), J Coward (Richmond Hawks), G Davey (Streatham) and A Stinchcombe (Streatham).

The undoubted hero of the British team was the Scottish born goaltender, Jimmy Foster, who played in all seven matches. He posted four shut-outs and conceded only three goals against some of the best teams in world ice hockey. His brilliant goaltending was an inspiration to the rest of the British side; his performances against Canada and the United States of America particularly stood out. Jimmy Foster had been born in Glasgow in 1905 but grew up in Winnipeg, Manitoba, where he learned to skate and play ice hockey. His career started in the local junior leagues before he moved to New Brunswick to join the Moncton Hawks of the Maritime Senior Hockey League where Percy Nicklin, was the coach.

Foster made his name with this club in the 1932 Allan Cup competition where he went an amazing 417 minutes of play without conceding a goal. He went on to win the Allan Cup, awarded to the amateur champions of Canada, with Moncton Hawks in 1933 and 1934. A year later, Foster moved to London to join Richmond Hawks of the English National League where Percy Nicklin was again the coach. He would later play for Harringay Greyhounds. Jimmy Foster would be the only Scot to win a gold medal at the Winter Olympic Games for the next 66 years!

The success of Great Britain stunned the ice hockey world. It was the first time that Canada had failed to win the Olympic title. They were not particularly gracious losers, having complained about both the group format of the competition and the composition of the British squad which they considered to be Canadian rather than British. It was not the first time the thorny issue of nationality had raised its ugly head at the various LIHG championships and it would not be the last.

Great Britain's achievement was testimony to the strength of the English National League. Indeed, it was considered by some ice hockey observers to be the strongest league competition in the world outside the professional National Hockey League in North America. That was quite a compliment, given the plethora of other professional and semi-professional leagues existing in Canada and the United States of America.

The English National League was attracting huge attendances to its big stadium type arenas. The various clubs were staffed in the main by Canadian imports who were semi-professionals in all but name. The standard of play was of a very high calibre. Many critics in Canada were irritated about the

Jimmy Foster, Scotland, the hero of Great Britain's Olympic, World and European Championship triumph of 1936.

Season 1935-1936

departure of their best amateur talent to play in England but many of these players obviously thought that the trip to the "mother country" was well worth the effort. The game in England was reaching heights of success it would never attain again.

In Scotland, Mohawks consolidated their position at the top of the league with an important victory over Kelvingrove on 11 February. The game had been the usual tense occasion, with the West End team close-marking their opponents and relying on the breakaway. Kelvingrove used both of their forward lines well, but it was Mohawks who secured the crucial goal when Wally Welch scored fifty seconds from full time to give them a 1-0 win.

The only other significant league result in February was Mustangs disappointing 1-1 draw with Glasgow University. They were without the influential Max Brennan for this match; in the end they were fortunate to take a point. Mustangs could ill afford to drop points in fixtures like this, given that their matches with Mohawks and Kelvingrove were such tight affairs.

They were back to full strength when they faced Kelvingrove in the first semifinal of the Mitchell Trophy on 21 February. In their two league championship matches to date each side had recorded a victory but 'Grove had prevailed in the recent President's Pucks semi-final. Mustangs decided to experiment in this tie by putting Max Brennan and W G McDonald in attack. It was a gamble which sadly backfired on them, as it left huge gaps in their defence. As expected it was a hard fought and gruelling encounter. The always busy and highly effective Alec Fullerton gave Kelvingrove the lead with a fortuitous goal after only three minutes. Mustangs pressed hard for the equaliser in the second period but were defied by Dave Cross who was in great form. Kelvingrove took a grip of the game in the final session and it was no surprise when Ken Hurll broke away and slipped a perfect pass to Bert Gemmell, whose first time shot found the corner of the net to seal a 2-0 victory.

The other semi-final between Mohawks and Glasgow University was no less exciting with a spirited and enterprising performance from Varsity. Indeed, the experienced A Rintoul gave them a 1-0 lead at the end of the first period; he then increased that lead at the beginning of the middle session with a shot that Greg Lennox badly misjudged. This set the alarm bells ringing and Mohawks finally got out of first gear. They scored two goals within a minute of each other to bring the score to 2-2 by the end of the second period. With Varsity defending gallantly in a dramatic third period it was left to John Fullerton to break the deadlock, then Wally Welch clinched the tie when he scored yet another last minute goal to give Mohawks a 4-2 win. It had been a very good contest with Glasgow University giving their best display of the season. Mohawks played without Billy Fullerton who was again on speed skating duties and they were also short of substitutes, so they had done well to come from 2-0 behind.

Mohawks would now meet Kelvingrove for the second time in a cup final this season the match to be played in early March. With the President's Pucks already won, Mohawks were now well on course for a unique treble if they could add the Canada Cup and the Mitchell Trophy. With three quarters of the league championship completed on 3 March, they retained first position with 21 points from twelve matches. They had scored 44 goals, far more than any other team in the competition, for the loss of only 10. Kelvingrove were hanging on to second place with 17 points from twelve matches but Mustangs were losing ground in third position with 14 points although they had played only eleven matches.

Kelvingrove and Mohawks met in the final of the Mitchell Trophy on 6 March. It was to be yet another epic contest between these two deadly rivals. The match attracted 2,400 spectators to Crossmyloof, one of the largest crowds ever for a domestic fixture at the venue. Mohawks were at full strength but Kelvingrove had to do without the injured Ken Hurll in attack.

Jim Kenny put Mohawks ahead after only three minutes when he skated through to fire a fast shot past Dave Cross, who was unsighted by one of his own players. The West End team tried hard to respond but again found the close body checking of Ronald MacDonald and Wally Welch a formidable barrier to overcome. The first period ended with Mohawks still in the lead.

"Inside Edge" described the second period as one of the most exciting sessions of ice hockey ever witnessed at Crossmyloof. Kelvingrove strove desperately for the equalising goal and at one point both teams were playing with two players each in the penalty box. Chances were made and squandered at both ends of the ice as the period ended goalless. The final period was a more scrappy affair as Kelvingrove began to tire. Mohawks asserted their overall superiority but failed to add another goal. No matter, they had beaten their old foes for the fourth successive time this season and for the second time in a cup final. There could be no dispute that Mohawks were the more polished and faster team throughout and deserved to retain the trophy.

Kelvingrove bounced back from their Mitchell Trophy disappointment only four days later when they defeated Mustangs 1-0 in a league match. It was a particularly good result for 'Grove since they took to the ice short of substitutes and had actually asked for a postponement of the fixture. Mustangs had objected to this request. A Sid Montford goal fifteen seconds from full time ensured that justice was done.

Life was breathed into the league championship a week later when Mustangs at last recovered some real form when they defeated the high flying Mohawks 3-0. The first period had ended goalless but in the second period W G McDonald and Johnny Kelly fired Mustangs into a 2-0 lead. In a fraught final session, Mohawks pressed their opponents relentlessly but found Billy Turnbull a real obstacle. It was left to N Andrews to add a third goal to leave Mohawks reflecting on a rare defeat.

Season 1935-1936

Greater excitement than normal preceded the home international fixture between Scotland and England at Crossmyloof on 14 March. Always an eagerly anticipated match even more spice was added on this occasion following the success of the Great Britain side in the recent European, World and Olympic Championships. The English side chosen for Glasgow contained no less than six players from the triple championship winning team.

The response of the SIHA to the challenge presented was to pick a number of Anglo-Scots for the home side. This strategy had been tried before in the home internationals of 1931 and 1935 but without success since Scotland had lost both fixtures. Despite that rather depressing precedence four players were selected from the English National League and these were the brilliant Great Britain goaltender, Jimmy Foster of Richmond Hawks, a back line duo of Ralph McAlpine and Paul McPhail of Earls Court Rangers and up front P S "Scotty" Cameron of Kensington Corinthians.

The Mohawks trio of Billy and John Fullerton and Jim Kenny along with Johnny Kelly of Mustangs were the only survivors from Scotland's previous match against England in 1935. Ronald MacDonald of Mohawks was the only new face to be selected from the Scottish League. The home squad was completed with the return to international duty of Sid Montford of Kelvingrove. The selection of the Anglo-Scots was as ever not without comment. Some observers were of the opinion that home developed talent should have been preferred even if the opposition was as daunting as this England team. It was certainly hard lines on regular players like Dave Cross or Bill Russell that they had to make way but one could see the logic of the SIHA position on this matter, given Scotland's poor international record.

The two teams were:

Scotland: J Foster (Richmond Hawks); R McAlpine (Earls Court Rangers) and P McPhail (Earls Court Rangers); W Fullerton (Mohawks), P S Cameron (Kensington Corinthians) and J Kenny (Mohawks). - W S Montford (Kelvingrove), J Fullerton (Mohawks), J Kelly (Mustangs) and R O MacDonald (Mohawks).

England: A Child (Wembley Lions); E J Ramus (Streatham) and C A Erhardt (Streatham); A Archer (Wembley Lions), E Brenchley (Richmond Hawks) and J Coward (Richmond Hawks). - J Kilpatrick (Wembley Lions), R Groome (Kensington Corinthians) and J Shannon (Wembley Canadians).

Referees: A S Dick (SIHA) and W G McDonald (SIHA).

The match attracted a bumper attendance to Crossmyloof, the spectators paying a set charge of 2s each for the privilege. In the event, the contest failed to live up to pre-match expectations. Despite an exciting climax, defences rather dominated although England had by far the better of the exchanges in attack.

The first period commenced with an early goal for England after Edgar "Chirp" Brenchley was left unmarked and beat Jimmy Foster from close range. This unfortunate start unsettled the Scots who took a number of penalties. While short-handed, Alex Archer scored a second goal but it was disallowed. Scotland had more of the game in the second period, though both sides had chances to score. Scotty Cameron came very close to grabbing an equaliser at the end of the session. The third period was noticeably faster and England had another goal disallowed, this time from Johnny Coward. Foster, who was having a magnificent game, prevented a certain goal with a sprawl save at the feet of Brenchley, before a clever solo move by Cameron ended with his shot rebounding of the pads of Art Child; following up, he slammed home the equalising goal amidst huge excitement. The match ended 1-1.

The result was the best achieved by Scotland against England in the five matches played between the two countries since the reorganisation of the sport north of the border in 1929. Indeed, "Inside Edge" regarded it as "the greatest thing that has happened in the history of Scottish ice hockey." That comment was going a little too far, but it had been an encouraging performance against a very strong English team and it fully justified the decision made by the SIHA to play the Anglo-Scots, all of whom played exceptionally well. Jimmy Foster and Scotty Cameron had been the best players on the ice.

A week later, Glasgow travelled to the Manchester Ice Palace again to play the home side in their third fixture of the season. Hopes were high of winning on this occasion following two reverses in the previous matches. Glasgow were on familiar lines, the only changes from their last fixture being the omissions of John Fullerton and Earl Muirhead, although Billy Fullerton available again, came back into the side.

Having played there only a month earlier Glasgow adapted much better this time to the smaller ice surface at Manchester and gave the home team a run for their money. It was an exciting encounter which see-sawed before ending 5-5. Glasgow were very unfortunate not to win, having two goals disallowed for reasons known only to the match officials. Of the legitimate goals scored by Glasgow, Billy Fullerton scored a hat-trick and Johnny Kelly, a brace.

Matters were drawing to a close in the league championship, not without some controversy. The match between Glasgow University and Kelvingrove on 20 March had to be scratched because of the inability of Varsity to ice a full team due to illness and injuries. An unsympathetic SIHA took a hard line and subsequently awarded Kelvingrove a 5-0 victory, a decision not without bearing on the final positions at the top of the league.

A week later, Kelvingrove met Mohawks in what was a virtual championship decider. Both teams now shared first place with 21 points. Crucially Mohawks had played a game less. Kelvingrove had to defeat Mohawks to have any chance of winning the league title. Mohawks could afford to draw the match, since they would expect to win their remaining fixtures against Lions and Glasgow University. Kelvingrove's final match was a much more tricky encounter against third place Mustangs.

Season 1935-1936

Scotland and England Teams, March 1936. Back Row; Sid Montford (Kelvingrove), Jim Kenny (Mohawks), J Coward (England), Billy Fullerton (Mohawks) and Ralph McAlpine (Earls Court Rangers) Middle Row; Jack Gilmour (SIHA), W G McDonald (Referee), Paul McPhail (Earls Court Rangers), Johnny Kelly (Mustangs), John Fullerton (Mohawks), E Ramus (England), J Shannon (England), Andy Dick (Referee) and Graham Fraser (Coach). Front Row; Scotty Cameron (Kensington Corinthians), Ronald MacDonald (Mohawks), C A Erhardt (England), Jimmy Foster (Richmond Hawks), A Child (England), J Groome (England), J Brenchley (England), A Archer (England) and J Kilpatrick (England

Frozen in Time

It was all set up for a thrilling contest. It did not disappoint. After a quiet and goalless first period, Charlie McMillan thought he had scored for Kelvingrove in the middle session but the match referees, Graham Fraser and Jack Gilmour, disallowed the goal for an infringement. Many observers were of the view that any infringement was actually against McMillan and that the goal should have stood. This decision seemed to rattle Kelvingrove who lost their discipline by taking a number of needless penalties. In an exciting third period the West End team pushed hard to make the breakthrough but it was the ever-dangerous Wally Welch who broke up the ice and scored for Mohawks. When Sid Montford took a penalty, Mohawks took full advantage for Jim Kenny to add a second power play goal to give his side a narrow but deserved 2-0 win.

Mohawks wrapped up the league championship four days later when they defeated Lions 3-0, Billy Fullerton grabbing a brace and Ronald MacDonald securing the other goal. With 25 points and a match still to play Mohawks could not now be caught and were worthy winners of the Canada Cup for the second time. They had now equalled the record of Kelvingrove and Bridge of Weir.

Mohawks became the first club though to win the "treble" of Canada Cup, Mitchell Trophy and President's Pucks in one season. It represented a quite remarkable achievement! The secret of Mohawks success was teamwork. The squad had a wonderful work ethic and every player in their team knew instinctively what the other was doing. Quality ran through the entire squad. Greg Lennox was a sound goaltender but he had a brilliant back line in front of him. Much of the attention naturally fell on Mohawks forward line but in Ronald MacDonald and Wally Welch the team had a defence second to none.

Wally Welch had been a revelation. Equally comfortable in defence or attack this superbly accomplished player had been the icing on the cake of Mohawks' season. His tricky stick-handling, effective body checking and incisive finishing had been a joy to watch and Ronald MacDonald had clearly benefited as a result of playing with him on the back line.

Mohawks were a team geared to attack and possessed the most effective forward line in the Scottish League - Billy and John Fullerton and Jim Kenny. The team finished the league campaign with 50 goals and their first line accounted for 33 of them. Most defences found it too difficult to cope not only with the puck control of their forwards but also with their speed. In Billy Fullerton, Mohawks had the fastest man on skates and his brother John was no slouch either.

There were still three league fixtures to play when Mohawks clinched the title. These matches were played out over the next three weeks, the most important being the final one between Kelvingrove and Mustangs to decide second place. It was Mustangs who prevailed with an emphatic 4-1 victory to finish three points behind the champions who rather carelessly lost their final match 3-1 to Glasgow University.

Season 1935-1936

On their game Mustangs were capable of beating anyone in the league as their results had demonstrated but they lacked that vital ingredient all successful teams needed; consistency. In Max Brennan, W G McDonald, Bill Russell and Johnny Kelly the club had players of real quality but in the end it was not enough. Given the squad at their disposal Mustangs would have been disappointed not to have won either of the two cup competitions. They never lost any more than two goals in any league match, and had the consolation of possessing the top marksman in the championship, Johnny Kelly, who finished with 15 goals, almost a third of his team's total.

For Kelvingrove, it was their second barren season in succession. The team had never quite resolved what its best formation was in attack but what was clear was the fact that new players were required to freshen things up a bit. Even their defence had not been as sound this season. The one bright spot at Kelvingrove was the success of their junior team in winning the junior league championship, a feat which bode well for the future.

Glasgow University finished the season where most observers expected them to be - in fourth position, quite a distance away from the "big three". Given the comparative playing strengths of the various teams there was really no great surprise about this. The club retained some very good players on an individual level but lack of coaching was a perennial problem at Varsity. Another problem had been a shortage of players with the team often having to take to the ice with only six players.

Lions ended the season in bottom position having lost 15 matches and drawn 1. The team had conceded a record 75 goals and had scored only 11 in reply. It had all proved too much, even for the ex-Bridge of Weir duo of Wilbur and Earl Muirhead, who were used to better things. If the SIHA was serious about persisting with a five-team league championship in the future something would need to be urgently done about strengthening this club.

The representative season ended with another round of matches between Glasgow and Manchester, the first at Crossmyloof on 3 April and the return at the Ice Palace a day later. These fixtures presented the SIHA with the opportunity to bring in some new players; unfortunately that opportunity was not taken. The selectors stuck with what they knew. It was an odd decision given that Glasgow had failed to beat Manchester on the three previous occasions the two sides had met this season.

Both matches were profoundly disappointing experiences for Glasgow. The home game was lost 8-4 and the return 8-2. Despite the best efforts of goaltender Dave Cross, defensive frailty was blamed for these defeats although "Inside Edge" also thought the absence of Billy Fullerton in both matches was another significant factor. It was notable that two of the other major players of the season, Wally Welch and Johnny Kelly, failed to make any impression in either match.

Billy Fullerton was the man of the moment. At 23 years of age he had blossomed into the complete athlete. Tall and rather slim built, Fullerton was a superb stick-handler and was of course possessed of lightning speed. A maker as well as a taker of goals he was also a very clean player despite the abuse he was often subjected to by opposing defenders. The talent of "The Flying Mohawk" was recognised south of the border when he was invited to join Earls Court Rangers of the English National League for a series of trial matches at the beginning of April. At the conclusion of these trials Fullerton was offered a semi-professional contract by the London outfit. It must have been a very difficult decision but he turned them down preferring to remain in Glasgow since he was reluctant to give up his security and his employment with a local stockbroking firm.

It was perhaps ironic that in a season when one club, Mohawks, totally dominated domestic competition in a league comprising only five teams, the popularity of ice hockey remained undiminished. Indeed, attendances at Crossmyloof had continued to rise, particularly in those matches involving Kelvingrove, Mohawks and Mustangs. The local game had also benefited by basking in the reflective glory of the British success in European, World and Olympic Championships.

Despite a general "feel good" factor in the Scottish game, the sport was confined to only one ice rink in the country. The Scottish League badly needed an injection of fresh talent but the signs were encouraging as plans were being put into action to introduce ice hockey at the new Perth Ice Rink in the season ahead. This was welcome news as at long last it seemed that the domestic game was about to expand beyond the confines of Crossmyloof.

There had been a nail biting end in the English National League with the Wembley Lions winning the title on goal difference from the Richmond Hawks. The ice hockey boom continued apace south of the border, particularly in London, where plans were announced to introduce the game in the new Harringay Arena, yet another North American style rink, capable of holding up to 8,000 spectators.

It all seemed rather unreal if one recalled that only a decade earlier Blaine Sexton's nomadic London Lions could not find an ice rink in England where they could play the game!

Season 1936-37

Although not fully appreciated at the time, the establishment of a senior club at the new Perth Ice Rink was to be the harbinger of things to come as ice hockey in Scotland took its first tentative steps towards semi-professionalism.

Since being revived in 1929 competitive ice hockey in Scotland had been strictly amateur and wholly concentrated at one venue. Now the sport was ready to expand its horizons beyond the confines of Crossmyloof Ice Rink in Glasgow. Perth was the start but others would follow and the game north of the border would never be the same again.

Semi-professionalism however would not occur overnight. The transition from the amateur game would be a long, and for some clubs, a painful experience but that slow evolution was nevertheless inevitable. The management at Perth Ice Rink made it quite clear that they would be obtaining most of their playing staff directly from Canada and so for the first time in Scotland a club would be importing Canadians specifically to play ice hockey rather than simply depending on any itinerant exiles who just happened to be resident in the country at the time. The die was cast.

The expansion of the domestic game presented real challenges to the SIHA. Very much tied to Crossmyloof in terms of both its composition and its focus, the ruling body would now be required to expand its own horizons if it was to adequately fulfil its mission of promoting and developing ice hockey in the country as a whole. The SIHA would have to forge effective links with the new men coming into the sport at venues like Perth and work with them in a spirit of co-operation and goodwill.

If the new club being established at Perth represented the future then the old Glasgow University club had become the latest icon of the past. Regrettably, Varsity had finally succumbed to the inevitable and had been obliged to disband. The club had struggled on occasion the previous season to ice a full team and had increasingly come to rely on alumni and outsiders rather than current students to staff their side.

They had fought a very good fight over the previous seven seasons in the Scottish League. Although never at any time serious contenders for the league championship, the club had enjoyed some periods of success, none more so than their two consecutive appearances in the final of the Mitchell Trophy in seasons 1933-34 and 1934-35. Varsity were always capable of springing a surprise or two indeed part of their charm had been their unpredictability.

Some excellent players had worn the colours of Glasgow University. The best of these was probably the Canadian international, Orvald "Snoops" Gratias, but others worthy of mention were J O McCabe, Felix McLernan, Ronald Milne and the brilliant Jack Easton. The latter player had been the heart and soul of the club and when he left for his native Canada early in 1934 the guiding spirit of this grand old club went with him.

At this point it is also important to remember the enormous contribution made by students at Glasgow University to the early development of ice hockey in Scotland at the end of the 19th century. As William Pollock Wylie noted, in 1897 they were at the very forefront of the Scottish Ice Hockey Club, which may well have evolved out of the Glasgow University Bandy Club in existence at least a year before. That was quite a heritage. The passing of Glasgow University Ice Hockey Club in 1936 was witness to the last vestiges of the "Corinthian" spirit so much a part of the early years of the Scottish game. An era had truly ended.

Yet as one door closes another opens and at least the Scottish League would still commence the new season with the same number of clubs as the season before. These five clubs were Kelvingrove, Lions, Mohawks, Mustangs and Perthshire Panthers. In very quick time this was changed to "Perth" Panthers. Beyond the fact that they would play in orange and black, Perth Panthers were as yet an unknown quantity and would remain so for the first month of the season, as they had not yet completed their recruitment of players. The club had employed the Ottawa-born and ex-Manchester star, Les Tapp, as their player-coach and he was looking to acquire other players with Canadian experience, either directly from Canada or from the various leagues in England.

Although the Perth club was not unnaturally looking for experienced personnel for its senior team, it also intended to develop local junior talent. With this laudable aim in view ambitious plans were made to establish a North of Scotland Ice Hockey League. Amongst the clubs being mooted to play in this league were Gallacs, Leuchars, Perth Airport, Perth Panthers Reserves, Perth Territorial Army and St Andrews University. Quite where all of the players would come from, to staff these teams, was another matter but enthusiasm was clearly the name of the game at Perth.

In the Scottish League, sometimes referred to as the Scottish National League now Perth were on board, each team would play the other on four occasions for the league championship. This gave each team sixteen fixtures commencing in early October and concluding in mid March. The running order of the two major cup competitions, the President's Pucks and the Mitchell Trophy, remained the same.

The SIHA did however introduce one important change to the format of the league championship. The team finishing in first position would be required to finish more than two points ahead of the team finishing second

Season 1936-1937

Billy Fullerton, the finest home bred player of his generation.

to be champions. If they did not finish more than two points ahead of the runners-up a play-off between them for the title would be required.

It is not immediately obvious why the SIHA came to this decision, since the whole point of having a league championship in the first place was surely to reward the most consistently good team all season, that being the team which finished in first position irrespective of their points margin over the team which finished second. Play-offs were popular in North America and it may be that this development was one result of the increasing Canadian presence in the Scottish game.

In reviewing the prospects of the various teams for the season ahead, one had to take account of the fact that there had been significantly more player movements than was normal and that this process was still ongoing as the season got officially underway. The Crossmyloof based clubs felt obliged to follow the example of Perth in recruiting players directly from Canada or from the English leagues.

Mohawks, the defending champions and double cup winners, were much affected by these processes. The biggest upheaval was at the back where the club lost its entire first line defence. Goaltender Greg Lennox had retired and his intended replacement, Tom Nicol of Lions, had moved to London. Duncan MacLachlan returned to the team but only as a stopgap since he was unable to play on Friday evenings due to business commitments.

The brilliant defensive partnership of Ronald MacDonald and Wally Welch was broken up as the former moved to Lions and the latter was enticed to join Mustangs. The loss of Welch in particular was keenly felt but on the plus side Alec Fullerton moved from Kelvingrove to join his brothers, John and Billy, to complete a unique family set-up at Mohawks. The club also acquired Don Edwards, who had struggled to find regular ice time at Mustangs, and Jack Johnston from Glasgow University.

Jim Kenny also remained at Mohawks, despite being appointed as the new SIHA coach, replacing the departed Graham Fraser. The decision of the ruling body to allow Kenny to remain as a player at Mohawks drew adverse comment from some quarters, since a number of observers thought there was a conflict of interest involved. An odd decision, it was a less expensive option for the SIHA. There was no argument that the diminutive and bespectacled Canadian was eminently qualified for the job.

Kelvingrove also started the season with several changes to their squad. The loss of Alec Fullerton was a blow since it ended a highly successful partnership with Andy Dick which had lasted for four seasons. Fullerton was replaced on the blue line by the accomplished and hard hitting Joe Collins who was returning to the club. In attack, the long serving Bert Gemmell had retired and it was unlikely that Charlie McMillan would be available for another season. Ken Hurll had won a scholarship to Oxford University so he would only be available from time to time.

Season 1936-1937

The West End club looked to Canada to replenish their depleted resources. Their first import was W (Bill) Moore, a forward who could play at centre or on the wing. More imports were expected in the next few weeks as Kelvingrove, who had not won anything for two seasons, sought to regain their position as one of the leading clubs in the country.

The ambitious Mustangs seemed to be the least affected by personnel changes their only real problem being the unavailability of star defender, W G McDonald, for an as yet undetermined amount of time. Team manager, Bob Gardiner, had moved quickly to find a replacement of equal ability when he signed Wally Welch from Mohawks. He also acquired Felix McLernan from Glasgow University and it was expected that further fresh talent would be arriving from Canada in due course.

Lions approached the new season in a more optimistic frame of mind. The SIHA had undertaken to seriously strengthen this team and had made a start by facilitating the move of Ronald MacDonald from Mohawks. Within weeks he would be joined by the Scotland and Great Britain international forward, Pete Stevenson, who arrived from Manchester. The capture of Stevenson was a major coup for Lions for not only was he a player of outstanding ability but he was also a born leader on the ice. He was the type of player who could attract other good players to join him at the club.

The season opened on 1 October with an exhibition match between Kelvingrove and Mohawks to officially open the Central Scotland Ice Rink at Perth. The new venue had a seating capacity of 2,300 and with standees, a total capacity of 3,100. The ice surface was 175 feet by 97 feet making it a very compact but noisy rink when it was full. For the record, Kelvingrove defeated Mohawks 2-1 although both teams iced guest players.

The league championship got underway on 2 October when Kelvingrove recorded an easy 5-0 victory over Lions. Four days later, in the first heavyweight contest of the new campaign, Mohawks drew 2-2 with Mustangs in what "Inside Edge" in the *Daily Record and Mail* described as a "splendid display of fast and spectacular ice hockey." Twice behind and without the injured John Fullerton and having only one substitute available, Mohawks did well in the circumstances. Wally Welch scored both Mustangs goals against his old team.

Mohawks had been working away to strengthen their squad and began by solving their goaltending problem by signing A (Art) Palfrey from Manchester. A goaltender of proven ability it was a sign of the changing times that a player of his quality was prepared to join the Scottish League. One can only speculate that the "expenses" now on offer in Glasgow had made it worth his while to move.

Mohawks did not finish there as G (Gordon) Galloway arrived from Toronto as a centre with a good reputation as a playmaker. The intention was that he would play on the team's second line with youngsters, Don Edwards and Jack Johnston. This signing greatly enhanced Mohawks prospects since it provided player-coach, Jim Kenny, with more options in attack.

Kelvingrove had not been idle either. They too had continued to look to Canada to further strengthen their squad. Two brothers, A (Archie) and M (Matt) Maxwell arrived from Winnipeg. They were both forwards and had been born in Glasgow but had emigrated to Canada as children. The Maxwell boys were of slim build but they were reported to be fast and good stick-handlers.

All of these players made their respective debuts when Kelvingrove faced Mohawks on 13 October. The champions were still without John Fullerton so Gordon Galloway joined the first line with Billy Fullerton and Jim Kenny while 'Grove took the ice with a first line of Sid Montford, Archie Maxwell and Bill Moore. It was an exciting match, Kenny putting Mohawks ahead in the first period before Moore scored an equaliser for Kelvingrove in the middle session. Dave Cross was in outstanding form throughout as Mohawks did the bulk of the attacking but there was no further scoring and it ended 1-1.

Three days later, Mustangs defeated Kelvingrove 3-1 to go to the top of the league table. Glen Braid put them ahead after only thirty seconds as Mustangs displayed superior teamwork and finishing power. Kelvingrove were disjointed which was not really surprising with so many new players in their team. Mustangs though were looking good with Wally Welch moving effortlessly into the left defence slot to partner Max Brennan.

Lions continued to strengthen their ranks with the signing of L (Len) McCartney from Port Arthur in Ontario. Some of the Canadians who were coming into the Scottish League at this time were of variable quality but that could not be said of McCartney who was a first class acquisition for the Glasgow club. Lions were now starting to look a competitive team for the first time. McCartney made a scoring debut for Lions in a 3-1 loss to Mohawks. In his next match against Kelvingrove on 23 October he scored again in a historic 2-1 win. This was Lions' first ever victory in competitive ice hockey. The team had gone 21 consecutive matches in all competitions without recording a single win. Now at long last they had broken their duck!

Mohawks took over leadership of the league four days later when they defeated their nearest rivals Mustangs 4-2. In a physical encounter, Mustangs were 2-0 down at the end of the first period but brought it back to 2-2 in the middle session. Some faulty judgement by Billy Turnbull allowed Mohawks two further goals, the returning John Fullerton securing the final and decisive goal of the game.

By the end of October, Perth Panthers were at last ready to make their debut in the Scottish League. The squad being assembled by player-coach Les Tapp would in time be a mixture of Canadian experience and Scottish youth. As yet, it was the latter trend which predominated and it included two good prospects for the future in D (Doug) Mitchell and T S (Tommy) McInroy.

Season 1936-1937

Perth Panthers opened their account against Kelvingrove at Crossmyloof with a hard fought 2-2 draw. Not unexpectedly the new boys took a while to settle into the match and combined poorly. They still managed to come from being behind twice, courtesy of a brace from Les Tapp, the best player on the ice. He was well aware that the squad required more quality and was attempting to bring additional players from Canada.

The first quarter of the league championship was concluded in early November when Mustangs defeated Lions 6-1, a result which returned them to the top of the table with 7 points from five matches. Mustangs had scored an impressive 18 goals, almost double that of any other team, the versatile Wally Welch accounting for half of that total. He was clearly enjoying life with his new team where his "rugged crashing style" was noted as a constant menace to opposing players.

Mohawks were in second position with 6 points, having played one match less than Mustangs. After a slow start they remained undefeated. Kelvingrove, on the other hand, were struggling to make an impact with only 4 points from five matches. It was taking time for their new team to settle down but they were continuing to recruit. Another Canadian, J (John) Cuthill, joined the club from Prince Albert, Saskatchewan, and he would certainly not be hard to notice being six feet in height and fourteen stones in weight.

Lions occupied fourth position with only 2 points from five matches but at least they had finally won a game. Despite their predicament the club was confident of some improvement in their fortunes now that Pete Stevenson and Len McCartney were settling in. With only one match played the jury was out on Perth Panthers but any team with a player as good as Les Tapp was worth the watching.

"Inside Edge" was of the view that the recent influx of Canadians into the Scottish League had done much to raise the standard of the local game. Most of the matches so far had been competitive and exciting affairs. Attendances were increasing and spectators were getting good value for money for the fare on offer. The Canadian players were bringing a bit of additional glamour into the sport and the increase in female and children's attendance at matches continued to be a feature.

The ice hockey correspondent of the *Glasgow Herald* agreed that the standard of play was generally improving except in one respect.

> "One would like to appeal to those in authority to enforce a stricter interpretation of illegal checking. It certainly appears to the observer that a great deal of ill-natured tripping and obstruction is allowed to go unpunished nor is the occasional meting out of one or two minutes in the penalty box for blatant offences likely to stamp out this evil."
>
> *(Glasgow Herald: 27 October 1936).*

Frozen in Time

It was the case that the current intake of Canadian talent had led to an increase in the more robust and physical side of the game. Such tactics were of course an integral part of ice hockey in Canada but perhaps enthusiasm for this type of play, while generally popular with the paying public, was less so with those players who remained strictly amateur. The risk of serious injury arising from overly physical play was always a worrying factor for players whose livelihoods were made outside of the sport.

Ice hockey was a dangerous enough sport to play without looking for trouble, as Alec Fullerton of Mohawks to name but one player found to his cost. In a recent match against Lions he had by accident got in the way of a hard shot from Pete Stevenson where the puck struck him fully on his mouth. The result was that Fullerton lost seven teeth from his lower jaw, but that did not put him off from continuing to play the game. Hardy individuals these ice hockey players!

Kelvingrove turned in their best performance of the season to date on 10 November when they defeated the league leaders Mustangs 2-0. Making his debut for the team was yet another recruit from Canada, R (Robert) Thomson, who while born in Scotland had been brought up in Winnipeg. Known as "Red" Thomson he was actually a nephew of the famous Celtic goalkeeper, John Thomson, who had tragically lost his life in an accident during a match against Rangers a few years earlier.

The following evening another milestone in the evolution of Scottish ice hockey was achieved when Perth Panthers made their long awaited home debut against Lions. It was the first time a competitive match had been played outside Crossmyloof Ice Rink since the revival of ice hockey in 1929.

A large and enthusiastic crowd of spectators sat enthralled as Perth battled back from being 3-1 down to grab a dramatic draw with two goals from right wing, J Wold, in the final three minutes of the match. Les Tapp was still in the process of building a competitive team at Perth and more players were due to arrive at the club in the near future.

Lions went one better two days later when they gave Mohawks their first defeat of the season. Although Jim Kenny scored after only forty seconds of play, Len McCartney secured an equaliser at the end of the period. Pete Stevenson then put Lions ahead at the start of the second period. Despite intense pressure from the champions their new goaltender, R H (Bobby) Henderson, conceded no more goals. Mohawks' chances were not improved by their lack of discipline in the final session as Lions closed the game down for a 2-1 win.

The first round of the President's Pucks competition was held on 17 November when holders Mohawks were paired with Mustangs. In their two league matches so far, Mohawks had recorded one win with the other game drawn. A keen cup-tie was expected and Mustangs were encouraged by the return of W G McDonald who would be playing his first match of the season.

Season 1936-1937

Les Tapp, Perth Panthers and Scotland

Described as the fastest game of the year, the first period was even, both teams having chances to take the lead. Mustangs exerted enormous pressure in the second period but found Art Palfrey in magnificent form. Early in the third period Gordon Galloway intercepted a stray pass, skated in on goal and fired a low shot past Billy Turnbull. Despite a hectic finish Mohawks held on for a just-about-deserved 1-0 victory.

In the league championship Perth Panthers were finding it hard going. They suffered two consecutive defeats in three days at Crossmyloof, at the hands of Mustangs and Mohawks respectively. Both matches were lost by the odd goal; in both Les Tapp had been outstanding, earning the applause of an appreciative audience. In the second match, two new Canadians had made their debut for Perth, B Burbridge and L (Les) Lovell, the latter scoring Perth's only goal and already catching the eye when it was noted "he gave good support and his accurate shooting impressed."

The first semi-final of the President's Pucks was played on 1 December between those old rivals Kelvingrove and Mohawks. The West End team had gone eight consecutive matches without a win against their opponents in all competitions losing six and drawing the other two. They were determined to put that right.

It was not to be. Mohawks continued their dominance with an emphatic looking 4-1 win although the score did not entirely reflect the way the match went. A poor first period from Kelvingrove saw them 3-0 down with Dave Cross having a rare off night. Again disjointed in attack 'Grove huffed and puffed for the remainder of a match they were always chasing. In contrast, the well-oiled Mohawks were clinical in their finishing and sound in defence.

Three days later Perth Panthers were a shade fortunate to beat Lions 3-2 in the other semi-final. A quiet first period was followed by an explosive start to the middle session as three goals were scored within the first minutes. Perth led 2-1 before Pete Stevenson scored as Lions came from behind for the second time. Stevenson was sitting in the penalty box when B Burbridge scored the winning goal for Perth in the third period, but the tie ended in controversy with Lions unhappy at the refereeing of Andy Dick and Bob Gardiner.

In the league championship a Jim Kenny goal after only two minutes gave Mohawks an important 1-0 win against Mustangs. A fine match was marred by a knee injury to Bill Russell. It kept him out of Mustangs next fixture, the first time for six years that Russell had missed a game, a truly remarkable record of consistency for a very good player.

On 9 December the improving Perth Panthers recorded their first victory in the league championship when they defeated Kelvingrove 6-4 in a thrilling contest at a packed Perth Ice Rink. Just over 3,000 spectators witnessed Les Tapp scoring a hat-trick and Les Lovell a brace. Kelvingrove iced Jack Logan, the ex-Dennistoun goaltender, who was deputising for the injured Dave Cross.

Season 1936-1937

The league championship reached the half way stage in mid-December with Mohawks having taken over from Mustangs at the top of the table. Mohawks had 12 points from eight matches. Always known more for their attacking flair the key to Mohawks current success was a formidable defence in which goaltender Art Palfrey had played consistently well behind a solid if unspectacular duo of Alec Fullerton and the underrated Archie Bogie.

Mustangs, only a point behind, were certainly pushing the champions hard but significantly they had played one more match. They were leading scorers with 25 goals and had the best defensive record in the league, having conceded only 16. They had a squad of outstanding individuals but often lacked combination; there was an impression that they were not getting the best out of the players they had at their disposal.

Their first line of defence, Max Brennan and W G McDonald, had hardly played together all season. That situation was about to get worse as Brennan had recently completed his studies and had qualified as a doctor. He was not expected to be at Mustangs very much longer. McDonald had rarely been available and although Wally Welch, Felix McLernan and Bob Gardiner had taken on the defensive duties it was considered that Welch was more effective when playing in attack. They had been quieter than usual on the transfer front, looking on as the other clubs continued to strengthen their squads. They finally decided to go down the same route by acquiring two new forwards from Canada, W (Bill) Boivin and H (Henry) Loane. Boivin arrived from Winnipeg and Loane had been a school friend of Johnny Kelly in the old country. The latter player had strongly impressed "Inside Edge" who had seen him in practice leading this keen observer to conclude that Mustangs were now the favourites to win the league championship.

Kelvingrove were in third position with 8 points from nine matches. Their form remained erratic which was hardly surprising given the almost constant additions to their squad. The West End side needed to start showing some consistency in the next quarter to have any chance of winning a third Canada Cup. At least the 'Grove junior team was making a splash with nine wins and one draw in ten matches.

Lions had only 5 points from nine matches but signs of improvement were starting to show. They had signed another Canadian forward in J (Jimmy) Lightfoot but their defence was the main problem area of the team despite the best efforts of Ronald MacDonald. Perth Panthers were bottom of the league a point behind Lions but they had played only five matches and had not yet settled down as a team.

In looking at the league championship as a whole, one is drawn to the conclusion that the four Crossmyloof teams were considerably stronger than they had been in the first quarter of the season. All of the clubs had recruited additional players from Canada or England and while some were clearly better than others it was considered that they were generally of a good

Frozen in Time

Joe Collins, one of the most accomplished home bred players of this era.

Season 1936-1937

standard. They were invariably young, fit, fast and skilful and had played the game at a decent level in the land of their birth.

There were now proportionately more players in the Scottish League who were either born in Canada, or who had learned to play the game in Canada, than at any time since the initial season of 1929-30. In this respect developments in Scotland were a mirror image of those in England, with the proviso that, in the English National League, the imports were semi-professionals who were paid a wage, whereas those in the Scottish League were classed as amateurs who were paid "expenses".

The boundaries between what constituted a semi-professional player from an amateur player were becoming increasingly blurred. More than mere semantics was involved here. It was clear from their inception that Perth Panthers intended recruiting their players directly from Canada or England and one must therefore assume that the expenses offered by the club made it well worth their while to come.

This development had led the Glasgow clubs to follow suit. All four clubs had sought to strengthen their teams by also directly recruiting players from Canada or England. It was a deliberate response to what was occurring at Perth but whether it was entirely feasible was another matter. The economics of the game, as they were structured in Glasgow, did not lend themselves to such extravagances at least in the long run.

The gate money accrued at Perth Ice Rink from attendances of around 3,000 per match and associated marketing made it possible for the club to recruit players from Canada or England. The situation was rather different at Crossmyloof Ice Rink, where all four clubs were in competition with each other for the same constituency and where the marketing opportunities were much more limited.

In such circumstances the four Glasgow clubs were not competing on an even playing field with Perth. They would require to exercise some financial prudence if they were not to bite off more than they could chew. This necessitated long term fiscal planning, but with ice hockey going through a boom period a heady optimism seemed to prevail amongst the sport's administrators and club officials.

No doubt with some income generation in mind, the SIHA decided that the final of the President's Pucks between Mohawks and Perth Panthers should be played over two legs for the first time in the history of the competition. Despite understandable objections from Perth both of these ties would be played at Crossmyloof, the first leg on 18 December and the return on 5 January. As anticipated, the first match drew a bumper attendance of 3,000 spectators to the Glasgow venue. In an exciting game Perth came from behind twice to draw 2-2 with a Mohawks side who were not at their best. This was primarily due to the close marking and heavy checking employed by the visiting side, and to Mohawks' surprising failure to utilise their speedy wing men to the best effect.

Frozen in Time

In the first period, the ever alert John Fullerton intercepted a stray pass and raced in on Mac Ross to score. Play was fairly even when B Burbridge secured a deserved equaliser for Perth late in the second period. Within minutes of the final session starting Gordon Galloway scored with a back-handed shot only for the brilliant Les Tapp to equalise in the final minutes, with a shot from the boards that some thought Art Palfrey might have saved.

The New Year commenced with the second leg of this final tie. It was to be an anticlimax as Mohawks recovered their form to thrash their opponents 9-1. Perth were certainly short-handed for this match, owing to an outbreak of influenza at the club, but even so the margin of their defeat was as emphatic as it was embarrassing. The match was all over as a contest in the first five minutes as Mohawks scored three goals without reply. They moved centre Gordon Galloway into the first line of attack, in place of John Fullerton, and it worked a treat as he bagged a hat-trick, as did Billy Fullerton. Thanks to great back-checking, particularly from the second line, and a solid defensive performance, the threat posed by the Perth danger men, Les Tapp and Les Lovell, was simply snuffed out. It was yet another highly impressive performance by Mohawks in a competition they had almost completely dominated since its inception five seasons ago. This was their third consecutive victory in the final of the President's Pucks and their fourth overall.

Mohawks followed up their success only three days later with a resounding 7-0 win against Kelvingrove in the league championship. The champions had now scored 16 goals in two matches, Billy Fullerton obtaining his second hat-trick in consecutive matches. In fairness to Kelvingrove they had not played a competitive match for almost a month and took to the ice in this game without any substitutes being available. Mohawks' margin of victory over Kelvingrove was the largest in the history of this particular fixture and it was the tenth consecutive match against the West End team without defeat.

The first representative match of the season was played on 23 January when Glasgow entertained Brighton Tigers of the English National League at Crossmyloof. Given the calibre of the opposition this fixture would normally have been designated as a full international match by the SIHA but it was obviously erring on the side of caution bearing in mind Scotland's poor record against English club sides in the past.

The squad chosen for Glasgow was on very different lines from those selected in the past. The almost ever present Dave Cross was replaced in goal by Art Palfrey and not one of the Fullerton brothers made the side although Billy would have done so had he been available. Of the ten players selected Joe Collins was the only one who had not learned to play the game in Canada.

On the blue line in front of Palfrey were Bill Boivin and Collins. The first line of attack was Pete Stevenson, Len McCartney and Jim Kenny. The second line was Johnny Kelly, Henry Loane and Robert Thomson. Cover for defence or attack was provided by Wally Welch. Glasgow looked a strong side but they lacked practice time together and they were facing a very settled and very good Brighton team.

Brighton had the better of the first period but it was Glasgow who took the lead when Len McCartney followed up on a rebounded shot from Pete Stevenson to open the scoring against the run of play. The second period was more even. Glasgow had chances to increase their lead with Jim Kenny and Henry Loane both coming close. At the other end, Art Palfrey was in outstanding form defying everything the speedy Brighton forwards could throw at him. The period ended goalless. The exchanges were even keener in the final period as Brighton went flat out. Their pressure finally paid off when the best player on the ice, Bobby Lee, scored the equaliser. With the minutes ticking away the same player made a breakthrough and swerving past Palfrey fired the puck into the net for the winning goal amidst great excitement.

Brighton had been the better team overall but Glasgow could take some satisfaction from a very encouraging performance. "Inside Edge" considered Brighton Tigers to be the best club side ever to have visited Crossmyloof, a side which included three players born in Scotland, Jimmy Kelly, Bob Purdie and S "Scotty" Cameron. The performance of the Glasgow team reinforced the view of most observers that some of the Canadian imports who had recently come into the Scottish League were indeed of a very good standard and had the ability to compete at this level.

Mohawks continued to set the pace in the league championship with successive wins over Lions and Perth Panthers. They were not resting on their laurels either having secured the services of another Canadian forward, G (Gerry) Strong, a native of Montreal. Mustangs, though, were not out of it yet and were continuing to push the champions hard.

The two teams met at the end of January in a vital match. If Mohawks won they would move six points ahead of Mustangs, and with only four matches left would seem almost certainties for the Canada Cup. It was a match Mustangs had to win if they wanted to keep their own championship aspirations alive. In their three previous league encounters, Mohawks had the edge with two wins and a draw.

Their latest confrontation lived up to all the pre-match expectations. It developed into a frantic contest played at great speed and characterised by robust exchanges. Play was evenly balanced with Wally Welch putting Mustangs ahead in the first period, only for Archie Bogie to equalise for Mohawks in the middle session. A simmering match finally exploded in the third period as both teams went all out for the winning goal. Bill Boivin put Mustangs ahead for the second time, before Art Palfrey and Bill Russell became embroiled in a fight which resulted in both of them being sent off. Mustangs took full advantage of Palfrey's absence when Henry Loane and Welch added to their team's goal tally to give them a rather flattering 4-1 victory.

With almost three quarters of the league campaign now completed Mustangs victory sent them to the top of the table with Mohawks on 18 points. However, the defending champions had played one match less and with that crucial game in hand they remained favourites to retain their title.

The match between Mohawks and Mustangs had been very physical. Two players, Alec Fullerton and Gerry Strong, required hospital treatment for their injuries. It had followed a particularly nasty confrontation between Mustangs and Lions only three days earlier, in another match tarnished by fighting amongst the players.

The SIHA was becoming increasingly concerned by the frequency of these incidents. Its president, Frank Stuart, remarked:

> "I know that in Canada scraps on the ice occur regularly and no one ever thinks much about it, but in Scotland there is a different outlook on these things and we simply must preserve our sporting traditions."
> *(Daily Record and Mail: 2 February 1937).*

The ice hockey correspondent of the *Glasgow Herald* reiterated his view that the referees had a duty to be stricter in their interpretation of what constituted a penalty, particularly in relation to illegal checking and tripping. He believed their failure in this regard was one of the root causes of the recent violence, since offended players were taking the law into their own hands by instigating retaliation on their unpunished aggressors.

Matches were still being refereed by a select pool of experienced club officials, all approved by the SIHA, almost all of whom were ex-players. The system was certainly open to abuse but complaints up until now had been few and far between. Yet it did seem rather incongruous that teams in competition with each other for major honours often had their important matches refereed by officials from their main rivals.

The higher incidence of physical play was entirely due to the increasing number of players with Canadian experience coming into the Scottish League.

This was, as Frank Stuart acknowledged, the way ice hockey was played in Canada but it was now giving the Scottish game a much more competitive edge it had not experienced before. Whether the SIHA liked to admit it or not, the domestic game was changing beyond all recognition. It was shedding more and more of the amateur ethos which had previously prevailed.

While some might lament the gradual passing of the game for the game's sake others in the sport positively embraced it. Along with the more robust style of play and semi-professionalism (in all but name) came much faster, more skilful and more entertaining matches, which were drawing record attendances to both Crossmyloof and Perth. The Canadian players were generally popular with the paying public and they undoubtedly added a bit of "show biz" to the sport.

Season 1936-1937

On the ice attention switched to the Mitchell Trophy, for which only the four Glasgow clubs would compete. The first semi-final between Kelvingrove and Lions was played on 5 February. The two sides had played in the league championship only three days earlier with the unpredictable Kelvingrove returning to form with a 6-3 win. It was therefore unfortunate for them that Joe Collins would not be available for the cup tie. In a dramatic match both teams shared a goal apiece in the first period. Lions had the better of the middle session and took a 3-2 lead into the final period. There were only five seconds remaining on the clock when Robert Thomson scored the equalising goal for Kelvingrove, taking the match into extra time. With tensions running high, both on and off the ice, Pete Stevenson capitalised on a defensive error to score the winning goal for Lions.

In the league championship Mustangs, having got themselves back into contention, then proceeded to lose three points in their next two matches. They were held 4-4 in a thrilling contest at Perth as the Panthers maintained their unbeaten home record. New signing, Jimmy Lightfoot, who had moved from Lions, was amongst the scorers. This was followed by an unexpected 2-1 defeat against Kelvingrove, a result which more or less administered the *coup de grace* to Mustangs' title ambitions. The main beneficiaries of these reverses were of course Mohawks.

The defending champions were determined not to slip up again. Unlike Mustangs, they had won their next two matches, yet again putting Kelvingrove to the sword with a 4-1 victory and then recording a thumping 6-1 win against Lions. This sequence of results meant that by the end of February, Mohawks were again sole leaders in the league championship with 22 points from fourteen matches compared to Mustangs with 19 points from fifteen matches. Mohawks now only had to remain unbeaten in their final two league matches to retain the Canada Cup. Both matches were potentially tricky, since their opponents were the ever improving Perth Panthers home and away. This "double-header" was almost guaranteed to provide an exciting climax to the season. Perth were currently in great form having just demolished Lions 12-4, with Jimmy Lightfoot and Les Tapp sharing five goals apiece!

Some consolation for Mustangs was provided by their 2-1 victory against Mohawks in the second semi-final of the Mitchell Trophy, played on 19 February. It drew another huge crowd to Crossmyloof for what was one of the most exciting matches of the season. Man of the match was Henry Loane whose "stick-handling genius and play making craft often threw Mohawks completely out of gear." There was no scoring in the first period although John Fullerton missed a great chance to put Mohawks ahead. With Alec Fullerton and Jim Kenny in the penalty box, Loane scored for Mustangs in the second period and shortly after Wally Welch made it 2-0. Kenny pulled a goal back shortly before the interval. Mohawks pressed very hard in the final session and were unlucky not to at least equalise but in the end few grudged Mustangs their success.

Mohawks were denied the opportunity of achieving their second consecutive "treble". The result meant that a new name would be engraved on the Mitchell Trophy, as neither Lions nor Mustangs had won it before. As with the President's Pucks this season, the final would be played over two legs commencing in early March.

Despite improved standards north of the border, no players from the Scottish League were selected for the Great Britain squad competing in the European and World Championships being held this year in London at the Empire Arena, Wembley and the Harringay Arena. Great Britain were of course the defending champions of both titles and there were great expectations that as the host nation they would be able to repeat the success of the previous year. Although there was no domestic involvement four players born in Scotland did make it into the British team and these were goaltenders Jimmy Foster and Ronald Milne of Harringay Greyhounds, defender Paul McPhail of Earls Court Rangers and forward Jimmy Kelly of Brighton Tigers.

The championships were again organised on a sectional basis. Great Britain had little difficulty qualifying for the next phase of the competition as they defeated Germany 6-0, Hungary 7-0 and Rumania 11-0. In the next round, Switzerland were beaten 3-0, Poland 11-0 and Hungary 5-0. Great Britain thus duly qualified for the final section having not lost a match and scoring an impressive 43 goals in the process. Jimmy Foster had enjoyed six consecutive shut-outs. Great Britain's three opponents in the final section were Switzerland, Germany and Canada, who were represented at this event by Kimberley Dynamiters from British Columbia. In the first match the Swiss were beaten 2-0 after extra time. Canada were next but they proved too good winning a dour contest 3-0. Great Britain then defeated Germany 5-0 in their final match to become European Champions for the second successive time but it was unbeaten Canada who won back the World Championship for the ninth time.

In the aftermath of the European and World Championships, Lions caused a major stir by signing the experienced Ronald Milne from Harringay Greyhounds, where he had been struggling to get a game as the understudy to the great Jimmy Foster. Lions had been shedding goals at an alarming rate all season. With an eye on the forthcoming Mitchell Trophy final the club had taken decisive action to plug its leaky defence. Ronald Milne was of course no stranger to the Scottish League, having previously turned out for Glasgow University prior to joining Manchester and then Harringay Greyhounds. As anticipated, Milne made his debut for Lions in the first leg of the Mitchell Trophy final on 2 March. However it was for a while touch and go. Mustangs protested about his inclusion in the Lions team, arguing that, in the absence of written confirmation from the BIHA regarding his transfer, they had selected an unregistered player. After some persuasion by SIHA officials a reluctant Mustangs agreed to play the tie but only under protest.

Season 1936-1937

Mustangs had some on-ice problems of their own to contend with. Bill Boivin had left the club to join Perth Panthers and Felix McLernan was missing through injury. With W G McDonald also unavailable Mustangs faced Lions with a sadly depleted defence, although they still presented a formidable challenge in attack. The match was a lively and thrilling affair characterised by outstanding performances from Ronald Milne for Lions and Henry Loane for Mustangs. Johnny Kelly scored for Mustangs after only five minutes when he capitalised on a defensive mistake. Only twenty seconds later Wally Welch made it 2-0. Lions recovered their composure and Len McCartney pulled a goal back just before the end of the first period. The second period was very even with both teams trading a goal, Welch making it 3-1 and McCartney again reducing the deficit. Lions went all out for the equaliser in the final session but found Milne in magnificent form defying the best efforts of their deadly duo, McCartney and Pete Stevenson. The match ended 3-2 for Mustangs and it set up an intriguing second leg on 12 March.

On 3 March, Mohawks faced Perth Panthers in a vital league match at Perth Ice Rink. The match attracted a full house. The spectators were not to be disappointed, as both teams served up a thrilling encounter. Mohawks took a bit of time to settle on the smaller ice surface at Perth, which allowed the Panthers to take an early advantage. The best player on the ice, Les Lovell, scored twice for Perth in the first period. Early in the middle session he made it a hat-trick with another outstanding solo goal. Gordon Galloway reduced the leeway before the interval. With Mohawks requiring a point to keep their league title ambitions on track they went out with all guns blazing in the final period. They pulverised the home goal and were finally rewarded when John Fullerton scored. In a breathtaking finish Jim Kenny secured that precious equalising goal minutes from full time. It ended 3-3.

The return match at Crossmyloof a week later was no less exciting. It started on a controversial note as Perth iced their latest signing, Bill Boivin, who then promptly scored after a minute of play. Mohawks protested about his selection, since the rules stated that a player changing clubs during a season could not play for his new club except in "special circumstances". The SIHA officials in attendance at the match agreed with this interpretation of the rules. Bill Boivin was benched for the remainder of the match and his goal was annulled. Perth were obviously not best pleased by these developments and the match then deteriorated into a physical contest. Mohawks however were not put off their stride as Gordon Galloway scored twice to give them a 2-0 lead at the interval - his first goal a brilliant individual effort. Jimmy Lightfoot, who (curiously) had also switched clubs during the season, pulled a goal back for Perth in the second period. A Jim Kenny strike in the final session sealed a 3-1 victory for Mohawks and with that, the Canada Cup!

It was Mohawks' second league championship win in successive seasons. They became the first team in the Scottish League to successfully defend their league title and it was their third title overall. They were now record winners of the Canada Cup. They had become champions again with the smallest playing squad in the league. It was a remarkable achievement owed primarily to their continued insistence on quality over quantity, and the excellent coaching skills of Jim Kenny. Mohawks finished the campaign with 25 points from sixteen matches and had the best defensive record in the league, the foundation of their success.

The champions employed a simple formula. A great goaltender, sound defence and two forward lines, one geared towards all out attack and the other more orientated towards back-checking when required. Alec Fullerton epitomised the spirit at the club. His previous feats of endurance have already been noted. He continued to play on in the latter half of the season despite being in constant pain with a broken bone in one of his feet.

There were still two league fixtures to be played when Mohawks wrapped up the title but the attention of most observers became focussed on the second leg of the Mitchell Trophy on 12 March. Mustangs held a 3-2 lead from the first leg but they suffered another blow to their seemingly diminishing ranks when star forward Henry Loane returned to Canada.

The return leg attracted 3,000 spectators to Crossmyloof but in an unprecedented development Mustangs refused to play the match! They were again furious about the inclusion of Ronald Milne in the Lions team, insisting that his selection contravened the rules. Despite assurances from the SIHA president Frank Stuart that Milne's registration with Lions was above board, Bob Gardiner, the captain and manager of Mustangs, refused to budge. He presented an ultimatum to the effect that if Milne was not withdrawn from the Lions team then Mustangs would not play.

The SIHA took the view that no rules were being breached by Milne's selection in the Lions team. In view of this the ruling body adopted a hard line. The only course of action left was to abandon the match and award the Mitchell Trophy to Lions since Mustangs were considered to have defaulted. The spectators eagerly expecting a keen contest had their admission money refunded, with fulsome apologies from embarrassed SIHA officials. A dreadful anti-climax to one of the showpiece games of the season.

Quite why such a protest was left to the eleventh hour with some 3,000 spectators in attendance defies logic. Mustangs must have known that Lions would select Ronald Milne so their action on the night seems both petty and mean spirited. Having played the first leg, surely they could have played the second as well, albeit under further protest.

On the other hand, the SIHA really needed to do something about tightening the rules around player movements during the season. The current system was open to abuse and on occasion was being abused. Although Lions had done nothing wrong under the existing rules, one might question how ethical

Season 1936-1937

it was for any club to hire players with specific matches in mind. The rules required clarification otherwise it would make a mockery of competition.

With the domestic season ending in something of a fiasco, a number of representative matches were arranged. On 16 March, Glasgow entertained Cambridge University at Crossmyloof on an evening when Mustangs were due to play Perth Panthers in the final match of the league programme. This fixture was re-arranged for the end of the month.

The squad selected by Glasgow was on similar lines to that which had taken the ice against Brighton Tigers in January. The only missing players were the departed Henry Loane, Bill Boivin - whose status remained unclear - and Robert Thomson, who was not selected on this occasion. Alec and Billy Fullerton returned to the team and Gordon Galloway, who was in great form, won his first representative honour.

Glasgow were anticipating a difficult match, but they outclassed their opponents as easily as the 10-2 score suggested. The "light blues" had no answer to the speed and individual ability of the Glasgow side for whom the Lions duo of Pete Stevenson and Len McCartney were in sparkling form. In truth this was not a vintage Cambridge University side, a fact reinforced when Perth Panthers demolished them 12-4 the following evening.

A much more formidable challenge was offered by Richmond Hawks of the English National League when a "double-header" was arranged against Scotland at Perth Ice Rink on 19 March and at Crossmyloof the following evening. Richmond Hawks were a talented outfit and included the Great Britain international, Johnny Coward, Harry McArthur, and the Scots-born George McNeil and Tommy Forgie. The Scottish squad selected for these matches bore very little resemblance to that which had taken the ice against England a year earlier. The only survivors from that team were Billy Fullerton and Jim Kenny and the only home developed players in the current squad were Fullerton and Joe Collins. No "Anglo-Scots" were considered for selection either, the bulk of the side comprising recent imports from Canada.

For the match at Perth, Art Palfrey was in goal behind a blue line of Joe Collins and Les Lovell. In attack, Bill Boivin, Les Tapp and Jimmy Lightfoot of Perth Panthers comprised the first line with Pete Stevenson, Len McCartney and Jim Kenny making up the second line. Gordon Galloway was held in reserve. For the match at Crossmyloof, Bill Boivin replaced Joe Collins in defence. In attack, the Stevenson, McCartney and Kenny line remained in tact but a new line was formed comprising Billy Fullerton, Gordon Galloway and Jimmy Lightfoot. Collins was held in reserve and Les Tapp was unavailable.

Scotland were trounced 8-3 at Perth and 10-3 at Crossmyloof. In reality these reverses should not have been unexpected, but the margin of defeat in both matches certainly rankled. Scotland completely failed to do themselves justice in either contest, relying far too much on individual ability but without any direction or game plan. Despite the loss of 18 goals it was considered that

Art Palfrey had done well in goal with Les Lovell and Len McCartney also gaining pass marks.

These results gave the SIHA much to ponder. It was difficult for the international team to find any continuity, given the almost constant player movements prevailing in the domestic game. Opportunities for team practice were almost nil so the players selected were often playing together for the first time. In such circumstances it was no surprise that lack of teamwork and combination, along with lack of stamina, were the defining factors in successive Scottish defeats.

The domestic season ended in yet more controversy when the one remaining league match between Mustangs and Perth Panthers was scratched. At a meeting on 23 March, the SIHA had decided to suspend Mustangs from further competition until next season. Perth Panthers were awarded the two points from this fixture.

The suspension of Mustangs was of course the result of their refusal to play in the second leg of the recent Mitchell Trophy final. The SIHA had certainly taken decisive action, but with the season all but over the punishment was not quite as bad as it seemed. A net result was that Perth Panthers leapfrogged Kelvingrove by one point in the league table to claim third place, a development which seemed a bit unfair on the West End club.

It had been a mixed season for Perth Panthers. They had seemed to spend most of it recruiting players, not quite managing to establish a settled side. This long process continued right up to the final weeks of the campaign when they made another three signings more with an eye to next season; A (Art) Schumann, a native of Gull Lake, Saskatchewan, and brothers, J (Jim) and R (Bert) Forsythe. In Les Tapp, Les Lovell, and Jimmy Lightfoot, Perth already had players of genuine quality. Tapp and Lightfoot, along with Len McCartney of Lions, finished joint top goal scorers in the league championship with 18 goals apiece. Indeed, Perth were the top scoring team in the championship with 58 goals, which was 10 more than the champions Mohawks managed but they also had the second worse defence in the championship and it was that which had let them down.

The season came to an exciting conclusion when it was announced that the world champions, Canada, represented by the Kimberley Dynamiters, would be visiting Crossmyloof on 25 March. At the end of a strenuous European tour, they had played 64 matches - won 56, lost 6 and drawn 2. The match in Glasgow was the last they would play before returning to Canada the following day. Given Scotland's recent performances against Richmond Hawks, not too much was expected. The local press urged the SIHA to include "Anglo-Scots" in the squad for this match. This advice was not heeded as the ruling body largely stuck with the same group of players, the only change being the exclusion of Joe Collins in favour of Lions latest Canadian import, J Dunsmore, who had played only one match for his club.

Season 1936-1937

Although everyone was fearing the worst, Scotland gave an excellent performance and were decidedly unlucky to lose the match 6-4. One is tempted to suggest that Canada were tired and weary after such a long haul on the Continent, but that would be ungracious and rather unkind to a Scottish team which at last played to something like its full potential. But for an understandably nervous start, Scotland may well have caused a sensation.

Canada made a fast start and took a 2-0 lead early in the match which made Scotland adopt more defensive tactics. Despite that Canada added a third goal before the end of the first period. Scotland opened up again in the middle session and were rewarded when Les Lovell went on one of his by now trademark rushes up the ice to score and reduce the deficit. Jim Kenny then scored with a back-handed shot and with great excitement mounting, Len McCartney broke away to score an equaliser at a time Canada were on a power play. Having clawed their way back into the match at 3-3, Scotland then lost a killer goal just before the end of the period.

The third period was end-to-end, but it was Canada who scored again. Pete Stevenson then reduced the leeway to 5-4 with a brilliant solo goal but the Canadians responded with a sixth goal near the end. With Canada having two players in the penalty box in the closing minutes, Scotland pounded their goal but an absorbing encounter ended 6-4 in Canada's favour.

Once again the official season had concluded somewhat prematurely, given that time had been set aside in April for ice hockey at both Crossmyloof and Perth. To fill this vacuum two local tournaments were held at each venue.

The final match of the Perth competition was notable for two main reasons. Firstly, Kelvingrove defeated Mohawks 2-1 - the first time they had defeated their old rivals in thirteen matches. Secondly, the match was the first in Scotland to be covered by a live radio broadcast. Jack Gilmour, secretary of the SIHA, provided the commentary. It was a measure of how far the game in Scotland had come that it was now deemed significant enough to attract the broadcast media.

The curtain came down at Crossmyloof with something of a novelty. A match was arranged between two ladies' teams. As the ice hockey correspondent of the *Glasgow Herald* somewhat ungallantly put it

> "A women's ice hockey match between sides designated "Eagles" and "Falcons" was played as an innovation at Crossmyloof last night. A slow, rather uninteresting game resulted in a draw, each side scoring a goal."
>
> *(Glasgow Herald: 1 May 1937).*

It is likely that most of the players in these two teams came from Kelvingrove Ice Hockey Club, as they were known to have a very active Ladies' Section. While the SIHA had been making encouraging noises in relation to developing the ladies' game, the lack of available ice time was a serious impediment to that aim ever being achieved.

Thus ended what "Inside Edge" considered to be the most colourful season in the history of the sport in Scotland. It was hard to disagree with this assessment. The Scottish game was witnessing the changing of the guards. The demise of Glasgow University at the beginning of the season and their replacement by Perth Panthers was symbolic. The amateur era was drawing to a close. Full semi-professionalism was just around the corner.

It was not just a question of how much each club was paying its players in "expenses" but the transition had been seen in other ways. The season had been marred to a certain extent over petty squabbling about player movements and registrations. In the past such matters would have been settled by the club officials concerned over a cup of tea or a pint of beer but these days had clearly gone. There was a harder edge to it all now as the clubs had become cash cows for the ice rink managements. A lot of money now rested on such decisions.

The game in England was already unrecognisable to that played only five years earlier especially in London. At venues like Wembley, Harringay and Earls Court matches were regularly attracting attendances of 7,000 or 8,000 spectators, who were watching and supporting teams almost wholly composed of imported players from Canada. The game was really professional in all but name, with the better players receiving "expenses" of £10 to £12 per week.

Some matches were being televised and others featured regularly on the radio. Press interest was enormous. This interest was underlined by the publication of a dedicated ice hockey newspaper, *Ice Hockey World*. Published weekly during the season, it had been founded by Canadian exile and entrepreneur, Robert Giddens, the season before and was proving to be a great success. It also covered the Scottish game though not in the same detail as that in England.

Wembley Lions won the English National League for the second season in succession by three points from their nearest challengers Harringay Racers. The champions were packed full of talent and included inspirational star defender, Lou Bates, as well as Great Britain internationals, Gordon Dailley and Alex Archer. Wembley's title win was especially meritorious since the league had expanded to eleven teams.

Season 1937-38

The winds of change continued to blow through Scottish ice hockey. After two seasons of only five clubs competing in the Scottish League or the Scottish National League as it was becoming increasingly known, the league championship was restored to six clubs with the inclusion of an additional team based in Perth. Four of these teams, Kelvingrove, Lions, Mohawks and Mustangs, continued to be based at Crossmyloof Ice Rink, Glasgow, while Perth Panthers and the newly formed Perth Black Hawks would be based at the Central Ice Rink, Perth. The establishment of Perth Black Hawks was yet more confirmation that the times were changing. Their arrival underlined the evolution towards a semi-professional league in Scotland. This trend had already commenced the season before with their rink neighbours, Perth Panthers, and it signalled the determination of the management at the Central Ice Rink to move the sport in a new direction.

Whether this was the direction in which the SIHA wanted the sport to go was still a moot point. In one sense the ruling body was no longer in control. The reality was that events were controlling it. Strong and dynamic commercial interests were driving the sport in Perth but in Glasgow the clubs ,as they were currently structured, were not at the same level of development - which for some was how they wanted it. Despite the prevailing optimism in the "Fair City" some observers had serious doubts regarding the feasibility of running two semi-professional teams from the same venue. As "Inside Edge" in the *Daily Record and Mail* pointed out

> "In many influential quarters it is felt that Perth with its population of only 35,000 is becoming somewhat ambitious in the proposal to run two first class teams and at the same time secure the services of many noted players to the disadvantage of Glasgow and other ice hockey centres.
>
> It is pointed out that Perth cannot maintain two first class football teams. Can it maintain two ice hockey teams? What Perth and the public really wants is one top notch team with a brood of reserve lads from which team selections can be made."
> (*Daily Record and Mail*: 29 September 1937).

If one was looking at the longer term then this was probably fair comment but semi- professional or fully professional ice hockey was to become a sport in Great Britain bedevilled by short term thinking and blatant opportunism. As things stood at the moment there was certainly no shortage of "top notch" players at Perth, the very proliferation of which had led to the creation of a second club.

In looking at the prospects of the various clubs for the season ahead, one is drawn to the inevitable conclusion that the two Perth teams were far and away better than anyone else. Although they had lost a number of important players to their new rink rivals, Perth Panthers remained a most formidable outfit. Their stock had been more than adequately replenished. The tall and imposing Robert Thomson had been acquired from Kelvingrove to play in defence and Len McCartney arrived from Lions. The club's ambition was highlighted by the signing of ex-Manchester left wing, J (Jack) Schofield.

While defensively not as strong, Perth Panthers had a potency in attack that rendered such a situation almost irrelevant. They now boasted a front line of Les Tapp, Len McCartney and Jimmy Lightfoot, who the season before had finished joint top goal scorers in the league championship. When one added Jack Schofield into the mix it was clear that Panthers had a forward line without equal in the country.

By contrast the strength of Perth Black Hawks appeared to lie more in defence where player-coach Les Lovell shared the blue line with Art Schumann. Both players also liked to attack whenever possible so goals from this area of the ice could also be expected. The club underlined its ambition by recruiting centre, R (Bob) Purdie, from Brighton Tigers who would partner Tommy McInroy and J (Jack) Stewart in the forward line. While Les Lovell had put together a very competitive looking first team, they appeared a bit light in reserve strength.

Mohawks, the defending champions, were the only Crossmyloof-based side which seemed capable of offering a realistic challenge to the two Perth teams. They had lost the services of both Gordon Galloway and Gerry Strong from the previous season but replacements were found when the useful Glen Braid moved from Mustangs and G (George) Baillie, left wing, arrived from Canada.

The backbone of Mohawks remained the three Fullerton brothers and player-coach Jim Kenny. Art Palfrey was the best goaltender in the Scottish League. They were a very proud club and it would therefore be premature to write off their chances of winning a third successive Canada Cup, but the opposition they faced from Perth this season was clearly of a much better standard than anything they had ever faced before.

By comparison, the three other Glasgow teams looked to be making up the numbers. The playing strength of Mustangs, runners-up in the league championship for the last two seasons, had been decimated. Star players, Wally Welch and Bill Russell had joined Lions, and Glen Braid had moved to Mohawks. While these were very serious losses it was not all doom and gloom, as Don Edwards was acquired from Mohawks, where he had now

Season 1937-1938

Jimmy Lightfoot, Perth Panthers and Scotland

been deemed surplus to requirements. In a surprising move, Bert Forsythe arrived from Perth Panthers.

Kelvingrove appeared to be stuck in a rut. This famous old club had not won a major honour for three seasons and it was difficult to see them doing any better this season. Most of the Canadian players they acquired the previous season had proved a disappointment - the one major exception being Robert Thomson but he had now moved to Perth Panthers. There was a familiarity about Kelvingrove; this was part of the problem. The squad badly needed an injection of fresh talent if it was to recapture its former glories.

Lions, already starting from a poor position, were badly depleted from last season. The loss of their star centre, Len McCartney, was of course a huge blow but the retirements of Ronald MacDonald, Tom Shearer and Wilbur Muirhead were no less regrettable. On the plus side, the club had acquired two very good players in Wally Welch and Bill Russell and had also signed a useful right defence in A (Alec) Purdie who had Canadian experience.

It was obvious at the outset of the season that if any of the Glasgow teams, with the possible exception of Mohawks, were to make any impact they would have to acquire more experienced Canadian talent. The Perth clubs had set the bar at a new level. Kelvingrove, Lions and Mustangs were acutely aware of this fact. As the season progressed, they all set about trying to improve the quality of their respective squads to meet the challenge.

The SIHA announced two important rule changes. They took action to regulate the movement of players between clubs during a season. This was in response to the controversy which had arisen the previous season over the legality of the registration of Ronald Milne at Lions. In future no one could play in the Scottish League without a new registration form issued by the SIHA. The second change introduced was more fundamental. In future all matches in the Scottish League would consist of three periods of twenty minutes duration each. At long last, after eight seasons of official competition, the Scottish game was brought into line with the rest of Europe and North America with matches being played in what was accepted as the regulation time by the LIHG.

It was hoped that this latter change would assist representative sides, in particular, to compete more effectively against their opposition. Crossmyloof-based players had been handicapped in the past by playing a shortened version of the game. Consequently, they had a propensity to tire badly in the third period of such matches. The rink management at the Glasgow venue were to be congratulated for finally agreeing to this change despite competing priorities for ice time from other sports.

Of course the growing popularity of ice hockey at Crossmyloof and the financial rewards that brought helped sway their decision. Pressure probably also came for the change from the rink management at Perth. Ice hockey matches at the Glasgow venue were now regularly attracting bumper crowds

Season 1937-1938

but despite this boom ticket prices for ordinary matches would remain at 9d for another season.

It would be the longest league championship ever in the history of the Scottish League. A total of 75 fixtures would be played between early October and early May. Each team in the competition would play the other on five occasions giving each side a total of 15 fixtures. As in the previous season, the team finishing in first position would require to finish more than two points ahead of the runners-up or otherwise face a play-off against them to determine the final destination of the Canada Cup.

The league championship opened on 1 October in controversial circumstances when Mohawks defeated Lions 3-1. Owing to some technical problems with the ice making equipment at Crossmyloof, the match was played in a mist which descended over the rink obscuring the visibility of the players, officials and spectators alike. The mist was apparently caused by the humidity in the building arising from the large attendance of spectators. Mohawks played the match under protest.

Resplendent in their new white and black kit, Perth Black Hawks made an impressive debut at Crossmyloof four days later with an emphatic 7-1 victory against Mustangs. Les Lovell scored a hat-trick for the visitors with Art Schumann and Bob Purdie each securing a brace. Mustangs had only one substitute available for the match. With the extended periods now in force they found the going very hard indeed.

Perth Panthers also made a fast start with a 5-0 home win against Kelvingrove, Len McCartney opening his account with a hat-trick. Perth Black Hawks returned to Crossmyloof for their next match against Lions and inflicted a 6-0 defeat, with Art Schumann joining the hat-trick club. Not to be outdone, Perth Panthers were next up at the Glasgow venue and thrashed a poor Mustangs side 10-0 with Jimmy Lightfoot helping himself to four goals and Len McCartney his second hat-trick in as many matches.

The alarm bells were already ringing. In their four fixtures to date the two Perth teams had scored 28 goals between them for the loss of only 1. These early results merely confirmed what a number of observers feared - that there was a huge gulf in class between the Glasgow teams and those in Perth. It led "The Blade" in the *Evening Times* to implore the SIHA to take the action needed to strengthen the Glasgow teams before the paying public tired of such one-sided matches.

The Crossmyloof based clubs had never stopped trying to strengthen their squads, but attracting players from Canada with the requisite experience and skill was difficult, given the competition emanating from Perth - not to mention from England. Of the players that did become available, it was agreed that the SIHA should take a hand in directing them to the most ailing teams.

In the brave new world of Scottish ice hockey, the fixture between those historic rivals, Kelvingrove and Mohawks, almost seemed a relic of a bygone age, but it did not lose its lustre to the clubs concerned or their numerous members and supporters. The two teams met in mid-October; it ended 1-1, Glen Braid scoring for Mohawks and Sam Stevenson for Kelvingrove. The match was notable for the return of Wally Welch to Mohawks from Lions but quite where that left the SIHA's new rules on inter-club transfers during a season was anyone's guess.

The first real showdown of the season took place on 19 October when Mohawks met Perth Panthers at Crossmyloof. It was an enthralling contest played at a fast and furious pace in front of a capacity attendance. The first period was goalless although Len McCartney missed an easy chance. Mohawks were the better team in the middle session with Glen Braid missing an open goal and Wally Welch clipping a post. The third period opened with a brilliant solo goal from Billy Fullerton but the best player on the ice, Les Tapp, secured the equaliser. It was no surprise when Robert Thomson scored what was the winning goal, close to the end of play. Perth finished the stronger side, and deserved their narrow victory. The usually sound Mohawks defence had been rather shaky throughout the game, although Art Palfrey in goal had played exceptionally well.

The difference in class between the top of the league and the bottom was amply demonstrated when Perth Panthers returned to Crossmyloof three days later and annihilated Lions 15-3! Their first line ran amok as Len McCartney bagged five goals. Les Tapp and Jimmy Lightfoot helped themselves to four apiece. The result constituted the highest scoring match in the history of the Canada Cup; no team had ever scored 15 goals in one game.

Mohawks, still smarting from their defeat by Perth Panthers, travelled to the Central Ice Rink at the end of October to face an unbeaten Perth Black Hawks. It was a close match until young Tommy McInroy scored in the second period to give Black Hawks a 3-1 lead. The home team became complacent in the final period and almost paid the price as first Jim Kenny pulled a goal back and then Billy Fullerton missed a great chance to level the scores in the final minute. It finished 3-2 for Black Hawks. It was the champions' second defeat to Perth opposition in consecutive matches, albeit by only one goal on both occasions. That was of little consolation to Mohawks who if they did not fully realise the enormity of the challenge which faced them certainly knew it now. It was going to be very difficult retaining their league title without more quality reinforcements being brought in to bolster their squad.

Following their harrowing defeat against Perth Panthers a new look Lions recorded their first win of the season when they defeated Kelvingrove 2-1. Lions had signed two new Canadians, left defence B (Bunt) Roberts and centre F (Frank) Chase, who scored both their goals on his debut. Chase, though born in London, England, had been brought up in Ottawa where he had played for a variety of local teams before joining Wembley Canadians for season 1935-36.

Season 1937-1938

The eagerly anticipated Perth derby took place on 5 November, appropriately enough an evening for fireworks. With both teams unbeaten and playing sparkling ice hockey, seats for the match were sold out weeks in advance. The capacity crowd was not to be disappointed. It was a match full of incident and played at a frenetic pace. The lead changed hands several times as Black Hawks went to the interval 4-3 ahead at the end of the second period. Play had been even but Panthers were the stronger side in the final period as their neighbours visibly tired. Les Tapp took control of the situation completing his hat-trick as Panthers clinched a 7-5 victory. The result was particularly sore on Art Schumann, who had scored four of his team's five goals.

The Perth derby concluded the first round of matches in the league championship. Perth Panthers remained the only undefeated team in the competition with five wins from five matches for a total of 10 points. They had scored an impressive 39 goals in the process for the loss of only 9, the best average in the league. Panthers first line of Les Tapp, Len McCartney and Jimmy Lightfoot seemed unstoppable.

Perth Black Hawks were in second place with 8 points from five matches. Their combination was not quite as good as Panthers although they were considered to be a faster team than their neighbours. Black Hawks relied more on the individual prowess of their star men, Les Lovell, Art Schumann and Bob Purdie. It was therefore very unfortunate that Schumann was about to leave the club to play part of the season in Germany. It represented a big loss.

The defending champions Mohawks were struggling to keep pace with the two Perth sides. It was not that they had a poor team, far from it, but the calibre of player being attracted to Perth was beyond anything seen in the Scottish game before. Despite the challenge posed it was obvious that Mohawks would have to collect some points from these teams if they were to have any chance of retaining their league title. They were just about managing to hold on to the coat tails of the Perth teams.

For Kelvingrove, Lions and Mustangs it was already clear that they were out of their depth. Lions had at least tried to improve the quality of their squad, but for the other two teams it seemed an uphill struggle. Each side had managed one win - but only against each other. In the absence of further recruitment it was difficult to see that situation improving.

Mustangs made a start in that direction by acquiring two new forwards, G Ney and G (Glen) Morrison, the latter from Wembley Lions. The biggest signing was made by Perth Black Hawks, who acquired international goaltender Ronald Milne. He was of course a well-kent figure in Scottish ice hockey circles, as well as being the central figure in the previous season's major controversy over player registration.

The first representative match of the season was arranged for Crossmyloof on 12 November, when Glasgow would play Birmingham Maple Leafs. They were currently unattached from any formal league competition in England.

Frozen in Time

The management at Birmingham Ice Rink had concluded that it was no longer financially viable to enter a team from the venue. Although now confined to playing challenge matches, the Birmingham team remained a very decent outfit.

For the first time ever a Scottish representative squad was selected which did not include a single home-developed player. Not even one of the Fullerton brothers made the side - confirmation, if any were needed, that the game in Scotland was undergoing profound change. There were five survivors from the Glasgow team which had beaten Cambridge University in March; Art Palfrey, Pete Stevenson, Jim Kenny, Wally Welch and Johnny Kelly.

Glasgow took the ice with Art Palfrey in goal behind a blue line of Bunt Roberts and Bert Forsythe. The first line was Wally Welch, Glen Morrison and Jim Kenny with the second line comprising Pete Stevenson, Frank Chase and George Baillie. Johnny Kelly was held in reserve. The Birmingham side contained three players who would later play in Scotland; Bill Lane, Howard "Biff" Smith and B "Breezy" Thompson.

While the match was disappointing, the result was positive. Glasgow secured a rare win at this level of competition. With defences on top the opening period was goalless although Birmingham had the better of it. At the start of the middle session an excellent three-man move culminated in Bunt Roberts, whose timely interceptions and solo thrusts were a joy to watch, scoring the first goal. He then set up Frank Chase for a second goal, which had just a hint of offside about it.

Birmingham redoubled their efforts in the final period but found Art Palfrey a tough nut to crack. The game ended 2-0 for Glasgow, a result all the more notable given that the following evening Birmingham travelled to Perth and defeated a combined Black Hawks and Panthers side 5-2. Certainly Les Lovell and Jimmy Lightfoot were missing from the Perth team but Glasgow's victory remained impressive by comparison.

On the domestic front Lions registered the first real upset of the season when they defeated Perth Black Hawks 4-3 in a thrilling encounter at Crossmyloof on 15 November. Pete Stevenson scored the winning goal to complete a well taken hat-trick in the final minute of the game. Black Hawks latest Canadian import, Jimmy Allan, made his debut in this match.

Four days later Kelvingrove met Mohawks in one of the most controversial matches ever in the history of this fixture. Kelvingrove entered this match with some fresh talent in their ranks having acquired two new forwards -a young student, Dean Steadman, from the University of Western Ontario Mustangs and the experienced Scotland international, Scotty Cameron, from Brighton Tigers.

Kelvingrove arrived late for the match; as a punishment they were required to play the first ten minutes without any substitutes during which time Billy Fullerton put Mohawks ahead. Jim Kenny made it 2-0 in the second period before 'Grove hit back in the final period when two quick goals from Archie

Season 1937-1938

Len McCartney, Perth Panthers and Scotland

Maxwell brought them level. Amidst great excitement Cameron scored again but the goal was disallowed, as it was considered the final whistle had blown a split second before he struck the puck into the net.

The growing popularity of ice sports in Scotland was underlined by the news that progress was underway towards building an ice rink in Dundee. A consortium of local businessmen had formed a company for this purpose and negotiations to find a suitable site within the city were well advanced. It was expected that the new rink would be open by next winter and the intention was to promote ice hockey at the venue. The further recruitment of players into the Scottish League continued unabated.

Mohawks made an excellent signing in the experienced G (George) Horne who had played with Southampton Vikings and Wembley Monarchs. He was a native of Alloa but had moved to Canada as a youngster with his family. Mustangs, who had lost the all-too-brief services of Glen Morrison, found a very good replacement in L (Laurie) Marchant, a native of Winnipeg. Perth Black Hawks also found a more than adequate replacement for the departed Art Schumann when they acquired Howard Smith from Birmingham Maple Leafs.

George Horne made his debut for Mohawks on 24 November, when the champions faced Perth Panthers at the Central Ice Rink. It was not to be a pleasurable experience for the Glasgow team as they were crushed 10-4, in front of 3,000 spectators. Panthers were in rampant form and were 8-1 ahead by the start of the third period. Robert Thomson and Len McCartney scored hat-tricks for Panthers while Horne got a brace for Mohawks. The result was really a terrible blow to the morale of Mohawks. With it came the realisation that, even at this stage of the season, their grip on the Canada Cup was looking increasingly tenuous.

They sought some consolation in the President's Pucks competition, which commenced on 30 November with a first round tie against Kelvingrove, who were still smarting from the recent league match between the two rivals and were more keen than usual to give a good account of themselves. In a rousing game, Archie Maxwell put them ahead in the first period but goals from Wally Welch and Glen Braid turned it around for Mohawks in the middle session. Despite incessant pressure in the final period the eager 'Grove attack could find no way past an inspired Art Palfrey and it finished 2-1.

Perth Panthers, riding the crest of a wave, were finally brought down to earth when they lost two matches in the space of three days. Lions inflicted their first reverse in the league championship when they travelled to Perth on 1 December and won 6-3. The Glasgow side scored three goals without reply in the first fifteen minutes and led 4-0 at the start of the second period. Although Panthers staged a spirited fight back in the final period it was not enough. Lions had now completed a unique double over both of the Perth teams. They were of course now a very different team to that humiliated by

Season 1937-1938

Perth Panthers only two months earlier. The addition of Bunt Roberts and Frank Chase to their side had led to an enormous improvement. They had subsequently improved their team further with the acquisition of F (Fiore) "Buster" Amantea, an outstanding goaltender from Winnipeg who had experience with Wembley Monarchs and Southampton Vikings. He made a winning debut in Perth.

Worse was to follow for Perth Panthers only two days later when they met their city rivals, Black Hawks, in the first round of the President's Pucks. Jimmy Lightfoot put Panthers ahead but Bob Purdie equalised with a brilliant solo goal a few minutes later. Jimmy Allan scored the only goal of the second period to give Black Hawks a 2-1 lead. The final period was a disaster for Panthers as Black Hawks took full control with four goals, Allan completing a hat-trick in a 6-1 victory. It is difficult to determine what went wrong for Panthers. They certainly missed Robert Thomson, who was injured and did not play in this match, but perhaps the strain of two matches in three days was just too much even for a side of their abilities.

Boosted by a derby win Perth Black Hawks were on a roll which was confirmed when they thumped Mohawks 5-0 in the league championship at the Central Ice Rink. Bob Purdie scored a hat-trick for the home side; while Mohawks huffed and puffed, they found Howard Smith and Les Lovell on the blue line too much of an obstacle to overcome.

Mohawks had no time to dwell on their fast disappearing title ambitions. Only two days later, they met a confident Lions in the first semi-final of the President's Pucks. Mohawks had defeated their opponents on the two occasions they had met in the league, but they were taking nothing for granted. It turned out to be an interesting and hard fought cup tie. Billy Fullerton put Mohawks ahead in the first period when he scored off a Jim Kenny rebound. The second period was goalless although both teams had good chances to score. Archie Bogie increased Mohawks lead at the start of the final period but soon after Pete Stevenson pulled a goal back. The remainder of the period developed into a frantic affair as Lions sought an equaliser and almost got it but in the end Mohawks held on for a deserved 2-1 win. Mohawks had now qualified for the final of the President's Pucks competition for the fourth consecutive time, a notable achievement.

Their three previous finals had all ended in victories; their opponents in this final would be Perth Black Hawks, who had little difficulty in disposing of Mustangs in the second semi-final played on 15 December. The Glasgow team had unfortunately just lost the valuable services of Bert Forsythe who had joined a club in Switzerland. He was certainly missed as Black Hawks won as easily as the 7-1 score line suggested, Bob Purdie grabbing four goals and Les Lovell a brace.

Astonishingly, it was decided that the first leg of the President's Pucks final was to be played only two days later. This was unfair to Perth Black

Hawks who had barely any time to recover from the semi-final; it was doubly unfair that both matches would be held at Crossmyloof. If Black Hawks were feeling hard done by, they kept their thoughts to themselves and did their talking on the ice.

The first leg of the final was an exciting contest played at a fast and furious pace. Mohawks were the better team in the opening period but only had one goal to show for their superiority when Glen Braid scored with a neat back flick. They were to pay for their failure to capitalise more fully because Black Hawks picked up the pace in the second period and started to take a grip on the proceedings. It was no surprise when Bob Purdie equalised with a great solo effort. Mohawks seemed rattled and even the normally reliable Art Palfrey blundered badly when he let Les Lovell in to score a second goal. Black Hawks dominated the third period as Howard Smith and Purdie added further goals to give them an impressive 4-1 win. That was quite an advantage to take into the second leg in a week's time.

It was unfortunate for Black Hawks that they had to play Perth Panthers in a league match sandwiched between their two President's Pucks final ties. Rather ominously for the rest of the league Panthers had just strengthened their squad by signing another experienced forward, A (Arnie) Pratt. In the derby match it was Len McCartney who stole the show when he secured a hat-trick in an important 4-2 victory.

The return leg of the President's Pucks final was played on Christmas Eve and was something of a damp squib. Leading 4-1 from the first leg, Black Hawks never looked like relinquishing their control of the tie, despite a much improved performance by Mohawks compared to the first leg. The match ended 0-0 to give Perth Black Hawks the first silverware of the season.

The SIHA announced that a "Scottish Select" side would undertake a short trip to Germany at the end of December. It would be the first time that a representative team had visited Europe since Scotland had played France in Paris in October 1932. The fact that such a tour was being organised at all was testimony to the growing confidence abroad in the Scottish game.

The reason it was a select side rather than a full Scotland side was because no players from either Perth Panthers or Kelvingrove were available owing to prior commitments. The tour party would be managed by two experienced ex-players and current referees, Ronald MacDonald and J O McCabe, both of whom were senior SIHA officials. The tour party was:

F Amantea (Lions); G Horne (Mohawks), B Roberts (Lions) and A G Bogie (Mohawks); W Fullerton (Mohawks), R Purdie (Perth Black Hawks), J Kenny (Mohawks), F Chase (Lions), L Marchant (Mustangs), G Baillie (Mohawks) and J Kelly (Mustangs).

Howard Smith and Les Lovell of Perth Black Hawks were originally selected for the squad but both had to withdraw because of injuries. This allowed George Horne and Archie Bogie to gain their first representative honours. Omissions from the squad were Pete Stevenson of Lions and Art Palfrey and Wally Welch of Mohawks. The only home developed players were Billy Fullerton and Archie Bogie.

The Scottish Select played three matches, all in Berlin, with the following results:

26 December 1937	Berlin	3-4
27 December 1937	German-Canadian All Stars	0-0
29 December 1937	Berlin Red and White Club	5-3

It is difficult to determine the standard of opposition faced by the tourists but on the evidence of the results obtained it appears to have been a mixed bag. The Scottish team were considered unlucky to lose the first match against Berlin; fatigue from a tiring boat and train journey finally catching up with them in the final minutes when they lost three goals. Against the German-Canadian All Stars, they should have won, George Horne hitting the post twice in the third period. It was third time lucky against Berlin Red and White Club, the tourists leading 5-0 before losing three final period goals as tiredness crept in again.

The first two matches were each played in front of 10,000 spectators. While there were no failures in the squad it was considered that Fiore Amantea and Bob Purdie had played consistently well in all three matches, but the real star of the trip was George Horne who was outstanding, both in his defensive duties and for setting up and contributing to attacks. There was little doubt that Mohawks had acquired not only a first class defender but a real character and born leader into the bargain.

At Crossmyloof, another ladies match between Falcons and Eagles took place in front of a large number of spectators on 28 December. "Inside Edge" offered a rather patronising view of the proceedings when he commented that while the ladies were genuine in their efforts "the entertainment they provided had more of a humorous element about it than any serious competition." The opinion of "The Blade" on the occasion was equally disparaging.

Male chauvinism aside the match does seem to have been played at a snail's pace though the spectators still appreciated the fare on offer. It ended as last season's match had in a draw, this time 0-0. Eagles were the better side and might have won - their centre, Lilian Reid, being the best player on the ice. Falcons right wing, Jean Herbertson, was also noted as being a cut above the rest.

The New Year opened with a representative match at the Central Ice Rink between Perth and Brighton Tigers. With Perth at full strength hopes were high that they would give a good account of themselves but these expectations were quickly dashed as they were comprehensively beaten 10-2 by an excellent Brighton team. The only player in the home side who passed muster was Howard Smith.

While it would be hasty to conclude too much on the evidence of this match, the result and the manner of the defeat did suggest that - despite an obvious overall improvement in playing standards north of the border - there remained a significant gulf in class between the Scottish (National) League and the English National League.

The New Year also opened badly for Mohawks who lost 4-3 against the improving Lions on 4 January. As if to prove a point to the Scottish selectors, Pete Stevenson scored all four of Lions goals! The match was again played in a thick mist which enveloped the rink.

With the second round of fixtures in the league championship now completed, Perth Panthers remained at the top of the table with 18 points from ten matches. They had scored an incredible 69 goals - almost as many as nearest challengers Perth Black Hawks and Mohawks put together. Now that Arnie Pratt had joined them, their attack looked even more awesome and it was hard to see past them for the title. Perth Black Hawks now appeared to be their only serious challengers. They were in second place with 14 points from ten matches but significantly they had already lost twice to Panthers in the championship. Mohawks were in third position with 10 points but already seemed to be out of genuine title contention. They remained a talented team, but events at Perth had simply overtaken them.

Lions had moved from bottom position in the league to fourth place as a result of the new signings they had made. Kelvingrove and Mustangs were struggling but they also continued to recruit when possible. Kelvingrove acquired another Canadian forward, D (Don) McLeod, while Mustangs signed a player from German ice hockey, E Nerlick.

The SIHA was disappointed to learn that no players from the Scottish League were being considered for the Great Britain squad taking part in the European and World Championships being held in Prague in mid February. There was of course nothing new about this but the fact that the British team this time was to be composed solely of "born and bred" players made the selection policy of the BIHA even more irritating than normal. While not suggesting that the standard of play in the Scottish League was the equal of that in the English National League, it certainly stood favourable comparison with that in the lower leagues in England. It was particularly galling that six out of the fourteen players selected for the British squad were from the English lower leagues and it smacked of parochialism that the BIHA had not seriously considered any home developed players from Scotland.

The SIHA submitted a formal letter of protest to the BIHA expressing its concern in this matter. The BIHA responded by asking the SIHA to select five players from the Scottish League and arrange for them to travel to the Harringay Arena in London where the final trials for the Great Britain squad were being held on 9 January. This somewhat hurried invitation was subsequently ignored by an outraged SIHA, who evidently felt that they had made their point.

Season 1937-1938

While the two ruling bodies were indulging in politics it was very unfortunate that players like Billy Fullerton, Joe Collins or Tommy McInroy were not after all going to have the opportunity to compete for places in the British team. Having made their point, and having received a favourable response, albeit belated, the decision of the SIHA to reject the offer of a trial for their players was petty and counter-productive.

News of a new ice rink being constructed in Dundee was followed by reports of a similar venture being planned for Edinburgh. The existing ice rink in the city at Haymarket was only used for skating and curling. While the current management at the venue wanted to promote ice hockey, it was realised the rink was not suitable for the sport.

Ambitious plans were announced for a new facility to be built on spare land adjacent to Murrayfield rugby stadium. It was hoped to have an ice surface measuring 190 feet by 96 feet with accommodation for several thousand spectators. The man behind these proposals was the Glasgow-born William Brown, who had moved to Canada as a child with his family and had played ice hockey for the famous McGill University Club in Montreal.

Perth Panthers started the third round of the league championship with a fortunate 2-1 away victory against Kelvingrove on 7 January. Unceremonious in their checking, the Glasgow team took the game to their opponents. They thought they had scored an equalising goal late in the third period; the match officials disallowed it for offside, amidst howls of derision from the sizable home support. Kelvingrove's new first line of John Cuthill, Scotty Cameron and Don McLeod not only impressed going forward but also with their back-checking qualities.

Kelvingrove took this better form into their next match against Mohawks. It was a proverbial game of two halves. Mohawks had the best of it initially by establishing a 2-0 lead with goals from Glen Braid and George Baillie by the middle of the second period. Don McLeod then pulled a goal back for Kelvingrove before Ken Hurll scored a deserved equaliser. The match ended 2-2, the third consecutive draw between these two teams in the championship.

Perth Panthers consolidated their lead at the top of the league when they defeated a feisty Mohawks 4-2 at the Central Ice Rink on 19 January. Weak finishing cost the visitors dear for they should have come away from Perth with at least a draw. Panthers raced into a 3-0 lead in the first period but never at any time were Mohawks completely out of the contest matching their opponents in every area of the ice except in the art of goal scoring.

Mohawks had just lost the services of international defender, Alec Fullerton, who had moved to Mustangs. He had found it difficult to retain a regular place on the blue line due to the outstanding form of George Horne and Archie Bogie. Fullerton though was too good a player to be warming the substitutes' bench every match so he was a most welcome addition to an ailing Mustangs side.

Frozen in Time

Ronald Milne, Perth Black Hawks and Scotland

Season 1937-1938

Lions upset the apple cart yet again when for the second time in the league this season they defeated Perth Panthers this time at Crossmyloof at the end of January. Frank Chase was unavailable for this match due to injury but Lions gave a debut to their latest Canadian recruit, N (Nelson) McCuaig, from British Columbia. He made an immediate impact by scoring a hat-trick in a deserved 5-3 victory.

Lions were quietly assembling a very talented squad well coached by Pete Stevenson. In the match against Panthers they preserved their energies by changing their forward lines at regular intervals, not flinching to ice their young and inexperienced second string - comprising D Jackson, D W (Dougie) McAlpine and D (Don) Cumming - when occasion demanded. Lions had left it too late in terms of the championship, but they had their sights firmly set on defending the Mitchell Trophy.

Perth Panthers' defeat still left them three points ahead of rink rivals Perth Black Hawks. The latter side had kept in touch by successfully negotiating a potentially tricky fixture at Mohawks, with a narrow 1-0 win courtesy of a Howard Smith goal in the second period. It was another match Mohawks could have won had their forwards been that bit sharper in front of goal.

Attention became focussed on two representative matches which had been arranged between Glasgow and Perth. The first match was at Crossmyloof on 29 January with the return at the Central Ice Rink on 12 February. Major James Simpson of Glencarse donated a trophy for the contests which were eagerly awaited by the paying public at both venues.

For the first match only four players survived from the Glasgow side which defeated Birmingham Maple Leafs in November and these were Bunt Roberts, Pete Stevenson, Jim Kenny and George Baillie. Art Palfrey lost his place in goal to Fiore Amantea and Joe Collins and George Horne joined Roberts on the blue line. In attack, Scotty Cameron, Laurie Marchant and Glen Braid were selected, the latter surprisingly in preference to Billy Fullerton.

The first team selected by Perth had an all Black Hawks defence of Ronald Milne in goal playing behind Howard Smith and Les Lovell. In attack, the deadly Panthers first line of Les Tapp, Len McCartney and Jimmy Lightfoot was intact. The substitutes comprised Robert Thomson, Arnie Pratt, Bob Purdie and Jimmy Allan.

Of the twenty players selected for Glasgow and Perth for this match only two, Joe Collins and Glen Braid, were home developed.

A packed Crossmyloof watched a thrilling spectacle between two very committed and evenly matched sides. Laurie Marchant put Glasgow ahead in the first period but Bob Purdie equalised for Perth in the middle session. Just before the end of that period Scotty Cameron scored a second goal for Glasgow, although there was some debate as to whether this goal was offside. Perth poured forward in the final period but Fiore Amantea was in brilliant form and Glasgow held on for a fortuitous 2-1 victory.

Frozen in Time

Perth Panthers, whose form had not been quite as convincing in recent matches, suffered another setback in the league championship when they were thumped 8-2 by Perth Black Hawks on 4 February. Panthers never recovered from losing the first three goals in an eighty seconds spell in the opening period and without the injured Jimmy Lightfoot they had only one substitute available. It was a heartening result for Black Hawks who, two days earlier, had lost at home to Mohawks.

This result completed the third round of the league championship. Perth Panthers remained top of the table with 26 points still 3 points ahead of Perth Black Hawks both teams having played sixteen matches. Mohawks were languishing in third place with 15 points and were effectively out of the running. The title was now a two-horse race between the Perth clubs.

Perth Panthers were starting to feel the pressure for in their next match away against Kelvingrove they lost 4-1. Panthers lost two goals within a minute in the second period and although Arnie Pratt pulled a goal back at the start of the final period their quest to find an equaliser only resulted in leaving gaps at the back which John Cuthill and Don McLeod fully exploited by scoring two breakaway goals.

The return representative match between Perth and Glasgow took place at the Central Ice Rink on 12 February. The huge interest in this match was clearly demonstrated by the fact that for the first time in the history of the sport in Scotland a special train was chartered to take approximately 400 supporters from Glasgow to Perth for the occasion.

Glasgow were obliged to make one change from the first match as Wally Welch replaced the unavailable Pete Stevenson. He had sustained a very nasty injury in a recent match against Mohawks when he was struck accidentally on the face with a stick and knocked unconscious. The unfortunate Stevenson had two teeth knocked out, six stitches inserted into his upper lip and a suspected broken nose. Perth also made one change to their side when Tommy McInroy came in for the injured Jimmy Lightfoot.

Glasgow held a 2-1 lead from the first leg. As expected, Perth opened the match in an aggressive fashion, but they found the visiting defence a formidable barrier to their ambitions. Adopting sound tactics, Glasgow were able to force the Perth centres out wide, with the result that their wing men repeatedly skated over the line ahead of the puck and were pulled up for offside. It was a frustrating evening for Perth who had by far the bulk of possession but with little end product. Robert Thomson put the home side ahead in the first period but the goal was disputed by a number of Glasgow players who were insistent that the puck had not entered the net. Following consultation with the goal judge the referee, Jack Gilmour, allowed the score to stand. Scotty Cameron equalised for Glasgow with a fine solo goal in the second period and despite desperate Perth pressure in the closing session the match ended 1-1 allowing Glasgow to collect the Simpson Trophy with a 3-2 aggregate victory.

Season 1937-1938

Hard on the heels of the new ice rinks being planned for Dundee and Edinburgh came news of a further development at Kirkcaldy. It was proposed to offer 30,000 ordinary shares at £1 each, 25,000 of which were offered for public subscription. The new rink would be a one story building comprising accommodation for about 4,000 spectators. Total costs of construction were estimated at £37,000.

The ice rink directors at Kirkcaldy were fully committed to promoting ice hockey at the new venue and were certainly not letting the grass grow under their feet. They immediately underlined their ambitions by securing the services of Les Lovell as the player-coach of the new team already being assembled for the season ahead. He was an inspiring leader, famed for his one man charges up the ice - an undoubted asset to his new club.

Until then Lovell would continue to wear the white and black colours of Perth Black Hawks and he led them to the top of the league championship table for the first time when they defeated Lions 3-1 on 15 February. That lead was short-lived. Perth Panthers had played one match less and they subsequently recaptured top spot when they defeated Mustangs 4-0 three days later. Making his debut for Panthers in this match was E (Earl) Morley, a native of Winnipeg.

That same evening at Crossmyloof, Mohawks defeated Kelvingrove 3-0 in the latest instalment of Scottish ice hockey's most enduring fixture. The score rather flattered the reigning champions as two of their goals came off deflections. Nevertheless, it was a disappointing performance by 'Grove who had been playing much better of late. They gave a debut to their latest Canadian import, R (Bob) Lightfoot; this led to the departure of Jack Johnston to Lions.

The first round of the Mitchell Trophy competition commenced on 22 February with a match between Mustangs and Perth Panthers at Crossmyloof. Unlike the situation last season the two Perth teams were taking part, which was only right and proper for the premier cup competition in the country. The league leaders had been off form recently, exhibiting a surprising lack of confidence leading Mustangs to believe they might have a chance. Laurie Marchant had missed a golden opportunity for Mustangs before Les Tapp put Panthers ahead in the opening period. Len McCartney increased the visitors' lead in the middle session against the run of play, but two minutes into the third period Johnny Kelly scored for Mustangs. They made a real fight of it in the time left but Panthers managed to hold on for a barely deserved 2-1 win.

Three days later Lions trounced Kelvingrove 6-1 in the second first round tie. Pete Stevenson returned from injury and along with Nelson McCuaig and Frank Chase formed a devastating attack, the latter player bagging a hat-trick. Lions first team was now entirely Canadian; they were simply too strong for Kelvingrove, who had no answer to their teamwork and finishing abilities.

Frozen in Time

In the European and World Championships held in Prague, Great Britain finished runners-up for the second consecutive year behind Canada, represented on this occasion by Sudbury Wolves from Ontario. Two Scottish-born players were selected for the British squad, goaltender Jimmy Foster of Harringay Greyhounds and forward Jimmy Kelly of Brighton Tigers.

In the preliminary section phase of the competition, Great Britain defeated Germany 1-0, Norway 8-0, Latvia 5-1 and then drew 1-1 with the United States of America. At the quarter-final stage the British team defeated Sweden 3-2 and Poland 7-1. Great Britain then defeated the host nation Czechoslovakia 1-0 with a goal in the final period to secure the European title for the third consecutive time and fifth overall.

Canada awaited Great Britain in the final. They raced into a 2-0 lead in the first period before Gerry Davey of Streatham pulled a goal back. The Canadians scored again just before the interval to make the score 3-1. There was no further scoring in either the second or the third periods. Canada won their tenth world title in front of 11,000 excited spectators.

On the domestic front, the league championship took another twist when Mohawks defeated Perth Panthers 4-2 at Crossmyloof on 1 March. It was the champion's first win over the league leaders this season. Much was owed to a solid defence, where Art Palfrey had been in great form, and the heavy checking of George Horne and Archie Bogie had upset the usual smooth rhythm of the slick Panther forwards.

Perth Black Hawks had the opportunity to overtake their neighbours at the top of the league the following evening, but in a quite remarkable turn of events they were beaten 5-1 by Kelvingrove at the Central Ice Rink. The Glasgow team's tactics were the key to their unexpected success. Their wing men closed marked their opposing wing men leaving Perth's centres to a strong checking defence. Don McLeod was the fastest player on the ice as Scotty Cameron helped himself to a well taken hat-trick.

Neither Perth side had much time to lick their wounds since they had been drawn against each other in the first semi-final of the Mitchell Trophy which was to be played at Crossmyloof on 4 March. In all competitions so far the teams had met on five occasions. Panthers had recorded three victories and Black Hawks two. Black Hawks made it three wins when they defeated Panthers 3-2. It was a hard match noted for its heavy and at times reckless checking a factor which told much more on Panthers who had a number of players already carrying injuries. When Les Tapp had to leave the ice with a shoulder injury their cause was effectively lost. Black Hawks had now completed a cup double over Panthers having earlier eliminated them from the President's Pucks.

The second semi-final of the Mitchell Trophy was played four days later between an on-form Lions and Mohawks. In a match full of incidents, mishaps and penalties, one particular incident of note occurred when George Baillie

Season 1937-1938

of Mohawks dropped his stick and pursued Bunt Roberts of Lions half-way up the ice before bringing him down with a perfect rugby tackle!

Mohawks' chances of winning this tie were not improved as serious injuries were sustained by Wally Welch and Jim Kenny in an even first period. Lions then struck twice within a minute in the middle session when Frank Chase and Pete Stevenson scored. Mohawks tried hard to rescue the situation in the final period but they found Fiore Amantea in unbeatable form. Pete Stevenson added a third goal in the final minute to give Lions a slightly flattering 3-0 win.

Lions, holders of the Mitchell Trophy, had now qualified for their second consecutive final where they would meet Perth Black Hawks at Crossmyloof on 15 March. The SIHA decided that the final should revert back to one match after the experiment of playing it over two legs the previous season.

Another important fixture at Crossmyloof was the eagerly anticipated international match between Scotland and Canada on 11 March. It was always a great event when Canada came to Glasgow and this occasion was no different. The Canadians were of course represented by Sudbury Wolves, winners of the recent World Championship, and this was their final match of an extensive European tour. Ticket prices for the match were fixed at a flat rate of 2s. It was a very different Scotland squad that was selected for this match to that which had taken the ice against Canada the previous season. The only survivors from that match were Les Lovell, Pete Stevenson and Len McCartney. Fiore Amantea would be in goal behind a blue line of George Horne and Les Lovell. The first line of attack was Pete Stevenson, Bob Purdie and George Baillie with the second line comprising Arnie Pratt, Len McCartney and Laurie Marchant. Bunt Roberts and Howard Smith would provide any cover.

The last time Scotland selected an entire squad composed only of players developed in Canada was against Germany in 1930. There were the usual arguments about who was in and who was out. Some observers thought that Art Palfrey was unlucky to lose his place to Fiore Amantea and the selection of George Baillie in preference to Jim Kenny, Jimmy Lightfoot or Don McLeod was certainly a subject of some debate. Although Scotland exceeded all expectations the match itself was disappointing. It was a scrappy affair characterised by disjointed passing and lengthy stoppages. The flow of the game was not helped by the reappearance of the troublesome mist which had plagued matches at Crossmyloof all season. It got worse as the match progressed and at times it blotted out play completely for the spectators.

Canada started brightly and, but for Fiore Amantea, they may have been a goal or two ahead in the first period. Scotland played much better in the middle session - so much so that Amantea did not have a save to make. Len McCartney almost put the home side in front, but his raking shot went inches past the post with the Canadian goaltender beaten.

The third period was more exciting as both teams went all out to establish an advantage. With only nine minutes of play left, Les Lovell went on one of his solo rushes up the ice and set up Arnie Pratt to score for Scotland. Shortly after, Len McCartney almost scored again. Only three minutes were left on the clock when Canada equalised in a dense fog. The match ended 1-1.

It was the best result Scotland had ever achieved at this level and it underlined the huge improvement in the standard of play existing in the Scottish League.

Given this situation it was very regrettable that two proposed matches against Earls Court Rangers had to be cancelled at almost the last moment. It would have been very interesting to see how this Scottish team would have fared against such top class opposition from the English National League.

Crossmyloof hosted another big match four days later when Lions met Perth Black Hawks in the final of the Mitchell Trophy. It is quite evident that the management of the Glasgow venue were becoming much more commercially aware of the popularity of ice hockey since ticket prices for this match were raised to 3s, 2s and 1s 6d. Given that standards of play had improved and matches were now of regulation duration, no one could really complain about higher prices for major matches.

One could never be entirely sure which Lions side would turn up, given the vagaries in their form. Perth Black Hawks were hoping to make it a cup "double" having already won the President's Pucks but they were very disappointing on the night, and only started playing in the final period. Lions managed to stifle the speed of the Perth team and the match was therefore played at a pace which suited them. Pete Stevenson put Lions ahead in the first period when he capitalised on a defensive error. Black Hawks had several good attempts in the second period but were stopped in their tracks by Fiore Amantea. As they continued to chase the game in the closing period they were hit on the break when Stevenson scored a second goal. Nelson McCuaig then clinched it when he pulled Ronald Milne out of his goal, shot the puck against him, picked up the rebound and coolly slotted the puck into the empty net. Lions had given a competent enough performance to defeat their more fancied opponents 3-0, and had won the Mitchell Trophy for the second consecutive season.

Scottish ice hockey received yet another boost with the news that a new ice rink was going to be constructed in Ayr. The building would cost £50,000 and it would be used for skating, curling and ice hockey with accommodation for about 4,500 spectators. One of the leading figures in the consortium behind the venture was Colonel Thomas C Dunlop, the founding father and ex-player of the long disbanded Doonside Ice Hockey Club.

In the league championship, Perth Black Hawks cast aside their recent Mitchell Trophy disappointment with a splendid 5-3 victory over neighbours Perth Panthers on 23 March. In a bruising contest Doug Mitchell of Panthers

Season 1937-1938

Don McLeod, Kelvingrove

had to retire with a facial injury - which subsequently required sixteen stitches. It was a significant win for Black Hawks since it took them back to the top of the league one point ahead of Panthers.

The recent form of the orange and black half of Perth was causing their supporters some concern. Panthers had lost a lot of ground lately having lost three of their previous four league matches. In fairness, a number of their star performers had been nursing long term injuries including Les Tapp, who had been forced to miss the recent Scotland match, Jimmy Lightfoot and Len McCartney. This seems to have led to a loss of confidence as the team was certainly missing its earlier zest.

With four-fifths of the league championship campaign now completed Perth Black Hawks sat proudly at the top of the league table with 31 points from 21 matches. They had lost fewer goals than any other side and in terms of winning the title appeared to be the form team. Black Hawks were greatly dependent on Howard Smith and Les Lovell not just for breaking up opposition attacks but also for setting up attacks for their own team. Indeed, Lovell was one of the leading goal scorers in the league.

Perth Panthers were only one point behind their neighbours but they had to find some way of recovering their past form. Both teams had only four matches left to play so every single point was now crucial. The final match between the two sides at the end of April was shaping up to be a title decider although both teams had a few potentially tricky fixtures to negotiate before then. It certainly guaranteed an exciting climax to the season particularly for the fans who congregated at the Central Ice Rink.

Perth Black Hawks commenced their cycle of matches by welcoming back Art Schumann who had returned from playing in Germany. The versatile German-Canadian made an immediate impact by setting up both goals scored by Bob Purdie in a 2-1 win against Lions on 1 April.

The response from Perth Panthers was an emphatic 12-5 victory at Mustangs four days later. Their deadly forward line was in full flow as Les Tapp scored four goals, Len McCartney a hat-trick and Jimmy Lightfoot a brace. It was a vitally important win for Panthers, who badly needed a really good result and performance to restore some confidence.

Following their failure to secure a match against England for another season the SIHA sought some consolation by arranging a short tour of England instead. The BIHA had seemingly found it impossible to offer the SIHA any suitable dates for a match because of fixture congestion in the English National League, but the Scots would not take no for an answer and therefore settled for the next best thing. Given these circumstances the SIHA made it quite clear that it would not be Scotland facing Brighton Tigers on 7 April and Earls Court Rangers on 9 April but a "Scottish League Select". In point of fact, semantics aside, there were only two changes in the touring party from the Scotland side which faced Canada in March. Howard Smith

Season 1937-1938

and George Baillie were unavailable and they were replaced by Les Tapp, now fully recovered from injury, and surprisingly, E Nerlick from Mustangs.

In the opening match at the Brighton Sports Stadium the Scottish-born Tommy Forgie gave the home side a two goal lead in the first period. Brighton increased their lead at the start of the middle session but goals from Les Lovell and Len McCartney brought the tourists back into the contest just before the interval. Brighton stepped up a gear in the third period scoring three further goals before Arnie Pratt pulled one back before the finish. It ended 6-3 for Brighton Tigers.

It was a much closer affair at the Empress Hall in London. In an exciting match, Earls Court Rangers just managed to edge out the Scottish League Select 8-6. Goals from Laurie Marchant and George Horne against the run of play gave the visitors a 2-0 lead before Earls Court pulled one back. Len McCartney made it 3-1 at the end of the first period. Play in the second period was fast and furious. Earls Court started in determined fashion and scored three goals in quick succession to take a 4-3 lead. Les Lovell then secured an equaliser with a typically brilliant solo goal. Earls Court responded with two further goals to lead 6-4 at the interval. Four further goals were traded in the final session, Len McCartney and Pete Stevenson scoring for the visitors.

Despite these two reverses most observers thought the Scottish League Select had performed reasonably well in both matches and were certainly not disgraced in either. "Inside Edge" was of the opinion that the touring party's speed and stick-handling were as good as that of Brighton and Earls Court but not their marking or sense of positional play. Given the highly encouraging performance against Canada there was however disappointment that both of these matches had been lost.

In the league championship Mohawks and Kelvingrove played out their fourth draw in the competition. John Fullerton and George Baillie put the champions two goals ahead only for Kelvingrove to hit back in an exciting finale. Both of their goals were scored by Don McLeod his second a great individual effort in the final minute of the game. In the six matches played between Kelvingrove and Mohawks this season four had been drawn and Mohawks had won the other two.

Perth Panthers went to the top of the league again on 12 April when they defeated Mohawks 3-2 at Crossmyloof in a potentially difficult fixture. Jimmy Lightfoot bagged a brace and Len McCartney got the other goal. A day later, Perth Black Hawks resumed first place when they thumped Kelvingrove 6-2 at the Central Ice Rink, Les Lovell and Bob Purdie each scoring a brace.

It was neck and neck between the two Perth teams and with each side having only two fixtures left the pressure was palpable. Something had to give and it did.

Perth Panthers leapfrogged their neighbours yet again on 15 April when they defeated a lacklustre Lions 6-2 at Crossmyloof with a hat-trick from

Arnie Pratt. Panthers had strengthened their team with the signing of the experienced Norman McQuade who would now partner Robert Thomson in defence. McQuade was an excellent addition to the Panthers side as he could play equally well in defence or attack as he had amply demonstrated with Wembley Monarchs and Great Britain.

A week later, Mohawks visited the Central Ice Rink to play a vital match against Perth Black Hawks and they returned to Glasgow with both points following a truly dramatic 5-4 win. The result was a devastating blow to the title prospects of Black Hawks; the pressure simply got to them.

Mohawks opened the game in confident fashion by racing into a 4-1 lead by the start of the second period. In contrast, Black Hawks had been nervous but they began to regain their composure and scored three goals in five minutes to level the score, Art Schumann completing his hat-trick. It was 4-4 going into the final period and amidst almost unbearable tension George Horne completed his hat-trick to put Mohawks 5-4 ahead. Black Hawks threw everything but the kitchen sink at Mohawks in the time left, but to no avail. The match ended in bitter disappointment for them.

Everything now rested on the final confrontation between Perth Panthers and Perth Black Hawks on 27 April. If Panthers won they would win the league championship outright by the required three points. On the other hand, Black Hawks needed at least a draw to force a championship play-off. The entire scenario could not have been scripted better by Hollywood.

The Central Ice Rink was of course packed to the rafters for the match to decide the destination of the Canada Cup. Tickets had been sold out weeks in advance. The one thing that was certain was that a fourth new name would be engraved on the trophy. Whether it was Perth Panthers or Perth Black Hawks was about to be decided.

In the end it came down to form. Since losing to Black Hawks on 23 March, Panthers had largely recovered much of their early season form and had won their previous three league matches, demonstrating they could handle the pressure. Needless blunders were to cost Black Hawks dear but in the final analysis Panthers were the much more composed team on the night.

It was very unfortunate for Black Hawks that Ronald Milne had a rare off-night being largely responsible for the loss of two of his side's goals. He should have done better in preventing Panthers first goal ten minutes after the start, but could do little to stop Jimmy Lightfoot adding a second before the end of the period. Arnie Pratt and Len McCartney were causing all kinds of mischief in the Blacks Hawks defence. Blacks Hawks were galvanised into action in the second period. Art Schumann scored with a surprise shot and three minutes later Jimmy Allan equalised. They now took charge of the game and Panthers were on the back foot struggling to cope with the thrilling dashes of Les Lovell and the speedy Black Hawks forwards. The period ended 2-2. Panthers made a strong start to the final period and went ahead again

Season 1937-1938

when Jimmy Lightfoot scored his second goal. Black Hawks fought back and Bob Purdie secured an equaliser. With ten minutes left and excitement at fever pitch Arnie Pratt fired in a simple shot outside the blue line which bounced gently on the ice but somehow eluded Ronald Milne who seemed to have it covered. The closing stages were frantic and filled with penalties but Panthers managed to close the game down and won 4-3. Perth Panthers had won the Canada Cup for the first time!

It had been the most competitive and exciting league championship in the history of the competition. Over the whole piece Perth Panthers had been the most accomplished team although the Black Hawks had pushed them to the wire. In the five head to head league clashes between the two sides, Panthers had won three and Black Hawks had won two. In the final analysis it was really Panthers' superior fire-power which had ultimately prevailed. No team came anywhere near the 131 goals they scored. Their first line of Les Tapp, Len McCartney and Jimmy Lightfoot were simply awesome, accounting for 97 of these goals between them. The signing of Norman McQuade, although tough on the home-developed Doug Mitchell who had a splendid season, was a master stroke, as his expertise and confidence rubbed off on the rest of the team at exactly the time they most needed it.

For the runners-up it was a case of what might have been. They had the best defence in the league and were no slouches in attack either with 95 goals, Bob Purdie scoring 28 and Les Lovell with 23, an astonishing total for a defender. Black Hawks' real problem had been a lack of offensive depth. It was no co-incidence that Lovell and line-mate, Howard Smith, were required to set up and often finish so many attacks as the squad lacked an effective second line.

Mohawks had endured a season of frustration. A record of 11 wins, 10 defeats and 4 draws underlined the team's inconsistency. Most of their defeats had come at the hands of the two Perth sides but they did manage to exact a terrible revenge on Black Hawks at the most critical part of the season. George Horne had proved a revelation; had he arrived earlier in the season Mohawks may have pushed the Perth teams much further.

There were still four league matches, all of which involved the other three teams, to be played when Perth Panthers wrapped up the title. The one result of note was Lions 9-0 demolition of Kelvingrove in which Frank Chase helped himself to six goals!

Once the dust had settled it was Lions who occupied fourth position. Their first team was as good as any in the league but their squad lacked depth. One is left with the nagging suspicion that this was a team which could have done even better. Often brilliant, often lacklustre, they were utterly contrary. At least Lions had the consolation of retaining the Mitchell Trophy.

Ahead of Kelvingrove on goal difference, Mustangs managed to finish in fifth position. Their season had been blighted more than any other team with

Les Lovell, Perth Black Hawks and Scotland

Season 1937-1938

players coming and going. It never allowed them to ice a settled formation. In Bert Forsythe, Johnny Kelly and Laurie Marchant they were not without quality, but there was simply not enough of it in the squad.

And what of bottom place Kelvingrove? It had been this great old club's worst season. Despite the energetic efforts of the talented Joe Collins, Scotty Cameron and Don McLeod, Kelvingrove had an ageing squad lacking the necessary quality in depth to mount any sort of sustained challenge over the long haul of a championship season. Many of the Canadians brought to the club over the past two seasons had not been up to the mark. Kelvingrove had scored only 52 goals and that sad statistic told its own story.

There was further good news for Scottish ice hockey with the announcement that a new ice rink was to be constructed in Falkirk and that it would be ready for the new season. The building would cost £37,500 and it would have a spectator capacity of about 4,000. The intention would be to use the venue for other events outwith the winter sports season by covering the ice area with retractable flooring.

This had been a landmark season in the history of the Scottish game. A process which commenced the previous season came to fruition in this one as the last vestiges of the amateur code which had previously governed the sport north of the border were finally discarded in favour of semi-professionalism no matter how it was dressed up. Clubs continued to award their players "expenses", at various rates of generosity, but no-one was fooled. The game had changed beyond all recognition.

How much it had changed can be seen in the composition of the regular first teams of the six clubs comprising the Scottish League. Of the 36 players concerned, 29 had learned to play the game in Canada. The vast majority of these players had been either recently imported from Canada or from clubs in England or Germany. The only home-developed players who had regularly played in their first teams this season were Joe Collins, Archie Bogie, Billy Fullerton, Billy Turnbull, Alec Fullerton, Tommy McInroy and Doug Mitchell.

If the SIHA were concerned about this nothing was being said in public. Optimism prevailed and standards of play had improved immensely. Interest in the sport from the public and the media had never been greater. For the future there was the prospect of new teams entering the Scottish (National) League from Dundee, Falkirk and Kirkcaldy and new ice rinks were also planned for Ayr and Edinburgh. Indeed, it was the same Charles Fergusson, now Sir Charles Fergusson of Kilkerran and Lord Lieutenant of the County, who opened - and patronised with his family - the new Ayr rink. It was clear that Scottish ice hockey had entered a new era.

In England, Harringay Racers won the English National League for the first time.

Frozen in Time

Season 1938-39

As the Scottish Ice Hockey Association, formally reconstituted in 1929, looked forward to its tenth season in operation it did so with a curious mixture of hope and trepidation. For the first seven seasons it had governed the sport according to a strict amateur code but that worthy adherence to the principle of "the game for the game's sake" had started to erode in season 1936-37, a process well on the way to completion by the end of season 1937-38.

As season 1938-39 dawned it brought forth a revolution in Scottish ice hockey. The evolution towards semi-professionalism in Scottish ice hockey reached its acme with the establishment of three new clubs in Dundee, Falkirk and Kirkcaldy. Along with one club in Perth and two in Glasgow both the landscape and the profile of the sport in Scotland had changed beyond all recognition. The birth of this brave new world was not without pain. Three clubs had been obliged to disband from the season before, Perth Black Hawks - having played for only one memorable season - joining two Glasgow based clubs, Mustangs and Lions, on the scrap heap.

It was decided that with another new club being established on Tayside in Dundee it was really no longer financially viable or even sensible to operate two teams from the Central Ice Rink in Perth. In their short life Black Hawks had done remarkably well winning the President's Pucks and finishing runners-up in the Mitchell Trophy. They had also pushed their rink neighbours Panthers all the way in the league championship, finishing in second place. Perth Black Hawks had certainly made an impression both on and off the ice and their place in the history of the domestic game was assured.

Mustangs had entered the league in season 1935-36 with great ambitions to seriously challenge for the major honours. Their first season was their best when they finished second three points behind Mohawks. They finished runners-up again the following season but became embroiled in a furious row with the SIHA over player registration in the Mitchell Trophy final which led to the club being suspended from competition. Mustangs had struggled to compete in their final season when it was already evident that the writing was on the wall for them.

Lions also entered the league in season 1935-36 but in very different circumstances to those of Mustangs. The club was only created to make up the numbers and in its first season it had the dubious distinction of having the worst league record of any team in the history of the Canada Cup. The arrival of player-coach Pete Stevenson gradually turned things around and to their credit they managed to win the Mitchell Trophy on two occasions. Lions played their final season with an all Canadian team, and looked to have a real future, but the new realities of the Scottish game were about to catch up with them.

The owners of Crossmyloof Ice Rink were the Scottish Ice Rink Company. Two of its leading directors, Frank Stuart and Andrew Mitchell, were of course the president and the vice-president respectively of the SIHA. It was clear to them as both businessmen and sports administrators that four teams playing out of Crossmyloof was not a viable option in a semi-professional league. It was agreed that Mustangs and Lions had to go and that the rink should consolidate its available assets with the two better established clubs, Kelvingrove and Mohawks. This undoubtedly made commercial and sporting sense. In economic terms average attendances of between 1,500 and 2,000 per match at Crossmyloof could not sustain four teams playing at the venue within a semi-professional set-up. It may just be about possible to manage with two clubs but the margins would still be tight. Kelvingrove and Mohawks at least had the advantage of having large and enthusiastic supporters clubs which provided, albeit limited, revenue streams. Mustangs and Lions did not even have that. The new season would therefore commence with the following six teams; Dundee Tigers, Falkirk Lions, Fife Flyers, Kelvingrove, Mohawks and Perth Panthers.

Though some traditionalists mourned the passing of the amateur game there was little doubt that these were very exciting times for ice hockey followers in Scotland. The establishment of a genuinely national league for the first time organised on a semi-professional basis was an enormous leap of faith. The sport had come a long way and had overcome many obstacles. It would now require the goodwill and co-operation of all of its component parts if the new structure created was to prove a success and become a permanent fixture in the sporting firmament of the nation.

Central to this project would be the relationship between the SIHA and the new breed of businessmen and entrepreneurs running the clubs at the various ice rinks in the country. There was a potential for conflict here as the priorities of the sport's governing body were not necessarily those of the rink owners and their managers. The SIHA remained a product of the amateur era but in the new climate of professional and commercial interest fresh thinking and adaptable attitudes would be required if the sport was to progress.

With the advent of three new clubs and the need for the other three pre-existing clubs to seriously strengthen their playing squads, the search for the best Canadian talent available accelerated beyond anything previously witnessed in Scottish ice hockey. Dundee, Falkirk and Kirkcaldy were starting this process from scratch; they generally looked to recruit their players directly from Canada or from the English National League.

Season 1938-1939

In an attempt to protect the interests of home developed players the SIHA introduced a new rule restricting the number of imported players each club could recruit to seven. While this seemed a reasonable compromise in reality it meant that, apart from covering for injuries or suspensions, the number of home developed players actually appearing in the first team of each club would be very limited.

The "home player versus imported player" issue, long debated and agonised over in domestic ice hockey, was precisely the type of issue requiring that necessary degree of common sense and flexibility between the SIHA and the ice rink owners and managers if the new set-up was to operate successfully. To a certain extent the SIHA had already lost this argument. Even in the previous season, the number of home developed players regularly playing first team ice hockey was 7 out of a total of 36.

In the turmoil of player recruitment and transfers that took place prior to the new season opening, defending champions Perth Panthers had to suffer the break-up of their wonderful forward line as Len McCartney defected to Fife Flyers and Jimmy Lightfoot moved to Dundee Tigers. If this was not bad enough their defence was also seriously depleted following the departure of Robert Thomson to Falkirk Lions and Doug Mitchell to Dundee Tigers.

Indeed, Perth would start the season with an entirely new defence. Mac Ross was replaced in goal by Ronald Milne and the blue line would comprise Art Schumann and Bunt Roberts. Joining Les Tapp, Arnie Pratt and Jimmy Allan in attack would be Bob Purdie. Cover would be provided by the experienced veteran John Fullerton who had joined the club after nine seasons at Mohawks.

For the first time since the revival of Scottish ice hockey in 1929 the most successful club in the country, Mohawks or "Glasgow Mohawks" as some observers started to refer to them, would commence a season without any of the Fullerton brothers in their squad. If final proof were needed that domestic ice hockey had really changed then this surely was it. As noted, John was at Perth Panthers while Billy and Alec had both moved to Fife Flyers. An era at this famous old club had truly come to an end.

In addition to the loss of the Fullerton brothers, Mohawks would also be missing Jim Kenny who had decided to concentrate on coaching the juniors at Crossmyloof and Glen Braid who had moved to Dundee Tigers. On the plus side, Mohawks retained Art Palfrey in goal along with George Horne and Archie Bogie on the blue line. In attack, Glen Morrison and George Baillie were also retained.

Mohawks brought in three new players from Canada. On defence was A (Arthur) "Mickey" Shires who arrived after a number of seasons with Schreiber Colts. He was born in West Hartlepool in England but had moved to Port Arthur, Ontario, as a child. Another defender was G (Gordon) Cummine, a native of Saskatoon, Saskatchewan. In attack, C (Chester) Dawson arrived at Mohawks with a good reputation after a season with Streatham in the English National League. He was a native of Chatham, Ontario.

Mohawks also invested in young talent having acquired two ex-Lions, Don Cumming and Dougie McAlpine. Cumming was born in Glasgow but had emigrated to Canada as a child. His family returned to Glasgow in 1937 and he was actually still at school when he joined Mohawks at 16 years of age. Scottish born Dougie McAlpine had learned to play the game at Crossmyloof and was a second year medical student at Glasgow University.

Major change was also the order of the day at Kelvingrove. After nine seasons of loyal service to the club, Andy Dick and Sid Montford both retired. It was surprising that such a consistently good performer as the rugged and energetic Dick had never played for Scotland during his career. The home developed Montford had played three times for his country, curiously all against England, and had finished as joint leading goal scorer in the Canada Cup in season 1932-33. While both of these players would be missed, the remarkable Dave Cross was about to embark on his ninth consecutive season for Kelvingrove and tenth overall. The Glasgow police officer had been a model of consistency over the years and although he had lost his international place he was still highly regarded by everyone in the domestic game. Cover in this position would be provided by Billy Turnbull the ex- Mustangs goaltender. Kelvingrove managed to retain the services of the excellent Joe Collins and he would be partnered in defence by Bert Forsythe. In attack, Scotty Cameron and Don McLeod remained and they were joined by the talented Laurie Marchant another ex-Mustang. Kelvingrove recruited two forwards from Canada, W (Wilf) Cadieu and D (Don) Eaton. Both of these players were natives of Fort William, Ontario, and both had played for local teams in the area.

Of the new clubs, Dundee Tigers had assembled a very strong looking squad based on sound defence and incisive attack. W (Bill) Lane from Edmonton, Alberta, was brought in from the rootless Birmingham Maple Leafs to play in goal with Mac Ross formerly of Perth Panthers as his deputy.

On the blue line was the tall and red haired G (George) McNeil from Lourdes, Nova Scotia, who had come to England in 1936 to play for Richmond Hawks before moving to Earls Court Rangers the following season. "Gummy" McNeil was equally at home in defence or attack but was really known for his precise body-checking. His partner on defence was the impressive Howard Smith from Perth Black Hawks. Cover was provided by Doug Mitchell who had moved from Perth Panthers. Dundee were no less formidable in attack.

Player-coach and right wing, A (Albert) Rogers, arrived in the city of "jute, jam and journalism" after two seasons with Brighton Tigers. A native of Winnipeg, he was no stranger to European ice hockey, having played for Canada (Saskatoon Quakers) at the World Championships held in Milan in 1934. At centre was, M (Merrick) Cranstoun, a native of Merrickville, Ontario. He had played most of his formative ice hockey in Western Canada

Season 1938-1939

before moving to England in 1935 where he had turned out for Kensington Corinthians, Earls Court Rangers and Brighton Tigers.

At left wing was the speedy and predatory Jimmy Lightfoot who had moved from Perth Panthers. Dundee were not short of talented cover either, with Glen Braid arriving from Mohawks and J J (Jimmy) Shannon from Earls Court Rangers. A Londoner by birth, Shannon had moved to Toronto as a child and learned to play the game in Canada. Before joining Earls Court Rangers he had also seen action with Warwickshire and Wembley Canadians.

Fife Flyers had of course already fixed up their player-coach, Les Lovell, the previous season. He would be joined on the blue line by J (Jock) Stover from Chatham Maroons in Ontario and cover was provided by Alec Fullerton who had arrived from Mohawks. In goal was the slightly built, C (Chick) Kerr, a native of Saskatchewan.

The Kirkcaldy club had assembled an impressive array of forward talent. Right wing, T (Tommy) Durling, a native of North Battleford, Saskatchewan, had spent most of his recent career in England with Streatham. At centre was, J W (Jimmy) Chappell, who had arrived from Earls Court Rangers. He had been a key member of the Great Britain team which had won the European, World and Olympic Championships in 1936 scoring twice for his country in that tournament. A deadly finisher, the signing of Chappell was a major coup for Fife Flyers.

Norman McQuade and Len McCartney both arrived from Perth Panthers and from Perth Black Hawks the highly promising Tommy McInroy. Another home-developed player who arrived at Kirkcaldy was Billy Fullerton from Mohawks. Not quite the player he once was, he still represented an excellent acquisition to their squad. Fife appeared to have the most firepower in the Scottish League but the trick would be to get them playing together as a team.

Falkirk Lions were another club who commenced their recruitment by putting together a solid defence. Fiore Amantea arrived from the disbanded Lions and was in the opinion of some observers the best goaltender in the country. He was joined in defence by Robert Thomson, who moved from Perth Panthers and G (Gordon) Pantalone, a native of Ottawa, who had played the previous season with Streatham. Another ex-Lion, Alec Purdie, provided cover at the back.

Falkirk also pulled off a major coup when they signed the fast skating and tricky right wing, J G (Gerry) Davey, from Streatham where he had spent the previous five seasons. A native of London, England, he had grown up in Port Arthur, Ontario, where he had learned to play the game. Davey had been a team-mate of Jimmy Chappell in the triple championship winning Great Britain team in 1936, scoring a goal in the crucial 2-1 victory against Canada.

Davey would be joined in attack by the dangerous Nelson McCuaig, the ex-Lions left wing, and the experienced George McWilliams from Wembley Lions. Another player acquired from the English National League was, R

Frozen in Time

L (Chuck) Stapleford, from Streatham. The ex-Scotland international, Bill Russell, was yet another ex-Lion who would be putting on the red and white colours of Falkirk for this season.

The ice hockey correspondent of the *Glasgow Herald* was as excited as everyone else connected with the sport at the "galaxy of talent" which had been attracted to the Scottish (National) League. There was no doubt that it had raised the quality of the Scottish game to unprecedented levels. Players of the calibre of George McNeil, Gerry Davey and Jimmy Chappell, among others, were genuinely first class performers who would only enrich and enhance the local game. The proliferation of new players at all six clubs led the SIHA to the sensible decision to initiate what may be termed a "bedding-in" competition rather than go straight into the league championship. The Points Competition would therefore commence in early October with each team playing the other on four occasions for an overall total of sixty fixtures. It was anticipated that the Canada Cup would commence in early January. Not unexpectedly admission prices for ordinary matches at Crossmyloof Ice Rink were increased for the first time in some years. Prices were fixed at 1s and 1s and 6d. This still represented good value for money compared to prices in other sports and leisure pursuits. All matches at Crossmyloof would now commence at 8.00pm with the expectation that they would be concluded at approximately 9.30pm.

At Kirkcaldy Ice Rink, the admission prices for ordinary matches ranged from 1s to 3s 6d depending on the quality of the seat and its location. A season ticket to watch Fife Flyers would cost the committed follower 10s which looked a good deal. That price included a "tip-up" seat and free skating after the match. All matches would of course continue to be played in the evenings. Crossmyloof retained Tuesdays and Fridays for its matches; Dundee and Falkirk decided on Wednesdays; Kirkcaldy would use Thursdays and Perth decided on Saturdays. Falkirk Lions would however be obliged to play all of their earlier fixtures on the road since Falkirk Ice Rink would not actually be open and ready for business until the end of November.

In reviewing the prospects of the teams for the season ahead it was difficult to come to any firm conclusions, given the enormous turnover in playing staff at each club. In addition, the recruitment process was not yet over as some clubs were still trying to strengthen their squads as the season finally got underway.

Perhaps fittingly, it was those old rivals Kelvingrove and Mohawks who contested the first match of the Points Competition on 4 October. In what was described as a disappointing and scrappy match marred by penalties, Kelvingrove raced into a 3-0 first period lead before Mohawks pulled two goals back in the middle session. Each team traded a goal in the final period to give Kelvingrove a 4-3 victory and their first win against Mohawks for eighteen months.

Season 1938-1939

Dundee Tigers opened their campaign at home with a Tayside derby against Perth Panthers. The match attracted over 3,000 spectators to the Dundee-Angus Ice Rink and they were well entertained despite the "erratic shooting and ragged passing" of both teams. The first period was goalless before the wonderfully consistent Les Tapp put the visitors ahead in the second period. Dundee, resplendent in their yellow and black kit, fought back gamely and took the lead in the final session when the outstanding player on the ice, Jimmy Lightfoot, displaying dazzling stick-handling and quick-fire shooting, scored twice against his previous club. There were only fifteen seconds left when Tapp ruined the celebrations of the home crowd with a well-taken equaliser for Perth.

Over 3,000 spectators also witnessed Fife Flyers' opening match at Kirkcaldy Ice Rink when Falkirk Lions were the visitors. The home team were too individualistic in their efforts and lacked the combined movements of their visitors. The first period was goalless but strikes from Gerry Davey and Nelson McCuaig gave Falkirk a 2-0 lead by the second interval. Fife rallied in the third period and Norman McQuade pulled a goal back. As they continued to press forward for the equaliser, Chuck Stapleford hit them on the break to give Falkirk an encouraging 3-1 victory.

Mohawks got an early warning of a hard season ahead when Dundee Tigers visited Crossmyloof on 7 October and easily won 5-2. The visitors were leading 5-0 thanks to a brace from George McNeil and a hat-trick from Al Rogers before Mohawks scored two late goals to give the score a slightly more respectable look. The most striking feature of the match was the teamwork displayed by Dundee whose accurate passing had the Mohawks defence bewildered.

Kelvingrove fared better in their next test against one of the new teams when they held Fife Flyers 2-2 at Crossmyloof. Playing in their new uniform of green jerseys with a black and white border, stockings to match and black shorts, the smartly attired 'Grove came back from 2-0 down to snatch a deserved draw in the third period. The home team adopted a close marking and heavy checking game, tactics suited to playing a Fife side not quite working yet in combination with each other.

The two most impressive teams so far, Dundee Tigers and Falkirk Lions, faced each other on 12 October. Although "The Blade" in the *Evening Times* described the encounter as "poor stuff", Falkirk came away with both points following an emphatic 4-1 win. The result was a surprise to most observers as Dundee failed to get their favoured three men rushes going in attack and generally lacked ideas and inspiration against a well organised Falkirk team for whom Gerry Davey was outstanding.

While the normally perceptive ice hockey correspondent of the *Glasgow Herald* was enthused with the general level of excitement and spectacle being provided across the circuit he expressed some real concerns regarding the quite marked increase in physical and violent play.

"In every game I have seen this season there has been an appalling amount of unfair body checking, tripping, dangerous stick work and a host of other annoying infringements. A number of players appear to have no regard for the rules of the game. Something more severe than an occasional visit of a minute or two to the penalty box must be imposed to curb their unsporting behaviour."
(Glasgow Herald: 18 October 1938).

There remains a very fine line in ice hockey between what constitutes fair play from illegal play. Players are often permitted considerable leeway in checking but any offence involving the use of sticks, hands or feet is generally punished. Referees and other officials have very difficult decisions to make in what is the fastest team sport of them all and those decisions have to be made in seconds. It is not an easy task. There were now more Canadian-developed players in Scotland than at any time since 1929, and unlike then the game now was semi-professional. Canadians always tend to play a more physically robust game than Europeans. It was surely no great surprise that the domestic game would become more physical given the overwhelming Canadian presence and influence in all of the clubs.

The SIHA had largely the same pool of referees it had always had. Most of these referees were themselves Canadians or Canadian-developed. There was some implied criticism of them in that they were not being strict enough in interpreting the rules. That was quite possibly the case. Perhaps some of them were even in awe of some of the players now bestriding the Scottish game. Whatever the reasons, the officials would need to raise their game in line with the standards now prevailing generally within the sport. Perhaps the ice hockey correspondent of the *Glasgow Herald* was merely pining for the "good old days" of the amateur era at Crossmyloof when a league match could be postponed at a moment's notice simply because two players in an opponent's team were unavailable because they had to attend a relative's funeral. The times when physical contact between players in matches was kept to a minimum, with penalties being comparatively rare, were well and truly gone - for better or worse. It was the price of semi-professionalism.

The first quarter of the Points Competition was completed on 22 October. To the great surprise of most observers Falkirk Lions sat proudly at the top of the competition table with 8 points following four wins from four matches. Their performance was all the more meritorious when one considers that they had yet to play a home match.

Falkirk had the meanest defence in the competition, having lost only 3 goals despite "The Blade's" assertion that Fiore Amantea was easily beaten by low shots. If a solid defence was the key to their success their first line of attack were no slouches either. In Gerry Davey, Nelson McCuaig, who had been moved to centre, and George McWilliams, Falkirk's offence was a highly skilful combination of speed, skill and deadly finishing power.

Dundee Tigers were in second place with 7 points but with a match more played than Falkirk. They were a very strong and purposeful side who liked to go forward at every opportunity. Well coached by Al Rogers, it was noticeable that their home-developed players, Doug Mitchell and Glen Braid, had improved under his able tutelage. Dundee were the competition's leading goal scorers with 20, an average of 4 per match.

Perth Panthers, in third position with 6 points from seven matches played, were finding the new competition hard going. They had yet to defeat any of the new teams. Lack of an adequate second line of attack meant that Les Tapp had to play for longer stretches, a handicap in view of the increased pace of play this season. With this in mind the club signed another centre, B "Breezy" Thompson, from Birmingham Maple Leafs and a native of Vancouver.

Fife Flyers occupied fourth spot with 5 points from four matches. The team in blue and gold had not yet managed to settle into any effective combination. Their play was still dominated by too much individual effort; coupled with a "gung-ho" style it was something player-coach Les Lovell would need to seriously address. Fife had quality in abundance but an injury to Jock Stover would stretch their defensive capabilities.

Kelvingrove, in fifth place with 4 points from five matches played, also strengthened their squad with the acquisition of defender, A (Art) Seafred. A native of Winnipeg, he had experience in the English National League with Brighton Tigers and Earls Court Rangers and had also played in Germany.

Mohawks propped up the competition table with no points - five defeats from five matches. It was a desperate situation for a very proud club. The team was not actually as bad as their position in the table indicated, the major problems being in defence where they were yet to find the right blend. Neither a long term injury to Archie Bogie nor the inability or unwillingness of their forwards to back-check properly - a factor requiring the attention of their coach - had helped their situation.

The positions held by the two Glasgow teams were where most observers thought they would be. The general feeling was that they lacked teamwork and any real sense of tactical awareness. However, the ice hockey correspondent of the *Glasgow Herald* suggested that insufficient training and practice facilities at Crossmyloof were also to blame for the poor showing of the two teams. This was certainly a reasonable point as Kelvingrove and Mohawks did have more competition for ice time at their rink than any of their opponents.

The first representative match of the season was arranged for 12 November when a Scottish League Select would meet an English League Select at the Empress Hall, London.

The SIHA was careful not to designate this contest as a full international since certain players including Jimmy Foster of Harringay Greyhounds were

Arnie Pratt, Perth Panthers and Scotland

Season 1938-1939

not available for selection. Only three players survived from the Scottish League Select squad which had taken the ice against Brighton Tigers and Earls Court Rangers in April; Fiore Amantea, Bunt Roberts and Len McCartney.

The SIHA selected a strong squad on paper for this match. Fiore Amantea retained the goaltending position and in front of him were George McNeil and Gordon Pantalone. The first line of attack consisted of Gerry Davey, Len McCartney and Al Rogers with the second line made up of Art Schumann, Breezy Thompson and Wilf Cadieu. Bunt Roberts provided defensive cover.

Confidence was high that the Scottish League Select would be able to give a good account of themselves despite the lack of practice time playing together. Pride often comes before a fall. Few observers expected the visitors to be so completely outplayed as they were. The English League Select won the match 9-1, a score which accurately reflected the course of the play.

"Inside Edge" in the *Daily Record and Mail* was obliged to admit that the English game was still "too hot for our boys". The ice hockey correspondent of the *Glasgow Herald* suggested that it was difficult for any Scottish representative side to give of their best when one took into account the congested state of club ice hockey north of the border. He pointed out, for example, that the three Falkirk Lions players in the squad, Fiore Amantea, Gordon Pantalone and Gerry Davey, were playing their fourth match in five evenings!

While there was a good deal of truth in this assertion, team selection remained a significant factor. Selecting the right players was and remains a highly subjective matter, but there were certainly some really surprising omissions from the squad, particularly in the cases of Nelson McCuaig and Les Lovell, both of whom were in great form. Yet while all sorts of reasons could no doubt be put forward for the latest representative disappointment, the fact was that English ice hockey remained superior despite the obvious improvement in standards being witnessed in Scotland.

On the domestic front Falkirk Lions continued to set the pace. They recorded their seventh consecutive victory in the Points Competition with a dramatic 4-3 win at Dundee in early November. The Tigers were actually 3-0 ahead by the end of the second period and it would have been even more but for a great display from Fiore Amantea. Gerry Davey then took a hand in the final session as Falkirk scored four goals without reply as the capacity crowd looked on in disbelief.

At the other end of the table, Mohawks, who had endured the unprecedented indignity of nine consecutive defeats, finally broke their duck with a welcome 5-4 derby win against Kelvingrove in mid November. From a 2-0 deficit in the first period they fought back tenaciously to lead 5-2 in the third period before 'Grove pulled back two goals before the final whistle. Glen Morrison, who scored a brace, had his best match in a Mohawks jersey in what had been a typically rousing contest.

Mohawks faced their old rivals without the services of George Horne who had moved to Fife Flyers. The move was not entirely unexpected given that Mohawks had experienced defensive problems all season. A number of different partnerships had been tried on the blue line but the club finally settled on Mickey Shires and Gordon Cummine.

The latest Glasgow derby heralded the half way stage of the Points Competition. Falkirk Lions remained top of the table. They were still unbeaten, although they had only drawn their previous two matches, suggesting a slight dip in form. Falkirk had 18 points from ten matches and were now 5 points clear of their nearest rivals Dundee Tigers, whom they had already beaten twice at the Dundee-Angus Ice Rink.

Falkirk had set a very hot pace, but the notion that they might just be slipping was confirmed when they sustained their first defeat of the season at the hands of Fife Flyers on 17 November. The result signalled the end of a truly remarkable unbeaten run of ten matches on the road for the Falkirk side. It was George Horne's first match for Fife and he made an immediate impact, by assisting on their second goal and scoring the third and clinching goal himself in the third period for a 3-1 win. The defeat was partly blamed on the inability of Falkirk Lions to use their second line of attack properly. It meant that their first line was being asked to do too much with the result that tiredness was creeping into their play. Some observers also thought their defence was less mobile and slower than that of their main rivals. Despite this reverse Falkirk remained top of the table by one point from Dundee Tigers and as fate would have it their next match was in Dundee on 23 November.

Dundee Tigers therefore had the opportunity to overtake Falkirk Lions for the first time, and were very confident of doing so given that their first line of attack, Al Rogers, Merrick Cranstoun and Jimmy Lightfoot, were in sparkling form. The match was an enthralling encounter, dominated by a Dundee team who showered a total of 29 direct shots at Fiore Amantea in the Falkirk goal. However, Falkirk were the more tactically aware team. They fully exploited the tendency of George McNeil and Howard Smith to move forward too often and therefore leave goaltender Bill Lane exposed at the back. Nelson McCuaig capped a wonderful performance by contributing to the best goal of the season thus far, when he skated through the entire Tigers defence before back-handing a pass to Gerry Davey who coolly beat Bill Lane with a beautifully-placed shot. Falkirk had ultimately prevailed with an exciting 4-3 win.

Falkirk's victory seemed to indicate that the team had returned to its earlier season form, but in ice hockey as in other sports nothing can ever be taken for granted. The first round of the President's Pucks competition commenced on 29 November with a tie between Falkirk Lions and Mohawks at Crossmyloof. It looked as if a comfortable enough evening would be in prospect for the visitors but how wrong they were.

Season 1938-1939

Gerry Davey, Falkirk Lions and Great Britain

Mohawks had an outstanding record in this competition and they caused a major upset. The Glasgow club had managed to coax Jim Kenny back out of retirement and he provided the spark which had been missing all season. Mohawks took the game to their opponents who looked jaded in comparison. Both teams traded a goal in each of the first two periods. At the start of the final period Chester Dawson scored a quick goal to put the home side ahead. Falkirk poured forward in the time left even taking off Fiore Amantea in a desperate attempt to find the equaliser. With the clock ticking down it was Mohawks who applied the classic sucker punch when amidst great excitement George Baillie gathered the puck in his own end and skated two thirds of the rink before shooting it into the unguarded net for the clinching goal. Mohawks had won 4-2.

A day later Falkirk Lions made their long awaited home debut at Falkirk Ice Rink when they entertained Perth Panthers in the Points Competition. A capacity crowd of 4,500 was in attendance to cheer on the table toppers, but another shock was in store as the visitors skated off with both points in a deserved 3-2 win. It was a terrible anti-climax for the home players who had waited so long to play on their own ice. Coming on top of their exit from the President's Pucks, it again raised serious doubts about the team's stamina and recent topsy-turvy form.

The SIHA was becoming increasingly concerned about the steady rise in illegal and violent play; at last it took some decisive action when it handed out a number of one- and two-match suspensions to the offending players. The guilty men were George McNeil of Dundee Tigers, Gordon Pantalone of Falkirk Lions, Art Schumann of Perth Panthers and Don Eaton of Kelvingrove. It was hoped the example set to them would be a warning to other transgressors of the rules. The SIHA had been obliged to act, underlining the lack of confidence in a number of the officials refereeing matches in Scotland. As a result it was decided to dispense with the services of a number of referees. In future only four would be used to officiate matches in the Scottish (National) League. The chosen referees were Frank Chase, J O McCabe, Robert Gardiner and Captain J T Grassie, who was employed as the sports master of Perth Academy.

In the other first round tie of the President's Pucks competition Fife Flyers defeated Dundee Tigers 5-1 in a match played at Crossmyloof on 2 December. It was a quiet game, devoid of any serious body checking or general excitement. The Kirkcaldy team dictated play from the start against a rather disinterested looking Dundee side who struggled to get out of first gear. Although not amongst the goal scorers, Len McCartney was the man of the match, on account of his clever distribution of the puck.

In the Points Competition, Falkirk Lions returned to winning ways with two wins on the road at Perth Panthers and Kelvingrove, Gerry Davey scoring four of his team's seven goals in the latter match. In fact Falkirk were obliged

Season 1938-1939

to play three matches in four evenings at the beginning of December the last of which against Mohawks at home was lost 4-2. This sequence of fixtures closed the third quarter of the competition.

Despite losing further ground Falkirk Lions were still top of the table with 24 points from 16 matches. Although their recent form had been erratic neither of their main challengers, Dundee Tigers and Fife Flyers, had been able to take advantage of the situation, owing to their own inconsistencies. Dundee were sitting on 21 points and Fife were on 20 points, although the Kirkcaldy side had played one match less than the other two.

With four matches left Falkirk Lions looked favourites to win the Points Competition. Yet their seeming inability to win on their home ice must have been a concern to the club; all four matches were at Falkirk Ice Rink. These fears appeared well justified; Dundee Tigers defeated Falkirk 6-3 in the first of these fixtures in mid December. The result moved Dundee into joint top place although they had played one fixture more, a 2-2 draw at Kirkcaldy.

In the President's Pucks Mohawks faced Kelvingrove in the first semi-final played on 13 December. A typically close match was expected but it was marred by sixteen penalties, a record for the season. Mohawks incurred twelve of these penalties and it was really the failure of Kelvingrove to capitalise more on their numerous power-plays which cost them dear. Mohawks had been improving of late although the 7-2 score line flattered them.

Dundee Tigers took over the leadership of the Points Competition three days later when they thrashed a hapless Kelvingrove 8-1 at Crossmyloof. Both Al Rogers and Merrick Cranstoun scored hat-tricks as the visitors ran riot. With only one match left Dundee now had 26 points, 2 ahead of Falkirk, who still had three fixtures to play.

Kelvingrove appeared to be in free-fall as this reverse was their eighth consecutive defeat in all competitions. Indeed, 'Grove had not won a match since the end of October. While new players were required in all departments of the team it was their defence which was causing the most concern. Veteran goaltender Dave Cross, who was finding life much tougher this season, had been replaced on a few occasions by Billy Turnbull. The club had not adequately replaced the absent Bert Forsythe.

There was the usual mixture of excitement and apprehension for the visit of Canada to Crossmyloof Ice Rink on 17 December. The Canadians were represented this year by Trail Smoke Eaters from British Columbia. They were about to embark on a major tour of Europe prior to competing in the World Championships being held in Basle and Zurich, Switzerland, in February 1939.

It would again be a Scottish League Select team which would face Canada rather than the full Scotland international side. Unfortunately no players from either Fife Flyers or Perth Panthers would be considered for selection since they were contesting a Points Competition match the same evening. It says much for the state of the game in Scotland that the SIHA were unwilling to intervene by changing the date of this club fixture - as they would have done in the past - for fear of compromising the commercial interests of the two teams concerned.

The selectors relied heavily on Falkirk Lions for this match. Fiore Amantea was in goal behind a blue line of George McNeil and Gordon Pantalone. It was an all Falkirk first line of attack with Gerry Davey, Nelson McCuaig and George McWilliams. The second line was comprised of Al Rogers, Glen Morrison and Wilf Cadieu with the versatile Gordon Cummine providing the cover. The main pre-match debate over selection this time was the preference for Glen Morrison of Mohawks over his teammate, Chester Dawson.

Not too much was expected but the Scottish League Select gave a very impressive performance against their more illustrious opponents; with a bit of luck they might even have won the match. Canada raced into a 2-0 lead in the first period but in the middle session the home defence got to grips with their speedy visitors. The forwards responded with goals from Wilf Cadieu and Nelson McCuaig to level the scores. Canada reasserted themselves in the final period when they scored twice to give them a 4-2 win. A major difference between the two teams on the night was the ability of Canada to take the chances that came their way. The home team missed several good goal scoring opportunities - a tendency for the first line to shoot too much from long distance. George McNeil was a stalwart in both defence and attack and Fiore Amantea had a fine match in goal.

"Inside Edge" considered the home performance to be the best he had ever witnessed. He was also fulsome in his praise of Trail Smoke Eaters who he thought were the equal if not better than any of the other Canadian sides to have visited Crossmyloof in the past. Of course the "Scottish" squad was "made in Canada" but the fact that so many of its key players came from one club meant that the combination and the understanding so often missing in previous representative sides from Scotland was not as pronounced on this occasion. There was surely a lesson there for the future.

In the second semi-final of the President's Pucks a rapidly improving Perth Panthers defeated Fife Flyers 5-1 at Crossmyloof on 20 December. Len McCartney was injured and missed the match against his old team but Perth dominated the proceedings from the start. The star of the show was Breezy Thompson who apart from scoring two goals gave an outstanding performance of puck distribution and tactical awareness.

A day later Dundee Tigers completed their programme of matches in the Points Competition with a 5-1 victory at home against Kelvingrove. They had gathered 28 points and now had to sit and wait until Falkirk Lions, currently on 24 points, fulfilled their three remaining fixtures.

For Falkirk the objective was quite clear. If they won all three matches they would win the Points Competition - their remaining opponents were

Season 1938-1939

Gordon Cummine would be killed in action in 1943 whilst serving with the Royal Canadian Air Force, during the Second World War.

Frozen in Time

Falkirk Lions Ice Hockey Club, 1938-39. Left to Right; Tom Brown, Murray Newton, Red Thompson, W W (Bill) Russell, Bill Callander, Alex Purdie, George McWilliams, Charlie Stapleford, Gordon Pantalone, Jimmy Johnstone, Nelson McCuaig, Fiore Amantea, Gerry Davy and R J Buck

Season 1938-1939

Mohawks, Kelvingrove and Fife Flyers - but they could only achieve it by doing something they had not yet managed - winning matches on their own home ice. Having already played and lost three fixtures at home, they finally broke their duck with a 4-0 win against Mohawks on 21 December and followed that up a week later when Kelvingrove were despatched with the same score. They now had 28 points and were again level with Dundee at the top of the table. It all now depended on their final match with Fife Flyers on 4 January.

The final of the President's Pucks was played between Mohawks and Perth Panthers at Crossmyloof on 23 December. This was the seventh season of this competition and Mohawks were now making their sixth appearance in the final. They had won it on three occasions, including an aggregate final victory against Perth Panthers in season 1936-37, but alas for them there was to be no repeat this time. In an exciting first period Glen Morrison scored first for Mohawks only for Arnie Pratt and Art Schumann to score twice for Perth before Gordon Cummine restored parity before the first interval. Perth went ahead early in the second period through man of the match Bunt Roberts but Mohawks again hit back when Morrison got his second goal. Les Tapp then seized on a rebound off the pads of Art Palfrey to give Panthers a 4-3 lead going into the third period. Perth finally asserted themselves in the closing session as Mohawks visibly tired. Goals from Breezy Thompson and the home-developed N (Norrie) Andrews gave the visitors a deserved if somewhat flattering 6-3 win. Although Art Palfrey had faced 30 direct shots during the match Mohawks had made a real fight of it. Lack of a cutting edge proved their undoing. The signing of Breezy Thompson had rejuvenated Perth Panthers. They were now a much better balanced side with two good forward lines and a decent defence. In winning the first silverware of the season Perth had sent out a message to the other leading teams in the country that they were again becoming a force to be reckoned with.

The New Year led the ice hockey correspondent of the *Glasgow Herald* to reflect on certain aspects of the semi-professional game in Scotland.

> "The lack of home-bred players is becoming a problem in Scottish ice hockey. At the moment little more than a dozen home players are distributed among the six clubs and if any more of these players are forced out of the game by injury there seems little prospect of others being able to keep the sides at full strength.
>
> If the present rule regarding a maximum of seven Canadians in one club is to be observed, obviously a reserve of other players must be available to complete teams and to have a margin in case of accidents. Sides have recently had to take the ice with only one substitute to ring the changes.
>
> Frankly, there is little encouragement for Scots to participate in ice hockey under prevailing conditions. In several of the clubs they

are often kept shivering in the players box waiting to play one or two fleeting visits to the ice while in a critical match they may never appear at all. It certainly looks as if the day is not too far distant when sides will be entirely composed of Canadians.

Apart from other considerations the congested state of the fixtures and the consequent time spent in travelling make it more and more imperative for players to make the game a full time occupation."

(Glasgow Herald: 3 January 1939).

The sport did seem to be heading full steam in the direction of professionalism but there was a potentially fatal weakness. While attendances and marketing at most rinks could possibly sustain a limited form of professionalism, whereby clubs could have a mixed economy of full-timers, part-timers and amateurs, it remained the case that the basic infrastructure required to maintain a fully professional set-up on a long term basis in Scotland was simply not yet in place. The current ice hockey "boom" in Scotland was wholly dependent on relatively expensive Canadian imports premised on the expectation of sustained spectator interest. If the public tired of ice hockey, if it was indeed nothing more than a passing fad as some sports commentators thought, there was no real infrastructure being developed to cope with the resultant fall-out. Ice rink managers and owners saw the game as a commercial enterprise but if there was any falling-off of interest they would quickly turn to other more lucrative events they could promote at their venues to maintain their revenue stream.

Scottish clubs were playing an absurd number of matches and there was undoubtedly a danger of spectator fatigue creeping in. In addition to the Points Competition, itself far too long in duration, every rink was promoting its own individual cup competition. Teams were expected to challenge for the Coronation Cup at Perth, the Airlie Trophy at Dundee, the Bairns Trophy at Falkirk and the Anderson Cup at Kirkcaldy. The league championship was about to commence and the Mitchell Trophy was yet to be played for.

It was all starting to look like serious overkill. It was having a detrimental effect on the players, who were often required to play three matches a week leaving many of them jaded and more prone to injury. The SIHA was well aware of the situation, but it was difficult to curb the excesses of ice rink managers and owners whose primary aim was to make a quick return on their investment in the sport.

Falkirk Lions finally wrapped up the Points Competition when they defeated Fife Flyers 4-2 on 4 January. They finished the campaign with 30 points. Dundee Tigers finished in second place with 28 points and Fife Flyers third on 24 points.

Despite making heavy weather of it, few observers disputed that Falkirk deserved their success, particularly since they had only six home fixtures out

Season 1938-1939

of twenty matches played. Falkirk finished with a record of 14 wins, 2 draws and 4 losses. Much of the credit goes to a solid defence which had conceded the lowest number of goals in the competition and to a first line of attack, Gerry Davey, Nelson McCuaig and George McWilliams, who between them had scored 54 of their team's 71 goals in the competition.

The Points Competition had been a personal triumph for Gerry Davey. He finished as its leading marksman with 29 goals but his overall contribution to the Falkirk cause had been immense, both as a coach and as a catalyst of the team's success. The stocky but highly mobile Davey was a truly outstanding player whose skill and artistry on the ice was an inspiration to those around him.

The league championship would finally get underway on 11 January. The format for the competition would be exactly as that which had pertained in the recent Points Competition. Each team would play the other on four occasions giving each a total of twenty fixtures. The competition was expected to be completed by the end of April.

Falkirk Lions may still have been basking in the glory of their recent success because they lost their opening league match at home when Perth Panthers defeated them 2-1 with goals from Arnie Pratt and Breezy Thompson. On the same evening, Dundee Tigers gave early notice of their intentions when they annihilated Kelvingrove 11-2, Al Rogers helping himself to five goals.

Fife Flyers opened their league campaign with a typically disappointing performance against Mohawks who held them 4-4 at Kirkcaldy, Chester Dawson scoring a hat-trick for the visitors. Most observers felt that, given the quality of their squad, Fife had seriously underachieved so far. Much more was expected from the men in blue and gold who appeared to have almost an embarrassment of riches.

Mohawks had strengthened their squad with the introduction of new centre, W (Bill) Bodnar, who had played with Mickey Shires at Schreiber Colts the season before. A native of Port Arthur, Ontario, where Shires had also grown up, Bodnar came to the Glasgow club with a good reputation and a number of idiosyncrasies which included the wearing of glasses and a helmet while playing.

The question of imports generally was raised again when Fife Flyers made a request to the SIHA that in future each club should be permitted to sign eight Canadians with the caveat that only seven could be selected for any match. The matter was debated at the SIHA and held in abeyance but in an apparent attempt at compromise the concept of "intermediate" players was introduced.

The SIHA came to the view that in future players of Scottish parentage born in other countries should be regarded as native Scots provided they lived in Scotland for a few years and provided they were willing to accept the much more limited "expenses" paid to genuinely home-developed players.

Frozen in Time

Perth Panthers Ice Hockey Club, 1938-39. Left to Right; Scotty Milne, Bob Purdie, Johnny Scott, Les Tapp, Breezy Thompson, John Fullerton, Bunt Roberts, Arnie Pratt and Art Schumann.

Season 1938-1939

It was acknowledged that home-developed players were receiving expenses amounting to about £2 per week, whereas Canadian imports were receiving about £4 - perhaps even more.

This latest tinkering with the rules on nationality meant that intermediate players still residing in Scotland but without a senior club such as Johnny Kelly, Frank Chase or Jimmy Allan were now able to play again in the Scottish (National) League because of the increased quota. All three players were immediately fixed up, Kelly moving to Falkirk Lions, Chase, who had actually been refereeing, joined Kelvingrove and Allan was signed by Perth Panthers.

What was one to make of these developments? Obviously real pressure was being exerted by a number of clubs to increase the quota of Canadian imports, a pressure which the SIHA seemed either unwilling or unable to completely resist. Despite protestations to the contrary, the sport's ruling body was continuing to facilitate the erosion of home developed talent in the Scottish game. This latest sanctioning of even more Canadian developed players into the country's senior clubs simply beggared belief.

On a much more positive note Scottish ice hockey received a boost when three home-developed players were selected for the Great Britain squad being assembled to compete in the forthcoming European and World Championships being held in Basle and Zurich, Switzerland, in early February. The players chosen were Joe Collins of Kelvingrove, and Billy Fullerton and Tommy McInroy of Fife Flyers. These were the first players to be selected from the Scottish League for an official LIHG tournament since Pete Stevenson became the first in 1935.

"Inside Edge" considered Joe Collins to be the best home-developed player ever produced in Scotland - quite an accolade. Such opinions are of course always subjective but the term "best ever" could surely be equally applied to Billy Fullerton, whose call-up to the Great Britain was long overdue. The selection of Tommy McInroy, something of a surprise, constituted a really remarkable achievement for a young man who had only learned to skate barely two years earlier.

On the domestic front Dundee Tigers and Perth Panthers were making the early running in the league championship. It was doubly curious that both floundered at Kelvingrove in successive matches at the end of January. Dundee were held 2-2 and four days later 'Grove defeated Perth 4-1 to register the shock result of the season thus far.

Prior to the match with Dundee, Kelvingrove had suffered 14 consecutive defeats in all competitions and their win against Perth was their first victory for 18 consecutive matches. More remarkable still, since Panthers were themselves unbeaten in their previous ten matches and were very much the current form side in the competition.

The first quarter of the league championship was completed in early February. Dundee Tigers topped the league table with 8 points from five

Tommy McInroy, Fife Flyers, Scotland and Great Britain

Season 1938-1939

matches. They had scored 29 goals in the process although 21 of these goals had come against the two Glasgow teams in three of their matches. Dundee continued with their robust go-ahead style of play totally committed to all out attack but they did sometimes leave themselves exposed at the back.

Perth Panthers were in second place with 6 points from four matches. Apart from their shock defeat at Kelvingrove they had hardly put a foot wrong and had the best defence in the league. Fife Flyers were also sitting on 6 points but were as mercurial as ever. The Kirkcaldy cause had certainly not been helped following a very serious injury sustained by player-coach, Les Lovell, which was continuing to keep him out of the team for the time being.

Falkirk Lions had only 4 points from five matches to show for their efforts. They were continuing to disappoint both supporters and critics alike with their indifferent form. The ex-Mohawks veteran, John Fullerton, had recently joined them following the arrival of Breezy Thompson at Perth Panthers. It was difficult to determine what the problem was at Falkirk but they seemed to lack the spirit and the zest they had shown earlier in the season.

As expected neither of the two Glasgow teams were setting the heather on fire despite some better recent performances from Kelvingrove. The clear gulf in class between the Crossmyloof teams and those in the rest of the league was attracting unfavourable comment in a number of quarters but the situation was not quite as bad as was being presented. Kelvingrove and Mohawks were both capable of improvement; all that was needed was a bit of confidence allied to better coaching.

The European and World Championships commenced in Switzerland in early February but for Great Britain, composed mainly of home-developed players, it was to prove a disappointing tournament. It started well enough in the preliminary phase with a 3-1 victory against Belgium. The three British goals were all scored by Scots, Tommy McInroy, Billy Fullerton and Jimmy Kelly of Wembley Monarchs. McInroy scored again in a 1-0 win against Hungary which allowed Great Britain to progress into the semi-final stage of the competition.

Many observers had criticised the BIHA for selecting what they considered to be an inferior side and they felt vindicated when Great Britain lost all three of their section matches without scoring a single goal. Over 4,000 spectators witnessed Canada defeating Great Britain 4-0 in Zurich, all of the Canadian goals scored in the final period. The British team then lost 1-0 to Germany, thanks to another third period goal, and finished the tournament with a 2-0 defeat against Czechoslovakia. Great Britain finished the competition in eighth position, their worst performance in the World Championship since 1934.

At home the league championship was just beginning to look like a two horse race between Tayside rivals, Dundee Tigers and Perth Panthers, who met each other for the first time in a "double-header" in mid-February. Both matches ending not surprisingly in score draws. In the first match at the

Dundee-Angus Ice Rink, Perth were 2-0 ahead before the home team hit back to make it 2-2 by the end of play.

Dundee, playing their third league match in a week, then lost another point when they were held 3-3 by Mohawks at Crossmyloof in a match marred by controversy over the validity of the home team's second goal. The argument arising from this, and similar incidents elsewhere, led the SIHA to appoint neutral goal judges for all fixtures in the future. Up until then the practice had been for each rink to supply its own goal judges. While this system was potentially open to abuse, complaints had been few and far between.

After losing 7-3 to Mohawks in their previous match, Fife Flyers reminded everyone what they were capable of when they thrashed Falkirk Lions 9-1 on 23 February. One could never be sure which Fife would turn up for games, such was the level of their unpredictability. It was enormously frustrating that such an obviously talented squad of players found it so difficult to find the consistency required to mount a serious challenge for the major honours.

Mohawks were enjoying an improved run of form and rounded it off nicely with a convincing 7-2 derby win against Kelvingrove. The match was wholly dominated by an outstanding performance by Bill Bodnar, although Gordon Cummine scored a hat-trick. Mohawks took advantage of the new rule on signing intermediate players when they acquired young R (Raymond) Cheyne, who made a scoring debut against 'Grove. He had been training with Perth Panthers before joining the Glasgow club.

By the half way stage of the league championship in early March, Mohawks had overtaken Falkirk Lions in fourth position. On the face of it Falkirk's continued decline was baffling. There was undoubtedly still an over-reliance on their first line of attack, but their defence was not firing on all cylinders either. The team had also suffered from players missing through injury but this perhaps exposed a weakness in the overall quality of the squad.

Dundee Tigers retained top spot in the league with 17 points from eleven matches. With a frugal defence, they remained the only unbeaten team in the league championship. Perth Panthers, who had played one match less than their rivals, continued to push them hard with 16 points. Both sides were evenly matched and a keen contest between them was expected until the end of the campaign.

The Mitchell Trophy competition commenced at the end of February with a first round tie between Fife Flyers and Perth Panthers at Crossmyloof. Once regarded as the premier cup competition in Scottish ice hockey, it had become rather devalued in recent years due in the main to the insistence of the SIHA that all matches should be played at the Glasgow venue. The proliferation of rival cup competitions at the other rinks across the country had also contributed to its decline in status.

One had the feeling that the clubs outside Glasgow were not really taking the Mitchell Trophy as seriously as they ought and this was underlined by

Season 1938-1939

the lacklustre contest served up in this first round tie. In a match noted for lacking the urgency and vigour of a league encounter, Fife surprisingly but deservedly defeated Perth 2-1, their winning goal coming from Tommy Durling in the final period. It would be a month before the next tie in the competition would be played.

There was great interest around the circuit following the news that Canada, the newly crowned world champions, were returning to Scotland to play a number of matches throughout March. Represented by Trail Smoke Eaters, Canada had already defeated a Scottish League Select 4-2 in December but further matches between the two sides were now arranged for Dundee, Falkirk and Kirkcaldy as well as the new ice rink just being completed at Ayr.

Although the squads selected for these matches were on the usual lines the actual formations were changed according to the venues. Thus, at Falkirk, it would be the Lions first line which formed the Scottish League Select attack whereas at Dundee, it would be the Tigers first line and so on. The one permanent absentee from the home side was goaltender Fiore Amantea who was replaced by Bill Lane in all of the matches except at Ayr where Ronald Milne came in.

A total of five matches were played throughout March with the following results:

Falkirk Ice Rink	Scottish League Select 5	Canada 7
Dundee-Angus Ice Rink	Scottish League Select 0	Canada 4
Kirkcaldy Ice Rink	Scottish League Select 0	Canada 5
Ayr Ice Rink	Scottish League Select 2	Canada 4
Falkirk Ice Rink	Scottish League Select 2	Canada 3

The Scottish League Select had now played Canada on six occasions and had lost all six.

Yet, there was no real disgrace in this. Trail Smoke Eaters were arguably the best Canadian team to have ever visited Scotland. They conceded only one goal in the process of winning the World Championship. In their 46 match European tour, Canada had won an astonishing 44, drawn 1 and lost 1 - that to an all-Canadian London Select side. In a team of outstanding talent star forwards, Johnny McCreedy and Joe Benoit, would go on to play in the National Hockey League with Toronto Maple Leafs and Montreal Canadians respectively. The match at Ayr Ice Rink on 21 March was the first official ice hockey match at the new venue.

In the league championship Perth Panthers suffered an alarming slump in form - a draw and two defeats in consecutive matches. Their two defeats to Fife Flyers and Kelvingrove were both at home and by a single goal in each. The main benefactor of these unexpected reverses was, of course, Dundee Tigers who continued on their unbeaten run.

Kelvingrove had been playing better of late and were confident of recording their first win against Mohawks in six matches when the two sides met in the league at the end of March. It was a robust encounter full of needle which resulted in fifteen penalties being handed out. Kelvingrove were twice two goals behind but managed to level the match 3-3 thanks to Laurie Marchant's second goal of the game in the final period.

The second first round tie in the Mitchell Trophy competition was contested between Falkirk Lions and Kelvingrove on 28 March. It was a fast and exciting match where the lead changed hands several times but at no point did more than a single goal separate the two sides. While Falkirk were short-handed because of injuries, 'Grove played well and deserved their 4-3 victory, Wilf Cadieu scoring the decisive goal.

The first semi-final was played only three days later between Fife Flyers and Dundee Tigers. It was a very close affair which finished 4-4 at full time. Extra time consisting of five minutes each way was then played. Dundee were the more composed side and scored twice to secure a 6-4 victory with Jimmy Lightfoot completing his hat-trick. Dundee Tigers were now in a position to win the "double" of Mitchell Trophy and Canada Cup.

Dundee were certainly in pole position for the latter competition. By the end of the third quarter of the league championship in early April they still remained unbeaten with 21 points from thirteen matches. Perth Panthers also had 21 points but they had played fifteen matches. The two forthcoming fixtures between the sides were going to be crucial but Perth would have to play the rest of the season without the injured Art Schumann.

Injuries were now a major problem at most clubs. With players sometimes having to play as much as four times a week, owing to the ludicrous fixture congestion prevailing, it was inevitable that some would pick up injuries of varying severity. Some were only minor knocks but others were of more long term duration, such as those suffered by Robert Thomson and Chuck Stapleford at Falkirk Lions and Glen Morrison at Mohawks all of whom were out for the rest of the season.

Falkirk set about finding replacements for Thomson and Stapleford. There was real surprise when they signed, from Fife Flyers, Les Lovell, who had himself just returned from a lengthy spell of injury. Lovell had of course been the player-coach at Kirkcaldy, but their performances and results had been disappointing. There was a feeling that he had just not been able to get the best out of the available talent at the club.

Falkirk also acquired the experienced right wing, R (Bob) Beaton, from Streatham. A native of Port Hood, Nova Scotia, Beaton had also played for Brighton Tigers. He was an interesting character. A tobogganing accident when he was three years of age had robbed him of sight in his left eye but that had not stopped him taking up a career as a professional welterweight boxer for a time in the early 1930s.

The simmering tension slowly developing between those who administered ice hockey in Scotland and those who profited from it finally came to a head with

Season 1938-1939

the establishment of the Scottish Ice Rinks Association (SIRA). An initiative of the various ice rink owners and managers across the country, its aims were to unite behind an agreed programme of expansion and development of the sport and to maintain and enhance the semi-professional game.

The creation of a *de facto* owners' organisation was bad news for the SIHA since it represented a clear challenge to its authority. The SIRA formalised and reinforced the increasing divisions existing between the newer and brasher commercial interests in the sport and its more traditional elite, a remnant of the amateur era. It was difficult to visualise how the two groups would be able to work together, yet an attempt would have to be made if the sport in Scotland was not to descend into chaos.

A bridge of sorts between the two organisations was that man of many parts, Frank Stuart, who was appointed the president of the SIRA. He, therefore, had a foot in both camps and was in a unique position to see both sides of any issue which developed between them. The vice-president of the SIRA was J A W Simpson of Perth and Falkirk supplied both its treasurer and secretary, J Towers and F Moffat, respectively.

One issue was causing a great deal of conflict - the continuing difficulty over the number of Canadian imports that should be permitted to play at each club. The SIHA had attempted to restrict the numbers by use of quotas and other ruses but the SIRA were opposed to any restrictions preferring instead a free market approach. As a start they made it quite clear that they wanted the quota raised to eight for next season as previously suggested by Fife Flyers. Their argument was that the Canadians were crowd-pleasers. To restrict the numbers would be to deny the paying public what they wanted to watch, and that would result in fewer takings at the box office.

On the ice, the race for the league championship came to a head in more ways than one in mid-April when Dundee Tigers and Perth Panthers faced each other in the long awaited "double-header". The teams met for the first match at Dundee on 12 April. Both were sitting at the top of the league table on 23 points although Tigers still had one match in hand. In a thrilling contest it was Perth who prevailed 6-5, their goals coming from Breezy Thompson and new boy, E (Earl) Nicholson, who each secured a hat-trick.

And there lay the problem. Perth had signed Earl Nicholson from Harringay Racers. Dundee put in a protest that he should not have been allowed to play in this match because his transfer north of the border had not been registered by the BIHA. The SIHA quickly investigated the matter and found that this was indeed the case. As a consequence they declared the result of the match to be null and void. Perth Panthers refused to accept this ruling and informed the SIHA that Nicholson would be selected again for their match against Dundee scheduled for 14 April. That match was played and ended 1-1. The SIHA decided to take strong action at this latest challenge to their authority. For icing an "illegal" player in their two matches against

Frozen in Time

Dundee Tigers Ice Hockey Club, 1938-39. Back Row; Merrick Cranstoun, Doug Mitchell, ?, ?, Jimmy Lightfoot, George McNeil and Howard Smith. Front Row; Jimmy Shannon, Bill Lane, F Hill and Al Rogers.

Season 1938-1939

Dundee, Perth Panthers were docked the three points they had gained while Dundee Tigers were awarded all four points.

The upshot of this fiasco was that Dundee Tigers were virtually handed the Canada Cup; they had now acquired 27 points and with only two matches left were now in an almost unassailable position. The club were not entirely happy at gaining the advantage in this manner and would have preferred to re-play both fixtures against Perth. The SIHA were in no mood for compromise, perhaps seeing in this situation an opportunity to flex its muscles and re-assert itself by taking a hard line.

It was not one of Scottish ice hockey's finest moments. The league championship race had been building up to a grandstand finish but for it to end in this manner was an enormous anti-climax. Quite why Perth Panthers took such an obstinate line is hard to puzzle. They were clearly in the wrong. Perhaps the club saw it as defending some sort of principle but it was not a principle worth defending. The fact remained that they had iced an illegal player not once but twice and in the full knowledge that under existing rules that was illegal. Perth Panthers paid a heavy price for misplaced pride.

In the middle of the dispute between Dundee and Perth the second semi-final of the Mitchell Trophy was played on 13 April between Kelvingrove and Mohawks at Crossmyloof. Little did anyone realise at the time that this would be the final match between these old rivals in what had been the longest running and most enduring fixture in Scottish ice hockey. Kelvingrove had yet to register a win in their previous six matches. They were to be disappointed again;. Chester Dawson put Mohawks ahead in the first period, only for Don McLeod to secure the equaliser in the middle session. In an exciting third period George Baillie scored for Mohawks four minutes from full time and Mickey Shires added to that lead almost immediately thereafter. In a desperate finish Wilf Cadieu pulled a goal back for 'Grove but try as they might they could not find another as Art Palfrey defied them with a string of great saves in the final minutes. Mohawks won a robust contest 3-2.

The postscript to this match brought the really devastating news that Kelvingrove Ice Hockey Club, founder members of the revived SIHA in 1929 and one of the most successful clubs in the country, would be disbanding at the end of the season, an incredibly sad development. Kelvingrove had been a credit to the sport, becoming one of the great institutions in the local game, but times had obviously caught up with them. Most of their success had been achieved during the earlier years of the club's history in the amateur era, but it simply no longer had the necessary infrastructure in place to realistically compete in a semi-professional league.

This fine old club achieved the "double" twice when it won the Canada Cup and the Mitchell Trophy in seasons 1930-31 and 1933-34. They finished runners-up in the Canada Cup in season 1931-32 and were beaten finalists in the Mitchell Trophy in seasons 1931-32 and 1935-36. They were joint winners of the President's Pucks in season 1932-33 and beaten finalists in seasons 1933-34, 1934-35 and 1935-36. In their ten seasons of competition, Kelvingrove had played a total of 192 official matches for an overall record of 82 wins, 74 losses and 36 draws. In the two Points Competitions, Second Division and Canada Cup their record had been 64 wins, 60 losses and 31 draws out of a total of 155 matches played. In the Mitchell Trophy they played 22 matches with a record of 12 wins, 8 losses and 2 draws and in the President's Pucks they played 15 matches with a record of 6 wins, 6 losses and 3 draws.

A number of outstanding players had worn that famous green, black and white kit over the years, not the least of whom was goaltender Dave Cross who had been with the club since 1930. Sid Montford and Andy Dick had also been great servants to Kelvingrove, both having played nine seasons there. Other famous names included Alec Fullerton, Joe Collins, John Campbell, R L Noble, Scotty Cameron, Don Eaton and arguably the greatest of them all, Arthur Tingley.

The final of the Mitchell Trophy was contested between twice-winners Mohawks and Dundee Tigers at Crossmyloof on 21 April. It was the Glasgow club's fourth appearance in the final. The match may have been something of a distraction to Dundee (who had not yet quite wrapped up the Canada Cup in yellow and black ribbons) but that would be unfair to Mohawks, who gave the champions elect an almighty struggle.

Indeed, the match was not settled until after a period of extra time. As ever, Dundee were reluctant to change their first line of attack which meant that Al Rogers, Merrick Cranstoun and Jimmy Lightfoot played for 65 of the 70 minutes the match lasted. By comparison, Mohawks changed their front line frequently, skated faster but often to little effect due to wayward finishing. The first two periods were goalless but at the start of the third period George Baillie broke the deadlock by scoring for Mohawks on a power play while George McNeil was sitting in the penalty box. McNeil, ever eager to break forward, made amends by scoring an equalising goal before full time was called. In a tension packed period of extra time, Dundee were the better team. It was no real surprise when Merrick Cranstoun scored the winning goal with a long range shot, which some observers thought Art Palfrey might have dealt with.

A week later Dundee Tigers finally clinched the league championship and the Canada Cup at the Glasgow venue when they thrashed a dispirited Mohawks 10-3 with a scintillating performance of fast and controlled ice hockey. Player-coach Al Rogers scored five of his team's goals. Dundee won the title by five points from runners-up Perth Panthers, who crushed Kelvingrove 10-0 in the Glasgow club's last ever match.

Despite all of the late season controversy Dundee Tigers thoroughly deserved to win the title. They finished with a record of 12 wins, 6 draws and only 2 defeats. Dundee had scored 102 goals with 64 of them coming from their formidable first line although George McNeil and Howard Smith also contributed 30 goals between them from the defence. These statistics underlined the team's offensive qualities and the philosophy that they were always capable of scoring more goals than they would lose in any given match.

For Perth Panthers it was a question of what might have been. They must surely have regretted their actions over the Earl Nicholson affair which quite possibly cost them the league championship. Perth had easily the best defensive record in the league and at the other end of the ice they also had the leading marksman in Breezy Thompson who finished the campaign with 30 goals.

Fife Flyers were the great enigma, finishing in third position with 23 points. They were second-top goal scorers with 91, 11 more than second-place Perth but their defence had conceded 75, a staggering 29 more than Perth. Fife were capable of playing wonderful ice hockey one match yet could be ineffectual in the next. They undoubtedly had the strongest pool of forwards in the country but that perhaps had been their undoing since ex-coach, Les Lovell, had struggled to find the right blend.

The private battle between the two Glasgow clubs ended with a much improved Kelvingrove finishing in fourth position, three points ahead of Mohawks in fifth place. This was some consolation for 'Grove who had endured a poor head-to-head record against Mohawks, with two defeats and two draws. Kelvingrove had proved just a bit more resilient than Mohawks against the other teams in the league and had actually recorded one or two impressive results.

What of Falkirk Lions? Falkirk had incredibly gone from winning the Points Competition to finishing bottom in the league championship. Many observers were at a loss to quite understand how that had happened. Injuries to key players and at different parts of the campaign had certainly played havoc with their team selection but their appalling record at home - only two wins out of ten - was more difficult to explain.

Questions were also asked of a defence - on paper amongst one of the best in the league - which had lost 107 goals. The unwillingness of the first line to back-check was a major deficiency. There had also been a tendency to overwork their first line in matches, although Falkirk did seem to lack the overall quality and strength in depth of some other clubs.

So a momentous season for Scottish ice hockey finally came to an end. The sport was in the midst of an apparent boom despite remaining weaknesses in its infrastructure. In the overall enthusiasm permeating the semi-professional game no one was the least bit interested in listening to a "Cassandra". The future looked even brighter with more ice rinks being constructed at Dunfermline, Paisley and Aberdeen. As a result further expansion of the sport was likely in the season ahead.

For those of a more nostalgic disposition, the loss of Kelvingrove was an enormous disappointment. There were similar fears being expressed in some quarters regarding the future of Mohawks as well. Scottish ice hockey had obviously moved on from the old days of the "house league" at Crossmyloof yet something important had also been lost along the way. Perhaps this was simply yearning for the amateur era, but the ideals espoused by the twelve original clubs who established the revived SIHA in 1929 seemed a million miles away from the way the sport was being run now.

In England, Harringay Greyhounds won the English National League for the first time. They constituted a formidable side with the brilliant Jimmy Foster in goal and a number of players who would later play in the National Hockey League including Dick Behling, Hazen McAndrew, Joe Shack and Connie Tudin. The Greyhounds also boasted Joe Beaton, the brother of Falkirk's Bob Beaton.

Season 1939-40

In common with almost every other facet of social life in the country ice hockey was expected to be seriously curtailed by the outbreak of the Second World War. Just as the commencement of hostilities in 1914 had badly impeded the sport's development at that time, so this latest world conflict would eventually put a premature break on the boom period currently being witnessed in Scottish ice hockey. While the government was keen to do everything possible to encourage enlistment in the armed forces it was also well aware of the value of maintaining a spectator sports infrastructure as an important aid to public morale on the home front. Sporting events rendered the appearance of normality at a time when life was far from normal. Thus, sports such as football, cricket, rugby and racing were encouraged to continue as best they could albeit within a climate of wartime conditions and contingencies. The new ice hockey season had been due to commence on 1 October but that start time had to be postponed in the confusion and uncertainty following the declaration of war on 3 September. It was far from clear how many players would be available to participate in the sport not to mention how many ice rinks would be permitted to remain open for business. Ice rinks afforded valuable space for storage and bearing in mind what had occurred in 1914, Crossmyloof was certainly one rink likely to be requisitioned again for war purposes.

It was not until mid-October that some clarity on the situation was revealed by the ex-Kelvingrove star, Sid Montford:

> "Plans have now been completed for the start of organised ice hockey in Scotland. Competitive play will begin around 30 October. At a meeting of all interested parties it was decided to form a wartime emergency body under the rules and regulations of the Scottish Ice Hockey Association.
>
> Six teams, Ayr, Dundee, Dunfermline, Falkirk, Kirkcaldy and Perth, will take part. All of the players will be "pooled" with a view to equalising the balance of strength."
>
> *(Daily Record and Mail: 17 October 1939).*

The news that the Scottish (National) League would continue for another season was greeted with a certain amount of incredulity south of the border.

In what was a most peculiar reaction, the secretary of the BIHA, J F "Bunny" Ahearne, alleged that the SIHA was operating illegally and that neither it nor any of its competitions would be officially recognised. Whether Ahearne had the authority of the LIHG for taking this view is a moot point.

In any event, the response of the SIHA was simply to ignore the BIHA which in reality had no real jurisdiction for ice hockey matters in Scotland. Neither had the SIHA ever had any formal relationship with the LIHG. The SIHA did point out that it had previously gained formal recognition from the Canadian Amateur (Ice) Hockey Association to regulate the sport and organise competitions in Scotland. While such recognition was welcome, it had never been really essential.

The relationship between the SIHA and the BIHA had always been tenuous. It tended to fluctuate between grudging toleration and outright hostility according to circumstances. The BIHA undoubtedly saw the SIHA as an upstart at times. However, it could huff and puff all it liked; it had neither the authority nor the ability to impose its will in Scotland.

While there still remained a number of uncertainties as to exactly how many players would be available to each club, and to how exactly they would be "pooled" between them it was clear that the following six teams would compete in the new season; Ayr Raiders, Dundee Tigers, Dunfermline Vikings, Falkirk Lions, Fife Flyers and Perth Panthers. The semi-professional structure of the Scottish (National) League would also be maintained. Given the expected widespread movement of players and the establishment of two entirely new clubs at Ayr and Dunfermline, the SIHA decided to commence the new season with another Points Competition to be regarded as a "bedding-in" tournament. Each team would play the other on four occasions for a total of twenty fixtures and it was intended that no team would play more than twice a week. Match nights were arranged as follows; Dunfermline would play on Mondays, Falkirk and Dundee on Wednesdays, Kirkcaldy on Thursdays, Ayr on Fridays and Perth on Saturdays. The Points Competition would commence at the end of October and was expected to conclude by early January.

One very famous name was of course missing from the new season; Mohawks. They had reluctantly decided to follow the path of Kelvingrove by withdrawing from senior ice hockey. It was a most regrettable but entirely understandable decision, made in the full knowledge that as the club was currently structured it could not have continued to successfully compete in the wholly semi-professional game. Mohawks' demise was an inevitable consequence of the sport's recent development, but the expected closure of Crossmyloof in the near future was the final nail in the coffin. Leading members of the SIHA since 1929, Mohawks Ice Hockey Club had been the most successful team of the pre-war era. They had won the Canada Cup a record three times in seasons 1931-32, 1935-36 and 1936-37. The Mitchell Trophy was secured in seasons 1934-35 and 1935-36 and the President's

Season 1939-1940

Pucks a record four times in seasons 1932-33, 1934-35, 1935-36 and 1936-37. They remained the only team in the Scottish League to have won all three major trophies in one season when they achieved this singular honour during season 1935-36. In their ten seasons of competition, they had played a total of 197 official matches for an overall record of 106 wins, 66 losses and 25 draws. In the two Points Competitions, First Division and Canada Cup their record had been 81 wins, 55 losses and 18 draws out of a total of 154 matches played. In the Mitchell Trophy they played 20 matches with a record of 10 wins, 8 losses and 2 draws and in the President's Pucks they played 23 matches with a record of 15 wins, 3 losses and 5 draws.

A number of outstanding players had worn the famous blue, white and red colours over the years, none more so than Scottish ice hockey's premier family dynasty, Alec, Billy and John Fullerton, all locally developed players, and in their prime, the equal of any Canadian imports. Other great players who graced the club over the years included S A MacDonald, Art Brady, John Campbell, Jim Kenny, Art Palfrey, Ronald MacDonald, Wally Welch and George Horne. They had always been an exceptionally well run club never at any time having a large squad of players, always preferring quality to quantity as their record so clearly demonstrated.

So the Scottish Ice Rink, Crossmyloof, Glasgow, the spiritual home of Scottish ice hockey, no longer had any teams competing at senior level. Since 1929, a total of 14 different clubs had competed in the Scottish League out of this famous old rink. For the few romantics left in the game it was very sad to witness the end of that era. Mohawks, the last and the best of those clubs, had now gone too.

The SIHA managed to conclude the potentially tricky process of allocating unattached players between the various teams on schedule for the new season commencing on 30 October. This process was accomplished with the co-operation of the clubs, although it seems clear from the results that a "free market" had also been at work in determining which players went where. As expected in the circumstances, the actual number of players available to each team was reduced from that of previous seasons.

Dundee Tigers, the reigning champions, were one of the clubs least affected by player movements. The basic spine of the team - consisting of Bill Lane in goal, George McNeil in defence and player-coach Al Rogers and Merrick Cranstoun in attack - was retained. Glen Braid remained but on the down side the club had lost the services of Howard Smith - replaced by Bunt Roberts who joined from rivals Perth Panthers - and Jimmy Lightfoot, both of whom would be greatly missed. The forward line was significantly strengthened with the acquisition of the ex-Kelvingrove duo of Scotty Cameron and Laurie Marchant. They remained very strong in attack but appeared short of adequate cover at the back for what would be a long and no doubt bruising season ahead.

Ayr Raiders Ice Hockey Club, 1939-40. Left to Right; Fiore Amantea, Mickey Shires, Wally Welch, Ken Johnston, Gordon Cummine, Don Cummine, Chester Dawson, Frank Prock and Bill Bodnar.

Season 1939-1940

Perth Panthers had lost a number of key players including Bunt Roberts, Bob Purdie and Arnie Pratt. Remaining at the club were Ronald Milne in goal with Raymond Cheyne and Art Schumann in defence, both equally at home in attack. A reasonably strong forward line-up in Les Tapp, Breezy Thompson and Jimmy Allan was supplemented by the addition of Frank Chase. Cover on the blue line was provided by J (Johnny) Scott.

Fife Flyers were almost unrecognisable from the season before, with only George Horne and Tommy McInroy remaining at the club. It was the considered opinion of most observers that the Kirkcaldy team had seriously underachieved in the previous season and that wholesale changes were needed. Whether or not the introduction of a much smaller but more manageable squad would pay dividends remained to be seen.

The new goaltender was A G (Art) Grant, a native of Winnipeg where he had played for a number of local teams. Joining Horne on the blue line was that man of many clubs, Robert Thomson. In attack, Arnie Pratt arrived from Perth and Glen Morrison from Mohawks. The biggest signing though was Paul Rheault, a native of Lorette, Manitoba, who had played the previous season with Wembley Lions. Fife appeared to have recruited very well but they seemed particularly light in regard to substitutes.

Falkirk Lions were also a much changed side. Their entire defence from the previous season had departed. Billy Turnbull was recruited for the goaltending position. In front of him on the blue line were Alec Purdie and new boy, Clem Beaton, who was joining his older brother Bob at the club. Great Britain ace Gerry Davey remained for another season as did George McWilliams but their line-mate, Nelson McCuaig, had departed.

Of the two new clubs, Dunfermline Vikings, appeared to be the stronger. They had prized four players away from their local rivals at Kirkcaldy, which if nothing else promised some lively derby matches in the future. Goaltender Chick Kerr jumped ship, along with Fife's entire first line of attack, Tommy Durling, Jimmy Chappell and Norman McQuade.

On the blue line at Dunfermline were two players relatively unknown to Scottish ice hockey, "Pinky" Downs and E (Ernie) Batson. Also wearing the red, black and white colours of the new team were forwards L (Larry) Marsh and Jimmy Shannon who had played at Dundee the previous season. Obviously much would depend on how quickly these players blended but Dunfermline appeared to have a very decent squad.

Ayr Raiders drew most of their squad from the disbanded Mohawks although they registered something of a coup by signing Fiore Amantea as their goaltender. In front of him would be Mickey Shires and Gordon Cummine. The player-coach of the new team was Chester Dawson and joining him in attack were Bill Bodnar, Wally Welch and the ex-Kelvingrove star, Don McLeod. Ayr looked the weakest side in the league. Like all of the clubs, they would seek to recruit more players as and when they were able to do so.

Given the exceptional circumstances surrounding the new season the SIHA decided to allow teams to ice "guest" players if the occasion demanded it. This highly regrettable decision, taken mainly because of restrictions on transport and travelling, undermined serious competition but the SIHA further argued that since the public were paying for the privilege of watching first class ice hockey in equally difficult conditions it was incumbent on the clubs to play their fixtures with the best talent available. That may have been so but it was a system clearly open to abuse by the clubs and unfortunately that proved to be the case.

As noted, most of the teams operating in the Scottish (National) League this season did not have the size of player pool they would have liked. The average number of players in each squad was about nine or ten. This meant that the recognised first team players would be on the ice for longer periods than was desirable and were therefore more susceptible to injury and fatigue. In such circumstances the temptation to ice any available guest players was obviously very great.

Nevertheless, the SIHA should be given credit for organising a full programme of ice hockey despite the uncertain climate prevailing in the autumn of 1939. As luck would have it any potential disruption to the season ahead was largely ameliorated by the fact that it was played out during what came to be known as the "Phoney War". In actual fact, the autumn, winter and spring of 1939-40 were relatively quiet periods on the home front compared with what was to come thereafter.

One immediate consequence of the prevailing wartime conditions was the much reduced coverage of the sport afforded by the press. Newspapers were required to reduce their size in order to save paper; not unnaturally reporting on sports was greatly diminished. Ice hockey had benefited from regular and good coverage in the local and national press over the years. In future the coverage offered would be drastically reduced. The odd article might appear but essentially only the scores from matches would be recorded and even that was not always on a consistent basis.

The Points Competition got underway on 30 October when a packed Dunfermline Ice Rink witnessed the home team take on Dundee Tigers. In an exciting match George McNeil put the visitors ahead in the first period. In the middle session persistent Dunfermline pressure finally paid off when Tommy Durling equalised only for Al Rogers to score again for Dundee against the run of play. It was Durling who was the hero again in the final period when he tied the match 2-2 but the home side were just a shade unlucky not to have won.

Falkirk Lions dreadful home form followed them into the new season when they were crushed 5-1 by Fife Flyers. It could have been worse but for a brilliant display by Art Grant in the home goal. Arnie Pratt scored a hat-trick for the visitors, who seemed to have settled very quickly into their new formation. That same evening, Ayr Raiders made their debut at the Dundee-

Angus Ice Rink. The new boys arrived half an hour late, scored the opening goal but then ultimately lost the match 7-2, George McNeil scoring a hat-trick.

On 2 November, Fife Flyers and Perth Panthers fought out a 1-1 draw at Kirkcaldy. Fought being the operative word as George Horne and Art Schumman came to blows with each other and Arnie Pratt "floored" his ex-team-mate, Les Tapp. As for the ice hockey, Breezy Thompson put the visitors ahead in the second period before Tommy McInroy got the equalising goal for Fife in the final session.

A day later, Ayr Raiders, resplendent in their black and white kit, made their home debut when Dunfermline Vikings were the visitors. The match attracted about 3,000 spectators. The home side took to the ice with George Horne and Arnie Pratt as guest players. An exciting encounter ended 2-2 with Chester Dawson scoring twice for Ayr and Jimmy Shannon and Norman McQuade the marksmen for Dunfermline.

Falkirk Lions' disappointing start to the season - two defeats in two matches - led to the club strengthening its ranks with the acquisition of goaltender, M (Maurice) Gerth, and forward, T R (Tommy) Forgie. Gerth was a native of Kitchener, Ontario, and had played four seasons in England with Streatham. Forgie was born in Glasgow but had been brought up in Brantford, Ontario, where he had played for a number of local teams before joining Richmond Hawks and then Brighton Tigers.

The growing trend of Scottish clubs luring players away from the English National League did not go unnoticed by either the BIHA or ice rink owners and managers south of the border.

> "The BIHA is worried about the activities of Scottish ice rinks raiding England for star players. Meetings are being held but no official statement has yet been issued. An official in an interview stated that the Scottish rinks want to run their own affairs independent of the BIHA despite the fact that they cannot be affiliated to the international body or receive players from Canada.
>
> The Scottish way of building star teams is to come to our players and make big offers, stated a London rink manager. Any players who accept such an offer are outlawed but it is difficult to see what can be done about it."
>
> *(Daily Record and Mail: 8 November 1939).*

The already strained relationship between the SIHA and the BIHA can hardly have been helped by statements like this emanating from London. Ice hockey was now a semi-professional sport both north and south of the border and as such the free market prevailed. Some Scottish clubs were able to offer better terms and conditions to the available talent than their English counterparts; that was a consequence of the semi-professional game.

Frozen in Time

While the question of affiliation to the LIHG was something of a "red herring" the inference that Scottish clubs could not recruit players from Canada was incorrect. Some had already done so and would continue to do so as the season progressed. It would seem that some of the people involved in the game in England were simply ignorant of the way that the sport was run in Scotland.

On the ice the early pace setters in the Points Competition were Fife Flyers with four wins and a draw from their first five matches. Included in those four victories were two excellent derby wins against Dunfermline Vikings. These were a source of particular satisfaction to the vociferous Kirkcaldy support. Making a real impact at the club was centre, Paul Rheault, whose intelligence in distributing the puck and leading the line had been outstanding.

Fife Flyers good run of form however was halted in mid-November when they were defeated 5-3 by Perth Panthers, who were making extensive use of guest players. This contributed to an impressive unbeaten run of nine matches, which firmly established them at the top of the table by the end of December. Consistency of this sort would be a key factor for any team in a competition where on the day everyone seemed capable of beating everyone else.

The Points Competition was proving very competitive and was providing enjoyable entertainment for the large crowds flocking to the matches. Apart from Perth no team had been able to claim any real ascendancy, leaving the results of most matches difficult to predict. Dundee Tigers were the biggest disappointment in the competition, which led to some unfair criticism being directed against their goaltender, Bill Lane.

While Dundee Tigers were struggling, Falkirk Lions were decidedly improving as the campaign progressed. The club had strengthened their squad further with the signing of left wing, L (Lou) Savoie, a native of Winnipeg. Falkirk could now boast one of the best forward lines in the league with Gerry Davey, Tommy Forgie and Lou Savoie. While winning the Points Competition was now beyond them there were hopes of making a serious challenge in the league championship.

Perth Panthers' dominance was confirmed by the fact that they were able to lose three of their final four fixtures but still win the Points Competition by six points! Perth finished the tournament with 27 points with a record of 12 wins, 5 defeats and 3 draws. They had the meanest defence in the competition ,where goaltender Ronald Milne had been in brilliant form. Raymond Cheyne had done better than expected in defence, forming a solid partnership with Art Schumann and Johnny Scott.

Fife Flyers finished runners-up with 21 points, their inability to defeat Perth in four matches and two later derby defeats to Dunfermline Vikings costing them dear. The Kirkcaldy team were a formidable outfit at home; if that form could be harnessed to their away matches they would be real contenders for the forthcoming league championship. In Arnie Pratt, Paul

Season 1939-1940

Rheault and Tommy McInroy they possessed a wonderful forward line and this was allied to an abrasive and hard hitting defence.

Falkirk Lions finished third with 19 points confirming their steady progress. Both Ayr Raiders and Dunfermline Vikings finished just behind on 18 points and both could be reasonably satisfied with their performances in their first campaign. Dundee Tigers were shocked to finish in bottom position with 17 points. It was difficult to determine exactly why they had performed so poorly but there was little doubt that their defence had been seriously overstretched and needed reinforcements. The Points Competition concluded on 6 January.

For the New Year the SIHA introduced a new national knock-out trophy competition to be known as the Scottish Cup. Ties in this competition would be played on a home and away basis with the aggregate score determining the outcome. The arrangements for this tournament suited the rinks because it guaranteed extra income from staging a home game but if one team built up a commanding lead in the first match it negated the traditional cut and thrust excitement of a one-off cup tie for the spectator.

The Scottish Cup was intended to be the premier knock-out cup competition. In this respect it replaced the more traditional Mitchell Trophy, competition now apparently regarded as a relic of the amateur era. This change in status reflected the changes within the SIHA itself, which now seems to have moved its *modus operandi* to Falkirk Ice Rink, following the withdrawal of senior ice hockey at Crossmyloof.

The draw for the first round of the Scottish Cup produced some interesting ties with both a Fife and a Tayside derby in prospect. The first tie was played on 8 January when Dunfermline Vikings hosted Fife Flyers in a thoroughly bad tempered encounter. Dunfermline started strongly and were 2-0 ahead by the end of the first period, Fife hotly disputing Norman McQuade's second goal. Both teams exchanged goals and several punches in the middle session and while Fife turned the screw in the third period the home side held firm for a deserved 3-1 victory.

Falkirk Lions defeated Ayr Raiders 3-1 in their first round tie two days later. The home team were prevented from scoring more goals thanks to a brilliant display of goaltending from Fiore Amantea. Chester Dawson actually put Ayr ahead against the run of play before Gerry Davey recovered the situation with two quick goals in succession. He then completed his hat-trick in the final period.

In the Tayside derby, Dundee Tigers registered a welcome 5-3 victory against Perth Panthers. In the return Fife derby, Dunfermline Vikings surprised the home team at Kirkcaldy Ice Rink with a superb performance winning the match 6-4. Dunfermline progressed to the semi-finals with a 9-5 aggregate victory. Perth Panthers also overcame their first tie deficit at Dundee to progress to the semi-finals.

Frozen in Time

There was great excitement at Ayr Ice Rink as the home team defeated Falkirk Lions 6-3 to give them a 7-6 aggregate win to secure a semi-final place. Watched by a capacity crowd, the visitors almost rescued the match in the final period with two late Tommy Forgie goals. Only a wonderful save by Fiore Amantea in the last seconds of the match prevented the tie from going into extra time. Ayr gave a debut to Frank Prock in this match; he replaced Don McLeod who had left the club.

The semi-finals of the Scottish Cup paired Dunfermline Vikings with Ayr Raiders and Perth Panthers with Falkirk Lions. The latter team had qualified, courtesy of a two leg aggregate victory against Dundee Tigers in a tie described as the "second round". The semi-finals would be played on 29 January and 3 February.

The league championship would commence in mid January and was expected to finish in late April. As in the previous competition each team would play the other on four occasions, twice at home and twice away, giving each side a total of twenty fixtures. The teams would no longer compete for the Canada Cup because - like the Mitchell Trophy and the President's Pucks - this particular trophy was apparently now also regarded as a totem of the past. How very sad this was, in the brave new world of Scottish ice hockey.

The SIHA was keen to reduce the dependence of clubs on guest players, a practice which some observers had warned would lead to abuse. It was recognised that it had rather marred the Points Competition. To this end plans were announced to recruit a further batch of players from Canada who would be allocated to the various clubs in as fair a manner as possible. The thinking was that if the clubs had a larger squad of players to choose from it would cut down the need to borrow players from elsewhere.

The league championship got off to an exciting start on 15 January when Dunfermline Vikings fought out a thrilling 5-5 draw with Dundee Tigers, Al Rogers scoring a hat-trick for the visitors. Dundee followed this up with a good 8-5 victory against Ayr Raiders, Merrick Cranstoun grabbing four of his team's goals. This encouraging start in the league continued with a 3-1 win against Perth Panthers in their next match as Dundee sought to improve upon their miserable autumn campaign.

The promised batch of Canadians duly arrived in Scotland and the SIHA allocated them to the various clubs following a trial match played behind closed doors. H (Hugh) Williams from Winnipeg was allocated to Dundee Tigers; E (Eddie) McMillan also from Winnipeg to Fife Flyers; K (Ken) Johnston from Saskatoon to Ayr Raiders; L (Les) Vickery from Prince Albert to Perth Panthers; V (Verne) Reilly also from Prince Albert to Dunfermline Vikings and T (Tom) Allan from Wilcox to Falkirk Lions.

While all of these young men came to Scotland with good reputations they would most likely prove to be a mixed bag. It really was impossible for the

Season 1939-1940

SIHA to know how good any of them actually were on the basis of scouting reports and one trial match. Some teams benefited more than others.

The first semi-final tie of the Scottish Cup was played between Dunfermline Vikings and Ayr Raiders on 29 January. The star of the match was Tommy Durling who scored all three of the Viking's goals in a 3-1 victory but it was noted that the new left defence, the recently allocated Verne Reilly, was "a virile raider with beautiful stick work." It had been a physical encounter but it left Ayr with a reasonable chance of recovering the situation. In the return leg at Ayr Ice Rink, Dunfermline Vikings made their intentions quite clear by scoring some early goals to put the tie beyond the home side. The hugely experienced Tommy Durling was again the scourge of Ayr with another hat-trick as the visitors ran out 7-4 winners to clinch the tie 10-5 on aggregate. Dunfermline were quite comfortable in both matches and looked a good bet to win the trophy.

In the other semi-final tie, Falkirk Lions and Perth Panthers battled to an exciting 3-3 draw. Gerry Davey scored all three of his team's goals to put the Lions 3-0 ahead but slackness crept into their play allowing the Panthers to come back into the game. It was no great surprise when Art Schumann, who was enjoying a magnificent season, scored the equalising goal six minutes from full time.

Perth Panthers, who were enduring a terrible time in the league championship, were nevertheless hopeful of reaching the cup final. Having worked very hard to gain an unexpected draw at Falkirk, home advantage was to no avail as a highly organised Falkirk side turned in an excellent performance to win the match 4-1 after falling behind to an early goal. The visitors took the chances that came their way whereas Perth squandered theirs. Falkirk progressed to the cup final on a 7-4 aggregate.

So Dunfermline Vikings and Falkirk Lions would contest the first Scottish Cup final to be played over two legs on 19 February and 1 March.

In the league championship it was noticeable that many more goals were being scored in comparison to the previous Points Competition. This was probably the result of cumulative tiredness as players were on the ice for longer shifts but in addition good quality defenders seem to have been rather thinner on the ground. These factors had led to a lot of high scoring matches and while that was entertaining for spectators the overall standard of play was not as it should have been.

Dundee Tigers, who were unbeaten in their first six matches, suffered their first defeat in the league when they were thrashed 12-6 by Falkirk Lions on their own ice in mid February. In an extraordinary game, Merrick Cranstoun scored all six of Dundee's goals while Tommy Forgie and Gerry Davey each scored four goals for Falkirk. The result left Dundee, Falkirk and Fife Flyers sharing joint leadership of the league with 10 points from seven matches.

The eagerly anticipated first leg of the Scottish Cup final was played at Dunfermline Ice Rink on 19 February in front of an expectant capacity crowd of 3,400. It proved to be a pulsating encounter from the moment Tommy Durling first timed a pass from Jimmy Chappell into the net to put Dunfermline ahead after four minutes. Falkirk recovered from this early blow to take charge of the game and quickly rattled in three goals from J (Johnny) Taylor, Tommy Forgie and Lou Savoie, to lead 3-1 at the end of the first period.

At the start of the second period Gerry Davey scored to give Falkirk a 4-1 lead. Any complacency was certainly punished as Dunfermline finally got their game together. Norman McQuade and Jimmy Chappell scored within a minute of each other. Jimmy Shannon then had the misfortune to score an own goal to give Falkirk a 5-3 lead at the end of the period.

Roared on by a vociferous home crowd Dunfermline pressed Falkirk back in the final session. Durling scored his second goal and with only thirty seconds left on the clock McQuade got his second goal to tie the match 5-5. Falkirk had been the better side but great credit was due to Dunfermline for their never say die approach.

The continued unpredictability of the league championship was amply demonstrated when following their 12-6 drubbing at the hands of Falkirk, Dundee easily won their next two home matches. They thrashed Fife Flyers 12-6 with George McNeil and Merrick Cranstoun each scoring four goals and then they exacted a good measure of revenge on Falkirk when they were annihilated 12-3, Al Rogers scoring five goals with a hat-trick each for George McNeil and Merrick Cranstoun.

By the end of February, the half way stage of the league championship was reached. Dundee Tigers were sitting at the top of the table with 15 points from eleven matches their awesome fire-power and a very much improved defensive performance having done much to get them there.

Fife Flyers were in second position with 12 points from ten matches while Falkirk Lions were third with 11 points from ten matches. The biggest surprise had been the wretched form displayed by Perth Panthers who had amazingly lost their first eight matches despite comfortably winning the Points Competition in the autumn. They finally broke that sequence with a welcome 6-1 victory at Ayr Raiders.

Fife Flyers came within a point of Dundee Tigers at the top of the league when they defeated them 5-3 in a fine match at Kirkcaldy on 29 February, Paul Rheault scoring four of his team's goals. The following evening they took over the leadership of the league by one point when they travelled to Ayr and defeated the home team 8-5, Rheault again scoring four goals and line-mate, Arnie Pratt, a hat-trick. Fife were clicking into top gear the result at Dundee being the first of six consecutive wins in the league championship.

The same evening that Fife Flyers were taking top position in the league their county rivals Dunfermline Vikings were at Falkirk Ice Rink to play the home side in the second leg of the Scottish Cup final. The match attracted an attendance of 4,000 spectators and with the tie poised at 5-5 the home supporters were confident that their team would be lifting the silverware at the end of the evening. In an exciting first period six goals were exchanged between the two teams, Clem Beaton, Gerry Davey and Bob Beaton scoring for Falkirk and Tommy Durling with two goals and Jimmy Chappell replying for Dunfermline. The second period was then goalless as caution gripped both sides. In the third period, Tommy Forgie put Falkirk 4-3 ahead but Chappell then scored twice for Dunfermline while the home team were shorthanded due to penalties. The cup seemed to be heading to Fife but just before the end Forgie scored again to settle the tie 5-5. The game went into two periods of extra time but the two sides could not be separated. The SIHA decided that the two teams would replay the Scottish Cup final on a home and away basis no doubt with an eye on revenue maximisation. These matches would be played on 18 March and 20 March. It was agreed that should extra time be required in the second leg then the next goal scored would be the winner a development clearly taken from the North American game.

In the league championship Fife Flyers consolidated their position at the top of the league on 4 March when they defeated local rivals Dunfermline Vikings 8-3 on their own ice, Paul Rheault collecting five goals in this match. Observers were running out of superlatives to describe his performances. He was a one man demolition squad and an inspiration to his team. Rheault had built up an almost telepathic understanding with Arnie Pratt who was also in sensational form and along with Tommy McInroy, the Kirkcaldy first line seemed unstoppable.

Dundee Tigers lost ground two days later when they could only draw 2-2 with Perth Panthers on their own ice. This result left them in second place with 16 points. Fife Flyers had 18 points both sides having played thirteen matches. The two sides played in an attacking but highly aggressive style a point which was borne out by their respective penalty statistics.

Fife Flyers not only topped the league in points but also in the number of penalties they conceded. It came to a total of 104 minutes. Dundee Tigers were not far behind having racked up 88 minutes in penalties of which 31 were handed out to the skilful but combative, Merrick Cranstoun. The cleanest team in the league were perhaps not surprisingly, Perth Panthers, with only 45 minutes conceded a factor which may partly explain their disappointing league campaign.

Another team who were struggling were new boys, Ayr Raiders. They had lost six consecutive league matches and took decisive action in an attempt to stop the rot. The club released Wally Welch, Frank Prock and Don Cumming and in their places they acquired three new young Canadian forwards from Streatham in the English National League, R (Roy) McBride, H (Hedley) Marshall and J (Jack) McBeth. All three players were from the Winnipeg area and would become known as "The Three Ms".

Frozen in Time

By the three quarters stage of the league championship in mid March, Fife Flyers remained top of the table with 22 points from fifteen matches. Dundee Tigers were in second position and still in the hunt with 20 points. Falkirk Lions were in third place with 17 points and seemingly out of the running but they were to surprise everyone before the season was out.

The marathon that had developed into the Scottish Cup final resumed on 18 March when Falkirk travelled to Fife to play Dunfermline Vikings in the first leg replay following two 5-5 draws. Gerry Davey opened the scoring for the visitors with a rather fortuitous goal after only three minutes. The match was played at a hectic pace and several penalties were imposed. Falkirk led 1-0 at the end of the first period. Davey increased Falkirk's lead at the start of the middle session before Scotty Cameron, a guest player, pulled a goal back for Dunfermline. The home team went all out for the equaliser but ran into a brick wall in the shape of Maurice Gerth who was having a fine match in the Falkirk goal. Falkirk went 3-1 ahead early in the final period when Tommy Forgie capitalised on a defensive blunder. In a dramatic turn of events Norman McQuade then scored twice for Dunfermline to level the tie 3-3. As in the first match of the final at Dunfermline in February, Falkirk were the better side but once again they let their concentration and their lead slip in the closing minutes of the contest.

The second leg was played at Falkirk Ice Rink two days later and was described by Sid Montford writing in the *Daily Record and Mail* as the most amazing cup tie in Scottish ice hockey history. While it certainly was an enthralling encounter made all the more tension ridden by the introduction of "sudden death" overtime to decide the issue, it was actually dominated by an outstanding individual performance from Norman McQuade who scored a hat-trick for Dunfermline. Falkirk began the match as favourites and played as such with Tommy Forgie giving them a 1-0 first period lead. McQuade scored the first of his three goals early in the second period when he followed up on a rebound of Maurice Gerth's pads. Just before the second interval Lou Savoie restored the home team's lead when he took advantage of poor defensive work by Dunfermline. As in the previous match Falkirk went 3-1 ahead at the start of the final period when Bob Beaton scored. Larry Marsh then reduced the deficit with a long range shot from mid ice which Gerth really should have saved. In the closing minutes Dunfermline threw five forwards into the game and the gamble paid off when McQuade scored the equalising goal ninety seconds from full time to silence the noisy home crowd who had already started celebrating.

In almost unbearable tension a period of extra time commenced. Dunfermline had the psychological advantage of having come from behind so often in this final and Falkirk may also have felt more pressure since they were the home team. In any event both teams made chances but almost inevitably it was Norman McQuade who concluded the matter when he picked up a

Season 1939-1940

loose puck in front of Gerth and promptly netted. Dunfermline Vikings, in their first season, had won the Scottish Cup! It was a notable achievement for Dunfermline who were struggling badly in the league championship. They had a team better suited to the cut and thrust of cup competition and they had shown a lot of character, resilience and no little skill to come from behind in both replayed matches. Few observers grudged them their success but there was some sympathy for Falkirk Lions who had been the more accomplished side throughout all four matches of the final.

That same evening, an increasingly nervous Dundee Tigers dropped a crucial point in the league championship when they drew 4-4 at home to Ayr Raiders the visitors' new "M" line making an impact when they each scored a goal. Worse was to follow for Dundee a week later when they lost 4-3 at Falkirk a result which effectively ended their challenge for the league championship with two matches left. That result left Falkirk Lions still in third place with 21 points but with three matches still to play.

Fife Flyers also had three matches left and led the league with 24 points. Their next match was against Ayr Raiders at Kirkcaldy who were soundly beaten 8-5, Paul Rheault scoring five of these goals. Fife Flyers had the league title in their grasp but their next match was at Dundee who would certainly not be easy opposition despite their own disappointment. It was as expected a very close match but Fife eventually prevailed 4-3, the phenomenon that was Paul Rheault grabbing a priceless hat-trick.

The Kirkcaldy side could not be caught as they had now amassed 28 points with one match left to play at Falkirk. They had won the league championship with a record of 14 wins and 6 defeats scoring an impressive 120 goals in the process for the loss of 88. It had been a magnificent team effort from a club with one of the smallest playing squads in the country.

Paul Rheault had been the single biggest factor in Fife Flyers success. The champions were far from a one man team but his personal contribution to its overall success had been immeasurable. He had scored at least 49 goals in the championship the total figure is not known because the records are incomplete. Rheault had built up an almost uncanny relationship with linemates, Arnie Pratt and Tommy McInroy, and together they had presented a most formidable trio for any defence to handle.

It was difficult not to feel some real sympathy for Falkirk Lions, the "nearly men" of the season. Arguably unlucky to have been beaten in the Scottish Cup final, Falkirk defeated Fife Flyers 8-4 in the latter's final match of the season in the league championship, but finished with 27 points, only one point behind. They had won their last six matches. Had they found that form earlier in the campaign, the league title might have been wrapped in red and white ribbons.

Dundee Tigers ultimately finished in third position with 23 points. They had failed to win any of their final four matches, not the best time lose form.

Perth Panthers, after a truly dreadful start, recovered well to finish in fourth place with 16 points. The best defence in the league by far, they conceded only 69 goals; they also had the poorest attack, scoring only 55 goals all season.

Ayr Raiders had been very unpredictable but a losing sequence of six consecutive matches mid season had cost them dear. They had managed to spring the odd surprise or two and they finished in fifth position only a point behind Perth.

For Dunfermline Vikings, the season had been all about the Scottish Cup. Their league campaign had faltered badly as a result, but they were obviously a much better side than bottom place in the league indicated.

On 25 April, the sport in Scotland received a welcome boost with the official opening of Paisley Ice Rink. It was another arena-type venue with accommodation for 4,500 spectators. A large crowd watched two select teams play in a challenge match and the intention was that Paisley would enter a senior team in the Scottish (National) League when the time was right.

The expansion of ice hockey into the largest town in Scotland was good news. It would also help to redress the geographical imbalance of the Scottish (National) League which now had a pronounced east-central Scotland focus. In time, Paisley would become one of the real strongholds of the Scottish ice hockey and would furnish the country with a succession of successful and well supported teams at both the amateur and the semi-professional level.

In England, Harringay Greyhounds won the English National League for the second consecutive season. Jimmy Foster was still in goal for the champions and their team contained four players who would later feature in the National Hockey League, Dick Behling, Hazen McAndrew, Joe Shack and Connie Tudin. Shack, with 24 goals, was the leading goal scorer in the championship.

So ended the last organised season of ice hockey in Scotland until after the Second World War. Given the various circumstances surrounding the sport it was remarkable that a full season of competition had actually taken place at all. Spectators and ice rink managers and owners were certainly grateful for that, but in other respects it had been an unsatisfactory season. The widespread use of guest players by the teams had made a mockery of serious competition. The increase in the levels of violent and illegal play merely pandered to the baser instincts of those spectators perhaps not fully conversant with the finer points of the game.

Ice hockey matches would continue to be played on a purely unofficial and episodic basis throughout the remaining war years at those ice rinks not requisitioned by the government for emergency purposes. A number of challenge matches were arranged where it was possible to do so and these sometimes included teams from the Canadian armed forces either stationed in Scotland or visiting the country.

† † †

A number of players familiar to Scottish ice hockey enlisted in the armed forces before or during the war. Sadly, amongst those who would ultimately make the supreme sacrifice during that terrible conflict were Gordon Cummine of Mohawks and Ayr Raiders, Art Grant of Fife Flyers and the Glasgow born Jimmy Kelly of Brighton Tigers. No doubt there were many others.

The best known was perhaps Pilot Officer William (Billy) Fullerton, who would be tragically killed in 1941. A huge loss to his family and friends, Scottish ice hockey also lost one of its brightest stars. His career had spanned the entire amateur and semi-professional era of the pre-war game with three different clubs, Queen's, Mohawks and Fife Flyers, and included 12 appearances for Scotland and six for Great Britain.

Billy Fullerton was the finest home bred player of the entire era covered by this book and it is fitting that a final word on him should conclude this historical record of the sport he had so loved and so graced during his distinguished career.

Frozen in Time

Statistics

Frozen in Time

Glasgow Real Ice Skating Palace

"Bandy" or "Hockey on the Ice" Competitive Fixtures 1896 - 1897

6-6-1896	Glasgow	0	London Bandy Club	10
6-6-1896	Glasgow	0	London Bandy Club	4
8-6-1896	Glasgow	1	London Bandy Club	8
8-6-1896	Glasgow	0	London Bandy Club	6
3-7-1896	Scottish Bandy Club	?	Glasgow All Comers	?
21-12-1896	Scottish Bandy Club	?	Glasgow University Bandy Club	?
23-4-1897	Scottish Bandy Club "A"	2	Scottish Bandy Club "B"	3

Scottish Ice Hockey Association 1929

Challenge Matches

Date	Home		Away	
04-03-29	Bearsden	0	Glasgow Canadians	4
13-03-29	Bearsden	0	Kanderstag Bats	4
20-03-29	Achtungs	10	Glasgow Skating Club	0
23-03-29	Bridge of Weir	2	Glasgow High School	4
27-03-29	Achtungs	2	Doonside	3
30-03-29	Bridge of Weir	5	Mohawks	0
06-04-29	Achtungs	5	Glasgow Canadians	1
08-04-29	Glasgow Canadians	7	Bearsden	1
13-04-29	London Lions	4	United Services	3
16-04-29	Nomads	4	Wanderers	1
23-04-29	Kelvingrove	4	Mohawks	2
26-04-29	Doonside	1	Queen's	3

Scottish Ice Hockey Association

1929 Player Squads

Achtungs

First Team: H C Higginbotham; W R Higginbotham and R Rintoul; A Rintoul, N C MacKenzie and R A G Bennie
Substitutes: E M Cameron, F Tennent, R H Gardiner and C P Kerr.

Bearsden

First Team: R G Walker; A S Dykes and E R Smith; J R Gilmour, G C Scott and J G Carruthers.
Substitutes: J E Forrest, R O MacDonald and W G Munro.

Bridge of Weir

First Team: A R M Muirhead; A E McLeod and J K Woodrow; I S McLeod, W M Muirhead and M G Meikle.
Substitutes: W Bird, R E Muirhead, H J Telfer, G Neil and T Shearer.

Doonside

First Team: Colonel T C Dunlop; Colonel W A Collins and Commander K B S Greig; W H Dunlop, Rev H Horton and S K Lindsay.
Substitutes: F McLernan and D A Porter.

Glasgow Canadians

First Team: F McLernan; E R McLeod and G R Nodwell; S K Lindsay, H W Reid and D A Porter.

Glasgow High School

First Team: J Maitland; W A Strang and G L Melville; A Buchanan, J Buchanan and A S Knight.

Mohawks

First Team: J Fullerton; R C Brown and J Baird; R Patrick, G Holmes and S Stevenson.
Substitutes: J G Fyfe and T Shearer.

Scottish League Season 1929-30 Points Competition

Fixtures and Results

04-10-29	Bridge of Weir	2	Mohawks	1
08-10-29	Dennistoun	0	Kelvingrove	6
11-10-29	Doonside	5	Glasgow Skating Club	1
15-10-29	Queen's	2	Achtungs	2
18-10-29	Bearsden	5	Mohawks	4
22-10-29	Dennistoun	3	Glasgow University	3
25-10-29	Bridge of Weir	0	Glasgow Skating Club	2
29-10-29	Kelvingrove	1	Queen's	6
05-11-29	Bearsden	6	Doonside	1
08-11-29	Glasgow Skating Club	1	Mohawks	4
12-11-29	Dennistoun	0	Queen's	2
15-11-29	Bridge of Weir	4	Doonside	0
19-11--29	Kelvingrove	0	Achtungs	8
22-11-29	Glasgow University	0	Queen's	2
03-12-29	Achtungs	4	Dennistoun	0
06-12-29	Glasgow University	2	Kelvingrove	3
10-12-29	Bridge of Weir	2	Bearsden	3
13-12-29	Achtungs	8	Glasgow University	2
17-12-29	Glasgow Skating Club	2	Bearsden	3
20-12-29	Doonside	0	Mohawks	7

Final table

	P	W	L	D	F	A	Pts
Bearsden	4	4	0	0	17	9	8
Achtungs	4	3	0	1	22	4	7
Queen's	4	3	0	1	12	3	7
Mohawks	4	2	2	0	16	8	4
Bridge of Weir	4	2	2	0	8	6	4
Kelvingrove	4	2	2	0	10	16	4
Glasgow Skating Club	4	1	3	0	6	12	2
Doonside	4	1	3	0	6	18	2
Glasgow University	4	0	3	1	7	16	1
Dennistoun	4	0	3	1	3	15	1

Scottish League Season 1929-30 First Division

Fixtures and Results

03-01-30	Mohawks	3	Queen's	0
14-01-30	Achtungs	3	Bearsden	2
07-02-30	Bridge of Weir	1	Achtungs	3
28-02-30	Queen's	6	Achtungs	2
14-03-30	Bridge of Weir	0	Mohawks	3
18-03-30	Bearsden	2	Queen's	3
28-03-30	Achtungs	0	Mohawks	2
01-04-30	Queen's	8	Bridge of Weir	0
08-04-30	Bearsden	3	Bridge of Weir	1
15-04-30	Mohawks	4	Bearsden	1

Final table

	P	W	L	D	F	A	Pts
Mohawks	4	4	0	0	12	1	8
Queen's	4	3	1	0	17	7	6
Achtungs	4	2	2	0	8	11	4
Bearsden	4	1	3	0	8	11	2
Bridge of Weir	4	0	4	0	2	17	0

Scottish League Season 1929-30 Second Division

Fixtures and Results

07-01-30	Doonside	0	Glasgow University	8
10-01-30	Glasgow Skating Club	2	Kelvingrove	3
11-02-30	Dennistoun	0	Kelvingrove	4
04-03-30	Dennistoun	0	Doonside	1
07-03-30	Glasgow University	2	Glasgow Skating Club	5
11-03-30	Kelvingrove	1	Glasgow University	0
21-03-30	Glasgow Skating Club	8	Doonside	0
04-04-30	Doonside	0	Kelvingrove	5
11-04-30	Dennistoun	1	Glasgow Skating Club	2
18-04-30	Glasgow University	2	Dennistoun	2

Final table

	P	W	L	D	F	A	Pts
Kelvingrove	4	4	0	0	13	2	8
Glasgow Skating Club	4	3	1	0	17	6	6
Glasgow University	4	1	2	1	12	8	3
Doonside	4	1	3	0	1	21	2
Dennistoun	4	0	3	1	3	9	1

Statistics

Scottish League Season 1929-30

Player Squads

Achtungs

First Team: H C Higginbotham; H W Reid and W R Higginbotham; R Rintoul, A Rintoul and E M Cameron.

Substitutes: N C MacKenzie, T W K Moffat, A Tulloch, D M Somerville, G Donaldson, F Tennent and the Hon J S MacLay.

Bearsden

First Team: R G Walker; A S Dykes and E R Smith; J R Gilmour, G C Scott and J G Carruthers.

Substitutes: J E Forrest, R O MacDonald, J C Dykes, W G Munro and J W Adams.

Bridge of Weir

First Team: A N Macfie; J K Woodrow and R J G McDonald; I S McLeod, W M Muirhead and R E Muirhead.

Substitutes: A E McLeod, H J Telfer, A R M Muirhead, B G Downes, W Bird and D Buchanan.

Dennistoun

First Team: J C Weir; J S Hay and J H Borland; J F Logan, H Reid and A J Biggar.

Substitutes: W Waddell, F Martin, H A Clark, W W Russell, H Waddell and J M Frame.

Doonside

First Team: Colonel T C Dunlop; Colonel W A Collins and Commander K B S Greig; W H Dunlop, Rev H Horton and G D Parsons.

Substitutes: I K M Fair, G T Cunningham, D S Wilson, F H Dunlop, A Miller and C A Lambert.

Glasgow Skating Club

First Team: J B Wharrie; C H Borland and W Ritchie; H R Orr, J O McCabe and F McLernan.

Substitutes: I Borland, T C Brown, R W Reid, W T Lightbody, D S Dobson and R D Brand.

Glasgow University

First Team: J S Carlaw; J B Faison and C W de Visser; R T Myers, J A Easton and D W Lindsay.

Substitutes: J W R Murray, A Russell and J W Barclay.

Kelvingrove

First Team: D Croll; A S Dick and W M Phinney; R L Noble, J R McGeachie and E Fincham.

Substitutes: L Berlinquet, R H Gardiner, A Swan, D M C Mailer, W S Montford, J Buchanan, J Hardie, C Lamb, J Robertson, C Craig and G Wilson.

Mohawks

First Team: D Cross; A R Brady and T Shearer; J Fullerton, J Campbell and S A MacDonald.

Substitutes: S Stevenson, C Gammie, G Holmes, A Anderson and C B Baird.

Queen's

First Team: G Aitken; A R Bazin and V Carty; E R McLeod, A J Tingley and G R Forsyth.

Substitutes: D A Porter, S Helgregan, K Eddy-Larsen, E L Archibald, D H Stevenson, G Neil and J M McCreadie.

Scottish League Season 1930-31 League Championship - Canada Cup

Fixtures and Results

Date	Home		Away	
07-10-30	Glasgow Skating Club	3	Glasgow University	4
10-10-30	Achtungs	2	Dennistoun	0
14-10-30	Bridge of Weir	3	Bearsden	0
17-10-30	Kelvingrove	1	Mohawks	0
21-10-30	Glasgow Skating Club	3	Queen's	1
24-10-30	Glasgow University	5	Dennistoun	1
28-10-30	Bridge of Weir	2	Achtungs	0
31-10-30	Mohawks	3	Bearsden	0
04-11-30	Queen's	0	Kelvingrove	0
07-11-30	Dennistoun	1	Glasgow Skating Club	3
11-11-30	Achtungs	4	Glasgow University	2
14-11-30	Mohawks	0	Bridge of Weir	1
18-11-30	Bearsden	0	Kelvingrove	7
21-11-30	Queen's	1	Dennistoun	0
25-11-30	Bearsden	2	Glasgow Skating Club	1
28-11-30	Glasgow University	0	Bridge of Weir	2
02-12-30	Mohawks	2	Queen's	1
05-12-30	Kelvingrove	4	Achtungs	0
09-12-30	Dennistoun	5	Bearsden	1
13-01-31	Queen's	4	Glasgow University	1
16-01-31	Glasgow Skating Club	0	Bridge of Weir	0
20-01-31	Dennistoun	0	Kelvingrove	0
23-01-31	Bearsden	0	Glasgow University	2
27-01-31	Bridge of Weir	0	Queen's	2
30-01-31	Mohawks	6	Glasgow Skating Club	0
03-02-31	Achtungs	1	Bearsden	3
13-02-31	Kelvingrove	4	Glasgow University	0
17-02-31	Bridge of Weir	4	Dennistoun	3
24-02-31	Glasgow Skating Club	4	Kelvingrove	8
27-02-31	Glasgow University	1	Mohawks	1
03-03-31	Queen's	2	Bearsden	2
06-03-31	Achtungs	1	Queen's	2
10-03-31	Kelvingrove	1	Bridge of Weir	1
17-03-31	Glasgow Skating Club	1	Achtungs	5
24-03-31	Dennistoun	1	Mohawks	2
31-03-31	Mohawks	1	Achtungs	0

Frozen in Time

Final Table

	P	W	L	D	F	A	Pts
Kelvingrove	8	5	0	3	25	5	13
Bridge of Weir	8	5	1	2	13	6	12
Mohawks	8	5	2	1	15	5	11
Queen's	8	4	2	2	13	9	10
Glasgow University	8	3	4	1	15	19	7
Achtungs	8	3	5	0	13	15	6
Glasgow Skating Club	8	2	5	1	15	27	5
Bearsden	8	2	5	1	8	24	5
Dennistoun	8	1	6	1	11	18	3

Scottish League Season 1930-31

Player Squads

Achtungs

First Team: H C Higginbotham; H W Reid and W R Higginbotham; A Rintoul, G Reid and N C MacKenzie.
Substitutes: E M Cameron, D M Somerville, T W K Moffat, A Tulloch, C Gourley and G Shields.

Bearsden

First Team: R G Walker; J W Adams and R O MacDonald; J E Forrest, J R Gilmour and W G Munro.
Substitutes: R F McLean, E R Smith, L W Ross, F H Waters, G C Scott and J G Carruthers.

Bridge of Weir

First Team: A N Macfie; J K Woodrow and G D Rowley; I S McLeod, W M Muirhead and R E Muirhead.
Substitutes: R J G McDonald, A E McLeod, H J Telfer, A F Reid, D Buchanan and S Muhlbaur.

Dennistoun

First Team: J F Logan; T Nisbet and J H Borland; S Stevenson, H Reid and A J Biggar.
Substitutes: A Swan, J M Frame, J S Hay, J Baird and W W Russell.

Glasgow Skating Club

First Team: J B Wharrie; I Borland and T C Brown; F McLernan, J O McCabe and C H Borland.
Substitutes: R W Reid, F G Seligman and C Reid.

Glasgow University

First Team: J S Carslaw; J B Faison and C W de Visser; R H Gardiner, J A Easton and D W Lindsay.
Substitutes: R Parker, J W Barclay, R T Myers, A Russell, J C Henderson, W H Dunlop and G D Parsons.

Kelvingrove

First Team: D Cross; A S Dick and W M Phinney; W S Montford, J Campbell and R L Noble.
Substitutes: L Berlinquet, J Brown, E Fincham, J Buchanan, M Cohen, R D Gemmell and C A Franette.

Mohawks

First Team: W G Lennox; J G Fyfe and T Shearer; J Fullerton, T Craig and A R Brady.

Substitutes: W A Strang, A Gray, E K Reid and F Thomson.

Queen's

First Team: V Carty; F L Reardon and A R Bazin; W Fullerton, A J Tingley and M J Hall.

Substitutes: G R Forsyth, E L Archibald, R G Webster, P Peltier, J Barnes, I Stuart and G Aitken.

Scottish League Season 1931-32 League Championship - Canada Cup

Fixtures and Results

Date	Home		Away	
13-10-31	Achtungs	3	Glasgow University	2
16-10-31	Bridge of Weir	4	Bearsden	0
20-10-31	Mohawks	4	Dennistoun Eagles	2
23-10-31	Glasgow Skating Club	2	Queen's	4
27-10-31	Kelvingrove	1	Achtungs	0
03-11-31	Bearsden	2	Glasgow University	1
10-11-31	Mohawks	5	Glasgow Skating Club	0
13-11-31	Queen's	2	Kelvingrove	1
17-11-31	Achtungs	4	Bearsden	2
20-11-31	Glasgow University	1	Bridge of Weir	3
24-11-31	Dennistoun Eagles	3	Glasgow Skating Club	0
27-11-31	Bridge of Weir	1	Dennistoun Eagles	1
01-12-31	Queen's	0	Mohawks	1
08-12-31	Achtungs	0	Bridge of Weir	2
11-12-31	Glasgow University	2	Dennistoun Eagles	0
15-12-31	Glasgow Skating Club	0	Kelvingrove	3
18-12-31	Bearsden	2	Queen's	2
22-12-31	Mohawks	5	Achtungs	0
05-01-32	Bridge of Weir	6	Glasgow Skating Club	2
12-01-32	Dennistoun Eagles	0	Queen's	1
15-01-32	Bearsden	1	Mohawks	3
19-01-32	Glasgow Skating Club	2	Achtungs	0
22-01-32	Kelvingrove	2	Bridge of Weir	1
26-01-32	Queen's	6	Glasgow University	1
29-01-32	Achtungs	0	Dennistoun Eagles	3
02-02-32	Kelvingrove	0	Bearsden	0
23-02-32	Bearsden	2	Glasgow Skating Club	3
01-03-32	Mohawks	0	Kelvingrove	4
04-03-32	Bridge of Weir	6	Queen's	0
08-03-32	Glasgow University	3	Mohawks	9
15-03-32	Dennistoun Eagles	2	Kelvingrove	3
22-03-32	Achtungs	1	Queen's	3
25-03-32	Bearsden	1	Dennistoun Eagles	0
05-04-32	Glasgow Skating Club	1	Glasgow University	0
08-04-32	Mohawks	2	Bridge of Weir	1
12-04-32	Kelvingrove	2	Glasgow University	0

Final Table

	P	W	L	D	F	A	Pts
Mohawks	8	7	1	0	29	11	14
Kelvingrove	8	6	1	1	16	5	13
Bridge of Weir	8	5	2	1	24	8	11
Queen's	8	5	2	1	18	14	11
Bearsden	8	2	4	2	10	17	6
Glasgow Skating Club	8	3	5	0	10	23	6
Dennistoun Eagles	8	2	5	1	11	12	5
Achtungs	8	2	6	0	8	20	4
Glasgow University	8	1	7	0	10	26	2

Scottish League Season 1931-32 Player Squads

Achtungs

First Team: W H Dunlop; H W Reid and W R Higginbotham; R F Winfield, A Rintoul and G Reid.

Substitutes: N C MacKenzie, L W Sproule, D M Somerville, G Shields, C Gourley, A Tulloch, A Love, T W Kennedy and W G Dunstan.

Bearsden

First Team: R G Walker; J W Adams and J R Gilmour; W Steele, R O MacDonald and F Hems.

Substitutes: L W Ross, R F McLean, I Reid and W S Turnbull.

Bridge of Weir

First Team: A Ross; G D Rowley and J K Woodrow; I S McLeod, W M Muirhead and R E Muirhead.

Substitutes: R J G McDonald, A E McLeod, A F Reid, W S McLeod, L G Dixon and H R Peel.

Dennistoun Eagles

First Team: J F Logan; J H Borland and W W Russell; A J Biggar, S Stevenson and D Edwards.

Substitutes: A S Gray, J Allan, J Jarvie, H Reid and P Gignac.

Glasgow Skating Club

First Team: L Maxton; B Butters and R H Gardiner; F McLernan, J O McCabe and W J Towers.

Substitutes: F G Seligman, H S Finnie, D Buchanan, T Brodie and H Murray.

Glasgow University

First Team: J S Carslaw; J B Faison and D W Lindsay; C W de Visser, J A Easton and A F Thomson.

Substitutes: R Parker, J W Barclay, J C Henderson, T A Proost, C N Young and A E Robertson.

Kelvingrove

First Team: D Cross; A S Dick and J H Collins; K Hurll, W S Montford and J Campbell.

Substitutes: L Berlinquet, W M Phinney, E Fincham, J Buchanan, R D Gemmell and J McGeachie.

Mohawks

First Team: W G Lennox; J G Fyfe and T Shearer; J Fullerton, T Craig and A R Brady.

Substitutes: E K Reid and A Fullerton.

Queen's

First Team: V Carty; F L Reardon and A R Bazin; W Fullerton, A J Tingley and J Johnston.

Substitutes: G R Forsyth, R G Webster, E L Montford and I O Mathieson.

Scottish League Season 1932-33 League Championship - Canada Cup

Fixtures and Results

Date	Home		Away	
11-10-32	Kelvingrove	3	Mohawks	1
14-10-32	Bridge of Weir	0	Queen's	3
18-10-32	Juniors	2	Bears	1
21-10-32	Glasgow University	1	Dennistoun Eagles	1
25-10-32	Queen's	3	Kelvingrove	2
01-11-32	Mohawks	2	Bridge of Weir	4
04-11-32	Dennistoun Eagles	1	Juniors	0
08-11-32	Bears	3	Glasgow University	0
11-11-32	Kelvingrove	0	Bridge of Weir	1
15-11-32	Juniors	3	Mohawks	2
18-11-32	Glasgow University	3	Queen's	3
25-11-32	Dennistoun Eagles	0	Bears	3
29-11-32	Kelvingrove	2	Juniors	0
02-12-32	Bridge of Weir	3	Glasgow University	0
09-12-32	Queen's	0	Dennistoun Eagles	1
13-12-32	Glasgow University	3	Kelvingrove	1
16-12-32	Juniors	2	Bridge of Weir	2
27-12-32	Dennistoun Eagles	0	Bridge of Weir	2
06-01-33	Mohawks	2	Dennistoun Eagles	0
10-01-33	Bears	0	Queen's	3
13-01-33	Dennistoun Eagles	0	Kelvingrove	2
17-01-33	Glasgow University	1	Mohawks	2
20-01-33	Queen's	0	Juniors	1
24-01-33	Bridge of Weir	1	Bears	0
14-02-33	Bears	1	Mohawks	4
21-02-33	Mohawks	1	Queen's	0
28-02-33	Kelvingrove	1	Bears	1
07-03-33	Juniors	0	Glasgow University	2

Frozen in Time

Final Table

	P	W	L	D	F	A	Pts
Bridge of Weir	7	5	1	1	13	7	11
Mohawks	7	4	3	0	14	12	8
Queen's	7	3	3	1	12	8	7
Kelvingrove	7	3	3	1	11	9	7
Juniors	7	3	3	1	8	10	7
Glasgow University	7	2	3	2	10	13	6
Bears	7	2	4	1	9	11	5
Dennistoun Eagles	7	2	4	1	3	10	5

Scottish League Season 1932-33 Player Squads

Bears
First Team: W H Dunlop; R O MacDonald and J R Gilmour; A Rintoul, J Johnston and R F Winfield.
Substitutes: N C MacKenzie, L W Sproule, H W Reid, C J Russell, D Gerrard and R G Walker.

Bridge of Weir
First Team: A Ross; W M Muirhead and J K Woodrow; I S McLeod, W G McDonald and R E Muirhead.
Substitutes: W S McLeod, A F Reid, A E McLeod and D Buchanan.

Dennistoun Eagles
First Team: J F Logan; J H Borland and L Maxton; A S Gray, S Stevenson and W W Russell.
Substitutes: J Allan, L Holland and A Gilmour.

Glasgow University
First Team: C N Young; F McLernan and T A Proost; C W de Visser, J A Easton and J O McCabe.
Substitutes: R H Gardiner, D W Lindsay, J C Henderson, A F Thomson and B Butters.

Juniors
First Team: W S Turnbull; G D Rowley and J H Collins; D Edwards, A Gray and F Hems.
Substitutes: W Steele, E L Montford and A Love.

Kelvingrove
First Team: D Cross; A S Dick and A Fullerton; W S Montford, J Campbell and R D Gemmell.
Substitutes: E Fincham, J Beveridge, W J Towers, C McMillan and A J Tingley.

Mohawks
First Team: W G Lennox; J G Fyfe and T Shearer; J Fullerton, T Craig and E K Reid.
Substitutes: G Holmes, J Hanson, I Carruthers, D MacLachlan, J Campbell and W Fullerton.

Queen's

First Team: V Carty; R G Webster and G R Forsyth; W Fullerton, A J Tingley and H S Finnie.
Substitutes: I O Mathieson and B Watson.

Scottish League Season 1933-34 League Championship - Canada Cup

Fixtures and Results

Date	Home	Score	Away	Score
10-10-33	Bears	0	Bridge of Weir	3
13-10-33	Dennistoun Eagles	0	Kelvingrove	4
17-10-33	Mohawks	2	Juniors	0
20-10-33	Glasgow University	0	Bears	1
24-10-33	Bridge of Weir	1	Dennistoun Eagles	0
27-10-33	Juniors	0	Kelvingrove	3
31-10-33	Bears	0	Mohawks	5
07-11-33	Dennistoun Eagles	1	Glasgow University	0
14-11-33	Kelvingrove	1	Bridge of Weir	1
21-11-33	Juniors	1	Bears	2
24-11-33	Mohawks	3	Dennistoun Eagles	2
28-11-33	Bridge of Weir	1	Glasgow University	3
05-12-33	Bears	0	Kelvingrove	5
12-12-33	Dennistoun Eagles	2	Juniors	1
15-12-33	Bridge of Weir	1	Mohawks	0
19-12-33	Glasgow University	0	Kelvingrove	5
29-12-33	Bears	1	Dennistoun Eagles	2
06-01-34	Mohawks	1	Glasgow University	0
09-01-34	Juniors	0	Bridge of Weir	3
12-01-34	Kelvingrove	2	Mohawks	1
16-01-34	Glasgow University	1	Juniors	0
19-01-34	Bridge of Weir	4	Bears	2
26-01-34	Juniors	1	Mohawks	5
30-01-34	Bears	1	Glasgow University	3
02-02-34	Dennistoun Eagles	0	Bridge of Weir	2
06-02-34	Kelvingrove	2	Juniors	0
09-02-34	Mohawks	2	Bears	2
13-02-34	Glasgow University	3	Dennistoun Eagles	3
16-02-34	Bridge of Weir	0	Kelvingrove	1
20-02-34	Bears	1	Juniors	1
27-02-34	Dennistoun Eagles	1	Mohawks	5
06-03-34	Glasgow University	5	Bridge of Weir	1
13-03-34	Kelvingrove	2	Bears	2
16-03-34	Juniors	0	Dennistoun Eagles	0
20-03-34	Mohawks	4	Bridge of Weir	1

Frozen in Time

27-03-34	Kelvingrove	1	Glasgow University	2
03-04-34	Dennistoun Eagles	2	Bears	2
10-04-34	Bridge of Weir	3	Juniors	1
17-04-34	Mohawks	0	Kelvingrove	2
24-04-34	Juniors	2	Glasgow University	1
24-04-34	Kelvingrove	1	Dennistoun Eagles	1
28-04-34	Glasgow University	0	Mohawks	1

Final Table

	P	W	L	D	F	A	Pts
Kelvingrove	12	8	1	3	29	7	19
Mohawks	12	8	3	1	29	12	17
Bridge of Weir	12	7	4	1	21	17	15
Glasgow University	12	5	6	1	18	18	11
Dennistoun Eagles	12	3	5	4	14	23	10
Bears	12	2	6	4	14	30	8
Juniors	12	1	9	2	7	25	4

Scottish League Season 1933-34 Player Squads

Bears

First Team: W H Dunlop; R O MacDonald and J R Gilmour; A Rintoul, J Johnston and R F Winfield.
Substitutes: N C MacKenzie, L W Sproule, C J Russell and I O Mathieson.

Bridge of Weir

First Team: A Ross; M D Brennan and W G McDonald; W S McLeod, I S McLeod and W M Muirhead.
Substitutes: J K Woodrow, A F Reid, J Drew, D Buchanan, R E Muirhead and W MacLachlan.

Dennistoun Eagles

First Team: J F Logan; J H Borland and L Maxton; A S Gray, S Stevenson and W W Russell.
Substitutes: L Holland, A Gilmour, H S Finnie, W R Inglis, G Braid and R Mills.

Glasgow University

First Team: A G Garnock; R H Gardiner and F McLernan; J O McCabe, J A Easton and A J McCabe.
Substitutes: A F Thomson, I H Borland, J C Henderson and O A Gratias.

Juniors

First Team: W S Turnbull; E L Montford and J H Collins; W Steele, D Edwards and A Gray.
Substitutes: F Hems, G Henderson, N Andrews, A G Bogie, D Jackson and G D Rowley.

Kelvingrove

First Team: D Cross; A S Dick and A Fullerton; W S Montford, A J Tingley and C McMillan.
Substitutes: R D Gemmell, J Beveridge and W J Towers.

Mohawks

First Team: D MacLachlan; J G Fyfe and T Shearer; W Fullerton, J Fullerton and J Campbell.
Substitutes: T Craig and E K Reid.

Frozen in Time

Scottish League Season 1934-35 League Championship - Canada Cup

Fixtures and Results

09-10-34	Mohawks	3	Glasgow University	1
12-10-34	Dennistoun Eagles	2	Juniors	0
16-10-34	Bridge of Weir	2	Kelvingrove	0
19-10-34	Glasgow University	3	Dennistoun Eagles	1
23-10-34	Mohawks	1	Bridge of Weir	2
26-10-34[1]	Juniors	1	Kelvingrove	1
30-10-34	Bridge of Weir	5	Glasgow University	1
06-11-34	Juniors	1	Mohawks	12
13-11-34	Kelvingrove	1	Dennistoun Eagles	0
20-11-34	Glasgow University	2	Juniors	0
23-11-34	Dennistoun Eagles	1	Bridge of Weir	3
27-11-34	Mohawks	1	Kelvingrove	1
04-12-34	Bridge of Weir	6	Juniors	1
11-12-34	Kelvingrove	2	Glasgow University	1
18-12-34	Mohawks	0	Dennistoun Eagles	2
25-12-34	Juniors	2	Kelvingrove	4
28-12-34	Dennistoun Eagles	5	Juniors	1
04-01-35	Kelvingrove	0	Bridge of Weir	0
08-01-35	Glasgow University	1	Dennistoun Eagles	6
11-01-35	Bridge of Weir	1	Mohawks	2
15-01-35	Juniors	0	Kelvingrove	4
18-01-35	Glasgow University	1	Bridge of Weir	1
22-01-35	Mohawks	4	Juniors	0
25-01-35	Dennistoun Eagles	1	Kelvingrove	4
29-01-35	Glasgow University	2	Juniors	2
01-02-35	Bridge of Weir	3	Dennistoun Eagles	1
05-02-35	Kelvingrove	1	Mohawks	0
08-02-35	Bridge of Weir	2	Juniors	1
12-02-35	Kelvingrove	2	Glasgow University	2
15-02-35	Dennistoun Eagles	3	Mohawks	5
19-02-35	Mohawks	3	Glasgow University	1
26-02-35	Juniors	8	Dennistoun Eagles	1
05-03-35	Bridge of Weir	3	Kelvingrove	1
08-03-35	Kelvingrove	2	Juniors	3
12-03-35	Glasgow University	2	Dennistoun Eagles	1
19-03-35	Mohawks	3	Glasgow University	1
26-03-35	Glasgow University	1	Bridge of Weir	2
02-04-35	Juniors	3	Mohawks	7

Statistics

05-04-35	Kelvingrove	4	Dennistoun Eagles	0
09-04-35	Glasgow University	0	Juniors	5
12-04-35	Dennistoun Eagles	1	Bridge of Weir	7
16-04-35	Mohawks	4	Kelvingrove	4
23-04-35	Bridge of Weir	2	Juniors	2
24-04-35[2]	Bridge of Weir	7	Mohawks	2
30-04-35	Kelvingrove	3	Glasgow University	2
30-04-35[3]	Mohawks	11	Dennistoun Eagles	5

[1] Result null and void following a protest from Kelvingrove.
[2] Bridge of Weir forfeit both points to Mohawks.
[3] Scratched match, no points awarded to either team.

Final Table

	P	W	L	D	F	A	Pts
Bridge of Weir	15	10	2	3	39	14	23
Mohawks	14	9	3	2	45	21	20
Kelvingrove	15	8	3	4	33	21	20
Glasgow University	15	3	9	3	21	39	9
Dennistoun Eagles	14	4	10	0	25	42	8
Juniors	15	3	10	2	29	55	8

Scottish League Season 1934-35 Player Squads

Bridge of Weir

First Team: A Ross; M D Brennan and W G McDonald; W S McLeod, W M Muirhead and A F Reid.

Substitutes: J K Woodrow, I S McLeod, R E Muirhead, J Johnston, D Buchannan, J Collingwood and R G Walker.

Dennistoun Eagles

First Team: J F Logan; E L Montford and J H Collins; G Braid, R Mills and W W Russell.

Substitutes: S Stevenson, H S Finnie, W R Inglis, J M Newton, J Delaney and W Ross.

Glasgow University

First Team: P McKay; R H Gardiner and F McLernan; A Gray, D Edwards and J O McCabe.

Substitutes: R S Milne, O A Gratias, A Rintoul, A F Thomson, I H Borland and H H Johnston.

Juniors

First Team: W S Turnbull; P Stevenson and A G Bogie; J Scott, J Kelly and D Jackson.

Substitutes: N Andrews, J Strachan, N G Bennett, G Henderson, J Watson and K Hurll.

Kelvingrove

First Team: D Cross; A S Dick and A Fullerton; W S Montford, A J Tingley and C McMillan.

Substitutes: R D Gemmell, J Beveridge, R Brown, A Gray, I O Mathieson and C Nevitt.

Mohawks

First Team: D MacLachlan; R O MacDonald and T Shearer; W Fullerton, J Fullerton and J Kenny.

Substitutes: W G Lennox, R F Winfield, E K Reid, G A Porter, C J Russell, G Ayres and J R Gilmour.

Statistics

Scottish League Season 1935-36 League Championship - Canada Cup

Fixtures and Results

Date	Home		Away	
08-10-35	Glasgow University	1	Mustangs	2
11-10-35	Kelvingrove	3	Lions	0
15-10-35	Mohawks	5	Glasgow University	1
18-10-35	Mustangs	0	Kelvingrove	1
22-10-35	Lions	0	Glasgow University	5
25-10-35	Mohawks	2	Mustangs	1
29-10-35	Glasgow University	0	Kelvingrove	0
01-11-35	Mustangs	11	Lions	1
05-11-35	Kelvingrove	2	Mohawks	1
08-11-35	Lions	1	Mohawks	9
12-11-35	Mustangs	1	Glasgow University	0
15-11-35	Lions	0	Kelvingrove	4
22-11-35	Mohawks	4	Glasgow University	0
26-11-35	Kelvingrove	0	Mustangs	4
29-11-35	Glasgow University	1	Lions	0
10-12-35	Mustangs	0	Mohawks	0
13-12-35	Kelvingrove	2	Glasgow University	1
17-12-35	Lions	0	Mustangs	5
03-01-36	Mohawks	3	Kelvingrove	1
07-01-36	Mohawks	6	Lions	1
14-01-36	Kelvingrove	5	Lions	1
24-01-36	Lions	2	Glasgow University	2
28-01-36	Mohawks	2	Mustangs	0
04-02-36	Glasgow University	0	Kelvingrove	3
07-02-36	Mustangs	5	Lions	1
11-02-36	Kelvingrove	0	Mohawks	1
14-02-36	Lions	1	Mohawks	6
18-02-36	Mustangs	1	Glasgow University	1
28-02-36	Lions	0	Kelvingrove	4
03-03-36	Glasgow University	2	Mohawks	5
10-03-36	Kelvingrove	1	Mustangs	0
13-03-36	Glasgow University	2	Lions	1
17-03-36	Mustangs	3	Mohawks	0
20-03-36[1]	Kelvingrove	5	Glasgow University	0
24-03-36	Lions	2	Mustangs	4
27-03-36	Mohawks	2	Kelvingrove	0
31-03-36	Mohawks	3	Lions	0
07-04-36	Glasgow University	3	Mohawks	1

Frozen in Time

14-04-36	Glasgow University	1	Mustangs	3	
21-04-36	Mustangs	4	Kelvingrove	1	

[1] Result decided by SIHA as Glasgow University scratched.

Final Table

	P	W	L	D	F	A	Pts
Mohawks	16	12	3	1	50	16	25
Mustangs	16	10	4	2	44	14	22
Kelvingrove	16	10	5	1	32	17	21
Glasgow University	16	4	9	3	20	35	11
Lions	16	0	15	1	11	75	1

Statistics

Scottish League Season 1935-36 Player Squads

Glasgow University

First Team: D MacLachlan; F McLernan and J H Collins; A Rintoul, A Gray and R F Winfield.
Substitutes: P B Reid, R Brown, J Johnston, J Strachan, G Niven, J Peterson and J R Gilmour.

Kelvingrove

First Team: D Cross; A S Dick and A Fullerton; W S Montford, C McMillan and R D Gemmell.
Substitutes: C Nevitt, K Hurll, S Stevenson, E L Montford and I O Mathieson

Lions

First Team: T Nicol; J M Newton and W M Muirhead; R E Muirhead, D Jackson and D Harvie.
Substitutes: G Henderson, H S Finnie, C J Russell, J Beveridge, L W Sproule and W S McLeod.

Mohawks

First Team: W G Lennox; R O MacDonald and W Welch; W Fullerton, J Fullerton and J Kenny.
Substitutes: T Shearer, E K Reid, G A Porter, A G Bogie, P Stevenson and J R Gilmour.

Mustangs

First Team: W S Turnbull; M D Brennan and W G McDonald; G Braid, J Kelly and W W Russell.
Substitutes: D Edwards, R H Gardiner, N Andrews, J Scott, J Delaney and W Munro.

Frozen in Time

Scottish League Season 1936-37 League Championship - Canada Cup

Fixtures and Results

Date	Home		Away	
02-10-36	Kelvingrove	5	Lions	0
06-10-36	Mohawks	2	Mustangs	2
09-10-36	Lions	0	Mustangs	5
13-10-36	Kelvingrove	1	Mohawks	1
16-10-36	Mustangs	3	Kelvingrove	1
20-10-36	Mohawks	3	Lions	1
23-10-36	Lions	2	Kelvingrove	1
27-10-36	Mustangs	2	Mohawks	4
30-10-36	Kelvingrove	2	Perth Panthers	2
03-11-36	Mustangs	6	Lions	1
06-11-36	Mohawks	3	Kelvingrove	0
10-11-36	Kelvingrove	2	Mustangs	0
11-11-36	Perth Panthers	3	Lions	3
13-11-36	Lions	2	Mohawks	1
24-11-36	Mustangs	3	Perth Panthers	2
27-11-36	Mohawks	2	Perth Panthers	1
08-12-36	Mohawks	1	Mustangs	0
09-12-36	Perth Panthers	6	Kelvingrove	4
11-12-36	Kelvingrove	4	Lions	2
15-12-36	Lions	3	Mustangs	4
23-12-36	Perth Panthers	5	Lions	2
08-01-37	Kelvingrove	0	Mohawks	7
12-01-37	Mustangs	2	Kelvingrove	2
15-01-37	Mohawks	2	Lions	1
19-01-37	Mustangs	4	Perth Panthers	2
22-01-37	Mohawks	5	Perth Panthers	2
26-01-37	Mustangs	5	Lions	3
27-01-37	Perth Panthers	4	Kelvingrove	2
29-01-37	Mustangs	4	Mohawks	1
02-02-37	Lions	3	Kelvingrove	6
09-02-37	Mohawks	4	Kelvingrove	1
12-02-37	Perth Panthers	4	Mustangs	4
16-02-37	Kelvingrove	2	Mustangs	1
23-02-37	Lions	1	Mohawks	6
26-02-37	Lions	4	Perth Panthers	12
03-03-37	Perth Panthers	3	Mohawks	3
05-03-37	Kelvingrove	3	Perth Panthers	3
09-03-37	Mohawks	3	Perth Panthers	1

Statistics

10-03-37	Perth Panthers	8	Lions	9
26-03-37[1]	Mustangs	v	Perth Panthers	

[1] SIHA awarded Perth Panthers a win as Mustangs were under suspension.

Final Table

	P	W	L	D	F	A	Pts
Mohawks	16	11	2	3	48	22	25
Mustangs	16	8	5	3	45	30	19
Perth Panthers	16	5	6	5	58	53	15
Kelvingrove	16	5	7	4	36	43	14
Lions	16	3	12	1	37	78	7

Scottish League Season 1936-37 Player Squads

Kelvingrove

First Team: D Cross; A S Dick and J H Collins; W S Montford, R Thomson and A Maxwell.
Substitutes: C Nevitt, S Stevenson, E L Montford, K Hurll, I O Mathieson, W Moore, J Cuthill, M Maxwell, G Leckie, J Milne and J F Logan.

Lions

First Team: R H Henderson; R O MacDonald and J M Newton; P Stevenson, L McCartney and W M Muirhead.
Substitutes: D Jackson, H S Finnie, D Harvie, J Cannon, P B Read, T Shearer, J Lightfoot, R S Milne and J Dunsmore.

Mohawks

First Team: A Palfrey; A Fullerton and A G Bogie; W Fullerton, G Galloway and J Kenny.
Substitutes: D MacLachlan, J Johnston, J Fullerton, D Edwards and G Strong.

Mustangs

First Team: W S Turnbull; F McLernan and W Welch; J Kelly, H Loane and W Boivin.
Substitutes: M D Brennan, W G McDonald, R H Gardiner, G Braid, W W Russell, J Scott and N Andrews.

Perth Panthers

First Team: M Ross; D Mitchell and L Lovell; B Burbridge, L Tapp and J Lightfoot.
Substitutes: S Blackman, J Wold, A Watson, H Heap, S Smith, N Lawson, J Darling, T McInroy, W Boivin, J Stewart, A Schumann, J Forsythe and R Forsythe.

Statistics

Scottish League Season 1937-38 League Championship - Canada Cup

Fixtures and Results

Date	Home	Score	Away	Score
01-10-37	Mohawks	3	Lions	1
05-10-37	Mustangs	1	Perth Black Hawks	7
06-10-37	Perth Panthers	5	Kelvingrove	0
08-10-37	Lions	0	Perth Black Hawks	6
12-10-37	Mustangs	0	Perth Panthers	10
13-10-37	Mohawks	1	Kelvingrove	1
15-10-37	Mustangs	6	Lions	1
19-10-37	Mohawks	1	Perth Panthers	2
22-10-37	Perth Black Hawks	8	Kelvingrove	5
22-10-37	Lions	3	Perth Panthers	15
27-10-37	Kelvingrove	3	Mustangs	1
28-10-37	Perth Black Hawks	3	Mohawks	2
30-10-37	Lions	2	Kelvingrove	1
02-11-37	Mohawks	6	Mustangs	0
05-11-37	Mohawks	6	Lions	4
05-11-37	Perth Panthers	7	Perth Black Hawks	5
09-11-37	Mustangs	1	Perth Black Hawks	3
10-11-37	Perth Panthers	7	Kelvingrove	2
15-11-37	Lions	4	Perth Black Hawks	3
19-11-37	Kelvingrove	2	Mohawks	2
19-11-37	Perth Panthers	6	Mustangs	4
23-11-37	Mustangs	2	Lions	1
24-11-37	Perth Panthers	10	Mohawks	4
26-11-37	Kelvingrove	0	Perth Black Hawks	3
01-12-37	Perth Panthers	3	Lions	6
07-12-37	Kelvingrove	3	Mustangs	2
08-12-37	Perth Black Hawks	5	Mohawks	0
21-12-37	Mohawks	2	Mustangs	0
22-12-37	Perth Black Hawks	2	Perth Panthers	4
04-01-38	Lions	4	Mohawks	3
07-01-38	Kelvingrove	1	Perth Panthers	2
07-01-38	Perth Black Hawks	2	Mustangs	2
11-01-38	Lions	2	Perth Black Hawks	3
12-01-38	Perth Panthers	6	Mustangs	3
14-01-38	Mohawks	2	Kelvingrove	2
18-01-38	Mustangs	2	Lions	2
19-01-38	Perth Panthers	4	Mohawks	2
21-01-38	Kelvingrove	0	Perth Black Hawks	4

Frozen in Time

Date	Home		Away	
25-01-38	Lions	5	Perth Panthers	3
28-01-38	Mohawks	0	Perth Black Hawks	1
28-01-38	Perth Panthers	3	Lions	1
01-02-38	Kelvingrove	1	Lions	4
02-02-38	Perth Black Hawks	0	Mohawks	1
04-02-38	Perth Panthers	2	Perth Black Hawks	8
08-02-38	Mohawks	3	Lions	1
09-02-38	Perth Black Hawks	1	Mustangs	0
11-02-38	Kelvingrove	4	Perth Panthers	1
15-02-38	Lions	1	Perth Black Hawks	3
18-02-38	Perth Panthers	4	Mustangs	0
18-02-38	Mohawks	3	Kelvingrove	0
23-02-38	Mustangs	3	Lions	1
01-03-38	Mohawks	4	Perth Panthers	2
02-03-38	Perth Black Hawks	1	Kelvingrove	5
18-03-38	Mustangs	5	Mohawks	4
18-03-38	Lions	2	Kelvingrove	1
22-03-38	Mohawks	1	Mustangs	3
23-03-38	Perth Panthers	3	Perth Black Hawks	5
24-03-38	Mohawks	3	Lions	1
29-03-38	Mustangs	2	Perth Black Hawks	7
30-03-38	Perth Panthers	7	Kelvingrove	5
01-04-38	Lions	1	Perth Black Hawks	2
05-04-38	Mustangs	5	Perth Panthers	12
08-04-38	Kelvingrove	2	Mohawks	2
12-04-38	Mohawks	2	Perth Panthers	3
13-04-38	Perth Black Hawks	6	Kelvingrove	2
15-04-38	Lions	2	Perth Panthers	6
19-04-38	Kelvingrove	3	Mustangs	2
22-04-38	Perth Black Hawks	4	Mohawks	5
22-04-38	Kelvingrove	7	Lions	3
26-04-38	Mohawks	4	Mustangs	3
27-04-38	Perth Black Hawks	3	Perth Panthers	4
29-04-38	Lions	9	Kelvingrove	0
03-05-38	Mustangs	6	Kelvingrove	0
05-05-38	Kelvingrove	2	Mustangs	3
06-05-38	Lions	4	Mustangs	2

Final Table

	P	W	L	D	F	A	Pts
Perth Panthers	25	19	6	0	131	77	38
Perth Black Hawks	25	17	7	1	95	54	35
Mohawks	25	11	10	4	66	63	26
Lions	25	9	15	1	65	90	19
Mustangs	25	7	16	2	58	95	16
Kelvingrove	25	6	15	4	52	88	16

Statistics

Scottish League Season 1937-38 Player Squads

Kelvingrove

First Team: D Cross; A S Dick and J H Collins; J Cuthill, S Cameron and D McLeod
Substitutes: W S Montford, A Maxwell, C Nevitt, S Stevenson, K Hurll, J Johnston, D Steadman and R Lightfoot.

Lions

First Team: F Amantea; A Purdie and B Roberts; P Stevenson, F Chase and N McCuaig.
Substitutes: R H Henderson, J M Newton, D Jackson, J Cannon, W Welch, W W Russell, A McPherson, D Cumming, D McAlpine and J Johnston.

Mohawks

First Team: A Palfrey; G Horne and A G Bogie; W Fullerton, G Baillie and J Kenny.
Substitutes: J Fullerton, A Fullerton, W Welch, G Braid and G Morrison.

Mustangs

First Team: W S Turnbull; A Fullerton and R Forsythe; J Kelly, L Marchant and E Nerlick.
Substitutes: F McLernan, J Scott, N Andrews, R H Gardiner, D Edwards, G Ney, P B Read and G Morrison.

Perth Black Hawks

First Team: R S Milne; H Smith and L Lovell; T McInroy, R Purdie and J Allan.
Substitutes: A Schumann, F Hill, W Gellatly, J Stewart and D Rose.

Perth Panthers

First Team: M Ross; D Mitchell and R Thomson; L Tapp, L McCartney and J Lightfoot.
Substitutes: S Blackman, N Lawson, A Pratt, J Schofield, E Morley and N McQuade.

Frozen in Time

Scottish League Season 1938-39 Points Competition

Fixtures and Results

04-10-38	Kelvingrove	4	Mohawks	3
05-10-38	Dundee Tigers	2	Perth Panthers	2
06-10-38	Fife Flyers	1	Falkirk Lions	3
07-10-38	Mohawks	2	Dundee Tigers	5
08-10-38	Perth Panthers	0	Falkirk Lions	3
11-10-38	Kelvingrove	2	Fife Flyers	2
12-10-38	Dundee Tigers	1	Falkirk Lions	4
13-10-38	Fife Flyers	4	Perth Panthers	2
14-10-38	Mohawks	1	Falkirk Lions	3
15-10-38	Perth Panthers	2	Dundee Tigers	4
18-10-38	Kelvingrove	1	Perth Panthers	3
19-10-38	Dundee Tigers	8	Mohawks	2
20-10-38	Fife Flyers	8	Kelvingrove	1
21-10-38	Mohawks	0	Perth Panthers	1
22-10-38	Perth Panthers	1	Kelvingrove	1
25-10-38	Kelvingrove	1	Falkirk Lions	3
26-10-38	Dundee Tigers	9	Fife Flyers	7
27-10-38	Fife Flyers	4	Dundee Tigers	3
28-10-38	Mohawks	1	Kelvingrove	3
29-10-38	Perth Panthers	2	Falkirk Lions	4
01-11-38	Mohawks	1	Fife Flyers	2
02-11-38	Dundee Tigers	3	Falkirk Lions	4
03-11-38	Fife Flyers	4	Mohawks	2
04-11-38	Kelvingrove	2	Dundee Tigers	3
05-11-38	Perth Panthers	4	Fife Flyers	2
08-11-38	Mohawks	2	Falkirk Lions	6
09-11-38	Dundee Tigers	4	Kelvingrove	1
10-11-38	Fife Flyers	4	Falkirk Lions	4
11-11-38	Kelvingrove	1	Falkirk Lions	1
15-11-38	Mohawks	5	Kelvingrove	4
16-11-38	Dundee Tigers	5	Perth Panthers	2
17-11-38	Fife Flyers	3	Falkirk Lions	1
18-11-38	Mohawks	2	Dundee Tigers	3
19-11-38	Perth Panthers	5	Kelvingrove	3
22-11-38	Kelvingrove	1	Fife Flyers	5
23-11-38	Dundee Tigers	3	Falkirk Lions	4
24-11-38	Fife Flyers	3	Perth Panthers	4
26-11-38	Perth Panthers	1	Dundee Tigers	2
30-11-38	Falkirk Lions	2	Perth Panthers	3
30-11-38	Dundee Tigers	6	Mohawks	2

Statistics

01-12-38	Fife Flyers	6	Kelvingrove	4
04-12-38	Perth Panthers	3	Falkirk Lions	5
06-12-38	Kelvingrove	3	Falkirk Lions	7
07-12-38	Falkirk Lions	2	Mohawks	4
07-12-38	Dundee Tigers	3	Fife Flyers	4
08-12-38	Fife Flyers	2	Dundee Tigers	2
09-12-38	Mohawks	4	Kelvingrove	1
14-12-38	Falkirk Lions	3	Dundee Tigers	6
15-12-38	Fife Flyers	4	Mohawks	1
16-12-38	Kelvingrove	1	Dundee Tigers	8
17-12-38	Perth Panthers	7	Fife Flyers	4
21-12-38	Dundee Tigers	5	Kelvingrove	1
21-12-38	Falkirk Lions	4	Mohawks	0
27-12-38	Kelvingrove	2	Perth Panthers	5
28-12-38	Falkirk Lions	4	Kelvingrove	0
30-12-38	Mohawks	2	Perth Panthers	2
03-01-39	Mohawks	4	Fife Flyers	4
04-01-39	Falkirk Lions	4	Fife Flyers	2
06-01-39	Mohawks	4	Perth Panthers	7
07-01-39	Perth Panthers	8	Mohawks	5

Final Table

	P	W	L	D	F	A	Pts
Falkirk Lions	20	14	4	2	71	43	30
Dundee Tigers	20	13	5	2	85	52	28
Fife Flyers	20	10	6	4	75	62	24
Perth Panthers	20	10	7	3	64	58	23
Mohawks	20	3	15	2	47	81	8
Kelvingrove	20	2	15	3	37	83	7

Scottish League Season 1938-39 League Championship - Canada Cup

Fixtures and Results

11-01-39	Falkirk Lions	1	Perth Panthers	2
11-01-39	Dundee Tigers	11	Kelvingrove	2
12-01-39	Fife Flyers	4	Mohawks	4
17-01-39	Mohawks	3	Kelvingrove	1
18-01-39	Dundee Tigers	5	Fife Flyers	2
20-01-39	Kelvingrove	0	Fife Flyers	5
21-01-39	Perth Panthers	5	Falkirk Lions	4
24-01-39	Mohawks	1	Fife Flyers	4
25-01-39	Falkirk Lions	3	Dundee Tigers	3
26-01-39	Fife Flyers	0	Perth Panthers	1
27-01-39	Kelvingrove	2	Dundee Tigers	2
31-01-39	Kelvingrove	4	Perth Panthers	1
01-02-39	Dundee Tigers	8	Mohawks	3
01-02-39	Falkirk Lions	4	Fife Flyers	4
03-02-39	Mohawks	2	Falkirk Lions	3
04-02-39	Perth Panthers	7	Kelvingrove	1
07-02-39	Mohawks	2	Perth Panthers	4
08-02-39	Dundee Tigers	9	Falkirk Lions	2
09-02-39	Fife Flyers	8	Kelvingrove	3
14-02-39	Mohawks	7	Fife Flyers	3
15-02-39	Dundee Tigers	2	Perth Panthers	2
18-02-39	Perth Panthers	1	Dundee Tigers	1
21-02-39	Mohawks	3	Dundee Tigers	3
23-02-39	Fife Flyers	9	Falkirk Lions	1
24-02-39	Mohawks	7	Kelvingrove	2
25-02-39	Perth Panthers	9	Fife Flyers	2
01-03-39	Dundee Tigers	6	Mohawks	4
01-03-39	Falkirk Lions	4	Kelvingrove	4
02-03-39	Fife Flyers	4	Dundee Tigers	6
04-03-39	Mohawks	3	Perth Panthers	8
05-03-39	Perth Panthers	4	Mohawks	1
07-03-39	Kelvingrove	8	Fife Flyers	3
08-03-39	Falkirk Lions	5	Perth Panthers	5
09-03-39	Fife Flyers	3	Kelvingrove	3
10-03-39	Mohawks	5	Falkirk Lions	4
11-03-39	Perth Panthers	2	Fife Flyers	3
14-03-39	Kelvingrove	0	Dundee Tigers	2
15-03-39	Falkirk Lions	3	Fife Flyers	9

Statistics

16-03-39	Fife Flyers	10	Falkirk Lions	2
18-03-39	Perth Panthers	1	Kelvingrove	2
21-03-39	Kelvingrove	3	Mohawks	3
22-03-39	Dundee Tigers	6	Falkirk Lions	3
23-03-39	Fife Flyers	7	Mohawks	6
29-03-39	Falkirk Lions	2	Kelvingrove	2
01-04-39	Perth Panthers	4	Mohawks	1
04-04-39	Kelvingrove	4	Falkirk Lions	2
05-04-39	Dundee Tigers	3	Fife Flyers	5
06-04-39	Fife Flyers	1	Dundee Tigers	4
07-04-39	Kelvingrove	2	Mohawks	2
08-04-39	Perth Panthers	4	Falkirk Lions	3
12-04-39	Falkirk Lions	11	Mohawks	2
12-04-39[1]	Dundee Tigers	5	Perth Panthers	6
14-04-39[1]	Perth Panthers	1	Dundee Tigers	1
19-04-39	Dundee Tigers	6	Kelvingrove	6
25-04-39	Kelvingrove	7	Falkirk Lions	4
26-04-39	Falkirk Lions	4	Mohawks	6
27-04-39	Fife Flyers	5	Perth Panthers	3
28-04-39	Mohawks	3	Dundee Tigers	10
29-04-39	Perth Panthers	10	Kelvingrove	0
29-04-39	Falkirk Lions	11	Dundee Tigers	9

[1] Dundee Tigers awarded four points as Perth Panthers iced an illegal player.

Final Table

	P	W	L	D	F	A	Pts
Dundee Tigers	20	12	2	6	102	64	30
Perth Panthers	20	11	6	3	80	46	25
Fife Flyers	20	10	7	3	91	75	23
Kelvingrove	20	5	8	7	56	86	17
Mohawks	20	5	11	4	68	95	14
Falkirk Lions	20	3	12	5	76	107	11

Scottish League Season 1938-39 Player Squads

Dundee Tigers

First Team: W Lane; G McNeil and H Smith; A Rogers, M Cranstoun and J Lightfoot.
Substitutes: M Ross, D Mitchell, G Braid, J Shannon, J Schofield and F Hill.

Falkirk Lions

First Team: F Amantea; R Thomson and G Pantalone; G Davey, N McCuaig and G McWilliams.
Substitutes: A Purdie, J Fullerton, W W Russell, R Stapleford, J Kelly, J Johnston, L Lovell and R Beaton.

Fife Flyers

First Team: C Kerr; J Stover and L Lovell; T Durling, J W Chappell and N McQuade.
Substitutes: A Fullerton, G Horne, W Fullerton, L McCartney and T McInroy.

Kelvingrove

First Team: D Cross; A Seafred and J H Collins; S Cameron, D Eaton and W Cadieu.
Substitutes: W S Turnbull, C Nevitt, R Forsythe, L Marchant, D McLeod, F Chase and J Kenny.

Mohawks

First Team: A Palfrey; M Shires and G Cummine; G Baillie, G Morrison and C Dawson.
Substitutes: A G Bogie, G Horne, D Cumming, D McAlpine, W Bodnar, R Cheyne, B Brazier and J Kenny.

Perth Panthers

First Team: R S Milne; A Schumann and B Roberts; A Pratt, B Thompson and L Tapp.
Substitutes: R Purdie, J Fullerton, N Andrews, J Scott, J Allan and E Nicholson.

Scottish League Season 1939-40 Points Competition

Fixtures and Results

Date	Home		Away	
30-10-39	Dunfermline Vikings	2	Dundee Tigers	2
01-11-39	Falkirk Lions	1	Fife Flyers	5
01-11-39	Dundee Tigers	7	Ayr Raiders	2
02-11-39	Fife Flyers	1	Perth Panthers	1
03-11-39	Ayr Raiders	2	Dunfermline Vikings	2
04-11-39	Perth Panthers	6	Falkirk Lions	4
06-11-39	Dunfermline Vikings	2	Fife Flyers	3
08-11-39	Falkirk Lions	2	Ayr Raiders	4
08-11-39	Dundee Tigers	2	Perth Panthers	4
09-11-39	Fife Flyers	4	Dunfermline Vikings	2
10-11-39	Ayr Raiders	7	Falkirk Lions	4
11-11-39	Perth Panthers	2	Dundee Tigers	2
13-11-39	Dunfermline Vikings	2	Ayr Raiders	1
15-11-39	Falkirk Lions	3	Perth Panthers	1
15-11-39	Dundee Tigers	3	Dunfermline Vikings	3
16-11-39	Fife Flyers	4	Falkirk Lions	2
17-11-39	Ayr Raiders	2	Dundee Tigers	3
18-11-39	Perth Panthers	5	Fife Flyers	3
20-11-39	Dunfermline Vikings	5	Perth Panthers	3
22-11-39	Ayr Raiders	2	Fife Flyers	3
22-11-39	Dundee Tigers	1	Falkirk Lions	5
23-11-39	Fife Flyers	4	Dundee Tigers	3
24-11-39	Falkirk Lions	3	Dunfermline Vikings	2
25-11-39	Perth Panthers	3	Ayr Raiders	1
27-11-39	Dunfermline Vikings	2	Falkirk Lions	3
29-11-39	Falkirk Lions	3	Dundee Tigers	4
29-11-39	Ayr Raiders	0	Perth Panthers	0
30-11-39	Fife Flyers	6	Ayr Raiders	5
02-12-39	Perth Panthers	4	Dunfermline Vikings	1
02-12-39	Dundee Tigers	4	Fife Flyers	0
04-12-39	Dunfermline Vikings	3	Dundee Tigers	5
06-12-39	Falkirk Lions	4	Fife Flyers	2
06-12-39	Dundee Tigers	5	Ayr Raiders	6
07-12-39	Fife Flyers	1	Perth Panthers	4
08-12-39	Ayr Raiders	3	Dunfermline Vikings	3
09-12-39	Perth Panthers	4	Falkirk Lions	2
11-12-39	Dunfermline Vikings	3	Fife Flyers	2
13-12-39	Dundee Tigers	1	Perth Panthers	4
13-12-39	Falkirk Lions	4	Ayr Raiders	0
14-12-39	Fife Flyers	2	Dunfermline Vikings	3

Frozen in Time

15-12-39	Ayr Raiders	2	Falkirk Lions	3
16-12-39	Perth Panthers	5	Dundee Tigers	3
18-12-39	Dunfermline Vikings	3	Ayr Raiders	4
20-12-39	Falkirk Lions	0	Perth Panthers	1
20-12-39	Dundee Tigers	3	Dunfermline Vikings	6
21-12-39	Fife Flyers	5	Falkirk Lions	3
22-12-39	Ayr Raiders	2	Dundee Tigers	3
23-12-39	Perth Panthers	2	Fife Flyers	1
25-12-39	Dunfermline Vikings	2	Perth Panthers	0
27-12-39	Dundee Tigers	5	Falkirk Lions	8
28-12-39	Fife Flyers	6	Dundee Tigers	6
29-12-39	Falkirk Lions	2	Dunfermline Vikings	2
29-12-39	Ayr Raiders	4	Fife Flyers	1
30-12-39	Perth Panthers	2	Ayr Raiders	4
01-01-40	Dunfermline Vikings	2	Falkirk Lions	2
03-01-40	Falkirk Lions	2	Dundee Tigers	2
04-01-40	Fife Flyers	2	Ayr Raiders	2
05-01-40	Ayr Raiders	4	Perth Panthers	3
06-01-40	Perth Panthers	9	Dunfermline Vikings	3
06-01-40	Dundee Tigers	1	Fife Flyers	3

Final Table

	P	W	L	D	F	A	Pts
Perth Panthers	20	12	5	3	63	43	27
Fife Flyers	20	9	8	3	58	59	21
Falkirk Lions	20	8	9	3	60	61	19
Ayr Raiders	20	7	9	4	57	61	18
Dunfermline Vikings	20	6	8	6	53	60	18
Dundee Tigers	20	6	9	5	65	72	17

Statistics

Scottish League Season 1939-40 League Championship

Fixtures and Results

Date	Home		Away	
15-01-40	Dunfermline Vikings	5	Dundee Tigers	5
17-01-40	Dundee Tigers	8	Ayr Raiders	5
17-01-40	Falkirk Lions	6	Fife Flyers	4
18-01-40	Fife Flyers	11	Perth Panthers	5
19-01-40	Ayr Raiders	2	Dunfermline Vikings	4
20-01-40	Perth Panthers	1	Falkirk Lions	6
22-01-40	Dunfermline Vikings	3	Fife Flyers	8
24-01-40	Dundee Tigers	3	Perth Panthers	1
24-01-40	Falkirk Lions	3	Ayr Raiders	4
25-01-40	Fife Flyers	7	Dunfermline Vikings	5
26-01-40	Ayr Raiders	6	Falkirk Lions	2
27-01-40	Perth Panthers	3	Dundee Tigers	8
05-02-40	Dunfermline Vikings	6	Ayr Raiders	8
07-02-40	Falkirk Lions	2	Perth Panthers	1
07-02-40	Dundee Tigers	8	Dunfermline Vikings	8
08-02-40	Fife Flyers	4	Falkirk Lions	7
09-02-40	Ayr Raiders	1	Dundee Tigers	6
10-02-40	Perth Panthers	2	Fife Flyers	4
12-02-40	Dunfermline Vikings	7	Perth Panthers	2
14-02-40	Dundee Tigers	6	Falkirk Lions	12
15-02-40	Fife Flyers	8	Dundee Tigers	5
16-02-40	Ayr Raiders	4	Fife Flyers	3
16-02-40	Falkirk Lions	5	Dunfermline Vikings	6
17-02-40	Perth Panthers	1	Ayr Raiders	3
21-02-40	Falkirk Lions	5	Dundee Tigers	5
22-02-40	Fife Flyers	6	Ayr Raiders	1
23-02-40	Ayr Raiders	1	Perth Panthers	6
24-02-40	Dundee Tigers	12	Fife Flyers	6
24-02-40	Perth Panthers	3	Dunfermline Vikings	1
26-02-40	Dunfermline Vikings	1	Perth Panthers	1
28-02-40	Dundee Tigers	12	Falkirk Lions	3
29-02-40	Fife Flyers	5	Dundee Tigers	3
01-03-40	Ayr Raiders	5	Fife Flyers	8
02-03-40	Perth Panthers	4	Ayr Raiders	2
04-03-40	Dunfermline Vikings	3	Fife Flyers	8
06-03-40	Falkirk Lions	4	Ayr Raiders	3
06-03-40	Dundee Tigers	2	Perth Panthers	2
07-03-40	Fife Flyers	8	Dunfermline Vikings	2
08-03-40	Ayr Raiders	4	Falkirk Lions	5
09-03-40	Perth Panthers	0	Dundee Tigers	1

Frozen in Time

11-03-40	Dunfermline Vikings	6	Ayr Raiders	11
13-03-40	Falkirk Lions	2	Perth Panthers	5
13-03-40	Dundee Tigers	6	Dunfermline Vikings	1
14-03-40	Fife Flyers	6	Falkirk Lions	4
15-03-40	Ayr Raiders	2	Dundee Tigers	7
16-03-40	Perth Panthers	1	Fife Flyers	6
20-03-40	Dundee Tigers	4	Ayr Raiders	4
21-03-40	Fife Flyers	2	Perth Panthers	5
22-03-40	Ayr Raiders	5	Dunfermline Vikings	3
23-03-40	Perth Panthers	2	Falkirk Lions	3
25-03-40	Dunfermline Vikings	3	Falkirk Lions	10
27-03-40	Falkirk Lions	4	Dundee Tigers	3
28-03-40	Fife Flyers	8	Ayr Raiders	4
29-03-40	Ayr Raiders	1	Perth Panthers	3
30-03-40	Perth Panthers	7	Dunfermline Vikings	3
30-03-40	Dundee Tigers	3	Fife Flyers	4
08-04-40	Dunfermline Vikings	8	Dundee Tigers	3
10-04-40	Falkirk Lions	8	Fife Flyers	4
13-04-40	Falkirk Lions	7	Dunfermline Vikings	5
15-04-40	Dunfermline Vikings	4	Falkirk Lions	5

Final Table

	P	W	L	D	F	A	Pts
Fife Flyers	20	14	6	0	120	88	28
Falkirk Lions	20	13	6	1	103	88	27
Dundee Tigers	20	9	6	5	110	87	23
Perth Panthers	20	7	11	2	55	69	16
Ayr Raiders	20	7	12	1	76	97	15
Dunfermline Vikings	20	4	13	3	84	119	11

Scottish League Season 1939-40 Player Squads

Ayr Raiders

First Team: F Amantea; M Shires and G Cummine; W Welch, W Bodnar and C Dawson.
Substitutes: D McLeod, D Cumming, D McAlpine, F Prock, K Johnston, R McBride, H Marshall and J McBeth.

Dundee Tigers

First Team: W Lane; G McNeil and B Roberts; A Rogers, M Cranstoun and L Marchant.
Substitutes: S Cameron, G Braid and H Williams.

Dunfermline Vikings

First Team: C Kerr; P Downs and E Batson; T Durling, J W Chappell and N McQuade.
Substitutes: J Shannon, L Marsh and V Reilly.

Falkirk Lions

First Team: M Gerth; A Purdie and C Beaton; G Davey, T Forgie and L Savoie.
Substitutes: W S Turnbull, G McWilliams, R Beaton, J Taylor, D Cumming and T Allan.

Fife Flyers

First Team: A G Grant; G Horne and R Thomson; A Pratt, P Rheault and T McInroy.
Substitutes: G Morrison, G Ney and E McMillan.

Perth Panthers

First Team: R S Milne; R Cheyne and A Schumann; L Tapp, B Thompson and J Allan.
Substitutes: J Scott, F Chase and L Vickery.

Scottish League

Composition Season by Season

1929-1930	Achtungs; Bearsden; Bridge of Weir; Dennistoun; Doonside: Glasgow Skating Club; Glasgow University; Kelvingrove, Mohawks: Queen's.
1930-1931	Achtungs; Bearsden; Bridge of Weir; Dennistoun Eagles; Glasgow Skating Club; Glasgow University; Kelvingrove; Mohawks: Queen's.
1931-1932	Achtungs; Bearsden; Bridge of Weir; Dennistoun Eagles; Glasgow Skating Club; Glasgow University; Kelvingrove; Mohawks: Queen's.
1932-1933	Bears; Bridge of Weir; Dennistoun Eagles; Glasgow University: Juniors; Kelvingrove; Mohawks; Queen's.
1933-1934	Bears; Bridge of Weir; Dennistoun Eagles; Glasgow University: Juniors; Kelvingrove; Mohawks.
1934-1935	Bridge of Weir; Dennistoun Eagles; Glasgow University: Juniors; Kelvingrove; Mohawks.
1935-1936	Glasgow University; Kelvingrove; Lions; Mohawks; Mustangs.
1936-1937	Kelvingrove; Lions; Mohawks; Mustangs; Perth Panthers.
1937-1938	Kelvingrove; Lions; Mohawks; Mustangs; Perth Black Hawks: Perth Panthers.
1938-1939	Dundee Tigers; Falkirk Lions; Fife Flyers; Kelvingrove; Mohawks: Perth Panthers.
1939-1940	Ayr Raiders; Dundee Tigers; Dunfermline Vikings; Falkirk Lions: Fife Flyers; Perth Panthers.

League Championship

	First	Second	Third
1929 – 1930	Mohawks	Queen's	Achtungs
1930 – 1931	Kelvingrove	Bridge of Weir	Mohawks
1931 – 1932	Mohawks	Kelvingrove	Bridge of Weir

Statistics

1932 – 1933	Bridge of Weir	Mohawks	Queen's
1933 – 1934	Kelvingrove	Mohawks	Bridge of Weir
1934 – 1935	Bridge of Weir	Mohawks	Kelvingrove
1935 – 1936	Mohawks	Mustangs	Kelvingrove
1936 – 1937	Mohawks	Mustangs	Perth Panthers
1937 – 1938	Perth Panthers	Perth Black Hawks	Mohawks
1938 – 1939	Dundee Tigers	Perth Panthers	Fife Flyers
1939 – 1940	Fife Flyers	Falkirk Lions	Dundee Tigers

Mitchell Trophy Finals

1929 - 1930	Glasgow Skating Club	3	Bearsden	1
1930 - 1931	Kelvingrove	2	Mohawks	1
1931 - 1932	Queen's	0	Kelvingrove	0
Re-Play	Queen's	2	Kelvingrove	0
1932 - 1933	Bears	1	Bridge of Weir	0
1933 - 1934	Kelvingrove	8	Glasgow University	0
1934 - 1935	Mohawks	2	Glasgow University	1
1935 - 1936	Mohawks	1	Kelvingrove	0
1936 - 1937[1]	Lions	2	Mustangs	3
1937 - 1938	Lions	3	Perth Black Hawks	0
1938 - 1939	Dundee Tigers	2	Mohawks	1

[1] Final played in two legs but as Mustangs defaulted on second leg the trophy was awarded to Lions.

President's Pucks

1932 – 1933	Kelvingrove	0	Mohawks	0
Re-Play[1]	Kelvingrove	0	Mohawks	0
1933 – 1934	Bridge of Weir	3	Kelvingrove	0
1934 – 1935	Mohawks	2	Kelvingrove	1
1935 – 1936	Mohawks	1	Kelvingrove	1
Re-Play	Mohawks	3	Kelvingrove	0
1936 - 1937				
1st leg	Mohawks	2	Perth Panthers	2
2nd leg	Mohawks	9	Perth Panthers	1
1937 – 1938				
1st leg	Perth Black Hawks	4	Mohawks	1
2nd leg	Perth Black Hawks	0	Mohawks	0
1938 – 1939	Perth Panthers	6	Mohawks	3

[1] Pucks awarded to both teams.

Frozen in Time

Scottish Cup Final

1939 - 1940
1st leg   Dunfermline Vikings 5   Falkirk Lions 5
2nd leg   Dunfermline Vikings 5   Falkirk Lions 5

Replay 1st leg Dunfermline Vikings 3   Falkirk Lions 3
Replay 2nd leg Dunfermline Vikings 4   Falkirk Lions 3

Kelvingrove v Mohawks Competitive Record 1930 - 1939

17-10-30	League Championship	Kelvingrove	1	Mohawks	0
28-03-31	Mitchell Trophy Final	Kelvingrove	2	Mohawks	1
05-02-32	Mitchell Trophy First Round	Kelvingrove	1	Mohawks	0
01-03-32	League Championship	Kelvingrove	4	Mohawks	0
11-10-32	League Championship	Kelvingrove	3	Mohawks	1
14-04-33	President's Pucks Final	Kelvingrove	0	Mohawks	0
28-04-33	President's Pucks Final Replay	Kelvingrove	0	Mohawks	0
12-01-34	League Championship	Kelvingrove	2	Mohawks	1
23-03-34	President's Pucks Semi-Final	Kelvingrove	3	Mohawks	0
17-04-34	League Championship	Kelvingrove	2	Mohawks	0
27-11-34	League Championship	Kelvingrove	1	Mohawks	1
30-11-34	Mitchell Trophy Semi-Final	Mohawks	1	Kelvingrove	0
05-02-35	League Championship	Kelvingrove	1	Mohawks	0
16-04-35	League Championship	Kelvingrove	4	Mohawks	4
19-04-35	President's Pucks Final	Mohawks	2	Kelvingrove	1
05-11-35	League Championship	Kelvingrove	2	Mohawks	1
20-12-35	President's Pucks Final	Mohawks	1	Kelvingrove	1

03-01-36	League Championship				
	Mohawks	3	Kelvingrove	1
17-01-36	President's Pucks Final Replay				
	Mohawks	3	Kelvingrove	0
11-02-36	League Championship				
	Mohawks	1	Kelvingrove	0
06-03-36	Mitchell Trophy Final				
	Mohawks	1	Kelvingrove	0
27-03-36	League Championship				
	Mohawks	2	Kelvingrove	0
13-10-36	League Championship				
	Kelvingrove	1	Mohawks	1
06-11-36	League Championship				
	Mohawks	3	Kelvingrove	0
01-12-36	President's Pucks Semi-Final				
	Mohawks	4	Kelvingrove	1
08-01-37	League Championship				
	Mohawks	7	Kelvingrove	0
09-02-37	League Championship				
	Mohawks	4	Kelvingrove	1
13-10-37	League Championship				
	Kelvingrove	1	Mohawks	1
19-11-37	League Championship				
	Kelvingrove	2	Mohawks	2
30-11-37	President's Pucks First Round				
	Mohawks	2	Kelvingrove	1
14-01-38	League Championship				
	Kelvingrove	2	Mohawks	2
18-02-38	League Championship				
	Mohawks	3	Kelvingrove	0
08-04-38	League Championship				
	Kelvingrove	2	Mohawks	2
04-10-38	Points Competition				
	Kelvingrove	4	Mohawks	3
28-10-38	Points Competition				
	Kelvingrove	3	Mohawks	1
15-11-38	Points Competition				
	Mohawks	5	Kelvingrove	4
09-12-38	Points Competition				
	Mohawks	4	Kelvingrove	1
13-12-38	President's Pucks Semi-Final				
	Mohawks	7	Kelvingrove	2
17-01-39	League Championship				
	Mohawks	3	Kelvingrove	1
24-02-39	League Championship				
	Mohawks	7	Kelvingrove	2

Frozen in Time

21-03-39	League Championship			
	Kelvingrove	3	Mohawks	3
07-04-39	League Championship			
	Kelvingrove	2	Mohawks	2
13-04-39	Mitchell Trophy Semi-Final			
	Mohawks	3	Kelvingrove	2

Total Number of Matches   43
Mohawks   19 Wins
Kelvingrove   12 Wins
Drawn Matches   12

Statistics

Scotland

Competitive Record 1910 - 1938

Date	Venue	Home		Away	
26-03-10	London	England	11	Scotland	1
16-12-10	Glasgow	Scotland	8	England	3
22-11-30	Glasgow	Scotland	1	Germany	2
13-03-31	Glasgow	Scotland	1	Canada	11
06-11-31	Liverpool	London Lions	7	Scotland	0
07-11-31	Birmingham	London Lions	4	Scotland	1
12-12-31	Glasgow	Scotland	0	England	2
12-03-32	Glasgow	Scotland	2	Grosvenor House Canadians	1
29-10-32	Paris	France	7	Scotland	1
26-11-32	Glasgow	Scotland	1	Edmonton Superiors	8
24-02-33	Glasgow	Scotland	0	Grosvenor House Canadians	2
20-04-33	Oxford	England	4	Scotland	0
03-03-34	Glasgow	Scotland	1	England	3
27-12-34	London	Wembley Canadians	3	Scotland	1
29-12-34	Glasgow	Scotland	1	Richmond Hawks	8
16-02-35	Glasgow	Scotland	0	Wembley Canadians	7
16-03-35	London	England	6	Scotland	3
14-03-36	Glasgow	Scotland	1	England	1
19-03-37	Perth	Scotland	3	Richmond Hawks	8
20-03-37	Glasgow	Scotland	3	Richmond Hawks	10
25-03-37	Glasgow	Scotland	4	Canada	6
11-03-38	Glasgow	Scotland	1	Canada	1

Total Number of Matches   22
Scotland   2 Wins
Opposition   18 Wins
Drawn Matches   2

Scotland Player Squads 1910 - 1938

England 11 v Scotland 1

Princes Ice Rink, London 26 March 1910
First Team: J B Wharrie (Corinthians); A S Dunlop (King's); J Campbell (Corinthians); A J McGuffie (Wanderers); T Taylor (Wanderers), G Pettigrew (Star) and J D Strathearn (Beavers).
Substitute: J W Melvin (Wanderers).
Goal Scorer: J D Strathearn.

Scotland 8 v England 3

Crossmyloof Ice Rink, Glasgow 16 December 1910
First Team: J B Wharrie (Corinthians); A J McGuffie (Wanderers); J Campbell (Corinthians); A S Dunlop (King's); T Taylor (Wanderers), G Pettigrew (Star) and J D Strathearn (Beavers).
Substitutes: H Paul and S E Sage.
Goal Scorers: J D Strathearn (5), G Pettigrew (2) and T Taylor.

Scotland 1 v Germany 2

Crossmyloof Ice Rink, Glasgow 22 November 1930
First Team: F L Reardon (Queen's); T Nisbet (Dennistoun) and A R Bazin (Queen's); G D Rowley (Bridge of Weir), J A Easton (Glasgow University) and A R Brady (Mohawks).
Substitutes: J Brown (Kelvingrove), A J Tingley (Queen's) and R L Noble (Kelvingrove).
Goal Scorer: A R Bazin.

Scotland 1 v Canada 11

Crossmyloof Ice Rink, Glasgow 13 March 1931
First Team: F L Reardon (Queen's); G D Rowley (Bridge of Weir) and A R Bazin (Queen's); T Nisbet (Dennistoun), J A Easton (Glasgow University) and A R Brady (Mohawks).
Substitutes: H W Reid (Achtungs); J Fullerton (Mohawks); A J Tingley (Queen's) and R L Noble (Kelvingrove).
Goal Scorer: A J Tingley.

London Lions 7 v Scotland 0

Liverpool Ice Rink, 6 November 1931
First Team: D Cross (Kelvingrove); G D Rowley (Bridge of Weir) and J R Gilmour (Bearsden); J Fullerton (Mohawks), J A Easton (Glasgow University) and A J Tingley (Queen's).
Substitutes: J Campbell (Kelvingrove) and A Rintoul (Achtungs).

London Lions 4 v Scotland 1

Birmingham Ice Rink, 7 November 1931
First Team: D Cross (Kelvingrove); G D Rowley (Bridge of Weir) and J R Gilmour (Bearsden); J Campbell (Kelvingrove), J A Easton (Glasgow University) and A J Tingley (Queen's).
Substitutes: J Fullerton (Mohawks) and A Rintoul (Achtungs).
Goal Scorer: A Rintoul.

Scotland 0 v England 2

Crossmyloof Ice Rink, Glasgow 12 December 1931
First Team: D Cross (Kelvingrove); G D Rowley (Bridge of Weir) and A R Bazin (Queen's); D A Porter (Grosvenor House Canadians), K Thomson (Grosvenor House Canadians) and A R Brady (Mohawks).
Substitutes: J Fullerton (Mohawks), J A Easton (Glasgow University) and J Campbell (Kelvingrove).

Scotland 2 v Grosvenor House Canadians 1

Crossmyloof Ice Rink, Glasgow 12 March 1932
First Team: D Cross (Kelvingrove); G D Rowley (Bridge of Weir) and J R Gilmour (Bearsden); J Fullerton (Mohawks), J A Easton (Glasgow University) and A R Brady (Mohawks).
Substitutes: J Campbell (Kelvingrove), W M Muirhead (Bridge of Weir) and D Edwards (Dennistoun Eagles).
Goal Scorer: J Fullerton (2).

France 7 v Scotland 1

Palais des Sports, Paris 29 October 1932
First Team: D Cross (Kelvingrove); G D Rowley (Juniors) and J R Gilmour (Bears); J Fullerton (Mohawks), J A Easton (Glasgow University) and A R Brady (Liverpool).
Substitutes: J Campbell (Kelvingrove) and A J Tingley (Queen's).
Goal Scorer: J A Easton.

Scotland 1 v Edmonton Superiors 8

Crossmyloof Ice Rink, Glasgow 26 November 1932
First Team: D Cross (Kelvingrove); G D Rowley (Juniors) and J R Gilmour (Bears); J Fullerton (Mohawks), J A Easton (Glasgow University) and A R Brady (Liverpool).
Substitutes: J Campbell (Kelvingrove), A J Tingley (Queen's) and W Fullerton (Queen's).
Goal Scorer: J Fullerton.

Frozen in Time

Scotland 0 v Grosvenor House Canadians 2

Crossmyloof Ice Rink, Glasgow 24 February 1933
First Team: D Cross (Kelvingrove); J G Fyfe (Mohawks) and J R Gilmour (Bears); W Fullerton (Queen's), J Fullerton (Mohawks) and J Campbell (Mohawks).
Substitutes: J A Easton (Glasgow University), A J Tingley (Queen's), A R Brady (Liverpool), W M Muirhead (Bridge of Weir) and W G McDonald (Bridge of Weir).

England 4 v Scotland 0

Oxford Ice Rink 20 April 1933
First Team: D Cross (Kelvingrove); W M Muirhead (Bridge of Weir) and J R Gilmour (Bears); W Fullerton (Mohawks), J Fullerton (Mohawks) and J Campbell (Mohawks).
Substitutes: W G McDonald (Bridge of Weir), W S Montford (Kelvingrove), W W Russell (Dennistoun Eagles) and W S McLeod (Bridge of Weir).

Scotland 1 v England 3

Crossmyloof Ice Rink, Glasgow 3 March 1934
First Team: D Cross (Kelvingrove); A Fullerton (Kelvingrove) and J R Gilmour (Bears); W Fullerton (Mohawks), J Fullerton (Mohawks) and J Campbell (Mohawks).
Substitutes: W S Montford (Kelvingrove), W S McLeod (Bridge of Weir), C McMillan (Kelvingrove) and A J McCabe (Glasgow University).
Goal Scorer: W S McLeod.

Wembley Canadians 3 v Scotland 1

Wembley Arena, London 27 December 1934
First Team: R S Milne (Manchester); M D Brennan (Bridge of Weir) and W G McDonald (Bridge of Weir); W Fullerton (Mohawks), J Fullerton (Mohawks) and J Kenny (Mohawks).
Substitutes: W S McLeod (Bridge of Weir), W W Russell (Dennistoun Eagles) and P Stevenson (Juniors).
Goal Scorer: P Stevenson.

Scotland 1 v Richmond Hawks 8

Crossmyloof Ice Rink, Glasgow 29 December 1934
First Team: W S Turnbull (Juniors); A Fullerton (Kelvingrove) and J H Collins (Dennistoun Eagles); W Fullerton (Mohawks), J Fullerton (Mohawks) and J Kenny (Mohawks).
Substitutes: W S McLeod (Bridge of Weir), W W Russell (Dennistoun Eagles) and P Stevenson (Juniors).
Goal Scorer: P Stevenson.

Scotland 0 v Wembley Canadians 7

Crossmyloof Ice Rink, Glasgow 16 February 1935
First Team: D Cross (Kelvingrove); M D Brennan (Bridge of Weir) and W G McDonald (Bridge of Weir); W Fullerton (Mohawks), P Stevenson (Juniors) and J Kenny (Mohawks).
Substitutes: J Fullerton (Mohawks), W S McLeod (Bridge of Weir), W W Russell (Dennistoun Eagles) and A Fullerton (Kelvingrove).

England 6 v Scotland 3

Wembley Arena, London 16 March 1935
First Team: R S Milne (Manchester); P Stevenson (Juniors) and W M Muirhead (Bridge of Weir); W Fullerton (Mohawks), J Fullerton (Mohawks) and J Kenny (Mohawks).
Substitutes: W S McLeod (Bridge of Weir), W W Russell (Dennistoun Eagles), J Kelly (Juniors) and G Ayres (Mohawks).
Goal Scorers: W M Muirhead, W S McLeod and P Stevenson.

Scotland 1 v England 1

Crossmyloof Ice Rink, Glasgow 14 March 1936
First Team: J Foster (Richmond Hawks); R McAlpine (Earls Court Rangers) and P McPhail (Earls Court Rangers); W Fullerton (Mohawks), S Cameron (Kensington Corinthians) and J Kenny (Mohawks).
Substitutes: J Fullerton (Mohawks), W S Montford (Kelvingrove), J Kelly (Mustangs) and R O MacDonald (Mohawks).
Goal Scorer: S Cameron.

Scotland 3 v Richmond Hawks 8

Perth Ice Rink, 19 March 1937
First Team: A Palfrey (Mohawks); J H Collins (Kelvingrove) and L Lovell (Perth Panthers); W Boivin (Perth Panthers), L Tapp (Perth Panthers) and J Lightfoot (Perth Panthers).
Substitutes: J Kenny (Mohawks), P Stevenson (Lions), L McCartney (Lions) and G Galloway (Mohawks).
Goal Scorers: W Boivin, L Lovell and L McCartney.

Scotland 3 v Richmond Hawks 10

Crossmyloof Ice Rink, Glasgow, 20 March 1937
First Team: A Palfrey (Mohawks); W Boivin (Perth Panthers) and L Lovell (Perth Panthers); P Stevenson (Lions), L McCartney (Lions) and J Kenny (Mohawks).
Substitutes: W Fullerton (Mohawks), J H Collins (Kelvingrove), J Lightfoot (Perth Panthers) and G Galloway (Mohawks).
Goal Scorers: W Fullerton, J Lightfoot and P Stevenson.

Frozen in Time

Scotland 4 v Canada 6

Crossmyloof Ice Rink, Glasgow 25 March 1937

First Team: A Palfrey (Mohawks); W Boivin (Perth Panthers) and L Lovell (Perth Panthers); P Stevenson (Lions), L McCartney (Lions) and J Lightfoot (Perth Panthers).

Substitutes: W Fullerton (Mohawks), J Kenny (Mohawks), G Galloway (Mohawks) and J Dunsmore (Lions).

Goal Scorers: L Lovell, J Kenny, L McCartney and P Stevenson.

Scotland 1 v Canada 1

Crossmyloof Ice Rink, Glasgow 11 March 1938

First Team: F Amantea (Lions); G Horne (Mohawks) and L Lovell (Perth Black Hawks); P Stevenson (Lions), R Purdie (Perth Black Hawks) and G Baillie (Mohawks).

Substitutes: L McCartney (Perth Panthers), B Roberts (Lions), H Smith (Perth Black Hawks), A Pratt (Perth Panthers) and L Marchant (Mustangs).

Goal Scorer: A Pratt.

Scotland Players 1910 - 1938

Amantea, F (Fiore); (Lions); Canadian; goaltender; v Canada 1938 (1)

Ayres, G (Gilmour); (Mohawks); left defence; v England 1935 (1)

Baillie, G (George); (Mohawks); Scot; left wing; v Canada 1938 (1)

Bazin, A R (Arthur); (Queen's); Canadian; left defence; v Germany 1930; v Canada 1931; v England 1931 (3)

Boivin, W (Bill); (Perth Panthers); right wing/right defence; v Richmond Hawks 1937; v Richmond Hawks 1937; v Canada 1937 (3)

Brady, A R (Art); (Mohawks and Liverpool); Canadian; left wing; v Germany 1930; v Canada 1931; v England 1931; v Grosvenor House Canadians 1932; v France 1932; v Edmonton Superiors 1932; v Grosvenor House Canadians 1933 (7)

Brennan, M D (Max); (Bridge of Weir); Canadian; right defence; v Wembley Canadians 1934; v Wembley Canadians 1935 (2)

Brown, J (James); (Kelvingrove); Australian; right wing; v Germany 1930 (1)

Cameron, P S (Scotty); (Kensington Corinthians); Scot; centre; v England 1936 (1)

Campbell, J; (Corinthians); defence; v England 1910; v England 1910 (2)

Campbell, J (John); (Kelvingrove and Mohawks); Canadian; right wing; v London Lions 1931; v London Lions 1931; v England 1931; v Grosvenor House Canadians 1932; v France 1932; v Edmonton Superiors 1932; v Grosvenor House Canadians 1933; v England 1933; v England 1934 (9)

Collins, J H (Joe); (Dennistoun Eagles and Kelvingrove); Scot; left defence; v Richmond Hawks 1934; v Richmond Hawks 1937; v Richmond Hawks 1937 (3)

Cross, D (Dave); (Kelvingrove); Scot; goaltender; v London Lions 1931; v London Lions 1931; v England 1931; v Grosvenor House Canadians 1932; v France 1932; v Edmonton Superiors 1932; v Grosvenor House Canadians 1933; v England 1933; v England 1934; v Wembley Canadians 1935 (10)

Dunlop, A S (Archibald); (King's); Scot; defence/rover; v England 1910; v England 1910 (2)

Dunsmore, J, (Lions); Canadian; left defence; v Canada 1937 (1)

Easton, J A (Jack); (Glasgow University); Canadian; centre; v Germany 1930; v Canada 1931; v London Lions 1931; v London Lions 1931; v England 1931; v Grosvenor House Canadians 1932; v France 1932; v Edmonton Superiors 1932; v Grosvenor House Canadians 1933 (9)

Edwards, D (Don); (Dennistoun Eagles); Scot; right wing; v Grosvenor House Canadians 1932 (1)

Foster, J (Jimmy); (Richmond Hawks); Scot; goaltender; v England 1936 (1)

Fullerton, A (Alec); (Kelvingrove); Scot; right defence; v England 1934; v Richmond Hawks 1934; v Wembley Canadians 1935 (3)

Fullerton, J (John); (Mohawks); Scot; centre; v Canada 1931; v London Lions 1931; v London Lions 1931; v England 1931; v Grosvenor House Canadians 1932; v France 1932; v Edmonton Superiors 1932; v Grosvenor House Canadians 1933; v England 1933; v England 1934; v Wembley Canadians 1934; v Richmond Hawks 1934; v Wembley Canadians 1935; v England 1935; v England 1936 (15)

Fullerton, W (Billy); (Queen's and Mohawks); Scot; right wing; v Edmonton Superiors 1932; v Grosvenor House Canadians 1933; v England 1933; v England 1934; v Wembley Canadians 1934; v Richmond Hawks 1934; v Wembley Canadians 1935; v England 1935; v England 1936; v Richmond Hawks 1937; v Canada 1937 (11)

Fyfe, J G; (Mohawks); Scot; right defence; v Grosvenor House Canadians 1933 (1)

Galloway, G (Gordon); (Mohawks); centre; v Richmond Hawks 1937; v Richmond Hawks 1937; v Canada 1937 (3)

Gilmour, J R (Jack); (Bearsden and Bears); Scot; left defence; v London Lions 1931; v London Lions 1931; v Grosvenor House Canadians 1932; v France 1932; v Edmonton Superiors 1932; v Grosvenor House Canadians 1933; v England 1933; v England 1934 (8)

Horne, G (George); (Mohawks); Scot; left defence; v Canada 1938 (1)

Kelly, J (Johnny); (Juniors and Mustangs); centre; v England 1935; v England 1936; (2)

Kenny, J (Jim); (Mohawks); Canadian; left wing; v Wembley Canadians 1934; v Richmond Hawks 1934; v Wembley Canadians 1935; v England 1935; v England 1936; v Richmond Hawks 1937; v Richmond Hawks 1937; v Canada 1937 (8)

Lightfoot, J (Jimmy); (Perth Panthers); left wing; v Richmond Hawks 1937; v Richmond Hawks 1937; v Canada 1937 (3)

Lovell, L (Les); (Perth Panthers and Perth Black Hawks); Canadian; left defence; v Richmond Hawks 1937; v Richmond Hawks 1937; v Canada 1937; v Canada 1938 (4)

McAlpine, R (Ralph); (Earls Court Rangers); Scot; right defence; v England 1936 (1)

McCabe, A J; (Glasgow University); Canadian; left wing; v England 1934 (1)

McCartney, L (Len); (Lions and Perth Panthers); Canadian; centre; v Richmond Hawks 1937; v Richmond Hawks 1937; v Canada 1937; v Canada 1938 (4)

MacDonald, R O (Ronald); (Mohawks); right defence; v England 1936 (1)
McDonald, W G; (Bridge of Weir); Canadian; left defence; v Grosvenor House Canadians 1933; v England 1933; v Wembley Canadians 1934; v Wembley Canadians 1935 (4)
McGuffie, A J; (Wanderers); rover/defence; v England 1910; v England 1910 (2)
McLeod, W S (Walter); (Bridge of Weir); Scot; right wing; v England 1933; v England 1934; v Wembley Canadians 1934; v Richmond Hawks 1934; v Wembley Canadians 1935; v England 1935 (6)
McMillan, C (Charlie); (Kelvingrove); left wing; v England 1934 (1)
McPhail, P (Paul); (Earls Court Rangers); Scot; left defence; v England 1936 (1)
Marchant, L (Laurie); (Mustangs); Canadian; left wing; v Canada 1938 (1)
Melvin, J W; (Wanderers); v England 1910 (1)
Milne, R S (Ronald); (Manchester); Scot; goaltender; v Wembley Canadians 1934; v England 1935 (2)
Montford, W S (Sid); (Kelvingrove); Scot; right wing; v England 1933; v England 1934; v England 1936 (3)
Muirhead, W M (Wilbur); (Bridge of Weir); Scot; centre/left defence; v Grosvenor House Canadians 1932; v Grosvenor House Canadians 1933; v England 1933; v England 1935 (4)
Nisbet, T (Tom); (Dennistoun); Canadian; right defence/right wing; v Germany 1930; v Canada 1931 (2)
Noble, R L; (Kelvingrove); Canadian; left wing; v Germany 1930; v Canada 1931 (2)
Palfrey, A (Art); (Mohawks); Canadian; goaltender; v Richmond Hawks 1937; v Richmond Hawks 1937; v Canada 1937 (3)
Paul, H; v England 1910 (1)
Pettigrew, G (Gordon); (Star); centre; v England 1910; v England 1910 (2)
Porter, D A (Don); (Grosvenor House Canadians); Scot; right wing; v England 1931 (1)
Pratt, A (Arnie); (Perth Panthers); Canadian; right wing; v Canada 1938 (1)
Purdie, R (Bob); (Perth Black Hawks); Scot; centre; v Canada 1938 (1)
Reardon, F L (Fred); (Queen's); Canadian; goaltender; v Germany 1930; v Canada 1931(2)
Reid, H W (Hugh); (Achtungs); Canadian; right defence; v Canada 1931 (1)
Rintoul, A; (Achtungs); left wing; v London Lions 1931; v London Lions 1931 (2)
Roberts, B (Bunt); (Lions); Canadian; right defence; v Canada 1938 (1)
Rowley, G D (Gordon); (Bridge of Weir and Juniors); Canadian; right defence/right wing; v Germany 1930; v Canada 1931; v London Lions 1931; v London Lions 1931; v England 1931; v Grosvenor House Canadians 1932; v France 1932; v Edmonton Superiors 1932 (8)

Russell, W W (Bill); (Dennistoun Eagles); Scot; left wing; v England 1933; v Wembley Canadians 1934; v Richmond Hawks 1934; v Wembley Canadians 1935; v England 1935 (5)

Sage, S E; v England 1910 (1)

Smith, H (Howard); (Perth Black Hawks); Canadian; right defence; v Canada 1938 (1)

Stevenson, P (Pete); (Juniors and Lions); Canadian; right defence/centre; v Wembley Canadians 1934; v Richmond Hawks 1934; v Wembley Canadians 1935; v England 1935; v Richmond Hawks 1937; v Richmond Hawks 1937; v Canada 1937; v Canada 1938 (8)

Strathearn, J D; (Beavers); left wing; v England 1910; v England 1910 (2)

Tapp, L (Les); (Perth Panthers); Canadian; centre; v Richmond Hawks 1937 (1)

Taylor, T; (Wanderers); right wing; v England 1910; v England 1910 (2)

Thomson, K (Keith); (Grosvenor House Canadians); Scot; centre; v England 1931 (1)

Tingley, A J (Arthur); (Queen's and Kelvingrove); Canadian; centre; v Germany 1930; v Canada 1931; v London Lions 1931; v London Lions 1931; v France 1932; v Edmonton Superiors 1932; v Grosvenor House Canadians 1933 (7)

Turnbull, W S (Billy); (Juniors); Scot; goaltender; v Richmond Hawks 1934 (1)

Wharrie, J B (John); (Corinthians); Scot; goaltender; v England 1910; v England 1910 (2)

Players for Great Britain 1930-1939

Brady, A R (Art); (Mohawks and Liverpool); Canadian; left wing; v Canada 1930; v Edmonton Superiors 1933 (2)

Brennan, M D (Max); (Bridge of Weir); Canadian; right defence; v Canada 1935 (1)

Collins, J H (Joe); (Kelvingrove); Scot; left defence; v Belgium 1939; v Hungary 1939; v Canada 1939; v Germany 1939; v Czechoslovakia 1939 (5)

Cross, D (Dave); (Kelvingrove); Scot; goaltender; v Edmonton Superiors 1933 (1)

Easton, J A (Jack); (Glasgow University); Canadian; centre; v Canada 1930; v Edmonton Superiors 1933 (2)

Fullerton, J (John); (Mohawks); Scot; centre; v Edmonton Superiors 1933 (1)

Fullerton, W (Billy); (Mohawks and Fife Flyers); Scot; right wing; v Canada 1935; v Belgium 1939; v Hungary 1939; v Canada 1939; v Germany 1939; v Czechoslovakia 1939 (6)

Gilmour, J R (Jack); (Bears); Scot; left defence; v Edmonton Superiors 1933 (1)

MacDonald, S A; (Mohawks); Canadian; right wing; v Canada 1930 (1)

McDonald, W G; (Bridge of Weir); Canadian; left defence; v Canada 1935 (1)

McInroy, T (Tommy); (Fife Flyers); Scot; left wing; v Belgium 1939; v Hungary 1939; v Canada 1939; v Germany 1939; v Czechoslovakia 1939 (5)

McLeod, W S (Walter); (Bridge of Weir); Scot; right wing; v Canada 1935 (1)

Rowley, G D (Gordon); (Juniors); Canadian; right defence; v Edmonton Superiors 1933 (1)

Stevenson, P (Pete); (Juniors); Canadian; centre; v Canada 1935; v Latvia 1935; v France 1935; v Austria 1935; v Switzerland 1935; v Canada 1935; v Czechoslovakia 1935 (7)

Tingley, A J (Arthur); (Queen's); Canadian; centre; v Canada 1930; Edmonton Superiors 1933 (2)

Frozen in Time

Rules of Hockey (1900)

LAWS OF HOCKEY OF THE PROVINCE OF QUEBEC

Sec. 1. A team shall be composed of seven players who shall be *bona fide* members of the Clubs they represent. No player shall be allowed to play on more than one team in the same series during a season, except in a case of *bona fide* change of residence.

Sec. 2. The game shall be commenced and renewed by a face in the centre of the rink. Rink must be at least 112 feet by 58 feet. Goals shall be six feet wide and four feet high.

Definition of a face

The Puck shall be faced by being placed between the sticks of two opponents, and the Referee then calling "play."

The goals shall be placed at least ten feet from the edge of the ice.

Sec. 3. Two half hours, with an intermission of ten minutes between, will be the time allowed for matches, but no stops of more than fifteen minutes will be allowed. A match will be decided by the team winning the greatest number of games during that time. In case of a tie after playing the specified two half hours, play will continue until one side secures a game, unless otherwise agreed upon between the captains before the match. Goals shall be changed after each half hour.

Sec. 4. No change of players shall be made after a match has commenced, except for reasons of accidents or injury during the game.

Sec. 5. Should any player be injured during the first half of the match and compelled to leave the ice, his side shall be allowed to put on a spare man from the reserve to equalize the teams ; should any player be injured during the second half of the match the Captain of the opposing team shall have the option of dropping a player to equalize the teams or allow his opponents to put on a man from the reserve. In the event of any dispute between the Captains as to the injured player's fitness to continue the game, the matter shall at once be decided by the Referee.

Sec. 6. Should the game be temporarily stopped by the infringement of any of the rules, the Captain of the opposite team may claim that the puck be taken back and a face take place where it was last played from before such infringement occurred.

Sec. 7. When a player hits the puck, anyone of the same side, who at such moment of hitting is nearer the opponent's goal line is out of play, and may not touch the puck himself or in any way whatever prevent any other player from doing[1] so, until the puck has been played. A player should always be on his own side of the puck.

Sec. 8. The puck may be stopped but not carried or knocked on by any part of the body, nor shall any player close his hand on, or carry the puck to the ice in his hand. No player shall raise his stick above the shoulder, except in lifting the puck. Charging from behind, tripping, collaring, kicking or shinning shall not be allowed, and for any infringement of these rules, the Referee may rule the offending player off the ice for that match, or for such portion of actual playing time as he may see fit.

Sec. 9. When the puck goes off the ice or a foul occurs behind the goals, it shall be taken by the Referee to five yards at right angles from the goal line and there faced. When the puck goes off the ice at the sides it shall be taken by the Referee to five yards at right angles from the boundary line and there faced.

Sec. 10. The goal keeper must not during play, lie, kneel or sit upon the ice, but must maintain a standing position.

Sec. 11. Goal shall be scored when the puck shall have passed between the goal posts from in front below an imaginary line across the top of posts.

Sec. 12. Hockey sticks shall not be more than three inches wide at any part.

Sec. 13. The puck must be made of vulcanized rubber, one inch thick all through and three inches in diameter.

Sec. 14. The Captains of the contesting teams shall agree upon a Referee and two Umpires (one to be stationed behind each goal), which positions shall not be changed during a match, and two Timekeepers. In the event of the Captains failing to agree on Umpires and Timekeepers, the Referee shall appoint same.

Sec. 15. All disputes during the match shall be decided by the Referee, and he shall have full control of all players and officials from commencement to finish of matches, inclusive of stops, and his decision shall be final.

Sec. 16. All questions as to games shall be settled by the Umpires, and their decision shall be final.

Sec. 17. In the event of any dispute as to the decision of an Umpire or Timekeeper, the Referee shall have power to remove and replace him.

Sec. 18. Any player guilty of using profane or abusive language to any officials or other players, shall be liable to be ruled off by the Referee, as per section 8.

LAWS OF HOCKEY OF THE PROVINCE OF ONTARIO

Game

The game is placed on ice by teams of seven on each side, with a puck made of vulcanized rubber, one inch thick all through and three inches in diameter.

Sticks

Hockey sticks shall not be more than three inches wide at any part and not more than thirteen inches long in the blade.

Goal

A goal is placed in the middle of each goal line, composed of two upright posts, four feet in height, placed six feet apart, and at least five feet from the end of the ice.

The goal posts shall be firmly fixed. In the event of a goal post being displaced or broken, the Referee shall blow his whistle and the game shall not proceed until the post is replaced.

Match

Each side shall have a Captain (a member of his team), who, before the match, shall toss for choice of goals.

Each side shall play an equal time from each end. The duration of championship matches shall not be less than one hour, exclusive of stoppages. The team scoring the greater number of goals in that time shall be declared the winner of the match. If at the end of that time the game is a draw, ends shall be changed and the game continued for ten minutes, each side playing five minutes from each end with a rest of five minutes between, and if neither side has then scored a majority of games, similar periods of ten minutes shall be played in the same way until one side shall have scored a majority of goals,

Timekeepers

Timekeepers shall be appointed, one by each Captain, to keep the time during match.

Referee

There shall be only one Referee for a match, and in no case shall he belong to either of the competing Clubs. He shall enforce the rules, adjudicate upon disputes, or cases unprovided for by rule; appoint the Goal Umpires; control the timekeepers ; keep the score ; and at the conclusion of the match declare the result. The puck shall be considered in play until the Referee stops the game, which he may do at any time, and which he must do at once when any irregularity of play occurs by sounding[1] a whistle. His decision shall be final.

Score

A goal shall be scored when the puck shall have passed between the goal posts from in front and below an imaginary line drawn across the tops of the posts.

Goal umpires

Goal Umpires shall inform the Referee when a goal is scored. Their decision shall be final.

Face

The game shall be started and renewed by the Referee calling "play" after having placed the puck on its larger surface on the ice, between the sticks of two of the players, one from each team, who are to face it. After a goal has been scored the puck shall be placed on the centre of the ice.

Off-side

A player shall always be on his side of the puck. A player is off-side when he is in front of the puck, or when the puck has been hit, touched or is being run with, by any of his own side behind him (i.e., between himself and the end of the rink near which his goal is placed).

A player being off-side is put on-side when the puck has been hit by, or has touched the dress or person of any player of the opposite side, or when one of his own side has run in front of him, either with the puck or having played it when behind him.

If a player when off-side plays the puck, or annoys or obstructs an opponent, the puck shall be faced where it was last played before the off-side play occurred.

Knocking-on

The puck may not be stopped with the hand except by the goal-keeper (see Rule 11), but may be stopped, but not carried, or knocked on by any other part of the body.

Charging, tripping, etc.

No player shall raise his stick above his shoulder. Charging from behind, tripping, collaring, kicking, cross-checking, or pushing shall not be allowed. And the Referee must rule off the ice, for any time in his discretion, a player who, in the opinion of the Referee, has deliberately offended against the above rule.

When the puck leaves the ice

When the puck goes off the ice behind the goal line it shall be brought out by the Referee to a point five yards in front of the goal line, on a line at right angles thereto, from the point at which it left the ice, and there faced.

Rules

When the puck goes off the ice at the side, it shall be similarly faced three yards from the side.

Goal-keeper

The goal-keeper must not during play, lie, sit or kneel upon the ice; he may, when in goal, stop the puck with his hands, but shall not throw or hold it. He may wear pads, but must not wear a garment such as would give him undue assistance in keeping goal. The Referee must rule off the ice, for any time in his discretion, a player who, in the opinion of the Referee, has offended deliberately against this rule.

Change of players

No change of players shall be made after a match has commenced, except by reason of accident or injury during the game.

Injured player

Should any player be injured during a match, break his skate, or from any other accident be compelled to leave the ice, the opposite side shall immediately drop a man to equalize the teams. In event of any dispute, the matter shall at once be decided by the Referee.

Stoppages

Should the game be stopped by the Referee by reason of the infringement of any of the rules, or because of an accident or change of players, the puck shall be faced at the spot where it was last played, before such infringement, accident or change of players shall have occurred.

Frozen in Time

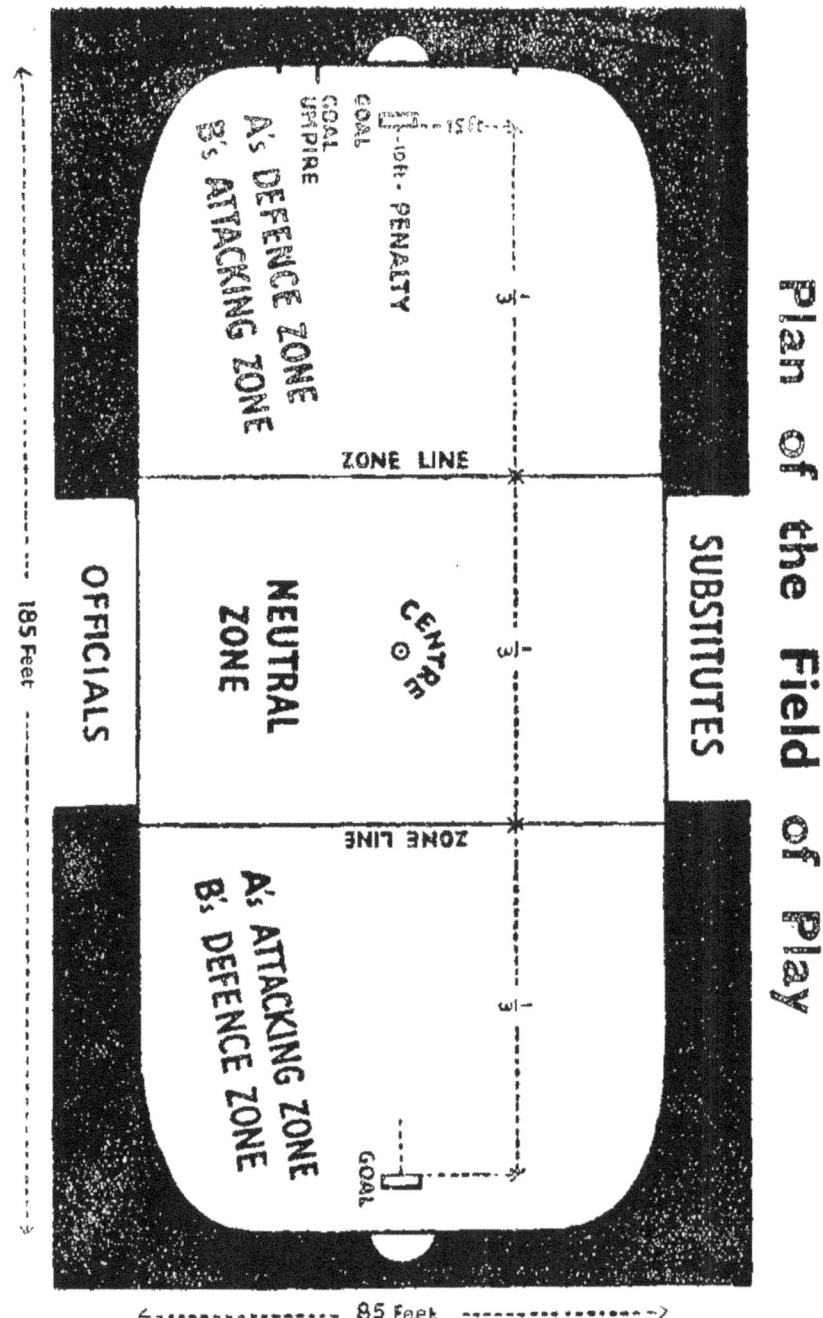

Rules of Ice Hockey (1936)

Contents

	Article
Note	1
I. Equipment.	
A. The Rink	3
B. The Goals	7
C. The Puck	13
D. The Sticks	14
E. The Goal-keeping Pads	15
F. The Players' Equipment	18
G. The Official Enclosures	19
II. The Players	
A. Their Positions	22
B. Substitutes	23
C. Substitutions	26
D. Reserves	33
E. Numbering	34
F. Colours	35
G. The Captain of the Team	38
III. The Officials	
A. Referee	45
B. The Timekeepers	56
C. The Penalty Timekeepers	62
D. The Goal Umpires	70
IV. The Play	.
A. Its Duration	76
B. Winners—Goals scored	83
C. Ends	87
D. Stoppages	89
E. Face-off	92
V. Infringements.	
A. General Infringements	97
B. Off-side	99
C. Carrying the Puck—Kicking	107

D. Prohibited Positions	109
E. Charging and Rough Play	111
F. Number of Players on Defence	114
G. Ragging	115
H. Other Infringements	116
VI. Penalties.	
A. Kinds of Penalty	118
B. Application	121
C. Duration—Suggestions for Penalties	128

Note

Art. 1.—This code of rules is only a synthesis of the previous rules, together with certain alterations made by the congresses of the L.I.H.G., the whole being completed by the addition of established practice, and arranged in a more rational order than previously.

Art. 2.—Ice-Hockey originated in Canada and should not be confounded with ' Bandy.' It is played on an ice rink between two teams of six members each who wear ice skates and push or slide by means of a Stick the Puck, which they try to get through the Goal of the opponents. The Match is played during a specified Time and the team which has scored most goals is the winner. A Referee (or two) is entrusted with the enforcement of the rules, watches over the game, and is helped by Timekeepers and Goal Umpires.

I. EQUIPMENT

A. The Rink

Art. 3.—The dimensions of the rink shall be at least 18 metres (60 feet) by 50 metres (165 feet), and at the most 33½ metres (110 feet) by 76 metres (250 feet). These proportions shall in every case be adhered to. The ideal dimensions of a rink shall be 26 metres (85 feet) by 56 metres (185 feet).

Art. 4.—The goals shall be placed at each end of the rink in the middle of the small side, the open part facing the centre, the goal line being parallel to the base line and at a distance of 1.50 m. (5 feet) minimum, and 4.50 m. (15 feet) maximum from it (according to the length of the rink).

Art. 5.—(a) A line of dark colour, 2.5 cm. (1 inch) wide shall be traced on or in the ice between the posts of each goal.

(b) Parallel to the goal-line, lines at least 5 cm. (2 inches) wide shall be traced across the whole width of the ice in the following places:

When the rink is 60 metres (200 feet) or more long, at 18 metres (60 feet) from the goal line;

Rules

When the rink is less than 60 metres (200 feet) long, at one-third of the distance separating the two goal-lines.

These lines, known as 'blue lines' or 'zone lines' shall divide the rink into three zones, known respectively as 'defence zone,' 'neutral or centre zone" and 'attacking zone' the latter being for each team the zone containing the opposing goal.

(c) A dark circle 30 cm. (1 foot) in diameter shall be marked out in the centre of the rink, that is to say, at the intersection of the imaginary diagonals.

(d) A circle of 3 m. (10 feet) radius, having as centre the middle of the goal-line and consisting of a stripe 5 cm. (2 inches) in width, shall be drawn around the goal, terminated behind it by a line running parallel to the goal-line and at a distance of 0.55 m. (22 inches) therefrom.

(The facing point for the special penalty imposed by Art. 119 shall be on the outer rim of this circle, perpendicular to the goal-line at its centre point.)

(e) A dark line shall be painted on the side boards defining the beginning of the end boards 5 metres (15 feet) from each goal-post (limit point for defence players to approach the face-off in case of application of the penalty specified in Art. 119).

Art. 6.—The rink shall be surrounded by a boarding which will form its limits. These boards shall be 25 cm. (10 inches) minimum in height and the corners of the rink shall as far as possible be rounded.

B. The Goals

Art. 7.—The goals shall consist of two vertical posts, 122 cm. (4 feet) in height and 183 cm. (6 feet) apart, the tops of which shall be connected by a horizontal bar.

Art. 8.—A cage, the front of which is formed by this framework, will support nets sufficiently strong to resist a powerful shot. This cage will be 40 cm. (16 inches) deep at the top, and at the bottom along the ice 55 cm. (22 inches).

The upper part of the goal shall be covered by netting, like the back and sides, and by nothing else that might obstruct the view of the goal umpire.

Art. 9.—The posts shall be fixed firmly in the ice and a dark line traced between them.

Art. 10.—In the event of the goal-net being torn or the posts broken or displaced, the umpire shall stop the game, which will be resumed only when the necessary repairs have been effected.

Art. 11.—It shall be the duty of the umpire to measure the goals on the occasion of each match.

Art. 12.—The home team shall be responsible for the marking of the rink and fixing of goals. The referee shall not allow the game to commence until these rules have been strictly carried out.

C. The Puck

Art. 13.—The puck is a flat round disc made of hardened vulcanized rubber measuring 2.54 cm. (1 inch) in thickness by 7.62 cm. (3 inches) in diameter. Its weight shall not be less than 141.5 grammes (5 ounces) nor more than 170 grammes (6 ounces).

D. The Sticks

Art. 14.—The sticks are square in section, and terminated at the lower end by a flat blade making an obtuse angle with the handle. They must not exceed 9 cm. (3½ inches) in width at any part. The length of the flat blade must not exceed 38 cm. (15 inches). The total length of the handle must not exceed 137 cm. (54 inches). These sticks are made entirely of wood, tape binding being permissible.

E. The Goal-keeping Pads

Art. 15.—The goal-keeper's pads are worn essentially for protection and are not intended to give him undue assistance in keeping goal.

The pad is placed round the leg and must not constitute a shield projecting on each or one side of the leg.

Art. 16.—When the two legs are together the pads must not under any circumstances take up more than 50 cm. (20 inches) in width.

Art. 17.—The umpire shall measure the pads before the match. He is entitled to do so at any time during the match.

F. The Players' Equipment

Art. 18.—The players, including the goal-keeper, may be provided with equipment for protection, but in no case with equipment that might give them any assistance during the match, or be capable of wounding another player. The other players shall not use the goal-keeper's equipment (with the exception of his stick as laid down in Art. 25).

G. The Official Enclosures

Art. 19.—An official enclosure shall be reserved for the officials and timekeepers close to the rink in the centre of the longer side. All necessary facilities shall be provided in it for the timekeepers, who shall be so placed as never lose sight of the referee at any time during the game.

Art. 20.—Another enclosure shall be reserved at the rinkside for the substitutes and penalty timekeeper. Other than these the team managers only are allowed access to this enclosure.

Art. 21.—Behind each goal enclosures shall be reserved for the goal umpire, who shall remain alone.

II. THE PLAYERS

A. Their Positions

Art. 22.—A team is formed of six players, named according to the position they occupy in the game: three forwards (right wing, left wing and centre), two defence (left and right) and one goal-keeper.

B. Substitutes

Art. 23.—In addition to the above-mentioned six players each team may have four additional players as substitutes, who will replace the players when desired but only under the circumstances mentioned below. At no time, however, may there be more than six players per team on the rink.

Art. 24.—Furthermore, it is also permissible to have a reserve goal-keeper, but the latter may only play in goal and the substitution may only be made at the beginning of a new period, or should occasion arise during the game if the goal-keeper has been the victim of an accident which in the opinion of the referee is sufficiently severe to prevent him from continuing to play; as soon as he has recovered, the referee shall authorize him to resume his place.

Any team whose goal-keeper has been injured shall return to the rink within not more than fifteen minutes after the interruption of the game (with the same or another goal-keeper) on penalty of forfeiting the match.

Art. 25.—Should the goal-keeper be penalized he shall be replaced by one of the players on the rink during the whole time of his enforced absence. The said player shall be authorized to play in the position of the goalkeeper, but shall not use any of the goal-keeper's equipment except his stick.

C. Substitutions

Art. 26.—A substitution may only be made during a stoppage of play, no matter what may be the reason for making the substitution.

Art. 27.—The referee must be advised of the impending substitution.

Art. 28.—In case of violation of these rules, the referee will impose the following penalties: two minutes' penalty for the two players who have carried out a substitution while the play was proceeding, or two minutes for the captain of the team having more than six players on the rink.

Art. 29.—The substitutes must be ready to play and must take their place in the team without delaying the game.

Art. 30.—The replaced player shall leave the rink simultaneously with the entry of the substitute.

Art. 31.—When not playing, the substitutes must cover their sweaters, so that the referee shall not mistake them for the players on the rink.

Art. 32.—If, from one of the two sides, more than four players (the goal-keeper excepted) are obliged to retire due to accidents, and if, consequently, it will no longer be possible to have six players on the rink, the other team will take off one or more players in order to equalize the strength of the sides on the rink.

D. Reserves

Art. 33.—The organizers of the meeting will fix the total number of players which will be admitted to take part in the meeting, on the understanding that, in accordance with Art. 23, only eleven players, inclusive of the four substitutes and the substitute goal-keeper, may be appointed for the one match. In cases where the organizers have not fixed this number, the teams may have a reserve for each player.

For World, European and Olympic Championships, the number of reserve players shall not exceed three.

E. Numbering

Art. 34.—All the players will be numbered and will carry the number prominently on their backs.

F. Colours

Art. 35.—While in play the teams will be attired in distinctly different colours, so as to avoid all confusion.

Art. 36.—Only the goal-keepers are exempt from wearing these colours which must be uniformly worn by all other members of the team.

Art. 37.—If two teams are found by the referee to be wearing colours which in his opinion are likely to prove confusing in play, the home club or alternatively the club drawn by lot will change colours.

G. The Captain of the Team

Art. 38.—Each team shall appoint a captain from among its members.

Art. 39.—He will wear on the right arm, between the elbow and the shoulder, an armlet of a different colour from the rest of his attire bearing the letter 'C.'

Art. 40.—The captain commands the other players; he is their official representative and takes all necessary decisions in the name of the team.

Art. 41.—He tosses up for the choice of ends, and if successful makes the choice,

Art. 42.—He decides in conjunction with the referee and the opposing captain upon the deviations from the rules necessitated by unforeseen circumstances, interpretations, prolongations, cancellations, the duration of periods, etc.; but in the case of non-agreement the ruling of the referee shall be final.

Art. 43.—After the match, he will submit any complaints which he considers well founded.

Art. 44.—If the occasion arises he 'scratches.'

III. THE OFFICIALS

A. Referee

Art. 45.—The referee is in absolute control of the game.

Art. 46.—He settles indisputably all matters in accordance with the rules of the game. He judges all disputes and makes the necessary decisions. In cases where no rules are applicable, he will act in accordance with usual practice and his own judgement.

Art. 47.—There is no appeal against the decisions of the referee. Any complaint against him, properly submitted, can have no consequence other than punishment (suspension or disqualification) if he is found to have acted wrongfully; it can never lead to a cancellation of his decisions.

Art. 48.—The referee is appointed by the organizers.

Art. 49.—His appointment cannot be contested if he is recognized as an international referee by the L.I.H.G.

Art. 50.—He must be neutral: if, however, it is impossible to obtain a neutral referee, then the appointment is subject to agreement between the captains of the teams.

Art. 51.—The referee appoints the timekeepers and the goal umpires, selecting them so far as is feasible from neutrals, He is responsible for them and may change them at any stage of the game. He is in no ways bound to follow their advice, and will settle out of hand any dispute regarding their duties.

Art. 52.—He will come to agreement with the captains of the teams regarding the interpretation of the rules and any alterations to be made in them owing to circumstances.

Art. 53.—He will referee with the necessary severity to ensure a correct game, free from rough play or deliberate infringements.

Art. 54.—He will move with the play.

Art. 55.—His duties are principally as follows:—

(a) Before the Match:

1. He will confirm that the lines of the rink are properly drawn on the ice and, if necessary, will have them altered and re-drawn.

2. He will examine the equipment of the players, the pucks (of which there shall be at least two), the pads of the goal-keeper, the sticks, the goals, the numbering and the identity of the players.

3. He will examine the enclosures reserved for the officials, the substitutes, and the goal umpires, and will ensure that none but authorized persons have access to same.

4. He will appoint the other officials, see that they are provided with the necessary instruments and that they are in their places, i.e. two ordinary and one or more penalty timekeepers, equipped with timepieces and ready in the

enclosure reserved for them; two goal umpires, one at each end behind the goals, standing in a position to see the puck entering the goal, and provided with small flags or white handkerchiefs.

5. He will get the captains to toss up for choice of ends.

6. He will advise the players of the rules applying to substitution, exhort them to keep calm, and inform them of the way in which penalties will be inflicted.

7. In case of bad weather the referee shall decide if the match shall be postponed; if there are two referees the match shall not be postponed unless both are in agreement; but a match once begun shall always be continued unless the referee (or referees) and both of the team captains agree otherwise.

(b) During the Match.

1. He will place the puck in play and show by blowing the whistle that play has commenced.

2. He will stop the game for any infringement and, if necessary, penalize the players at fault; he will not, however, stop play for an infringement if the stoppage would benefit the team of the player committing same, unless the referee considers a stoppage necessary in order to penalize the player at fault and so prevent the game from becoming rough;

3. He will inform the penalty timekeepers of the penalties inflicted;

4. He will stop play at the scoring of each goal and decide whether the goal is valid or not (by consulting the goal umpire, though without necessarily accepting the latter's opinion).

5. After each stoppage he will put the puck in play and show by blowing his whistle that play has recommenced.

6. He will settle disputes of all kinds.

7. He will stop play if one of the players is hurt, and also in the circumstances mentioned in Art. 10.

8. He will stop play as soon as the timekeepers inform him that the period is over.

(c) During the Rest.

1. He will remain in communication with the time-keepers and the players, and warn the latter three minutes before the end of the rest.

2. He will ascertain whether the lines of the rink are still sufficiently clear, and if not, will have them remade.

3. He will count up the goals scored during the preceding period.

(d) At the Resumption:

1. He will see to it that the penalized players whose time of punishment had not expired when the rest was taken, continue their absence.

2. He will recommence the game at the correct time, even if all the players are not yet on the rink, except in the case of circumstances beyond his control.

3. He will see that the teams change ends.

4. He will referee as before.

(e) At the end of the Match:
He will count up the goals scored by each team in the course of the match and, if necessary, order extra time to be played.

(f) After the Match:
He will examine and sign the report of the match, or ' referee's sheet.'

Art. 55 bis—Double Umpiring

(a) When there are two referees, each one shall in turn face off at the centre; the first referee, designated by drawing lots, shall face off during the first period and the first half of the third and of extra times; the other shall do so in the second period and the second half of the third play and of each extra time.

(b) One referee shall take up a position at one of the blue lines, against the railing; the other shall stay at the other blue line, against the other railing. They shall leave their positions as seldom as possible and shall return to them if obliged to move. Referees shall not change sides with the teams and shall referee during the entire game on the same blue line.

(c) Each referee shall be in charge of that half of the rink (between the centre and short side) where his blue line is; he shall give all decisions required for his half of the rink. He may at any time ask the other referee's opinion, but the final decision rests with him.

(d) Any fouls occurring at the division of the two halves, if not agreed on by the two referees, shall be decided in the last resort by the referee in charge of the face-off during the period.

(e) As an exception a referee may stop play because of any foul or other incident occurring in the half of the other referee whenever such foul or incident is serious and was not noticed by the other referee. The decision and penalty, if any, shall, however, rest always with the latter.

B. The Timekeepers

Art. 56.—Two timekeepers are appointed by the referee. They should, if possible, be neutral, but if this is not practicable, one belonging to each team should be chosen: however, if no neutral timekeepers are available, and if the two teams are unable each to appoint a timekeeper, the official timekeepers of the association in the country organizing the meeting will be appointed.

Art. 57.—Their duty is to inform the referee by blowing a whistle, ringing a bell, or beating a gong that the end of the period or of the rest has arrived.

Art. 58.—They will begin to count the time from the moment the referee blows the whistle for the first time when putting the puck into play.

Art. 59.—They will stop their watches during the stoppages of play, or, if they do not possess stop-watches, they will add to the playing time the time taken for each stoppage.

Art. 60.—They will advise the referee three minutes before the end of the interval.

Art. 61.—All disputes between them regarding the time will be settled there and then by the referee.

C. The Penalty Timekeepers

Art. 62.—The referee will appoint one timekeeper (if the latter is neutral, and two, one for each team, if a neutral timekeeper is not available), whose duty it is specially to keep time regarding the penalties inflicted on the players.

Art. 63.—The referee will tell them the duration of the penalty.

Art. 64.—They will commence to keep the time of the penalty only from the moment when the player sent off presents himself to them.

Art. 65.—They will add to the penalty all time lost for stoppages of play (as for the game).

Art. 66.—They will not permit the penalized player to return to play until he has completely served his sentence.

Art. 67.—When there is no stoppage of play, they will not allow another player to take the place of the penalized player at the moment that the latter is entitled to return to play.

Art. 68.—If, when the whistle goes for the rest, the player has not finished his sentence, he will finish it at the beginning of the following period. However, any penalty will be considered finished with the end of the match and will not be continued in the course of a later match.

Art. 69.—All disputes between the two penalty timekeepers will be settled forthwith by the referee.

D. The Goal Umpires

Art. 70.—The referee will appoint two goal umpires, if possible chosen from neutral persons, but if this is not practicable, one from each team.

Art. 71.—The goal umpires' duty is to inform the referee, by raising a flag or a white handkerchief, that the puck has entirely cleared the goal-line after passing over it from the front and that consequently a goal has been properly scored.

Art. 72.—This is his only duty and the only case in which he is called upon to make known his opinion; however, he must reply to the referee, if asked, as to whether in his opinion the goal has been properly scored (i.e. that there has been no kick, offside infringement, etc.), and shall also reply to any other question which the referee may consider it necessary to ask him.

Art. 73.—He will not change ends after the rest and will act as umpire alternately behind the goal of each team.

Art. 74.—He must place himself so as to be able to see the goal line perfectly.

Art. 75.—The referee is under no obligation to act on the judgement of the goal umpire, but shall in every case question him as to the validity of the goal scored.

IV. THE PLAY

A. Its Duration

Art. 76.—The teams will play during three periods of fifteen minutes each, separated by rests of ten minutes. Nevertheless, for matches which are not for the European or World Championships, periods may consist of twenty minutes each, if the opposing captains agree.

Art. 77.—All stoppages occurring in the game will be added to the actual playing time.

Art. 78.—If after the expiration of this time the game is undecided, i.e. if the two teams have each scored the same number of goals, or if neither of them has scored, extra time may be played; after a rest of ten minutes the match will be continued for ten minutes of playing time, each team playing five minutes from each end. No rest will be taken between these two periods of five minutes, but ends will be changed.

Art. 79.—If after this extra time the match is still undecided, extensions of ten minutes may be played in the same way, with a rest of five minutes between each extra time of ten minutes' duration, until a decision has been obtained.

Art. 80.—However, no match may be prolonged for more than thirty minutes of actual play, i.e. three periods of extra time. If after this time the match is undecided, it will be replayed.

Art. 81.—Should one of the teams refuse to play the required extra time, it will be declared to have lost.

Art. 82.—The Championships of Europe and of the World do not provide any exception to these rules.

B. Winners—Goals Scored

Art. 83.—The winning team of the match will be that which during the match, inclusive of extra time, has scored the greater number of goals.

Art. 84.—A goal is scored when the puck has entirely crossed from the front the plane formed by the goal-line, the posts, and cross-bar. The goal will not be allowed if the puck still touches the goal-line.

Art. 85.—In no case may the referee award a goal which has not thus been scored, no matter what infringement may have been committed by the defending team in preventing the goal from being scored.

Art. 86.—If, however, a goal has been scored through a foul, for instance after off-side, or through a kick, or through the goal-keeper being charged, etc., the referee will not allow the goal.

C. Ends

Art. 87.—Before the match, in the presence of the referee, the captains of the opposing teams will toss up. The successful captain may choose the end of the rink to be defended by his team in the first period.

Art. 88.—At each new period, after seven and a half minutes of the third period, or after five minutes' extra time, the teams will change ends.

D. Stoppages

Art. 89.—Play will only be stopped when the referee blows his whistle.

Art. 90.—The referee will stop play

(1) when the puck has gone over the lines. The puck shall be considered as having gone out of play if it touches a spectator and rebounds on to the rink, in the same way as if it had touched the referee.

(2) when an infringement has been committed (see Art. 97);

(3) when the puck has touched the referee;

(4) when a goal has been scored;

(5) for special reasons, such as injury to a player, damage to or breakage of the goal-posts, etc.;

(6) at the end of a period; after seven and a half minutes of the third period; and after five minutes of extra time.

Art. 91.—Play will not be stopped because a player has broken his stick, except when the player is the goalkeeper.

E. Face-Off

Art. 92.—In order to start playing the puck, two players, one from each team, will place themselves one opposite the other, at the spot indicated by the referee, the left-hand side turned towards the opposing goal and the blades of the sticks on the ice parallel and at 50 cm. (20 inches) distance from one another. The referee throws the puck between the two blades of the sticks, at the same time blowing his whistle to announce that play has begun. The players facing may not lift their sticks until the puck has touched the ice.

Art. 93.—At the face-off every player, except the two players who are facing off, shall be on-side (between the puck and the base of their zone) and at least 3 metres (10 feet) from the point of the face-off, except for the goal-keeper, who shall remain in his usual position in front of his own goal.

Art. 94.—At the beginning of a period, or when a goal has been scored, the referee faces the puck in the centre of the rink (marked by a dark circle).

Art. 95.—In the course of the game he (the referee) faces the puck at the spots hereinafter specified, according to why and where the game was stopped:—

(a) In the Central Zone:—

1. For off-side (i.e. whenever a player in the central zone received the puck from a team-mate who remained in the defence zone): at the spot from which the puck came before the off-side.

2. For any other infringement: at the spot where the infringement was committed.

3. When the puck goes off the rink: at 3 metres (10 feet) from the long side, opposite the point where the puck left the rink.

(b)In the End Zones:—
A. For an infringement committed by an attacking player:—
  1. For off-side (i.e. when a player not in possession of the puck crosses the blue line before the puck): at the spot where the puck was when the player crossed the line.
  2. For any other infringement, for an infringement committed jointly by a player from either team or because the puck went over the lines: on the blue line, at 3 metres (10 feet) from the long side nearest the spot where the infringement occurred or the puck went off,
B. For infringement by a defending player:—
  1. For a minor infringement by the goal-keeper (Art. 110) and for ragging (first offence) (Art. 115): at the spot marked on the ice in front of the goal (Art. 119);
  2. For penalizing a defence player in excess (Art. 114): in the centre of the rink;
  3. For any other infringement: at the spot where the infringement occurred.

Art. 96.—Nevertheless, whenever a face-off occurs in an end zone, in front of the goal, the point of face-off shall be carried 3 metres (10 feet) to one side of the goal at the same distance from the goal-line as the spot where the infringement occurred.

V. INFRINGEMENTS

A. General

Art. 97.—In general, the referee shall stop play for any infringement, whether intentional or not; however, he will not stop play if such stoppage is to the advantage of the team which has committed the infringement: but if the infringement is one which calls for a penalty he will stop play at the conclusion of that phase of the game in order to penalize the offending player.

Art. 98.—The referee must carry out his duty sufficiently severely to maintain correct play, without, however, upsetting the players and rendering play impossible by continuous stoppages.

B. Off-side

Art. 99.—A player whose position is between the puck and his own goal is said to be ' on-side.' If he is between the puck and the opposing goal he is 'off-side.' Players of the same team shall be known as 'team-mates' and 'opponents' of the other team.

Art. 100.—A player may always pass the puck to a team-mate who is on-side. He may also pass it to a teammate who is off-side, provided that this team-mate is in the same zone as himself; he may not, however, pass the puck to a team-mate who is off-side in another zone.

Art. 101.—Nevertheless, a puck once having entered the centre zone from the defence zone may be picked up by any of the players who were in the defence zone at the moment of the pass, that is to say, they may chase the puck into the centre zone.

Art. 102.—If the puck, at the moment it passes from the defence zone into the centre zone, is played by a teammate who was not in the defence zone at the moment when the pass was given, the game shall be stopped and a face-off shall take place at the point whence the pass originated.

(The game, however, shall not be stopped if the pass comes from the opponent who is at the time in the defence zone of the player receiving it, the defence players not being obliged to follow the puck into their defence zone.)

Art. 103.—A second defence zone is the goal area (Article 5 (d)). This bears the same relation to the remainder of the rink as the defence zone itself bears to the two other zones, that is to say:—

1. That an attacking player can only enter the goal area after the puck has entered it, even if he is on-side.

2. That nevertheless, if an attacking player after having transgressed in entering it leaves it again before the puck enters the area the game shall not be stopped; and finally,

3. That once within the goal area players who have lawfully entered it may pass to one another even in an off-side position.

Art. 104.—Even in the attacking zone, players who are off-side may join in the game provided always that they do not impede the view or interfere with the movements of the goal-keeper. In the event of any such infringement the game shall be stopped and any goal scored thereby shall be void.

To mark the portion of the rink within which off-side players may be considered likely to interfere with the goalkeeper, a special section, known as the ' goal-crease,' shall be outlined on the ice: a circle of 3 m. radius (10 feet) having as centre the middle of the goal-line and consisting of a stripe 5 cm. (2 inches) in width, shall be drawn around the goal, terminating behind it on a line running parallel with the goal-line and at a distance of 0.55 m. (22 inches) therefrom).

Art. 105.—Defending players may harass attackers, even those not in possession of the puck, but without using sticks or tackling, body checking being permitted only against players in possession of the puck.

Art. 106.—In the event of a pile-up in the goal-crease such that the referee loses sight of the puck, he shall stop the game.

Rules

C. Carrying the Puck—Kicking

Art. 107.—All players may stop the puck with any part of the body; but they must let it fall on the rink; it is not permitted to carry the puck or to play it in any other way but with the stick, but the players shall be able to use their sticks as they like, to hit the puck, to push it with the stick or carry it on the stick, on condition that they do not raise the stick higher than their shoulder.

Art. 108.—Nevertheless, in the defence zone and the centre zone a player shall be permitted to ' foot-lag ' the puck on to his stick, but shall not be allowed to kick it or to pass it in this way to a team-mate.

D. Prohibited Positions

Art. 109.—No player, except the goalkeeper, may lie down, sit, kneel or intentionally fall on the ice. The player who has accidentally fallen may not take part in the play and must make every effort to get up immediately.

A player who plays in one of the prohibited positions commits an infringement which is punishable should it impede a goal being scored.

Art. 110.—Only the goal-keeper or the player who replaces him while he is penalized, may stop the puck in any position (sitting, kneeling, falling) and clear it as he thinks best (kicking, throwing, etc.), with the one restriction that he may only throw it behind himself and not forward, and that he shall not hold the puck, lie, kneel or sit on it. Any minor infringement by the goal-keeper shall be penalized by the special face-off described in Art. 119.

E. Charging and Rough Play

Art. 111.—All rough play is prohibited. It is particularly prohibited to charge, to trip, or to grapple with one another, to hit with the skates or sticks, or to push, hold or impede an opponent by hand.

However, body checking will be allowed if carried out under the following conditions:—Cleanly, body to body, in the defence zone only, by any defence player against any attacking player in possession of the puck; it can be done with the chest, the back, the shoulder or the hip, but not with the knee or elbow or with the stick pushed out in front. A player who body checks may throw his weight slightly forward towards the attacking player but without gathering momentum for the charge; but he may not attack in the back a player who has just passed him, and body checking may not be done within five feet of the boarding.

Art. 112.—It is particularly prohibited to charge the goal-keeper while he is defending, and a goal scored under such circumstances should be declared void; however, such defence shall be deemed lacking if the goal-keeper leaves his goal-crease.

Art. 113.—In no case may a player not playing the puck be ' body checked,' even though he may be a potential receiver of the pass.

F. Number of Players on Defence

Art. 114.—No more than three team-mates, including the goal-keeper, shall be in their defence zone when the puck is not in that zone; but where the puck has just left the defence zone, no infringement shall have been committed if the extra players leave the zone immediately the puck has done so; similarly a fourth defending player may enter his defence zone in front of the puck with the aim of impeding an opponent in possession of the puck provided he is not more than one stick's length in front of the other. For the first offence, the game shall be stopped and the puck faced off in the centre of the rink; for the second offence, the first extra player to enter his defence zone shall be penalized one minute; for the third offence, the penalty shall be two minutes, and so on, each new offence increasing the penalty by one minute. Where several extra players enter their defence zone before the puck, the captain of the offending team shall designate the player to be penalized.

G. Ragging

Art. 115.—The team which, in order to gain time, for any reason deliberately plays a defensive game, by not carrying a puck forward but circling round the same spot, carrying the puck behind the goal, etc., without any player of the offending team being in their defence zone, commits an infringement. The first offence shall be penalized by the referee facing off the puck as set out in Art. 119; for the second offence, he shall penalize the player at fault.

H. Other Infringements

Art. 116.—It is prohibited to play a 'Dirty' or savage game, to use improper or coarse language, to have an argument with a spectator or another player, to raise the stick above the shoulder or to throw it on the ice.

Art. 117.—When the referee is of the opinion that a defending player intentionally commits a slight infringement in order to stop play at a critical moment, he will not stop play for this infringement and will penalize the player at the first stoppage following.

VI. PENALTIES

A. Kinds of Penalty

Art. 118.—Notwithstanding the stoppage of the game necessitating the stoppage of the puck, the referee may exclude from the game for varying periods of time a player committing an infringement, without it being permissible for the latter to be replaced during the period of his enforced absence.

Art. 119.—A special penalty shall be applied in the two cases considered under Art. 110 (minor infringement by a goal-keeper) and 115 (ragging—first offence). The referee shall face off the puck at 3 metres (10 feet) in front of, and perpendicular to, the middle of the goal of the offending team without any player of the defending team, except the goal-keeper and the player facing off, being within 5 metres (15 feet) of the nearest goal-post at the time of the face-off. A special spot shall be marked on the ice and lines painted on the boards for these distances (see Art. 5).

Art. 120.—Generally, the referee will give a warning before inflicting a penalty.

The referee will inflict penalties with the severity required to ensure a correct game free from intentional infringements. He will avoid upsetting the players by exaggerated penalties.

B. Application

Art. 121.—When in the opinion of the referee a player commits a punishable infringement, the former will, after having stopped the game, inform the player as well as the penalty timekeepers of the sentence inflicted, i.e. of the duration of the exclusion.

Art. 122.—The penalized player will at once leave the game and put on clothing of neutral colour.

Art. 123.—The time of the punishment will commence as soon as the game is resumed, after the sent-off player has placed himself at the disposal of the penalty timekeeper.

Art. 124.—All stoppages of play will be added to the time of punishment, which will therefore only be counted for the time actually played.

Art. 125.—As soon as the punishment is over, the penalized player (but not a substitute) will again take up his place in the game, without play being stopped. The penalty timekeeper will inform the player when his sentence is over.

Art. 126.—Such player shall skate back to his defence zone before he can again participate in the game.

Art. 127.—Should half-time arrive before the sentence has been fully served, the player will finish his sentence at the beginning of the following period; however, in the case of a tournament, when a sentence has not been fully served by the end of the match, it will not be carried forward to the following match.

C. Duration—Suggestions for Penalties

Art. 128.—The referee will penalize for the time thought suitable by him, one, two, five minutes, or even for the whole period if the infringement is exceptionally bad, such as intentionally causing injury to an opponent, or striking the referee.

Art. 129.—He will inflict the penalty in accordance with the importance of the infringement, its repetition, and its effect on the outcome of the game, etc.

Frozen in Time

Art. 130.—Under these circumstances it is very difficult to fix a scale of penalties; but for guidance a few penalties may be suggested to the referees to serve as a basis, without, however, the referees being obliged to act accordingly, as the infliction of penalties is entirely subject to their judgment.

Art. 131.—Below are mentioned some penalties which might serve as an index for the referees, and these suggestions have the advantage of giving the international referees an index of a fairly equal degree of firmness:—

One Minute

To all players, except the goal-keeper, who throw the puck.
To the player who intentionally kicks the puck or pushes it with the hand or arm.
To the player holding the puck in his hand, or against the edge of the rink or any other spot along the rink by the body or foot.
To the goal-keeper who strikes an adversary with the stick or who trips him.
To the player who is intentionally off-side.
To the player who trips an opponent with the stick.
To the player who shall be in the defence zone when there arc already three team-mates there (second offence).
To the player who shall 'rag' the puck (second offence).

Two Minutes

To the player who unintentionally trips.
To the player who throws his stick.
To the player who throws an opponent's stick to the ground.
To the player who is intentionally off-side (repeated offence).
To the player who charges an opponent otherwise than by 'body checking.'
To the player who lifts his stick above his shoulder.
To the player who disputes with the referee.
To the player who trips with his stick (repeated offence).
To the player who argues with the spectators.
To the player who contravenes the rules relating to substitution.

Three Minutes

To the player who uses his stick when ' body checking.'
To the player who intentionally trips an opponent.
To the player who throws his stick in order to avoid a score.

Five Minutes

To the player who injures the officials.
To the player who uses foul language.
To the player who kicks an opponent with his skate.
To the player who hits an opponent on the head with his stick.

Ten Minutes

To the player who intentionally injures an opponent.
To the player who attacks an official.
To the player who strikes an opponent with the handle of his stick.

Bibliography

Books

Giddens, R, "Ice Hockey World Annual 1950-1951", London, 1951
Gordon, D, "Raiders of the Lost Rink; Ice Hockey in Ayr", Stroud, 2004
Gordon, D, "Scotch on Ice; Scotland's Ice Hockey Heroes", Stroud, 2006
Harris, M C, "Homes of British Ice Hockey", Stroud, 2005
Harris, M C, "The British Ice Hockey Hall of Fame", Stroud, 2007
Patton, B M, "Ice Hockey", London, 1936
Stocks, B, "Ice Hockey Herald Annuals 1968-1969 to 1972-1973", Glasgow
Szemberg, S and Podnieks, A, "World of Hockey; Celebrating a Century of the IIHF', Bolton, Canada, 2007

Newspapers

The Daily Record and Mail
The Evening Times
The Glasgow Herald
The Scotsman
The Sketch Magazine
The Sunday Mail
The Times

Websites

A to Z Encyclopaedia of Ice Hockey - www.azhockey.com
Hockey Archives - www.hockeyarchives.info
Ice Hockey Journalists UK - www.ihjuk.co.uk
International Ice Hockey Federation - www.iihf.com
Society for International Hockey Research - www.sihrhockey.org

Index

A

Aberdeen 283
Achtungs Ice Hockey Club 47, 51, 54, 57, 60-61, 64-66, 69, 74, 76, 81-82, 89, 93, 96, 102, 104-105, 113-115, 127, 153-154, 306-309, 311, 313-315, 317-319, 350, 356-357, 363
Adamson, Christopher A 34
Ahearne, J F 286
Airlie Trophy 270
Aitken, Pat 153, 154, 157, 162-164, 167, 173, 175, 312, 316
Alberta 118, 154, 254
Allan Cup 187
Allan, J 319, 323
Allan, Jimmy 228, 231, 237, 246, 253, 273, 289, 339, 344, 349
Allan, Tom 294
Amantea, Fiore 231-233, 237, 241-242, 255, 258, 261-262, 264, 266, 268, 277, 288-289, 293-294, 339, 344, 349, 360-361
Amateur Skating Club 4
Anderson, A 57, 312
Anderson Cup 270
Andrews, Norrie 190, 198, 269, 327, 330, 333, 336, 339, 344
Archer, Alex 187, 191-193, 220
Ardinning 46
Argyll, Duke of 2
Argyll Ice Hockey Club 4, 36
Armstrong, Howard 65, 113
Arnot, William ii, 27, 31
Atlantic Fleet Canadians Ice Hockey Club 59
Austin-Smith, A F 29, 31
Austria (National Team) 365
Ayr xi, 28, 54, 74-75, 242, 249, 277
Ayr Ice Rink 24, 277, 294
Ayr Raiders Ice Hockey Club 285-286, 288-291, 293-297, 299-301, 345-350, 391
Ayres, Gilmour 161, 165, 169, 170, 184, 330, 359, 361
Ayrshire Polo Club 54

B

Baillie, George 222, 228, 232, 235, 237, 240-241, 245, 253, 264, 281-282, 339, 344, 360-361
Baird, C B 57, 312
Baird, J 307, 315
Bairns Trophy 270
Ball, Gerhard 70
Ball, Heinz 70
Ball, Rudi 79
Bandy 1, 4, 10, 12, 13, 14, 17, 18, 19, 21, 22, 26, 28, 31
Barclay, J W 78
Barnes, J 85, 316
Barrow, Lieutenant-Colonel 11, 12
Bates, Lou 143, 220
Batson, Ernie 289, 349
Bayne, Jack 11-12, 15, 17
Bayswater 116
Bazin, Arthur 62-63, 67, 69-70, 76, 79-81, 85, 87, 89, 94, 98-103, 105-107, 109, 113, 115, 125-126, 312, 316, 320, 356-357, 361
Bears Ice Hockey Club 113-117, 121-129, 134, 137-139, 143-144, 146-148, 153-155, 159, 170, 177-179, 321-323, 325-327, 350-351, 357-358, 362, 365
Bearsden 46, 53
Bearsden Ice Hockey Club 45, 47-48, 51, 53, 58, 60-61, 64, 66-69, 74, 80, 82, 84, 86-87, 93, 102-105, 113-115, 153-154, 159, 306-309, 311, 313-315, 317-319, 350-351, 356-357, 362
Beaton, Bob 278, 284, 289, 297-298, 344, 349
Beaton, Clem 289, 297, 349
Beaton, Joe 284
Beavers Ice Hockey Club 25, 27-28, 31, 32, 356, 364
Behling, Dick 284, 300
Belgium 26, 33
Belgium (National Team) 33-35, 275, 365

Benoit, Joe 277
Berlin 33, 35, 77, 100, 107, 233
Berliner Schlittschuh Club 77
Berlinquet, Lorne 66, 68, 76-77, 79, 81, 88, 94, 115, 312, 315, 319
Bessone, P 117
Beveridge, Joe 135, 140-141, 154, 178, 180-181, 323, 327, 330, 333
Biggar, A J 65, 311, 315, 319
BIHA see British Ice Hockey Association
Birmingham Ice Rink 98, 148, 228, 357
Birmingham Maple Leafs Ice Hockey Club 179, 227, 230, 237, 254, 259
Bodnar, Bill 271, 276, 288-289, 344, 349
Bogie, Archie 178, 207, 211, 231-233, 235, 240, 249, 253, 259, 327, 330, 333, 336, 339, 344
Bohemia 26, 33, 35
Bohemia (National Team) 35
Boivin, Bill 207, 210-211, 215, 217, 336, 359, 360-361
Bonnycastle, Dick 38,
Bonnycastle, Larry 100, 102, 109, 131
Borland, Ian 158, 178, 311, 315, 330
Borland, J H 68, 115, 123, 311, 315, 319, 323, 327
Borland, Jimmy 146, 151, 187
Bosanquet, Bernard 3
Brady, Art 62-63, 65, 67-70, 75, 76-77, 79, 82, 86-87, 89, 94, 98, 100-102, 106, 108-110, 113, 115, 117-119, 121, 129, 287, 312, 316, 320, 356-358, 361, 365
Braid, Glen 156, 173, 176, 202, 222, 226, 230, 232, 235, 237, 253, 255, 259, 287, 327, 330, 333, 336, 339, 344, 349
Brantford 291
Brelter, R 48
Brenchley, Edgar 186-187, 191-193
Brennan, Max 137-138, 140, 145, 147-150, 155-156, 157, 159, 162, 167-170, 172, 176-177, 179, 182, 184-185, 189, 195, 202, 207, 327, 330, 333, 336, 358-359, 361, 365

Bridge, H N 140
Bridge of Weir Curling Club 53
Bridge of Weir Hockey Club 53
Bridge of Weir Ice Hockey Club 47, 51, 53-54, 57-58, 61, 64, 66, 69, 74, 77, 79-88, 93-94, 96-97, 99-100, 102-108, 114-118, 120-127, 129, 134-135, 137-140, 142-150, 154-160, 162, 164-173, 176-177, 179-180, 184, 194-195, 306-309, 311, 313-315, 317-319, 321-323, 325-330, 350-351, 356-359, 361, 363, 365
Bridge of Weir Leather Company 53
Brighton Ice Hockey Club 3
Brighton Sports Stadium 245
Brighton Tigers Ice Hockey Club 187, 210-211, 214, 217, 222, 228, 233, 240, 244-245, 254-255, 259, 261, 278, 291, 301
British Columbia 214, 237, 265
British Ice Hockey Association (BIHA) 33, 35, 37, 63, 65, 70, 81, 90-91, 97, 100, 122, 143-144, 166, 169, 214, 234, 244, 275, 279, 286, 291
British League 70-71
Brown, Bobby 158, 167, 330
Brown, Jimmy 77, 79-80, 89-90, 94, 109, 315, 356, 361
Brown, T C 307, 311, 315
Brown, W H 48
Brown, William 235
Bruce, R 48
Buck, R J 268
Buckingham Palace 1
Burbridge, B 206, 210, 336
Bury Fen Bandy Club 18
Bushell, H W 48, 70, 98

C

Cadieu, Wilf 254, 261, 266, 278, 281, 344
Calgary 154
Callander, Bill 268
Cambridge University 54
Cambridge University Ice Hockey Club 1, 3-4, 35-36, 38, 41, 96, 169, 217, 228

Cambridge University Rugby Club 87
Cameron, Scotty 191-193, 211, 228, 230, 235, 237-238, 240, 249, 254, 282, 287, 298, 307, 311, 315, 339, 344, 349, 359, 361
Campbell, Archibald Sir (Lord Blythswood) 15
Campbell, J ii, 27-29, 31, 356, 361
Campbell, John 59, 61, 69-70, 75-76, 79, 81-82, 86-89, 94, 98, 100-101, 103, 105, 107, 109-110, 117, 119, 123, 126, 129, 135, 142, 145-147, 149, 155, 282, 287, 312, 315, 319, 323, 327, 356-358, 361
Campbell, Clarence S 48
Canada xii, 1, 13, 19, 26, 38-39, 52, 59, 60-61, 67, 73-75, 94, 99, 113, 115, 129, 142, 145, 153-154, 156-157, 159, 164, 167, 170, 186-187, 197-198, 200-204, 207, 209-210, 212, 216-218, 220, 222, 225, 230, 235, 241, 249, 252-255, 266, 291-292, 294
Canada Cup xiii, 74, 76, 80, 86, 88, 93-94, 102, 108-109, 121, 125-126, 129, 134, 144, 147-149, 155, 171-172, 177, 190, 194, 207, 211, 213, 215-216, 222, 225-226, 230, 246-247, 251, 254, 256, 278, 281-282, 286-287, 294, 313, 317, 321, 325, 328, 331, 334, 337, 342
Canada Cycle and Motor Company 73-74
Canada (National Team) 5, 37, 41, 65-66, 79, 86-88, 89, 91, 98, 103, 111, 118, 120, 130, 143, 166, 168-169, 187, 214, 218-219, 240-245, 265-266, 275, 277, 355-356, 360-365, 391
Canadian Amateur (Ice) Hockey Association 286
Canadians xii, 3-5, 19, 24, 28, 32, 34, 36, 38-39, 45-46, 51, 59-60, 65-67, 75, 79, 87, 91, 93, 102, 109, 114, 124, 131, 134-135, 143, 145, 151, 155, 164, 172, 187, 197, 202-203, 206, 219, 240-241, 249, 258, 265, 269-271, 277, 279, 294
Cannon, J 336, 339
Cannon, T G 36
Carr, J G 129, 169, 170
Carruthers, E D 48

Carruthers, J G 45, 60, 65-66, 69, 81, 307, 311, 315, 323
Carslaw, J S 53, 78, 114, 315, 319
Carty, Dave 47-48, 63, 71, 79-80, 83, 108, 127, 158-159, 312, 316, 320, 324
Carty, Val 99, 109, 116, 125, 312, 316, 320, 324
Cawthra, Jack 3
Celtic Football Club 204
Central Ice Rink, Perth 174, 196-197, 201, 204, 206, 209, 215, 217, 219, 221, 226, 230-231, 233, 235, 237-238, 240, 244-246, 251, 359
Chamonix 33, 38
Chappell, Jimmy 187, 255-256, 289, 296-297, 344, 349
Charlton, Sidney 43
Chase, Frank 226, 228, 231-232, 237, 239, 241, 247, 264, 273, 289, 339, 344, 349
Chatham 254
Chatham Maroons Ice Hockey Club 255
Cheyne, Raymond 276, 289, 292, 344, 349
Child, Art 187, 191-193
Cholette, J 117
Churchill, Peter 122
Claret, M 117
Clark, H A 311
Clark, John 14
Club de Patineurs de Paris 33
Cock, Joe 60, 96
Cohen, Mark 66, 141, 175, 315
Collins Joe, 84, 94, 98, 114-115, 121, 139-140, 143-144, 150, 156, 162-164, 168-169, 173, 176, 179, 182, 184, 200, 208, 210, 213, 217-218, 235, 237, 249, 254, 273, 282, 307, 311, 319, 323, 327, 330, 333, 336, 339, 344, 358-359, 361, 365
Collins, W A Colonel 54, 307, 311
Cooper, S B 11-12
Cooper, WB 11-12
Corinthians Ice Hockey Club 25, 27-28, 31, 76, 96, 356, 361, 364
Coronation Cup 270
Couldray, R W 146, 169

Coward, Johnny 187, 191-193, 217
Cox, Bevan C 34
Cox, P Sydney 34
Craig, Tom 84, 94, 108, 147, 312, 316, 320, 323, 327
Cranstoun, Merrick 254, 262, 265, 280, 282, 287, 294-295, 296-297, 344, 349
Cricket pads 26, 31
Croll, D 66-68, 70, 73, 76-77, 312
Cross, Dave 60, 69, 75-77, 79, 81, 84, 87, 94, 96, 98, 100-101, 103, 107-110, 116-117, 120-122, 125, 129-130, 135, 137, 140-141, 143, 145-146, 149, 154, 162, 167-168, 171, 183-184, 189-191, 195, 202, 206, 210, 254, 265, 282, 312, 315, 319, 323, 327, 330, 333, 336, 339, 344, 356-359, 361, 365
Crossmyloof Ice Rink, Glasgow xi, 21-27, 30-32, 37, 41-42, 44-49, 51-53, 55, 57-62, 65-67, 69, 71, 73-77, 79, 84, 87-91, 93, 96-97, 99, 103-107, 109, 111, 113, 115, 118, 120, 122-123, 125-126, 133, 135, 140, 143-144, 150, 154, 162, 164, 167-169, 171, 174-175, 177, 181, 184, 190-191, 195-197, 200, 203-204, 206, 209-213, 215-219, 221- 222, 224-228, 232-233, 237, 239-242, 245, 252-254, 256-259, 262, 264-266, 269, 275-276, 281-282, 284- 287, 293, 356-360
Cummine, Gordon 253, 262, 266-267, 269, 276, 288-289, 301, 344, 349
Cumming, Don 237, 254, 288, 297, 339, 344, 349
Cunningham, George 54, 311
Curling 9, 13, 17, 20-22, 24-25, 30, 37, 41, 43, 52, 58, 62, 75, 93, 133, 235, 242
Cuthbert, C R Captain 48
Cuthill, John 203, 235, 238, 336, 339
Czechoslovakia (National Team) 39, 186, 240, 275, 365

D

Dailley, Gordon 187, 220
Davey, Gerry 129, 169-170, 173, 186-187, 240, 255-258, 261-264, 266, 268, 271, 289, 292-293, 295-298, 344, 349

Davis, H A Lieutenant 48
Davos 39, 166
Dawson, Chester 253, 264, 266, 271, 281, 288-289, 291, 293, 344, 349
Delesalle, M 117
de Marwicz, F A 100, 129, 146
Denmark 18
Dennistoun (Eagles) Ice Hockey Club 47, 51, 53-55, 58, 61, 64-68, 74, 76-77, 79-82, 84-86, 89, 93-94, 97-99, 105, 107, 109, 114-116, 120-124, 126-127, 129, 134, 137-138, 144, 154-158, 162, 164-168, 170, 172-173, 175-179, 206, 308, 310-311, 313-315, 317-319, 321-323, 325-330, 350, 356-359, 361, 363
de Visser, C W 53, 63, 65, 68, 78, 114, 116, 135, 312, 315, 319, 323
Dick, Andy 38, 68, 75-76, 89, 94, 115, 135-136, 140-141, 143-145, 149, 154, 170, 184, 191, 193, 200, 206, 254, 282, 284, 300, 312, 315, 319, 323, 327, 330, 333, 336, 339
Doonside Estate, Ayr 28
Doonside Ice Hockey Club 30, 47, 51, 53-54, 61, 63-69, 73-74, 77, 127, 153, 242, 306-308, 310-311, 350
Douglas, George 12, 14-15
Downes, B 57, 311
Downs, Pinky 289, 349
Duden, Harold H 34
Duncanson, Albert 143
Dundee xi, 230, 235, 239, 249, 251
Dundee Tigers Ice Hockey Club xiii, 252-257, 259, 261-262, 264-266, 269-271, 273, 275-282, 285-287, 289-290, 292- 299, 340-351
Dunfermline xi, 283
Dunfermline Vikings Ice Hockey Club 285-286, 289-300, 345-350, 352
Dunlop, Archibald S ii, 27-29, 31, 356, 361
Dunlop, Billy 54, 77, 105, 121, 127-128, 307, 311, 315, 319, 323, 327
Dunlop, Frederick 54, 311
Dunlop, Thomas C Colonel 2, 30, 54, 74, 242, 307, 311
Dunne, J J 48

Dunsmore, J 218, 336, 360-361
Durling, Tommy 255, 277, 289-290, 295-297, 344, 349
Dykes, Andrew S 45, 53, 65, 307, 311
Dykes, Jimmy C 53, 311

E

Eagles Ladies Ice Hockey Club 219, 233
Earls Court 151, 220
Earls Court Rangers Ice Hockey Club 187, 191, 196, 214, 242, 244-245, 254-255, 259, 261, 359, 362-363
Easton, Jack 52, 60-61, 63, 65, 68-70, 76-80, 84, 87, 96, 100-101, 103, 110, 114, 116-117, 119-120, 126, 129, 139, 142, 155, 198, 312, 315, 319, 323, 327, 356, 357, 358, 361, 365
Eaton, Don 254, 264, 282, 344
Eddy-Larsen, K 60, 312
Edinburgh 18-19, 37, 62, 66, 91, 99, 115, 138, 235, 239, 249
Edmonton 254
Edmonton Superiors Ice Hockey Club 118, 120, 122-123, 142, 254, 355, 357, 361-365
Edwards, Don 84, 105, 107, 109-110, 114, 155, 159, 165, 176, 179, 200-201, 222, 319, 323, 327, 330, 333, 336, 339, 357, 361
Eglinton Hunt 54
Elkins, J 107
England xiii, 1, 3-4, 12, 22, 25-26, 35-39, 41-42, 48, 70-71, 74, 79, 88, 90-91, 97, 102, 108-109, 111, 114, 121-122, 131, 143, 151, 155, 164, 173-174, 179, 186, 189, 196, 198, 207, 209, 220, 225-227, 234, 244, 249, 253- 255, 284, 291-292, 300
England (National Team) xi, 5, 27-29, 31-33, 47, 53, 96, 99-100, 103, 107, 116, 129-130, 142, 144, 146, 151, 162, 169-170, 191-193, 217, 244, 355-359, 361-364
English National League 168, 173, 186-187, 191, 196, 209-210, 217, 220, 234, 242, 244, 249, 252, 254-255, 259, 284, 291, 297, 300
Erhardt, Carl 129, 146, 169, 173, 186-187, 191, 193

F

Faculty of Medicine, University of Edinburgh 115
Fair, Ian 53, 66, 68, 311
Fair, Peter, 48, 81, 107, 129
Faison, J B 78
Falcons Ladies Ice Hockey Club 219, 233
Falkirk xi, 249, 251,
Falkirk Lions Ice Hockey Club 252-253, 255-258, 261-266, 268, 270-271, 273, 275-276, 278, 283, 286, 289-296, 298-299, 340-352
Fawcett, Bernard H 96, 100
Fenwick's Ice Hockey Club 3
Fergusson, Charles, General Sir 2, 249
Fife Flyers Ice Hockey Club xiii, 252-253, 255-257, 259, 262, 264-266, 269-271, 273-279, 283, 286, 289-299, 301, 340-351, 365
Fincham, E 84, 115, 125, 312, 315, 319, 323
Finnie, H S 125, 178, 181, 319, 324, 327, 330, 333, 336
Forgie, Tommy 217, 245, 291-292, 294-298, 349
Forrest, J E 45, 53, 307, 311, 315
Forsyth, G R 116, 312, 316, 320, 324
Forsythe, Bert 218, 224, 228, 231, 249, 254, 265, 336, 339, 344
Forsythe, Jim 218, 336
Fort William, Ontario 254
Foster, Jimmy 186-188, 191-193, 214, 240, 259, 284, 300, 359, 362
France xi, 17, 26, 33
France (National Team) 116-118, 120, 123, 142, 232, 355, 357, 361-365
Franette, C A 86-87, 315
Fraser, Graham 175, 181, 183, 193-194, 200
Fullerton, Alec 54, 108, 115-116, 129, 135, 140-141, 145-147, 149, 154, 162-164, 169, 171, 183-184, 189, 200, 204, 207, 210, 212-213, 216-217, 222, 235,

249, 253, 255, 282, 287, 323, 327, 330, 333, 336, 339, 344, 358-359, 362
Fullerton, Billy 54, 76, 84, 94, 106, 108-109, 115-116, 118-119, 121, 123-127, 129, 135, 140, 143-144, 146-150, 155, 157-158, 160-163, 165-167, 169-172, 180-185, 189, 191-196, 199, 200, 202, 210, 217, 222, 226, 228, 231-233, 235, 237, 249, 253, 255, 273, 275, 287, 301, 316, 324, 327, 330, 333, 336, 339, 344, 357-360, 362, 365
Fullerton, John 54, 57, 67, 69, 76, 82, 84, 86-87, 89, 94, 96, 98, 100-102, 106-108, 110, 117-120, 123-124, 127, 129, 135, 138, 140, 144, 146-147, 149-150, 155, 157-158, 161-163, 165, 167, 169-171, 181, 183-185, 189, 191-194, 200-202, 210, 213, 215, 222, 245, 253, 272, 275, 287, 307, 312, 316, 323, 327, 330, 333, 336, 339, 344, 356-359, 362, 365
Fyfe, J G 108, 123-124, 135, 143, 150, 307, 316, 320, 323, 327, 358, 362

G

Gallacs Ice Hockey Club 198
Galloway, Gordon 201-202, 206, 210, 215, 217, 222, 336, 359, 360, 362
Gammie, C 57, 312
Gardiner, Robert H 78, 114, 176, 179, 201, 206-207, 216, 264, 307, 312, 315, 319, 323, 327, 330, 333, 336, 339
Gardner, Vic 48, 100
Garmisch-Partenkirchen 186
Garnock, A G 139, 155, 157, 327
Gemmell, Bert 115, 123, 135, 140-141, 142, 154, 166-167, 180, 189, 200, 315, 319, 323, 327, 330, 333
Geran, G 117
Germany 26, 33, 77, 186, 227, 232, 244, 249, 259
Germany (National Team) 33-34, 79, 81, 89, 91, 98, 107, 186, 214, 240-241, 275, 355-356, 361, 363-365
Gerth, Maurice 291, 298-299, 349
Giddens, Robert 220
Gillis, John 34
Gilmour, Jack 24, 26, 31, 46, 60, 66, 69, 81, 84, 98, 100, 103, 107, 110, 114, 117, 119-120, 122-129, 137-138, 144, 146, 148, 154, 159, 161, 165, 169, 175, 183-184, 193-194, 219, 238, 307, 311, 315, 319, 323, 327, 330, 333, 356-358, 361-362, 365
Gittens, W H 13-15
Glanfield, Stanley 14-15
Glasgow xi, xiii, 7-15, 17-19, 21-22, 24-25, 27-28, 30-32, 37, 41-43, 45-49, 51-55, 57-70, 73-74, 76-77, 79-82, 84-87, 89-91, 93, 96-97, 99-100, 102-106, 108-109, 111, 113-118, 120, 122-124, 126-127, 133-135, 137, 138-140, 142, 145-148, 150, 153-160, 164-171, 173, 175-182, 184-187, 189, 191-192, 194-198, 200-203, 209-214, 217-222, 224-225, 227-228, 230-231, 235, 237-238, 240-242, 246, 251, 253-254, 256-259, 261-262, 264, 269-271, 275-276, 282-283, 287, 291, 301, 305-308, 310-315, 317-319, 321-323, 325-333, 350-351, 355-362, 365, 391
Glasgow Academicals Rugby Club 53
Glasgow Academy 62
Glasgow Canadians Ice Hockey Club 45-49, 51, 306-307
Glasgow High School 62
Glasgow High School Ice Hockey Club 47, 51, 58, 153, 306-307
Glasgow Real Ice Skating Palace xi, 7-10, 12-14, 17-19, 21-22, 45, 305
Glasgow Skating Club Ice Hockey Club 28, 47, 51, 53, 58, 61, 64-68, 73-74, 76-77, 81-82, 85, 93, 96, 102, 104-106, 109, 114-115, 306, 308, 310-311, 313-315, 317-319, 350-351
Glasgow Speed Skating Club 181-182
Glasgow University Bandy Club 14, 19, 198
Glasgow University Hockey Club 53
Glasgow University Ice Hockey Club 51-53, 60-61, 63, 65-68, 74, 76-79, 82, 84-86, 93, 96, 100, 103-106, 114-118, 120, 123-124, 126, 134-135, 137, 140,

142, 145-147, 150, 154-160, 164-167, 169-170, 173, 175-176, 178-180, 182, 184-185, 189, 192, 194-195, 197-198, 200-201, 220, 308, 310, 312-315, 317-319, 321-323, 325-333, 350-351, 356-358, 361-362, 365
Golders Green Ice Rink, London 39, 70, 103
Gourock 17
Graham, Jimmy 118
Grant, Art 289-290, 301, 349
Grassie, J T Captain 264
Gratias, Orvald 142, 147, 150, 155, 157-159, 173, 198, 327, 330
Gray, Andrew 84, 89, 114, 116, 155, 159-160, 169, 183, 316, 319, 323, 327, 330, 333
Gray, Arthur 154
Great Britain xiii, 1, 3, 12-13, 18, 20, 33, 35, 37, 117, 220, 222
Great Britain (National Team) 33-36, 38-39, 41, 48, 60, 65, 70, 74, 79, 86, 96-98, 100, 107, 117, 122, 142, 145, 151, 166, 168-169, 171, 178, 180, 186-187, 191, 201, 214, 217, 220, 234, 240, 246, 255, 273, 275, 289, 301, 365
Greenway, R 29, 31
Greig, Kenneth B S Commander 54, 307, 311
Groome, J 191, 193
Grosvenor House Canadians Ice Hockey Club 39, 91, 99-100, 103, 106-107, 123-124, 129, 131, 143, 146, 151, 357-358, 361-364
Grosvenor House Hotel, London 39
Gull Lake 218

H

Haarlem 18
Hagnauer, J P 117
Haig, Nigel 28
Halford, P 146, 169-170
Halifax, Nova Scotia 175
Hall, Martin J 82, 85, 87, 94, 316
Hamilton, George 22
Hamilton, Ontario 165

Hammersmith Ice Drome, London 39, 84
Hanley, John 129
Harby, J A 14-15
Harding, D A Flying Officer 48
Harringay, London 151
Harringay Arena, London 196, 214, 220, 234
Harringay Greyhounds Ice Hockey Club 187, 214, 240, 259, 284, 300
Harringay Racers Ice Hockey Club 220, 249, 279
Harvie, D 181, 333, 336
Haslam Foundry and Engineering Company, Derby 21
Hay, J S 65, 311, 315
Haymarket Ice Rink, Edinburgh 37, 62, 235
Heinrich, A 79
Helgregan, F 60, 312
Hems, Fred 84, 114, 319, 323, 327
Henderson, Bobby 204, 336, 339
Henderson, G 178, 180, 327, 330, 333
Henderson, J C 78, 315, 319, 323, 327
Henglers Ice Rink, London 2, 4, 12
Henry, Howard R L 34
Herbertson, Jean 233
Higginbotham, H C 54, 307, 311, 315
Higginbotham, W R 54, 82, 307, 311, 315, 319
Higgins, John G 34
Hill, Fred 280
Holland 18, 135
Holme, W J Captain 48
Holmes, A 129
Holmes, Gregor 57, 71, 307, 312, 323
Holsbaur, Dr 79
Horne, George 230, 232-233, 235, 237, 240-241, 245-247, 253, 262, 287, 289, 291, 339, 344, 349, 360, 362
Horton, Harry Rev 54, 307, 311
Howell, C M G 28
Hungary (National Team) 79, 186, 214, 275, 365
Hurll, Ken 84, 115, 178, 183-185, 189-190, 200, 235, 319, 330, 333, 336, 339
Hutchins, Walter H 12

I

India 158
International Ice Hockey Federation (IIHF) 33, 391

J

Jackson, D 178, 237, 327, 330, 333, 336, 339
Jackson, Ted 146, 151
Jaenecke, Gustav 79
Japan (National Team) 186
Johnson, Gordon H 129-131, 169, 186
Johnston, Jack 84, 109, 114-115, 128, 155, 200, 202, 239, 268, 320, 323, 327, 330, 333, 336, 339, 344
Johnston, Ken 288, 294, 349
Jowett, J L 14-15
Junior Mohawks Ice Hockey Club 62
Junior Queen's Ice Hockey Club 62
Juniors Ice Hockey Club 113-118, 121, 123-124, 126, 130, 134, 138-139, 140, 142-144, 147, 150, 154-158, 160, 162, 164-173, 175-179, 184, 321-323, 325-330, 350, 357-359, 362-365
Justice, James Robertson 98

K

Kay, Martyn B 12, 14-15
Kellough, T M Dr 84
Kelly, Jimmy 211, 214, 240, 275, 301
Kelly, Johnny 158, 160, 169-170, 173, 176, 180, 185, 190, 191-193, 195, 207, 210, 215, 228, 232, 239, 249, 273, 330, 333, 336, 339, 344, 359, 362
Kelvingrove Ice Hockey Club xiii, 47, 51, 55, 58, 61, 64-68, 70, 73-77, 79-82, 84-90, 93-94, 96, 98, 100, 103-109, 114-118, 120-127, 129-130, 134-135, 137-151, 154, 156-160, 162, 165-171, 173, 175-185, 189-192, 194-196, 198, 200-204, 206-208, 210, 213, 218-219, 221-222, 224-228, 230, 232, 234-235, 238-240, 243, 245, 247, 249, 252, 254, 256-257, 259, 261, 264-266, 269, 271, 273, 275- 278, 281-283, 285-287, 289, 306, 308, 310, 312-315, 317-319, 321-323, 325-344, 350-354, 356-359, 361-365
Kelvinside Academy 62
Kenny, Jim 157-158, 160-163, 165, 167, 169-170, 180, 184-185, 190-194, 200, 202, 204, 206, 210-211, 213, 215-217, 219, 222, 226, 228, 231-232, 237, 241, 253, 264, 287, 330, 333, 336, 339, 344, 358-359, 360, 362
Kensington Corinthians Ice Hockey Club 191, 255, 359, 361
Kerr, C P 307
Kerr, Chick 255, 289, 344, 349
Kilpatrick, Jake 187, 191, 193
Kimberley Dynamiters Ice Hockey Club, 214, 218
King's Ice Hockey Club 25, 27-28, 31, 356, 361
Kingston 10
Kinross 11, 17
Kirkcaldy xi, 239, 249, 251
Kirkcaldy Ice Rink 239, 256-257, 277, 285-286, 293
Kitchener 291
Knightsbridge, London 2
Korff, W 79
Kummets, G 79

L

Lambert, Percy 29, 31, 311
Lammie, Johnny 118
Lancashire Ice Hockey Club 103
Lanctot, Gustave 34-35
Lane, Bill 228, 254, 262, 277, 280, 287, 292, 344, 349
Latvia (National Team) 166, 240, 365
Le Cron, Robert 34
Lemay, Albert 169
Lemay, Tony 169
Lennox, Greg 77, 84, 90, 108, 118, 165, 183, 185, 189, 194, 200, 316, 320, 323, 330, 333
Les Avants 28, 33-34
Leuchars Ice Hockey Club 198
Lightfoot, Jimmy 207, 213, 215, 217-218, 222-223, 225-228, 231, 237-239,

241, 244-247, 253, 255, 257, 262, 278, 280, 282, 287, 336, 339, 344, 359-360, 362
Ligue Internationale de Hockey sur Glace (LIHG) 33-35, 37-38, 45, 58, 100, 133, 135, 144-145, 156, 187, 224, 273, 286, 292
Lincoln, Lord 48
Lindquist, Vic 169
Lindsay, D W 63, 78, 135, 312, 315, 319, 323
Lindsay, S K 45-46, 307
Linton, G P Colonel 88
Lions Ice Hockey Club 177-182, 184-185, 192, 194-195, 198, 200-204, 206-207, 211-218, 221-222, 224-228, 230-234, 237, 239-242, 244-245, 247, 251-252, 255-256, 331-339, 350-351, 359-364
Little, Herbie 109, 131
Liverpool Ice Hockey Club 117, 121, 357-358, 361, 365
Liverpool Ice Rink 96-98, 103, 355-356
Loane, Henry 207, 210-211, 213, 215-217, 336
Loch Leven 17, 181, 185
Logan, Jack 126, 144, 156, 206, 311, 315, 319, 323, 327, 330, 336
London Bandy Club 10, 305
London Canadians Ice Hockey Club 3-4, 36
London Lions Ice Hockey Club 39, 48, 65, 70, 80-81, 90-91, 96, 98-100, 103, 129, 196, 306, 355-357, 361-364
London Scottish Rugby Club 87
Lorette 289
Lourdes, Nova Scotia 254
Lovell, Les 206, 210, 215, 217-219, 222, 225, 227-228, 231-232, 237, 239, 241-242, 244-248, 255, 259, 261, 275, 278, 283, 336, 339, 344, 359-360, 362

Mac, Mc

McAlpine, Dougie 237, 254, 339, 344, 349
McAlpine, Ralph 191,193, 359, 362

McAndrew, Hazen 284, 300
McArthur, Harry 217
McCabe, A J 135, 139-140, 145-147, 155, 327, 358, 362
McCabe, J O 65, 67-68, 81, 102, 105, 114, 135, 139, 147, 158-160, 179, 198, 232, 264, 311, 315, 319, 323, 327, 330
McCartney, Len 202-204, 210-211, 215, 217-219, 222, 224-227, 229-230, 232, 237, 239, 241-242, 244-247, 253, 255, 261, 264, 266, 336, 339, 344, 359-360, 362
McCreedy, Johnny 277
McCuaig, Nelson 237, 239, 242, 255, 257-258, 261-262, 266, 268, 271, 289, 339, 344
McDonald, J 57
McDonald, R J G 57, 311, 315, 319
MacDonald, Ronald O 45, 128, 138, 148-149, 155, 158, 160-161, 165, 184-185, 190-194, 200-201, 207, 224, 232, 287, 307, 311, 315, 319, 323, 327, 330, 333, 336, 359, 362
MacDonald, S A 62-63, 65, 67-70, 73, 76, 312, 365
McDonald, W G 115, 117, 122, 124-125, 129, 137-138, 145, 147-150, 155-156, 162, 167-170, 172, 176-177, 184-185, 189-191, 193, 195, 201, 204, 207, 215, 323, 327, 330, 333, 336, 358-359, 363, 365
Macfie, Norman 53, 83, 85, 94, 311, 315
McGill, David ii, 31, 47
McGill University Ice Hockey Club, Montreal 235
McGuffie, A J ii, 27-29, 31, 356, 363
McGuire, W 129
McInnes-Shaw, Archibald D Lieutenant-Colonel 88
McInroy, Tommy 202, 222, 226, 235, 238, 249, 255, 273-275, 289, 291, 293, 297, 299, 336, 339, 344, 349, 365
McKay, Peter 165, 178, 330
MacKenzie, N C 128, 307, 311, 315, 319, 323, 327
MacKenzie, W H 48, 70
MacLachlan, Duncan 127, 129, 135, 139,

143, 149, 160, 165, 179, 182, 200, 323, 327, 330, 333, 336
McLaurin, A G 11, 14-15
Maclay, John S Honourable 54, 311
McLeod, Alistair E 53-54, 57, 83, 307, 311, 315, 319, 323
McLeod, Don 234-235, 238, 240-241, 243, 245, 249, 254, 281, 289, 294, 339, 344, 349
McLeod, Eric R 45-46, 51, 59, 61, 69-70, 73, 76, 126, 307, 311
McLeod, Ian S 53-54, 57, 69, 83, 108, 118, 120-122, 127, 137-138, 155, 159, 172, 176, 307, 311, 315, 319, 323, 327, 330
McLeod, Walter S 83-84, 94, 106, 123-125, 127, 129, 135, 137-138, 146, 148, 150, 156, 159, 162-163, 166-170, 172, 176-177, 182, 319, 323, 327, 330, 333, 358-359, 363, 365
McLernan, Felix 45-46, 51, 66-67, 102, 105-106, 114, 173, 179, 198, 201, 207, 215, 307, 311, 315, 319, 323, 327, 330, 333, 336, 339
McMillan, Charlie 135, 141, 144-146, 148-149, 154, 158, 166-167, 170, 180, 194, 200, 323, 327, 330, 333, 358, 363
McMillan, Eddie 294, 349
McNeil, George 217, 254, 256-257, 261-262, 264, 266, 280, 282-283, 287, 290-291, 296, 344, 349
McPhail, Paul 191, 193, 214, 359, 363
McQuade, Norman 246-247, 255, 257, 289, 291, 293, 296, 298, 339, 344, 349
McWilliams, George 255, 259, 266, 268, 271, 289, 344, 349

M

Magnus, Louis 33
Magwood, John C P 48, 70, 81, 97-98, 100
Manchester 2, 159, 180
Manchester Ice Hockey Club 36, 38-39, 60-61, 65, 67-69, 81, 87-90, 96, 103, 140, 162, 169-170, 184-186, 192, 195, 198, 201, 214, 222, 358-359, 363

Manchester Ice Palace 36-37, 61, 67, 69, 81, 89, 90, 186, 192, 195
Manitoba University Graduates Ice Hockey Club, 86-88
Marchant, Laurie 230, 232, 237, 239, 241, 245, 249, 254, 278, 287, 339, 344, 349, 360, 363
Maritime Senior Hockey League, Canada 187
Marsh, Larry 289, 298, 349
Martin W M 34
Mason, George 145, 146, 169
Mavogodato, E E 33
Maxwell, Archie 202, 230, 336, 339
Maxwell, Matt 202, 336
Mayes, Harry E Flight-Lieutenant 100, 107, 129, 146, 151
Meagher, George A 9-10, 12, 17-18, 20
Melland, Neville 60, 65, 81, 98, 100
Melvin, J W 27, 31, 356, 363
Merrickville 254
Michaelis, C 117
Michener, Roland 38
Milan Ice Hockey Club 129
Milford, Jake 162
Mills, Bobby 156, 167, 173, 327, 330
Milne, Ronald S 157, 159, 160, 162, 165-166, 169-170, 173, 198, 214-216, 224, 227, 236-237, 242, 246-247, 253, 272, 277, 289, 292, 330, 336, 339, 344, 349, 358, 359, 363
Mitchell, Andrew 46-47, 49, 175, 252
Mitchell, Doug 202, 249, 253-254, 259, 280, 336, 339, 344
Mitchell Trophy xiii, 47, 63, 65-69, 73, 75-76, 82, 85-86, 89-90, 93, 105, 106-107, 109, 114-115, 123-127, 129, 134, 137-140, 144, 147-149, 153-154, 157-160, 171, 177-178, 185, 189-190, 194, 197-198, 213-14, 216, 218, 237, 239-242, 247, 251-252, 270, 276, 278, 281-282, 286-287, 293-294, 351-354
Moffat, F 279
Moffat, T W K 311, 315
Mohawks Ice Hockey Club xiii, 47, 51, 55, 57-65, 67-71, 73-77, 79-80, 82, 84, 86, 89-90, 93-96, 98-100, 102-106,

108-109, 115-118, 122-127, 129-130, 134-135, 138-140, 142-144, 146-150, 154-162, 164-173, 175-186, 189-192, 194, 196, 198-204, 206-207, 209-216, 218-219, 221-222, 224-228, 230-235, 237-241, 245-247, 251-257, 259, 261-262, 264-266, 269, 271, 275-278, 281-284, 286-287, 289, 301, 306-309, 312-314, 316-318, 320-323, 325-344, 350-354, 356-363, 365
Mohicans Junior Ice Hockey Club 62
Moncton Hawks Ice Hockey Club 187
Montford, Arthur 81
Montford, Eric 84, 144, 156, 178, 312, 320, 323, 327, 330, 333, 336
Montford, Sid 75, 81, 84, 86, 88-89, 94, 103, 105-107, 109, 118, 121, 123, 129-130, 135, 137, 139-141, 146-149, 154, 156, 168, 178, 180, 183-185, 190-194, 202, 254, 282, 285, 298, 312, 315, 319-320, 323, 327, 330, 333, 336, 339, 358-359, 363
Montgomery, Matthew Sir 88
Montreal 18, 77, 158, 211, 235
Montreal Amateur Athletic Association Ice Hockey Club 99
Montreal Canadians Ice Hockey Club 277
Montreal Victorias Ice Hockey Club 41
Montrose, Duke of 42-43
Moore, Bill 201-202, 336
Morley, Earl 239, 339
Morrison, Glen 117, 227-228, 230, 253, 261, 266, 269, 278, 289, 339, 344, 349
Morrison, J 117
Muirhead, Earl 53-54, 57, 83, 97, 105, 107, 127, 135, 155, 165, 178, 180, 185, 192, 195, 307, 311, 315, 319, 323, 327, 330, 333
Muirhead, Ramsay 53-54, 57, 83, 307, 311
Muirhead, Wilbur 53-54, 57, 69, 80-83, 87, 94, 97, 110, 115, 118, 121-124, 129, 137, 140, 144, 155, 169, 172, 177, 180, 195, 224, 307, 311, 315, 319, 323, 327, 330, 333, 336, 357-359, 363
Mulholland, N D 70
Munro, Ernest A 34
Murren 35, 37

Mustangs Ice Hockey Club 175-176, 178-185, 189-192, 194-196, 198, 200-204, 206-207, 211-218, 221-222, 224-225, 227-228, 230-232, 234-235, 239, 244-245, 247, 249, 251-252, 254, 331-339, 350-351, 359-360, 362-363
Myers, R T 82, 312, 315

N

Napier, Charlie 28
National Bandy Association 12
National Skating Association of Great Britain 10, 12-13, 17, 33, 35, 182
National Skating Club 2
National Skating Palace, London 2
Nerlick, E 234, 245, 339
Nesbitt, Ivor 122, 169
Nevitt, C 170, 330, 333, 336, 339, 344
New Brunswick 187
Newfoundland 35, 37
Newton, J M 178, 330, 333, 336, 339
Ney, G 227, 339, 349
Niagara Hall Ice Rink, London 2, 9-10
Niagara Ice Hockey Club, London 2-4, 36
Nicholson, Earl 279, 283, 344
Nicklin, Percy 186-187
Nicol, Tom 180, 185, 200, 333
Nisbet, Tom 77, 79, 80-82, 84-87, 89, 94, 176, 315, 356, 363
Noble, R L 68, 75, 79, 82, 88-89, 94, 109, 282, 312, 315, 356, 363
Nodwell, G R 45, 307
North Battleford 255
North of Scotland Ice Hockey League 198
Norway 18, 60
Norway (National Team) 240
Nova Scotia 175, 254

O

Oblonsky, R D 117
Ontario 10, 165, 182, 202, 228, 240, 253-255, 271, 291
Orr, H R 53, 67, 76, 311
Ottawa 61, 198, 226, 255
Ottawa Shamrocks, Ice Hockey Club 143

Oxbridge Universities 1, 35, 37-38
Oxford 143
Oxford Canadians Ice Hockey Club 4-5, 28, 31, 34-37, 91, 151
Oxford Ice Rink 103, 121, 129-130
Oxford University 142, 200
Oxford University Ice Hockey Club 1, 3-4, 35-39, 48, 81, 87, 91, 100, 109, 121, 129, 131, 142

P

Paisley Ice Rink 283, 300
Palais de Glace, Paris 18
Palais des Sports, Paris 117
Palfrey, Art 201, 206-207, 210-211, 217-218, 222, 226, 228, 230, 232-233, 237, 240-241, 253, 269, 281-282, 287, 336, 339, 344, 359-360, 363
Pantalone, Gordon 255, 261, 264, 266, 268, 344
Paris xi, 10, 17-19, 33, 117, 142, 232, 355, 357
Parker, R Dr 78
Parsons, Guy 53, 77, 311, 315
Partick Curling Club 9
Patton, Bethune M Major 1-4, 17, 20, 24, 27-29, 31, 33-34, 36, 38-39, 41, 46, 70, 391
Paul, H 29, 31, 356, 363
Pearson, Lester 38
Peltier, P 85-86, 316
Perth xi, 200, 204, 219, 225, 227, 239, 251
Perth Airport Ice Hockey Club 198
Perth Black Hawks Ice Hockey Club 221-222, 225-228, 230-232, 234, 236-242, 244-247, 251, 254-255, 337-339, 350-351, 360, 362-364
Perth Ice Rink see Central Ice Rink, Perth
Perth Panthers Ice Hockey Club 198, 202-204, 206-207, 209-211, 213, 215, 217-218, 220-222, 224-228, 230-232, 234-235, 237-240, 242, 244-247, 252-255, 257, 259, 264-266, 269, 271-273, 275-279, 281-283, 286-287, 289, 291-297, 300, 334-351, 359-364

Perth Panthers Reserves Ice Hockey Club 198
Perth Territorial Army Ice Hockey Club 198
Pettigrew, Gordon ii, 27-29, 31-32, 356, 363
Philadelphia 180
Phinney, William 68, 75-76, 88, 94, 115, 312, 315, 319
Pitblado, Edward 38
Planque, Robert 33
Points Competition 57-58, 60-61, 69, 75, 114, 126, 177, 256, 258, 261-262, 264-266, 270-271, 283, 286, 290, 292-296, 308, 340, 345, 353
Poland 86, 97
Poland (National Team) 79, 214, 240
Port Arthur 182, 202, 253, 255, 271
Port Arthur Bearcats Ice Hockey Club 186
Port Hood 278
Porter, Don 45-46, 51, 59-60, 99-101, 107, 126, 162, 307, 312, 330, 333, 357, 363
Porter, G A 161
Pratt, Arnie 232, 234, 237-238, 241-242, 245-247, 253, 260, 269, 271-272, 289-292, 296-297, 299, 339, 344, 349, 360, 363
President's Pucks xiii, 125-127, 130, 134-135, 144, 147-149, 151, 153-154, 156, 167, 169-171, 177-178, 182-183, 185, 189-190, 194, 198, 204, 206, 209-210, 214, 230-232, 240, 242, 251, 262, 264-266, 269, 282, 286-287, 294, 351-353
Prince Albert 203, 294
Prince Albert Mintos Ice Hockey Club 157
Princes Ice Hockey Club 2-5, 27-28, 31, 33-39, 70, 100, 103, 129, 131, 151
Princes Ice Rink, London 2-4, 28, 34, 36-37, 356
Princes Skating Club 3
Prock, Frank 288, 294, 297, 349
Proost, T A 135, 319, 323
Purdie, Alec 224, 255, 268, 289, 339, 344, 349

Purdie, Bob 211, 222, 225, 227, 231-233, 237, 241, 244-245, 247, 253, 272, 339, 344, 360, 363
Purley Ice Hockey Club, London 145-146

Q

Queen's Ice Hockey Club 47, 51, 59-66, 69-70, 73-74, 76, 79-82, 84-87, 91, 93-94, 96, 98-100, 102-109, 114-118, 120-126, 131, 134, 153, 171, 301, 306, 308-309, 312-314, 316-318, 320-322, 324, 350-351, 356-358, 361-365
Queens Ice Rink, London 116
Queen's Park Football Club 96

R

Ramus, Ernie 100, 146, 169, 173, 191, 193
Rangers Football Club 96, 157, 204
Reardon, Fred 76, 79-80, 87, 94, 98-99, 102, 105-106, 109, 113, 115, 125-126, 316, 320, 356, 363
Reichenheim, D 79
Reid, A F 149, 315, 319, 323, 327, 330
Reid, E K 147, 161, 316, 320, 323, 327, 330, 333
Reid, George 89, 319
Reid, Harry 65, 68, 77, 84, 311, 315, 319
Reid, Hugh 45-46, 49, 51, 57, 61, 69, 76, 80, 82, 86-87, 100, 105, 107, 113-114, 119, 128, 307, 311, 315, 319, 323, 356, 363
Reid, Lilian 233
Reilly, Verne 294-295, 349
Rheault, Paul 289, 292-293, 296-297, 299, 349
Rice-Jones, Art 169
Richmond Hawks Ice Hockey Club 162, 164, 166, 169, 186-187, 191, 196, 217-218, 254, 291, 355, 358-359, 361-364
Rintoul, A 54, 61, 69, 81-82, 98, 103, 114, 121, 127-128, 138-139, 154, 166, 179, 189, 307, 311, 315, 319, 323, 327, 330, 333, 356-357, 363
Rintoul, R 54, 61, 307, 311
Ritchie, W 53, 67, 76, 311

Roberts, Bunt 226, 228, 231-232, 237, 241, 253, 261, 269, 272, 287, 289, 339, 344, 349, 360, 363
Roemer, E 79
Rogers, Al 254, 257, 259, 261-262, 265-266, 271, 280, 282, 287, 290, 294, 296, 344, 349
Rogers, Bob 107
Ross, Angus 94, 108, 127, 159, 165, 170, 172, 319, 323, 327, 330
Ross, Mac 210, 253-254, 336, 339, 344
Rowley, Gordon 77, 79-80, 83, 85, 87, 94, 99-101, 103-107, 110, 113-120, 122-124, 126, 129, 138-139, 142-143, 150, 177, 315, 319, 323, 327, 356-357, 363, 365
Royal Caledonian Curling Club 41
Royal Engineers Ice Hockey Club 3, 36
Rumania 214
Russell, Bill 68, 115-116, 120, 126, 129-130, 144, 156, 162-163, 167, 169-170, 173, 176, 180, 182, 191, 195, 206, 211, 222, 224, 256, 268, 311, 315, 319, 323, 327, 330, 333, 336, 339, 344, 358-359, 363
Russell, Charlie 128, 155, 161, 178, 323, 327, 330, 333
Russia 33

S

Sage, S E 31, 356, 364
Saskatchewan 142, 203, 218, 253, 255
Saskatoon 253, 294
Saskatoon Quakers Ice Hockey Club 143, 254
Savoie, Lou 292, 296, 298, 349
Schofield, Jack 222, 339, 344
Schreiber Colts Ice Hockey Club 253, 271
Schumann, Art 218, 222, 225, 227, 230, 244, 246, 253, 261, 264, 269, 272, 278, 289, 292, 295, 336, 339, 344, 349
Scotland xi, xii, xiii, 1, 7, 9, 10-11, 13, 18-22, 24, 26, 28, 32, 35, 37, 41-43, 45-48, 52, 55, 60, 62, 65, 71, 75, 85, 91, 96, 104-105, 113, 133-134, 143, 145-146, 154, 157, 164, 166, 174, 186, 189, 197, 209, 211-212, 214, 220-221,

230, 234, 238, 251-252, 258, 261, 264, 269-271, 273, 277-279, 285-286, 292, 294, 300
Scotland (National Team) ii, xi, xii, xiii, 27-29, 31-32, 35, 47, 101, 106-107, 110-111, 113, 116-120, 122-124, 129-131, 134, 142, 144-146, 151, 159-160, 162-163, 167-171, 173, 176, 180, 191-193, 201, 210, 217-219, 228, 232, 241-242, 244, 254, 256, 265, 301, 355-361, 391
Scott, Bell 14-15,
Scott, G C 45-46, 53, 60, 67, 307, 311, 315
Scott, Johnny 272, 289, 292, 330, 333, 336, 339, 344, 349
Scottish Bandy Club 13-15, 17, 305
Scottish Corinthians Ice Hockey Club 47-48, 51, 53, 58, 153
Scottish Cup 293-300, 352
Scottish Ice Hockey Association (SIHA) xi, xii, 21, 25, 27, 31-33, 35, 47-48, 51-53, 55, 57-67, 71, 73-75, 77, 79, 81, 84-85, 87, 89-91, 93, 96-100, 102, 104, 106-107, 111, 113, 116-118, 120-122, 124-125, 129-130, 133-135, 138, 140, 142-146, 150-151, 153-154, 156-160, 167-169, 172, 175-178, 180-181, 191-192, 195, 197-198, 200-201, 209-210, 212, 214-216, 218-219, 221, 224-226, 232, 234-235, 241, 244, 249, 251-253, 256, 258-259, 261, 264, 266, 270-271, 273, 276, 279, 281, 284-287, 290-291, 293-295, 297, 306-307, 332, 335
Scottish Ice Hockey Club 18-20, 198
Scottish Ice Rink see Crossmyloof Ice Rink
Scottish Ice Rink Company 21-22, 41, 46-47, 71, 175, 252
Scottish Ice Rinks Association (SIRA) 279
Scottish League xii, xiii, 55, 58, 60-62, 64-65, 68-69, 76, 79, 86, 93, 97, 100, 102, 106, 109, 126-127, 135, 138, 142, 145, 149-151, 155, 157, 164-166, 168-169, 173, 177, 180-181, 184, 191, 194, 196-198, 201-203, 209, 211-212, 214-215, 221-222, 224-225, 230, 234, 242, 249, 255-256, 264, 273, 285-287, 290, 300, 308-311, 313, 315, 317, 319, 321, 323, 325, 327-328, 330-331, 333-334, 336-337, 339-340, 342, 344-345, 347, 349-350
Scottish League Select xii, 102-103, 107, 111, 121, 150, 244-245, 259, 261, 265-266, 277
Scottish National League see Scottish League
Scottish Select 232-233
Scottish Speed Skating Association 84
Seafred, Art 259, 344
Sexton, Blaine N 38-39, 48, 65, 70, 91, 98, 100, 196
Shack, Joe 284, 300
Shannon, Jimmy 191, 255, 280, 289, 291, 296, 344, 349
Shearer, Tom 57, 69, 84-85, 99, 108, 123, 135, 142, 158, 161, 224, 307, 312, 316, 320, 323, 327, 330, 333, 336
Shires, Mickey 253, 262, 271, 281, 288-289, 344, 349
SIHA see Scottish Ice Hockey Association
Simpson, James Major 237, 279
Simpson Trophy 238
Sioux Junior Ice Hockey Club 62
SIRA see Scottish Ice Rinks Association
Sloan, J 11-12, 15
Smith, Howard 228, 230-233, 237, 241, 244, 247, 254, 262, 280, 283, 287, 307, 311, 315, 336, 339, 344, 360, 364
Sopwith, Thomas O M 28, 34
Southampton Vikings Ice Hockey Club 230-231
Speed skating 17, 52, 66, 75, 77, 84, 93, 109, 143, 181, 189
Sproule, L W 128, 178, 319, 323, 327, 333
St Andrews University Ice Hockey Club 198
Stapleford, Chuck 256-257, 268, 278, 344
Star Ice Hockey Club 25, 27-28, 31, 222, 356, 363
Steadman, Dean 228, 339
Stevenson, Pete 158, 160, 162-164, 166-170, 172-173, 178-180, 182, 184, 186, 201, 203-204, 206, 210-211, 213, 215,

217, 219, 228, 231, 233-234, 237-239, 241-242, 245, 252, 273, 330, 333, 336, 339, 358-360, 364-365
Stevenson, Sam 57, 77, 84-85, 115, 156, 178, 226, 307, 312, 315, 319, 323, 327, 330, 333, 336, 339
Stewart, Jack 222, 336, 339
Stinchcombe, Archie 187
St Moritz 1, 37-38, 41, 48
Stoner, Hugo 28-29, 31, 34
Stover, Jock 255, 259, 344
Strathearn, J D ii, 27-29, 31-32, 356, 364
Streatham Ice Hockey Club 146, 169, 173, 187, 191, 240, 254-256, 278, 291, 297
Streatham Ice Rink, London 103, 181
Strong, Gerry 211-212, 222, 336
Strubbe, G A 48, 84
Stuart, Frank 46-48, 125, 134, 154, 175, 212, 216, 252, 279, 316
Sudbury Wolves Ice Hockey Club 240-241
Sursock, Harold 122
Sweden 18, 60
Sweden (National Team) 39, 41, 186, 240
Switzerland 1, 3, 17, 26, 33, 35, 37, 39, 43, 46, 52, 54, 116, 166, 231, 265, 273, 275
Switzerland (National Team) 33-34, 41, 79, 166, 214, 365

T

Tait, Robert 34
Tait, Victor H Flight-Lieutenant 48
Tapp, Les 184, 186, 198, 202-206, 210, 213, 217-218, 222, 226-227, 237, 239-240, 244-245, 247, 253, 257, 259, 269, 272, 289, 291, 336, 339, 344, 349, 359, 364
Taylor, Ken 38
Taylor, Johnny 296
Taylor, T ii, 27-29, 31-32, 356, 364
Tebbutt, Charles G 18
Telfer, H J 53, 57, 307, 311, 315
Thompson, Breezy 228, 259, 261, 266, 269, 271-272, 275, 279, 283, 289, 291, 344, 349

Thomson, Keith 99-101, 107, 151, 289, 357, 364
Thomson, Robert 204, 210, 213, 217, 222, 224, 226, 230-231, 237-238, 246, 253, 255, 268, 278, 336, 339, 344, 349
Thomson, W 11-12, 15
Tingley, Arthur J 61, 65-66, 68-70, 76, 79-80, 82, 84-89, 94, 98-100, 103, 105-107, 109-110, 115-117, 119, 123, 125-127, 129, 135, 137, 140-142, 145, 147-148, 150, 154, 156, 158, 168, 170-171, 178, 185, 282, 312, 316, 320, 323-324, 327, 330, 356-358, 364-365
Toronto 201, 255
Toronto CCM Ice Hockey Club 65, 74, 79
Toronto Granites Ice Hockey Club 38
Toronto Maple Leafs Ice Hockey Club 277
Towers, J 279
Towers, W J 109, 135, 140-141, 319, 323, 327
Trail Smoke Eaters Ice Hockey Club 265-266, 277
Tudin, Connie 284, 300
Turnbull, Billy 114, 144, 162-164, 176, 178, 184, 190, 202, 206, 249, 254, 265, 289, 319, 323, 327, 330, 333, 336, 339, 344, 349, 358, 364
Tye, Major 9
Tyler, A H 11-12

U

Unite, Thomas J 28
United Services Ice Hockey Club 41, 48, 70, 81, 306
United States of America 52
United States of America (National Team) 38, 143, 186-187, 240
University of Toronto Ice Hockey Club 41
University of Western Ontario Mustangs Ice Hockey Club 228

V

Vancouver 259

Vickery, Les 294, 349
Vienna 88, 129
von Trauttenberg, H Baron 98, 129

W

Waddell, H 53-54, 311
Waddell, W 53-54, 311
Waite, B R 29, 31-32
Walker, R G 45, 60, 128, 170, 307, 311, 315, 319, 323, 330
Wanderers Hockey Club 25
Wanderers Ice Hockey Club 25, 27-28, 31, 356, 363-364
Warwickshire Ice Hockey Club 148, 150, 159-160, 164, 179, 255
Waters, F H 53, 87, 315
Watson, Blake Dr 88, 111, 115-117, 324
Webster, Roy 116, 125, 316, 320, 324
Welch, Wally 182, 184-186, 189-190, 194-195, 200-203, 207, 211, 213, 215, 222, 224, 226, 228, 230, 233, 238, 241, 287-289, 297, 333, 336, 339, 349
Wembley Arena, London 151, 169, 358-359
Wembley Canadians Ice Hockey Club 162, 166-167, 169, 173, 187, 191, 226, 255, 355, 358-359, 361-364
Wembley Lions Ice Hockey Club 173, 187, 191, 196, 220, 227, 255, 289
Wembley Monarchs Ice Hockey Club 230-231, 246, 275
Wengen 35
Westminster Ice Palace, London 39, 41
West of Scotland Rugby Club 53
Wharrie, John B ii, 27-29, 31, 53, 67, 76, 96, 311, 315, 356, 364
Whyte, R H 11-12
Wiener EV Ice Hockey Club 88
Wilcox 294
Williams, Hugh 294, 349
Winfield, R F 127-128, 137, 155-157, 165, 179, 319, 323, 327, 330, 333
Winnipeg 187, 202, 204, 207, 230-231, 239, 254, 259, 289, 292, 294, 297
Winnipeg Monarchs Ice Hockey Club 166, 168-169

Wold, J 204, 336
Woodrow, Jimmy 53, 57, 83, 137, 139, 155, 172, 176, 307, 311, 315, 319, 323, 327, 330
Wylie, William Pollock xi, 7, 10-13, 15-17, 19-20, 198
Wylie and Lochhead, Glasgow 7
Wyman, Bob 151, 169, 186-187

Y

Yellowlees, Norm 169
York, Duke of 2
Young, Cowan 135, 319, 323

www.ingramcontent.com/pod-product-compliance
Lightning Source LLC
Chambersburg PA
CBHW081157230426
43666CB00016B/2838